Current estimates are that around 3,000 of the 6,000 languages now spoken may become extinct during the next century. Some 4,000 of these existing languages have never been described, or described only inadequately. This book is a guide for linguistic fieldworkers who wish to write a description of the morphology and syntax of one of these many under-documented languages. It uses examples from many languages both well known and virtually unknown; it offers readers who work through it one possible outline for a grammatical description, with many questions designed to help them address the key topics. Appendices offer guidance on text and elicited data, and on sample reference grammars which readers might wish to consult. The product of fourteen years of teaching and research, this will be a valuable resource to anyone engaged in linguistic fieldwork.

Describing morphosyntax

Describing morphosyntax

A guide for field linguists

THOMAS E. PAYNE

University of Oregon and Summer Institute of Linguistics

CAMBRIDGE UNIVERSITY PRESS

PUBLISHED BY THE PRESS SYNDICATE OF THE UNIVERSITY OF CAMBRIDGE
The Pitt Building, Trumpington Street, Cambridge, United Kingdom

CAMBRIDGE UNIVERSITY PRESS
The Edinburgh Building, Cambridge CB2 2RU, UK
40 West 20th Street, New York, NY 10011–4211, USA
477 Williamstown Road, Port Melbourne, VIC 3207, Australia
Ruiz de Alarcón 13, 28014 Madrid, Spain
Dock House, The Waterfront, Cape Town 8001, South Africa

http://www.cambridge.org

First published 1997
Reprinted 1999, 2001, 2002, 2003

Printed in the United Kingdom at the University Press, Cambridge

Typeset in Concorde 9/13.5pt (with Formata headings), in QuarkXPress™. [GC]

A catalogue record for this book is available from the British Library

Library of Congress Cataloguing in Publication data applied for

ISBN 0 521 58224 5 hardback
ISBN 0 521 58805 7 paperback

To Stephanie, Claire, and Doris

Contents

Acknowledgments

This work began as course notes and handouts for syntax and semantics courses at the University of Oregon. Over the years many students and colleagues have contributed discussions, data, and insights, without which this book would not have been possible. I have attempted to acknowledge contributions of data at the places where the data appear. However, certainly some important acknowledgments have been omitted, for which I am truly sorry.

As I am sure is true for the linguists who have published the original research that this book is based upon, my first thanks go to the speakers who have contributed the language samples that are cited in the text. There are too many to acknowledge individually, and I am only acquainted with a few of them personally. Nevertheless, my highest hope is that this book will in some small measure serve the needs of these individuals and their communities.

For guidance and many suggestions on earlier drafts of portions of this work, I wish to thank Tod Allman, Joan Bybee, Bob Carlson, Wally Chafe, Bernard Comrie, Scott DeLancey, R. M. W. Dixon, Matt Dryer, Jack Du Bois, T. Givón, Colette Grinevald (Craig), John Haiman, Bernd Heine, Paul Hopper, Christian Lehman, Marianne Mithun, Johanna Nichols, David Payne, Doris Payne, Keren Rice, Sandy Thompson, Russ Tomlin, and David Weber. Although all of these individuals contributed greatly to my thinking and writing as the book evolved, Doris Payne, Keren Rice, and Sandy Thompson stand out as deserving special appreciation for efforts above and beyond what I could possibly have expected.

Many individuals also contributed to the preparation of the document. In particular I would like to thank Kay Beckford for her painstaking work on the abbreviations and bibliography. I also thank Tod Allman and Doris Payne for their help in refining my chaotic thinking and convoluted prose.

Abbreviations

The linguistic examples in this book come from a variety of sources, published, and unpublished, as well as original fieldwork. The transcription and annotation systems used vary considerably from one author to the next. I have kept abbreviations to a minimum by using glosses consistent with the following list. This has required regularization of the spellings of certain abbreviations, but not analyses. For example, the gloss "subject" is abbreviated in a number of different ways in the literature. I have reduced all of these to SUB, but I haven't called anything a "subject" that is not called a subject by the author of the source.

Occasionally two abbreviations appear for the same gloss, e.g., INTRNS and INTR for "intransitive." Conversely, sometimes one abbreviation represents two distinct concepts, e.g., S for "only argument of a single argument clause" and "sentence." I consider these abbreviations to be so common, and their meanings so distinct, that any potential ambiguity is negligible.

1	first person	ADV	adverb
1INC	first person inclusive	AGR	agreement
1PL	first person plural	AN	animate
1SG	first person singular	ANT	anterior
2	second person	AP	antipassive
2DL	second person dual	APL	applicative
2PL	second person, plural	ART	article
2SG, 2S	second person, singular	ASP	aspect
3	third person	ASSOC	associative
3DL	third person, dual	ATR	advanced tongue root
3FSG	third person, feminine singular	AUG	augmentative
3MSG	third person, masculine singular	AUX	auxiliary
3PL	third person, plural	BEN	benefactive
3POS	third person, possessor	CAUS	causative
3SG, 3S	third person, singular	CENT	centric
A	most agent-like argument of a multi-argument clause	CL, CLS	classifier
		CM	case marker
ABS	absolutive case	CN	connective ('and then . . .')
AC	anticausative	COMP	complementizer
ACC	accusative case	COMPL	completive
ACT	actor	COND	conditional
ADJ	adjective	CONT	continuative

CONTR	contrast	LD	left-dislocation
COP	copula	LNK	linker
COR	coreference	LOC	locative
DAT, D	dative	MASC, M	masculine
DC	deictic center	MID	middle voice
DECL	declarative	MIR	mirative
DEF	definite	MKR	marker
DEM	demonstrative	MOD	modifier
DEP	dependent	MSG	masculine singular
DERIV	derivational	MVMT	movement
DET	determiner	N	noun
DETRANS	detransitive	NEG	negative
DIM	diminutive	NEU	neuter
DIR	directional	NF	non-finite
DISJUNCT	disjunction	NOM	nominative case, nominalizer
DIST	distributive	NONFUT	non-future tense
DO	direct object	NONPERF	non-perfective aspect
DR	downriver	NONSPEC:I	non-specific aspect, intransitive
DS	different subject		verb
DUR	durative	NP	noun phrase
E	epenthetic morph	NP_{rel}	relativized noun phrase
ERG	ergative	NS	non-subject
EVID	evidential	OBJ	object
EXIST	existential	OBL	oblique
EXO	exocentric	OBV	obviative
FEM, F	feminine	OPT	optative mode
FOC	focus	P	least agent-like argument of a
FRUST	frustrative		multi-argument clause
FUT	future	PART	participle
GEN, G	genitive	PASS	passive
GF	goal–focus	PAST	past tense
GNO	gnomic	PAST1	first past tense (immediate past)
HAB	habitual	PAST3	third past tense (distant past)
HSY	hearsay	PAT	patient
IMPER, IMP	imperative	PERF	perfective aspect
IMPERF	imperfective aspect	PL	plural
INAN	inanimate	PN, PRN	pronoun
INC	inclusive	POSS	possessive
INCHO	inchoative	POT	potential
INCOMPL	incompletive	PP	prepositional phrase
INCORP	incorporation	PPERF	past-perfective aspect
IND	indicative	PR	participant reference
INDEF	indefinite	PRED	predicate
INDIC	indicative	PREF	prefix
INF	infinitive	PRES	present tense
INFER	inferential mode	PROG	progressive aspect
INFL	inflectional	PROX	proximate
INST	instrumental	PURP	purpose
INTER	interrogative	QM	question marker
INTR,	intransitive	QP	question particle
INTRNS		QUAL	quality
INV	inverse	RECIP	reciprocal
INVIS	invisible	REDUP	reduplication
IRR	irrealis	REF	referential
ITER	iterative	REFL	reflexive

REL	relativizer	SW	soundword
REP	repetitive	TAM	tense, aspect, mode
S	only argument of a single-argument clause, Sentence	THM	theme
		TNS	tense
SEQ	sequence, sequential	TOP	topic
SG	singular	TRANS,	
SIM	simultaneous	TRNS	transitive
SM	subject marker	TVF	truth-value focus
SPEC	specifier	UNDGOER	Undergoer
SS	same subject	UR	upriver
STAT	stative	V	verb
STD	standard	VBLZR	verbalizer
SUB	subject	VER	veridical mode
SUBJ	subjunctive mode		

An asterisk (*) before an example indicates that the example is not a grammatically acceptable expression in the language. A question mark (?) before an example indicates that the example is marginally acceptable.

Introduction

....

Deer says, "So how am I going to cross over?" He goes looking for a tree bridge.
Finally he encounters Squirrel. "There you can cross on my tree bridge. Right over
there is my tree bridge." From a good distance Squirrel leaps. "Yuun!" Squirrel does
not leap from nearby. He says to him, "Just from there leap! Just from there I always
leap." Deer doesn't have the courage to try it. Finally he goes way out. He is close to
the end, when he jumps "cadaquin!" There inside the water boa he falls. Too bad.
(from *The One-eyed Warriors, a Yagua Folktale*, by Laureano Mozombite
[Powlison 1987])

0.1   The purpose of this book

This book is a guide and a bridge. I hope it will be a better guide
than Squirrel, and a better bridge than the water boa. It is a guide for linguistic fieldworkers who desire to write a description of the morphology
and syntax of one of the many under-documented languages of the world.
It is a bridge designed to bring the extensive knowledge of linguistic structure that exists in the literature to bear on the complex and often confusing
task of describing a language.

As this introduction is being written, there are reported to be
about 6,000 languages spoken on Earth (Grimes 1992). About 2,000 of
these have received close attention by linguistic researchers. The other
4,000 (roughly speaking) have only sporadically been described by linguists, and many have not even been recorded in written form for future
generations. Krauss (1992) estimates that 3,000 of the 6,000 or so languages spoken today will become extinct in the next century. The human
and intellectual tragedy of language extinction has been well articulated by
Krauss, Hale (1992), and others. It is not surprising that the 3,000 languages facing extinction come overwhelmingly from the 4,000 or so that
have not been consistently described.

Though descriptive linguistics alone will not solve the problems of
language and culture extinction, it is an important part of the solution. The
mere existence of a good dictionary and grammatical description confers a

certain status on a language that may have previously been despised as having "no grammar" or being "just a dialect," or even "primitive." Furthermore, the products of descriptive linguistic research constitute part of the reference material necessary to develop indigenous educational materials and written literature. Good linguistic research communicates to minority-language speakers and to surrounding communities that the language is viable and worthy of respect. Furthermore, when a language does become extinct, as is inevitable in many cases, the linguistic description and other materials remain as a central part of the cultural heritage of descendants of the language's speakers, as well as of all humanity. Without this documentation, the language, along with the cultural traditions and wisdom embodied in it, is lost forever.

For these reasons, hundreds, if not thousands, of individuals around the world are engaged in primary linguistic description. Not all of these individuals have been trained in the principles of descriptive linguistics, but all share a deep commitment to the vitality and intrinsic value of every human language and culture. An increasing number are native speakers of the under-described language themselves. These fieldworkers often find themselves at a loss as to how to approach the description of a language. This book was conceived with these fieldworkers in mind, and was developed under their guidance.

Experiencing a new language might be likened to arriving in an unfamiliar city with no guide or map to help you find your way around. Writing a grammatical description is like trying to draw your own map, based on your experiences hiking up and down the main roads and back alleys of the city. This book is intended to be a kind of "Michelin Guide to Cities" for the traveler who finds herself in this kind of situation. It is not a map of any particular "city," but it describes the principles and processes according to which cities are known to be designed, and suggests a systematic way of approaching the description of any city from the inside out.

The table of contents of this "Michelin Guide" itself suggests one possible outline for the grammatical description of a language.[1] Beginning with chapter 2, the section headings and subheadings propose one possible system for interpreting, categorizing, and describing grammatical structures (chapter 1 discusses important ethnolinguistic and other background information). Section headings that contain zeros, e.g., "section 4.1.01," are not part of the suggested outline for a grammatical description. Rather, they are extended commentary related to the next-higher outline heading (e.g., section 4.1.01 is extended commentary on section 4.1). At the end of each major section there appear questions that are meant to stimulate thought on key topics in morphosyntactic description. The answers to these questions could constitute the substantive portions of a grammar sketch or full reference grammar. Occasionally a section consists entirely of questions (e.g., section 1.6.1). These are important sections that should not be omitted in a grammatical description, but the topic is judged to be sufficiently self-explanatory as to require no further explanation. In all such cases, references are provided to additional readings for those who may want to pursue the issue further.

Thus, the outline of this guide is like a helicopter ride above the complexities of the city below. The chapters are neighborhoods that can be explored one-by-one, and the subsections are streets likely to be found within particular neighborhoods. However, even as a map cannot be produced only from the vantage point of a helicopter, so a grammar cannot be produced simply on the basis of an outline. The fieldworker must walk the streets and get to know the particular buildings, landmarks, and idiosyncrasies of this individual city. Although there are similarities among cities, so there are also many differences. The same is true for languages. One outline will not fit every language exactly. It takes sensitivity, creativity, and experience to create a description that is consistent with the properties of the language itself, and not wholly dependent on a preconceived outline. A basic assumption of the book is that the best way to understand language, as well as any particular language, is intense interaction with data. For this reason, text and extensive examples are provided, showing how similar neighborhoods in other cities are arranged. However, it is possible that the language you are studying exhibits some new pattern, or some new complexity not illustrated in the text and examples. It is important, in such cases, to document the unusual pattern as explicitly as possible, and to describe it in relation to the known range of variation.

While the known range of variation should not be perceived as a straitjacket that every language must be forced into, it is a valuable tool for organizing one's thoughts about language and communicating those thoughts to others. After all, a great deal is already known about what languages are like. In fact, there is so much literature available that one can not possibly be familiar with all of it. Furthermore, field linguists often work in isolated settings where access to library resources is limited. In this sense the book is intended to be a bridge as well as a guide. It is a bridge that will take you, the linguistic researcher, to the specific literature on the particular descriptive issue you are facing, and bring the valuable knowledge available in the literature to bear on the technical task of describing a particular language.

Insofar as possible, I have tried to suggest a system of organization that is consistent with general principles of late twentieth-century linguistic science. That is, the categories, terms, and concepts found in this book should be understandable to linguists from a variety of theoretical orientations, even if the linguists do not use the particular terminology themselves. I have noted alternate terminological usages whenever possible, but have undoubtedly not covered all possibilities. As you work through the grammar of a language using the outline of this book as a guide, questions will undoubtedly arise as to the appropriateness of particular definitions and interpretations to the language you are describing. This is good. It is only through honest interaction with data that linguists learn where our theoretical conceptions need to be revised. It might be said that one purpose of this book is to encourage field linguists to find holes in current theoretical understandings of linguistic structures. To the extent that it makes such understandings accessible, then it has accomplished its task.

In the remainder of this chapter, I will introduce some of the central concepts, metaphors, and terminology that appear throughout this book.

0.2   Some terminology and recurring metaphors

0.2.1   Language is a symbolic system

It is very important for field linguists to have a healthy respect for the difference, and interdependence, between **meaning** and **form**. Some of the most strident controversies and misunderstandings in linguistics can be boiled down to an argument between someone who believes that linguistic form, or structure, derives directly from meaning, and someone else who believes that form is entirely autonomous of meaning, or language in use. At several points in the following pages, this distinction will be illustrated

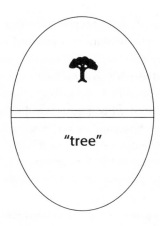

Figure 0.1 The form–function composite

and reiterated. As a preliminary characterization, meaning refers to what a language is used for, and form is the linguistic expressions themselves.

Linguists engaged in grammatical description commonly assume that language consists of elements of form that people employ to "mean," "express," "code," "represent," or "refer to" other things.[2] Although linguists (even good descriptive linguists) often imply that the linguistic forms themselves express concepts, this must be taken as a shorthand way of saying that speakers *use* linguistic forms (among other things) to accomplish acts of expressing, referring, representing, etc. (Brown and Yule 1983: 27ff.). For example, a word is a linguistic form. In and of itself it is just a noise emitted from someone's vocal apparatus. What makes it a *word* rather than just a random noise is that it is uttered intentionally in order to express some idea, or concept. When used by a skilled speaker, words can combine with other elements of linguistic form, such as prefixes, suffixes, and larger structures, to express very complex ideas. While the linguistic forms may aid in the formulation of ideas, or may constrain the concepts that can be entertained, the language itself is logically distinct from the ideas that might be expressed.

Langacker (1987), building on Saussure (1915), describes linguistic units as consisting of form–meaning composites. This property can be diagrammed as in figure 0.1. The upper half of the diagram in figure 0.1 represents the meanings, concepts, or ideas expressed in language, while the bottom half represents the linguistic units themselves. The double line across the center represents the relationship, or the **bond** between the two. Various terms can be and have been used to refer to the components of this composite. Terms associated with the top half include "signified," "meaning," "semantics," "pragmatics," "function," "conceptual domain," and "content." Terms associated with the bottom half include "signifier," "symbol," "structure," "form," "formal domain," and "grammar." Other terms are associated with the relationship between the two halves, B(ottom) and T(op). These include B "means" T, B "expresses" T, B "embodies" T, B "realizes" T, B "codes" T, B "represents" T, B "symbolizes" T, T "is a function of" B, etc.

As descriptive linguists we assume that the bond between symbol and signified item is **intentional**. That is, the language user intends to establish a representational link between form and meaning. From this it follows that the forms used to represent concepts will be structured so as to make the link obvious, within limits of cognition, memory, etc. This is not to deny the possibility that certain aspects of language may actually have no relation to the conceptual domain or may even serve to *conceal* concepts. However, we make it a working assumption that in general language users expect and want linguistic forms to represent concepts to be expressed.

In any symbolic system, form and meaning cannot be randomly related to one another. In other words a system is not a symbolic system at all if there is no consistency in the relationship between the symbols and categories or dimensions in the symbolized realm. Ideal symbolic systems (e.g., computer "languages") maximize this principle by establishing a direct, invariant coding relationship between every form and its meaning or meanings. However, real language is not an ideal symbolic system in this sense. It exists in an environment where variation and change are the rule rather than the exception. New functions for language appear every day in the form of new situations and concepts that speakers wish to discuss. Vocal and auditory limitations cause inexact articulations and incomplete perceptions of messages. These and many other factors lead to variation in the form of language, even in the speech of a single speaker. The bond between form and meaning in real language, then, is neither rigid nor random; it is direct enough to allow communication, but flexible enough to allow for creativity, variation, and change.

0.2.2   Prototypes and "Fuzzy Categories"

The notion of **prototype** in linguistics stems from the work of psycholinguist Eleanor Rosch (Rosch 1977, Rosch and Lloyd 1978, Mervis and Rosch 1981) and others on the human tendency to categorize the universe. A prototype is the best example of a category. So, for example, the prototypical "bird" for most English speakers is probably something like a sparrow – it has all the properties we think of as being appropriate to the category we have called "bird." A chicken is less than a prototypical bird, since it doesn't really fly all that much, and has a specific barnyard function. Similarly, a kiwi is even further from the prototype since it has no wings.

In linguistics, the notion of prototype has been very useful insofar as language is the aspect of human behavior through which categorization is most apparent. When we speak, we of necessity categorize the conceptual universe (the upper half of the form–function composite). For example, there is a very large number of things in the world that can be designated with the word "tree." In fact, if we include hypothetical worlds and plausible metaphorical extensions, there is an infinite number of referents for the word "tree." It is actually quite amazing that there is one word that refers to this tremendously large and varied category of items. Of course, there are kinds of trees, and modifiers can be added to clarify the intended referent. But still, in the process of speaking, one must decide whether a given concept "qualifies" as an instance of the category "tree" or not. The research mentioned above (Rosch *et al.*) has shown that people identify the category of a concept on the basis of an image, a "mind-picture" if you will, that typifies the entire category. Other concepts are then identified with the category because of their perceived similarity to the image, or prototype. Examples of the linguistic use of the principle of prototypes will be presented at various points throughout this book.

0.2.3   Morphosyntactic operations and operators

The terms **operation** and **operator** will come up often in the following discussions of linguistic form. A morphosyntactic operation is a relation between one linguistic form and another that correlates with a conventionalized meaning distinction.[3] The relation is normally ordered from simpler to more complex forms. The simplest forms can be termed **roots**. In most cases the presence of a morphosyntactic operation is evinced by a formal operator, e.g., a prefix, a suffix, a stress shift or a combination of two or more of these (see section 2.3 for a detailed exposition of the morphological means that languages employ to express operations). However, some operations exist independently of any overt expression. One method of noting the existence of a morphosyntactic operation that has no overt expression is to posit a zero morpheme.

0.2.4   Discourse is like a play: scenes, scripts, and the discourse stage

Throughout this book we will be using such terms as **message world** and **discourse stage** in discussing the conceptual part of linguistic communication. We can understand these terms as metaphors for the conceptual domain expressed in language. As mentioned above, it is crucial to keep this domain separate from the formal domain of linguistic structure. Concepts exist even if no one ever expresses them in language. The structure of language is certainly influenced by the concepts expressed, just as the structure of a nail, for example, is influenced by the nature of the task of attaching pieces of wood. However, a nail is not the task, and the nail does not accomplish the task on its own. So the linguistic expression, be it a word, a clause, or a discourse, is not itself the concept being discussed. It is a tool used by someone to express that concept.

From this perspective, discourse can be described metaphorically as a stage on which a play is being acted out. Much research on discourse comprehension and production has used some form of this metaphor to formulate substantive hypotheses and claims about how people communicate. For example, Minsky (1975) uses the term **frames** to refer to stereotyped situations within which knowledge is categorized and stored in memory, e.g., the "restaurant" frame consists of tables, chairs, waiters/ waitresses, food, a check, etc. Schank and Abelson (1977), building on Schank (1972), introduced the notion of **scripts**. Whereas a frame is a static set of entities in a particular arrangement, e.g., a restaurant, a script is a potentially dynamic set of events and situations, e.g., the process of sitting down, ordering, and dining at a restaurant. Fillmore (1976, 1977) suggests that verbs with their unique case frames activate **scenes** in the minds of language users. Lakoff's (1987) notion of **cognitive model** is an extension and elaboration of the notion of scene. What frames, scripts, scenes, and cognitive models have in common is that all are idealized mental structures, "pictures" if you will, that the human mind uses to categorize and store experience and knowledge. These approaches capture the fact that all knowledge is acquired and stored embedded in a context. One way of thinking about such a context is in terms of the metaphor of a **discourse stage**.

0.2.5   Building a message is like building a building

At several points in this book we will describe three methods by which languages are used to accomplish communicative tasks. These methods are **lexical**, **morphological**, and **analytic** (or **periphrastic**). In describing how these methods are used, it is sometimes helpful to think of the process of building a message as similar to the process of building a building. In the rest of this section we will briefly explore this simile.

Every building has a unique function. The proposed function of a particular building affects its form from the earliest design stages and throughout the construction process. If I am building a building, I have at my disposal certain raw materials, and an idea (perhaps a blueprint) of what the building is supposed to become. For now, let us suppose the raw materials are irregularly shaped stones. The construction process consists of taking stones from a resource pile and placing them judiciously into locations in the emerging wall of the building, being constantly conscious of the blueprint (i.e., I don't randomly pile stones together). The locations have certain shapes because of the stones I have already placed there, and the stones in my resource pile also have various shapes. My task is to match resource stones to locations in such a way that the result is a building that serves the intended purpose.

So, what do I do in the many situations where a particular stone does not quite fit the current location? The three main processes, it seems, would be:

1   Look for another stone.
2   Reshape the current stone or the location.
3   Combine two or more stones.

Other possible processes that have occurred to members of various classes I have taught are:

4   Get a stone from a different pile.
5   Use a lot of mortar.
6   Change the blueprint.
7   Give up.

Perhaps there are others. If this is a good simile for the process of building a message, then all (or at least many) of these procedures should have analogs in message-building.

All messages have a function. This follows from the assumption that language behavior is intentional. People normally do not use language randomly (though I think I know some who do). The form a message takes is affected by the function of the message. The resources available to the message builder are an idea of what is to be communicated and a store of conventionalized structures, e.g., vocabulary items, sentence structures, and morphological operators. The task of message-building involves judiciously fitting together existing structures in a unique way to create the particular message that is needed. At any given point in the process there is a partially complete message and a range of possible structures available to build the message in the intended direction. What processes are available to the communicator if a particular unit, say a vocabulary item, does not fit the message context?:

1 Get another lexical item.   (lexical)
2 Modify the first one, or the context. (morphological)
3 Combine lexical items.   (periphrastic)

For example, if my message requires the semantic notion of CAUSE(x, DIE(y)), i.e., something caused something else to die (see section 8.1 for an explanation of the predicate calculus notation), English offers me two strategies for accomplishing that function. I can use the verb *kill* or I can use the expression "cause to die." *Kill* is a lexical solution to the problem because it is a lexical item that embodies all the needed information within its conventionalized semantic makeup. "Cause to die," on the other hand, is a periphrastic strategy for accomplishing essentially the same task (though see section 8.1.1 for a discussion of common functional differences between periphrastic and lexical causatives). Some languages, e.g., Turkish, use a special morpheme to indicate causation. This is added to the root meaning "die" to form a new root meaning "kill." This is a morphological causative.

This triad of lexical, morphological, and periphrastic strategies is relevant to many different functional tasks in language. Some tasks that are typically accomplished by one strategy in one language may be accomplished by one of the other strategies in the next language. For example, past tense is expressed morphologically in English by a verb suffix. In other languages the time of a situation is expressed periphrastically by temporal adverbial phrases such as "two days ago," etc. Furthermore, languages invariably allow certain functions to be accomplished by more than one strategy. This is the case with *kill* and *cause to die* in English. Usually, however, when such a choice exists there is usually some slight difference in function between the various possibilities.

But what about the other possible strategies for building a building? Are there relevant analogies in message-building to the strategies suggested by students for building a stone building? How good is this simile anyway?

1 Go to a different pile. How about going to the lexicon of some other language? Sometimes the right English word just doesn't come to mind at the right time, but there is a perfect Spanish word just waiting to be used. If I judge my interlocutor will understand, I may just use that Spanish word. This is referred to as **code mixing** and is very common around the world, as most societies are multilingual.

2 Use a lot of mortar. Well, er, um, I dunno, maybe . . . I mean it's like you just kinda slop your message together a little, ya know?

3 Change the blueprint. Conceivably I may have so much trouble expressing a particular message, that I may just decide to say something a little different instead.

4 Give up. This strategy has a direct analog in message-building.

0.3   Conclusion

In summary, language is both a tool used by people for communication and a formal symbolic system. Any approach to linguistic description must be aware of both of these properties. The art of conceptualizing and describing a language involves analyzing its formal systematic properties, and interpreting them in light of the language's essentially human and communicative character. As a linguistic researcher, my understanding of the formal systematic properties of language must be informed by an understanding of the purposes language serves and the human environment in which it exists. Similarly, my understanding of the functions of particular morphosyntactic forms in communication must be informed by an under-standing of the ways in which those forms relate to one another in the for-mal system of the language. My understanding on either front is enriched as I concentrate on understanding the other.

As so aptly stated by Squirrel: "Just leap. Just from there I always leap."

1 Demographic and ethnographic information

The first task of a grammar or grammar sketch is to identify the language being described, and to provide certain particulars concerning its ethnolinguistic context. It is also important to orient the reader to previous literature and other research that has been done on the language.

1.1 The name of the language

Self-referent or **auto-denomination** are the anthropological terms for the name a group of people uses to refer to themselves. Often this name can only be translated as "people," or "human beings." It may also have hierarchically related meanings. For example, the word *e'ñapa* in Panare (a Carib language of Venezuela) means "person" when used in opposition to the term *në'na* "wild animal" or "evil spirit." The same term means "indigenous person" when used in opposition to the term *tato* "outsider"/"white person." Finally, the term can also refer strictly to Panares, when used in opposition to terms referring to neighboring indigenous groups. Only the context can disambiguate.

The terms by which language groups are known to outsiders are usually drawn from the outsiders' language, and are often derogatory in nature, e.g., in Peru the group now known as the Urarina used to be called the *Chimaco*, a Quechua term meaning "unreliable." Such terms are often not recognized by the people themselves, and, as in the case with Urarina, the self-referent can sometimes be substituted for the outsiders' term. On the other hand, the term *Panare* mentioned above is a Tupí word meaning "friend." So the outsiders' form of reference is not always derogatory. If there is a well-established tradition in the literature of using the outsiders' term, a linguistic researcher should not try to change it, unless the people themselves are offended by the general term and clearly would prefer to be known by the self-referent.

> **?**
>
> What is the language known as to outsiders?
> What term do the people use to distinguish themselves from other language groups?
> What is the origin of these terms (if known)?

1.2   Ethnology

The linguistic researcher may be tempted to spend a lot of time describing the material culture and cosmology of the people who speak the language being described. Careful ethnographic notes should be taken throughout your fieldwork, since an essential aspect of knowing a language is knowing the people who speak that language. However, the amount of space dedicated to this topic in a grammatical description should be limited. A detailed ethnography is a worthy topic for a separate monographic study. Some grammatical descriptions that include good, informative, and culturally sensitive ethnological introductions include Dixon (1972), Craig (1977), and Austin (1981). All too often descriptive grammars contain no ethnological information whatsoever, or it is consigned to footnotes.

> **?**
>
> What is the dominant economic activity of the people?
> Briefly describe the ecosystem, material culture, and cosmology (these will
> be intimately related).

1.3   Demography

A map of the area in which the language is spoken is usually helpful in a grammatical description. Be sure to include the locations of other language groups.

> **?**
>
> Where is the language spoken, and how are the people distributed in this area?
> Are there other language groups inhabiting the same area?
> What is the nature of the interaction with these language groups? Economic?
> Social? Friendly? Belligerent?
> In social/economic interactions with other groups, which groups are
> dominant and which are marginalized? How so?

1.4   Genetic affiliation

It is important to situate the language among its genetic relatives. In this section, describe previous research that has attempted to establish genetic relationhips within the language family, as well as external connections.

> **?**
> What language family does this language belong to?
> What are its closest relatives?

1.5   Previous research

It is very important to be aware of *all* work that has been done on a particular language or language family. If possible, you should get to know personally the prominent scholars in the field. True scholars are always eager to interact with anyone who shows a sincere interest in their work. You should become thoroughly familiar with all historical/comparative work done on the language and/or its family. There are few language families for which no previous work exists. Diachronic and comparative observations will then inform the grammatical description at every point, and you will have a good idea of where your own work fits within the general scheme of investigation on this language. However, previous work must be evaluated closely before you assume that the linguistic work has "been done."

The following sources will provide a good general introduction to the languages and language families of the world. These should be seen as starting points for detailed and exhaustive research into the specific literature relating to the language being studied: Voegelin and Voegelin (1977), B. Grimes (1992).

> **?**
> What published and unpublished linguistic work has been done in this language and/or its close relatives?

1.6   The sociolinguistic situation

1.6.1   Multilingualism and language attitudes

> **?**
> What percentage of the people are monolingual? (Treat men and women separately.)

What language(s) are people multilingual in, and to what degree?
As far as you can tell, what is the attitude of the speakers of this language toward their language, as opposed to other languages they may know? If possible, give evidence for your claims even though it may be anecdotal.

References: Sankoff (1980), Baugh and Sherzer (1984), Fasold (1992a, chs. 1 and 6).

....

1.6.2   Contexts of use and language choice

?..

In what contexts are multilingual individuals likely to use the language described in this sketch? When do they use other languages?

References: Sherzer (1977), Bauman and Sherzer (1974), Besnier (1986), Baugh and Sherzer (1984), Fasold (1992a, ch. 7).

....

1.6.3   Viability

Here I will suggest some rules of thumb for assessing the viability of a language that may be on the verge of extinction. These should not be considered definitive by any means, since a language's viability may be affected by any number of extralinguistic factors. Factors that lead to language extinction include assimilation to another culture and language, migration, disease, genocide, and insensitive government policies. Factors that lead to language maintenance and preservation include literacy campaigns, nationalistic movements within the group, and humanitarian government policies. With these qualifications in mind, here are the rules of thumb:

1 If there are no, or extremely few, children under the age of ten who are learning the language as their only language, the language will become extinct in the lifetime of the youngest mother-tongue speakers (i.e., sixty to seventy years).

2 If there is more than a handful of ten-year-old children who are monolingual in the language, and who have regular contact with each other (i.e., they live in the same community), the language will be taught to the next generation. This means that in sixty years the language will still be used as a regular means of everyday conversation in some communities. The viability of the language may still improve or deteriorate depending on sociological and other factors.

3 If many children are learning the language monolingually and essential economic activity (e.g., buying, selling, and/or distributing of essential goods) is conducted in the language, extinction is not imminent – the language could persist indefinitely.

The topic of language death and viability relates to the question of whether someone can be a "partially competent" native speaker of a language. It is clearly possible to have a native-like knowledge of one part of a language system and be lacking in another part. For example, one can have native-like phonology and syntax, but lack a wide vocabulary and have imperfect gender and case morphology, or satisfactory phonology and morphology but gaps in the syntax and vocabulary. It also appears that items heard in early childhood can persist in long-term memory and reappear in consciousness only decades later (Wayles Browne, p.c.). Also, there are cases where individuals appear to lack full fluency in any language. Such individuals are sometimes referred to as **semilinguals**, though this term is considered by some to be insulting, and therefore should be avoided if possible. For example, among the Yagua people of northeastern Peru, certain younger women who are partially culturally assimilated to the national culture do not apparently have full command of Spanish or Yagua. These women stand out in comparison to (a) older culturally assimilated women who speak Yagua fluently and some Spanish, (b) non-assimilated women of all ages who speak only Yagua fluently, and (c) all men, who speak Yagua fluently and Spanish to varying degrees of fluency. In all situations that I was able to observe, including conversations with their husbands, these younger, assimilated women would not speak Yagua at all, and would only speak rudimentary Spanish, even though their husbands and others would address them in Yagua. It is hard to imagine that these women were fluent but "latent" speakers of Yagua.

Because people may be partially competent speakers, it is often difficult to assess whether children are really becoming native speakers of a language. They may be becoming "partial" speakers, thus complicating the issue of how long the language is likely to remain viable as an everyday means of communication.

?

Are children learning the language as their first language? If so, how long do they remain monolingual?

What pressures are there on young people to (a) learn another language, and (b) reject their own language? How strong are these pressures?

Are there partially competent speakers?

References: Dorian (1981), Fasold (1992a, ch. 8).

1.6.4   Loan words

Languages "borrow" words from other languages under various circumstances. The references provide discussions of the sociological circumstances of linguistic borrowing. Multilingual speakers will, of course, borrow words and whole constructions for the nonce from another language if a native term is not readily available. This practice is termed **code mixing** or **code switching**, and is extremely common in multilingual societies. However, a vocabulary item from another language can be considered a borrowing only if it is recognized by otherwise monolingual speakers in appropriate native contexts. In other words, a word has been borrowed into another language only when it has become part of the lexical system of that language, as recognized by monolingual speakers. For example, the word *canoe* can be considered an English word, even though it is of Carib origin, because English speakers who have no knowledge of a Cariban language will use the term freely with no sense that it is a "foreign" word. However, if I use a Yagua term like *sámirya*, meaning "OK," in the middle of a discourse that is otherwise in English, this is not a borrowing. It can only be used between people who have some knowledge of Yagua, hence it would more appropriately be classified as code switching.

?
Does the lexicon of this language contain many words from other languages? If so, in what semantic domains do these tend to occur? Give examples.

References: Fasold (1992b, vol. II, ch. 2), Hill and Hill (1980).

1.7   Dialects

The common sociolinguistic distinction between **language** and **dialect** is the following: two speech varieties are said to be dialects of one language if speakers of the two varieties can understand one another immediately, i.e., with no period of familiarization on the part of either speaker. Conversely, two speech varieties are said to be two distinct languages if speakers cannot understand one another (i.e., communication is severely impaired) until they have adjusted their production and comprehension to allow for the variation. As yet there is no standard definition that is more explicit than this.

Variation is a fact of every language. Variation can be individual, as in variant pronunciations of the word *economics* or *either* in English. It can be sociological: e.g., I might pronounce the word *often* with the *t*, avoid certain terms or sentence structures, etc., in formal contexts. Occasionally it can be geographical, e.g., in Britain the term *pants* typically refers to what in America is referred to as *underpants*, whereas the same word *pants* in America corresponds, in its most common sense, to the British term *trousers*.

Often people assume a "dialect" is a form of speech used in a certain geographic area. However, geographic separation is only one source among many of linguistic variation. For the purposes of a grammar sketch, it is helpful to include some brief information on known geographically defined dialects. Nevertheless, most variation is not primarily defined geographically. That is, it is usually not the case that a particular variant form is restricted to or characteristic of a particular geographic region, though many are. In support of this claim we need only reflect on the source of variation. People's speech (and behavior generally) tends to become more like that of those people with whom they identify and interact. Even within a geographic region there are typically several sociologically distinct groups (defined by age, occupation, culture, interests, etc.). Members of each group unconsciously (and occasionally consciously) imitate the norms of their particular group and ignore the norms of other groups. This is true of traditional societies, as well as more complex societies. If such an "identification group" centers in a geographic area to the exclusion of others, the speech that characterizes a group can be said to be a geographically defined dialect. Geographical variation, therefore, can be considered to be but one kind of sociological variation.

Language variation can occur at any of the traditional levels of linguistic analysis, i.e., phonetics, phonology, morphology, syntax, and discourse. If dialects are mentioned in the sketch, it helps to specify at which of these levels the major observed differences lie, and give examples. In any case, one should not dwell on this section in a linguistic grammar. Again, there is usually enough complexity in the area of linguistic variation to constitute a monographic study in and of itself.

?

Is there significant dialect variation? What kinds of differences distinguish the dialects? Give examples.

What dialect is represented in the sketch?

References: Chambers and Trudgill (1980), Nelson (1983), Simons (1983), Trudgill (1986), Fasold (1992b, ch. 8).

2   Morphological typology

2.0   Historical background and definitions

Morphology is the study of shapes. For example, one can talk about the morphology of camels – different species of camels have different morphologies, i.e., they have different body shapes. Morphology in linguistics has to do with the shapes of words. How are words shaped in such-and-such a language? What systematic rules determine when and how they may adjust their shapes? Traditionally, morphology has also been concerned with the "categories" (i.e., "operations" or "functions") represented by adjustments in the shapes of words, as distinct from those operations represented by lexical or analytic processes (see Introduction, section 0.2.3).

In the rest of this section I will briefly define some terms used in discussions of morphology. After that, an outline for a possible chapter on morphological typology will be suggested.

A **morpheme** is a minimal shape. The classical definition of a morpheme is a minimal formal shape or piece that expresses meaning. For example the English word *dogs* contains two morphemes: *dog*, which embodies the main semantic content of the expression, and *-s*, which embodies the meaning of plurality. The form *dog* itself is not further divisible into meaningful component pieces, therefore it is a morpheme – a minimal shape. In most situations this definition works fine. However, more current approaches acknowledge the fact that particular meanings are not necessarily directly linked to particular pieces of form. For example, in Maasai (an Eastern Nilotic language of Kenya and Tanzania) many morphemes are not pieces of form at all; rather, they are tone patterns. Example 1a is in the active voice while 1b is the contrasting "middle" voice (examples courtesy of Jonathan Ololoso). The only difference between these two clauses is the tone patterns indicating voice on the verb and case on the noun:

(1)   a. ɛ́yɛ́tá   ɛmʊtí
            remove.meat pot.ACC
            "She removed meat from the pot."

       b. ɛyɛ́ta   ɛmóti
            remove.meat.MID pot.NOM
            "The pot is 'de-meated.' "

Furthermore, the meaning contributed by a morpheme may vary depending on other morphemes in the immediate environment. The whole message may be more than, less than, or simply different from the sum of the "meanings" of all the morphemes in the message. Therefore in this book we will conceptualize morphology as a system of adjustments in the shapes of words that contribute to adjustments in the way speakers intend their utterances to be interpreted. This is the basis of the operator/operation terminology introduced in the Introduction, section 0.2.3.

The forms of words in messages are shaped in a variety of ways, including but not limited to the addition of pieces of form. The precise meaning inferred by the hearer is developed via interaction among the linguistic context, the extralinguistic context, and the conventionalized meaning of the morphological operator or operators employed. It does not reside solely in the morphological operators. This view is consistent with the "Word and Paradigm" approach to morphology proposed by Anderson (1982). Anderson and others working in the Word and Paradigm framework conceive of morphemes as rules involving the linguistic context rather than as isolated "chunks" of linguistic matter. Ideally, the descriptive linguist should be able to go beyond the linguistic context to specify how a morpheme interacts with the non-linguistic context as well (see, e.g., Sperber and Wilson 1986 for hints in this direction). Unfortunately, such a worthy undertaking is beyond the scope of most reference grammars. In writing a reference grammar, one should be concerned with the conventionalized effects each morpheme has in its most common linguistic contexts.

A **bound morpheme** is a morpheme that must be attached to some other morpheme in order to be integrated naturally into discourse. It can be an **affix**, a **root**, or a **clitic**. The suffix -*s* in *dogs* is an example of a bound morpheme, since it could never be uttered by itself. The root, *dog*, on the other hand, is a **free morpheme** since it does not have to attach to some other form. In many languages roots are bound morphemes in the sense that they cannot be integrated into discourse without having something attached to them, e.g., the Spanish root *habl-* "speak" must be inflected before it can be used in discourse.

A **clitic** is a bound morpheme that functions at a phrasal or clausal level, but which binds phonologically to some other word, known as the **host**. Clause-level clitics often bind to either the first or the last element of a clause, whether that element is a noun, a verb, an adverb, an auxiliary, or any other word class. If the clitic occurs on the first element, it can attach to either the front or the end of that element. If it attaches to the end of that element it can be termed a "second-position" clitic. Clitics occurring on the last element of a clause always cliticize to the end (Klavans 1985).

The articles *a* and *the* in English are clitics, because (a) they cannot be integrated into standard discourse without being bound to some other form, and (b) they function on the phrase level; therefore their host can be any of several noun-phrase constituents:

(2)   the dog   cliticized to head
        the big dog   cliticized to modifier
        the two big dogs   cliticized to numeral

Evidence that these forms are bound to the element that follows includes the fact that in most spoken varieties, morphophonemic rules affect the boundary. The vowel of *the* is unreduced when appearing before a vowel-initial element and reduced when appearing before a consonant-initial element:[1]

(3)   [ði æpl]   "the apple"
        [ðə dɔg]   "the dog"

The article *a* takes a final nasal when appearing before a vowel, and takes no nasal but reduces to ə when appearing before a consonant:

(4)   [æn æpl]   "an apple"
        [ə dɔg]   "a dog"

It is arguably the case that all formatives that have been called "grammatical particles" are in fact clitics (Zwicky 1973). However, it is most common to use the term clitic for morphemes that express participant reference (anaphoric clitics) and clause level modality (epistemic or "discourse" clitics). It is not common to use the term clitic for, e.g., adpositions, case markers, tense/aspect particles, auxiliaries, semantic role or pragmatic status markers.

An **allomorph** is a variant pronunciation of a morpheme. For example the plural morpheme usually written as -*s* in English has at least three allomorphs: [-s] as in [hæts] "hats," [-z] as in [dɔgz] "dogs," and [-ïz] as in [báksïz] "boxes." Sometimes morphemes are conceived of as sets of allomorphs. Determining the "underlying" or "basic" form of a morpheme is important for developing a writing system and for glossing texts, but it is not a major theoretical issue that need occupy a great deal of space in a grammar sketch or reference grammar. The references cited below contain many suggestions for determining underlying forms and rules for deriving surface forms. Sometimes in the literature the terms "morph" or "formative" are used to refer to particular morphological shapes if it is unknown or unimportant whether they constitute morphemes or allomorphs of other morphemes.

Morphophonemic rules have the form of phonological rules, but are restricted to particular morphological contexts. The allomorphs of a particular morpheme are derived from phonological rules and any morphophonemic rules that may apply to that morpheme. For example, the allomorph [-s] of the plural morpheme /-z/ in English is determined by a general phonological rule that can be represented in generative notation as follows (see Burquest and Payne, 1994, for an explanation of this notation):

$$C \rightarrow [-\text{voice}] \, / \, [-\text{voice}]\_\_\_\_$$
$$[-\text{son}]$$

This is a phonological rule because it applies to all non-sonorant segments, not just the plural marker. On the other hand, the allomorphs [il] and [ir] of the prefix /in-/, meaning "not" in English, are determined by a morphophonemic rule. This is evidenced by the fact that not all examples of /n/ become [l] or [r] when occurring before /l/ or /r/. It is only the /n/ of the prefix /in-/:

(5)   irrational   /in+ræšənəl/
         irrespective   /in+rɪspéktɪv/
         irresponsible /in+rɪspánsɪbl/

illegal   /in+ligl/
illogical   /in+lajɪkl/
illiterate   /in+lɪtərət/
etc.

The prefixes /un-/ and /non-/, for example, do not exhibit this pattern:

(6)   unresponsive (*urresponsive)
         unreliable (*urreliable)
         unreached (*urreached)
         unlimited (*ullimited)
         unleash (*ulleash)
         non-lethal (*nol-lethal)
         etc.

Therefore the rules n → l / __ l and n → r /__ r are not phonological rules. They must be specified as occurring only with the prefix /in-/. Whenever such morphological information is required to specify the environment for an allophonic rule, the rule is morphophonemic.

Morphophonemic rules may be presented in the sections dealing with particular morphological operations. The notation used to represent the rules is normally compatible with the notation used to express phonological rules. The Word and Paradigm framework provides a notational system that is uniquely suited to languages with a great deal of morphophonemic variation and to languages that are highly fusional (see section 2.1.2 below).

A **root** is an unanalyzable form that expresses the basic lexical content of the word. Yet a root does not necessarily constitute a fully understandable word in and of itself. An inflectional operation, often involving a prefix or a suffix, may be required. For example, the form *habl-* in Spanish is a root.

A **stem** consists minimally of a root, but may be analyzable into a root plus derivational morphemes (see below). Like a root, a stem may or may not be a fully understandable word. For example, the form *tyajtépe* in Panare is a stem composed of the root *tyaj-* "to listen/hear," plus a derivational suffix *-tépe* meaning "want to." This stem cannot be integrated into natural discourse without the addition of further inflectional operations. In English, the forms *construct* and *destruct* are stems in that they inflect like other verbs but are themselves analyzable into a root, *-struct*, plus a derivational prefix.

Derivational operations are defined as operations which derive an inflectable stem from a root or an intermediate stem. However, a root plus derivational operation alone may or may not be a fully formed word (see Anderson 1985a for a definition of the term "word"). In the following example from Panare (Cariban, Venezuela), the verb root is *aamë* "raise." This root has two derivational morphemes, *s-* "DETRANS" and *o-* "INTRans." These are clearly derivational because they are not required (*yaamëñe* alone means "he raises it"), and when they do occur, they are not sufficient to allow the verb form to be integrated into discourse (**saamë*, **osaamë*):

(7)   Tée   y-o-s-aamë-n   e'ñapa tyityasa'
        s.w.appear 3-INTR-DETRANS-raise-NONSPEC:I person one
        "There someone stood up." (i.e., raised himself)

In effect, then, these derivational prefixes take the root meaning "raise" and convert it into another verb meaning "stand up." This operation may be termed **reflexivization** and is a very common sort of function for derivational morphology (see sections 3.2.2 and 8.2.1).

The prefix–suffix combination *y-* . . . *-n* seen in example 7, on the other hand, consists of inflectional operators. First, they (or other members of the same **paradigm**) are required in order for the verb to be properly integrated into discourse. Second, they are sufficient to allow the verb to be integrated into discourse. No other affixation is necessary.

According to Bybee (1985) derivational operations tend to be more **relevant** to the situation expressed in the root than do inflectional operations. Derivational operations consist primarily of the following:

1 Operations that change the grammatical category of a root, e.g., denominalization (changing a noun into some other category) and nominalization (changing a form of any grammatical category into a noun; see sections 5.2 and 9.1).
2 Operations that change the valence (transitivity) of a verb root, e.g., detransitivization, causativization, and desiderative (see section 3.2.2 and chapter 8).
3 Operations which in other ways significantly change the basic concept expressed by the root, e.g., distributive, diminutive (see section 9.7).

Characteristics of derivational operations include the following:

1 They are "non-obligatory" insofar as they are employed in order to adjust the basic semantic content of roots and are not themselves determined by some other operation or element in the syntactic structure.

2 They tend to be idiosyncratic and non-productive.
3 They tend not to occur in well-defined paradigms.

Inflectional operations are those which are required by the syntactic environment in which a root appears. Inflectional operations do not normally alter the basic meaning of the concept expressed; rather, they ground the concept expressed by a root according to place, time, participant reference, etc. That is, they specify *when* the event or situation took place, *who* or *what* were the participants or possessors, and sometimes *where*, *how*, or *whether* an event or situation really took place. According to Bybee (1985), inflectional operations tend to be less **relevant** to the concept described by the root. Typical inflectional operations include:

1 Person, number, gender, etc. (see section 9.5).
2 Tense, aspect, mode (see section 9.3).

Characteristics of inflectional operations include the following:

1 They are grammatically required in certain syntactic environments, e.g.,
   the main verb of an English sentence must be inflected for subject and
   tense.
2 They tend to be regular and productive (at least in comparison to
   derivational operations).
3 They tend to occur in paradigms, i.e., sets of forms of which one form must
   be selected in certain environments. For example, there are two
   morphological tenses in English, one of which must be specified for all
   independent verbs.

In summary, inflectional operations create fully formed words that are able to be integrated into discourse, whereas derivational operations create stems that are not necessarily fully grounded, and which may still require inflectional operations before they can be integrated into discourse.

As with all functional oppositions, inflection vs. derivation is less a distinction than a continuum. Some operations fall in between the prototypical extremes, and operations tend to migrate diachronically from one type to the other. Also, a given form may sometimes accomplish an inflectional task and other times a derivational task. Nevertheless, the prototypes of the extremes of this continuum do seem to be instantiated in many languages, and are therefore often worth discussing briefly in a grammar sketch or reference grammar.

2.1   Traditional morphological typology

One of the first items of business in analyzing the grammar of a language is determining what sort of language it is in terms of its morphology. This section will provide a framework and suggestions for understanding the morphological typology of a language.

A **typology** is simply a division of a range of phenomena into types. To "typologize" a phenomenon is to categorize it into types. For example, a typology of motorized vehicles might consist of a list containing trucks, automobiles, buses, etc. The value of a typology to those who study natural phenomena, such as language, is dependent on the extent to which the proposed typology makes **predictions** regarding important characteristics of the individuals represented by the types. For example, it would make little sense to typologize motor vehicles according to color. There are no important properties that correlate with (are predicted by) the color of a motorized vehicle. On the other hand a cluster of important formal and functional properties distinguishes buses from automobiles, tractors, etc. That is to say, there is far more coherence and substance to the concept of "bus" than there is to the concept of, for example, "maroon-colored motor vehicle."

Several typologies of language have been proposed in the history of linguistic science. The first typology that has maintained lasting interest is **morphological typology**. This typology refers primarily to the extent to which words in the language are divisible into clearly individuated morphemes. The first proposals recognized three morphological language types: (1) isolating, (2) agglutinating, and (3) inflectional or fusional. In this section I will describe an extension of this typology as proposed by Comrie (1989).

2.1.1   Synthesis

The index of **synthesis** (Comrie 1989) has to do with how many morphemes tend to occur per word. This index defines a continuum from **isolating** languages at one extreme to highly **polysynthetic** languages at the other. A strictly isolating language is one in which every word consists of only one morpheme. The Chinese languages come close to this extreme. A highly polysynthetic language is one in which words tend to consist of several morphemes. Quechua and Inuit (Eskimo) are good examples of highly polysynthetic languages. The following is an example of a polysynthetic structure in Yup'ik Eskimo (thanks to Eliza Orr):

(8)   tuntussuqatarniksaitengqiggtuq
       tuntu-ssur-qatar-ni-ksaite-ngqiggte-uq
       reindeer-hunt-FUT-say-NEG-again–3SG:IND
       "He had not yet said again that he was going to hunt reindeer."

Greenberg (1954) provides a quantitative method for measuring the morphological typology of a language. However, descriptive linguists rarely consider it helpful to apply Greenberg's method. This is probably because, as mentioned above, morphological typology is not predictive enough of other characteristics of the language to be of much value to readers of a grammar sketch. A more useful, though non-quantitative, rule is that if the language can express a whole sentence with just a verb, it is polysynthetic. If it cannot, then it is isolating. Adjectives such as "somewhat" or "highly" can then be added depending on the investigator's intuitions, e.g., English is "somewhat isolating," Chinese is "highly isolating." Korean is "somewhat polysynthetic" while Inuit is "highly polysynthetic." The payoff in terms of predicting other structural aspects of the language is simply not great enough to spend much time being more precise than this.

2.1.2   Fusion

The index of **fusion** (Comrie 1989) has to do with the degree to which units of meaning are "fused" into single morphological shapes. A highly **fusional** language (sometimes called "inflectional," but since this has other connotations, we will use the term fusional) is one in which one form can simultaneously embody several meanings, e.g., Spanish -ó in *habló* expresses indicative mode, third person, singular, past tense, and perfective aspect. If any one of these meaning components changes, the form of the verbal suffix must change. Turkish is a language for which each component of meaning is expressed by its own morpheme. Hence Turkish is a highly **agglutinative** language. Again, there is no quantitative method for precisely establishing the index of fusion for a given language. For highly isolating languages, the index of fusion just does not apply. If anything, English is agglutinative rather than fusional, e.g., in *anti-dis-establish-ment-ari-an-ism* each morpheme has a specific and fairly straightforward meaning. But then, such words are all of Latin origin. One hint of fusion in English is certain "strong" verb forms, e.g., *sang, thought, brought*, etc., in which a past tense morpheme cannot be strictly separated out from the root.

Nilotic languages express some morphological operations by way of a contrast between advanced tongue root (+ATR) and normal (–ATR) vowels. For example, in Sabaot, a Southern Nilotic language of Kenya and Uganda, the following two words contain the same "chunks" of morphological form. The only difference between the two is that in 9a a suprasegmental morpheme (ATR) is manifested by changes in the vowel quality and tone of the entire word:

(9)   a. kɔɔmnyɔɔnɔɔté
           ka-a-mnyaan-aa-tɛ-ATR
           PAST–1SG-be.sick-STAT-DIR-IMPERF
           "I went being sick (but I am not sick now)."

       b. káámnyáánáátɛ́
           ka-a-mnyaan-aa-tɛ
           PAST–1SG-be.sick-STAT-DIR
           "I became sick while going away (and I'm still sick)."

English strong verbs and Sabaot aspect are examples of fusion, not because many components of meaning are associated with a single form, but because specific chunks of morphology cannot be isolated.

?

Is the language dominantly isolating or polysynthetic?
If the language is at all polysynthetic, is it dominantly agglutinative or fusional?
Give examples of its dominant pattern and any secondary patterns.

References: Comrie (1989, ch. 2.3), Anderson (1982, 1985a, 1985b), Bybee (1985), P. Matthews (1991), Doris Payne (1985b), Pike (1947).

2.2   Morphological processes

There are six basic morphological processes by which stems can be formally altered to adjust their meanings to fit their syntactic and communicational context. These six processes are (1) **prefixation**, (2) **suffixation**, (3) **infixation**, (4) **stem modification**, (5) **reduplication** and (6) **suprafixation** (also, **suprasegmental modification**). A seventh process, **suppletion**, may not appropriately be called morphological since it involves the replacement of one stem by another. Nevertheless any of the operations that are typically coded by the six basic processes can also be coded by suppletion, therefore it deserves at least passing mention in this section.

Prefixes are bound morphemes that attach to the front of stems, e.g., *un-* in *unselfish*. **Suffixes** are bound morphemes that attach to the ends of stems, e.g., the *-ed* past tense marker of English. **Infixes** are bound morphemes that occur within stems. There are none of these in English, but they are fairly common in Austronesian languages, e.g., Bontok (Philippines) *um* in *fumikas* "become strong" (cf. *fikas* "be strong"). **Stem modification** is what happens in the *sing, sang, sung* paradigm of English. **Reduplication** is where a piece of a root (possibly the whole root) is repeated, e.g., Ilokano (Philippines) *pingan* "dish," *pingpingan* "dishes;" *talon* "field," *taltalon* "fields." **Suprasegmental modification** is where the tone or stress pattern of a word signals a particular morphological operation. English makes some use of stress patterns to signal the difference between certain nouns and related verbs, e.g., *pérmit* (noun) vs. *permít* (verb), *cónvert* (noun) vs. *convért* (verb), etc. Some languages, especially in Africa and Meso-America, use tone modification to signal very common morphological operations like tense and aspect. As mentioned above, **suppletion** is the replacement of one stem by another. In English the verb *be* is notoriously suppletive; *is, am,* and *are* derive from one historical root, *were* and *was* from another, and *be* from a third.

Most languages that are at all agglutinative employ suffixes; some of these also employ prefixes; some of these also employ infixes. Very few languages employ only prefixation, and none employs only infixation or any of the other types of morphological processes mentioned above. Bybee (1985) thoroughly describes the patterns of morphological expression of various kinds of operations in a randomized sample of fifty languages. She proposes that morphological processes, like syntactic processes, are at least somewhat motivated by universal cognitive principles. From this point of view, the role of semantics, pragmatics, and cognition in motivating morphological structures is an area of theoretical concern.

?

If the language is at all agglutinative, is it dominantly prefixing, suffixing, or neither?

Illustrate the major and secondary patterns (including infixation, stem modification, reduplication, suprasegmental modification, and suppletion).

References: Greenberg (1978, vol. III), Anderson (1985a), P. Matthews (1991), Bybee (1985).

2.3   Head/dependent marking

The **head** of a phrase is (under most definitions) the element that determines the syntactic function of the whole phrase. So, in a noun phrase the head is the noun that refers to the same entity that the whole phrase refers to, e.g., *crown* in *the Queen of England's crown*. An adposition is the head of an adpositional phrase because the presence of the adposition is what gives an adpositional phrase its particular syntactic properties – without the adposition the phrase would simply be a noun phrase. Other elements in a phrase are sometimes referred to as **dependents**.

Some languages tend to mark the relationship between a head and a dependent on the head, while others tend to mark the relationship on the dependent. For example, English is predominantly a dependent-marking language. This is illustrated by the fact that in possessive noun phrases, the head noun is not marked to indicate that it is possessed; rather, the possessor is marked: "John's book." Other languages, e.g., Farsi (Indo-Iranian, Iran), typically mark the head, e.g.,

(10)   Zhon kitab-é
        John book-POSS
        "John's book"

Languages will tend to follow one pattern or the other across various phrase types, i.e., noun phrases, verb phrases, and adpositional phrases. Head-marking languages are common throughout the Americas, Africa, Asia, Siberia, and in the Middle East. Dependent-marking languages are less common, and are found primarily in Europe, though some Amerindian languages are dependent-marking.

?
If the language is at all polysynthetic, is it dominantly "head-marking," "dependent-marking," or mixed?
Give some examples of each type of marking the language exhibits.

References: Nichols (1986).

3   Grammatical categories

In traditional grammar, **grammatical categories** are called "parts of speech." Every language has at least two major grammatical categories – noun and verb. Two other major categories, adjective and adverb, may or may not be instantiated in any given language, though they usually are to some extent. Most languages also have minor grammatical categories such as **conjunctions, particles**, and **adpositions**. As with most categorization schemes in descriptive linguistics, grammatical categories tend to be interestingly untidy at their boundaries. Nevertheless, core notions, or **prototypes**, can usually be identified. Another interesting property of grammatical categorization is that the category membership of any given form varies according to how that form is used in discourse (see Hopper and Thompson 1984 and the discussion in sections 5.2 and 9.1 of this book). Such variation in category membership may or may not be directly reflected in the surface morphosyntax. Therefore, sometimes subtle morphosyntactic tests are needed to determine formal category membership, and other times the category membership of a given form can only be inferred from the discourse context.

Grammatical categories are distinct from formal relational categories such as subject, object, and predicate, or functional categories such as AGENT, topic, or definite NP. They are the building blocks of linguistic structure. They are sometimes called "lexical categories" since many forms can be specified for their grammatical category in the **lexicon**. However, we will not use the term lexical category here because (1) the term grammatical category is more widely understood, and (2) the category of a word depends as much on how the word is used in discourse as on its conventionalized (lexical) meaning.

It is important to present empirical evidence for each grammatical category posited in a grammatical description. Sections 3.1 and 3.2 list and describe the formal characteristics that tend to distinguish nouns and verbs. For the other categories, however, there are too many possible language-specific properties to offer a compendium of all possibilities here.

3.1   Nouns

For the major grammatical categories, noun and verb, prototypes can be identified semantically. The class of **nouns** in any language includes words that express the most **time-stable** concepts, e.g., "rock," "tree," "mountain," "house," etc. (Givón 1984: 51). These are concepts that characteristically do not vary appreciably over time. Prototypical nouns, then, are words that express highly and obviously time-stable concepts. A concept like "fist" does not characteristically persist over a long period of time, therefore one would not want to use the morphosyntactic properties of the word "fist" to define nouns in general. Some languages may not express this concept with a simple noun. In determining whether any given word is a noun or not, one must first determine the morphosyntactic characteristics of prototypical nouns (see below for examples). Then the grammatical category of a questionable word can usually be determined according to how closely the word follows the morphosyntactic pattern of prototypical nouns. However, there will always be some truly ambiguous examples as well as words that function sometimes as a verb and sometimes as a noun depending on the context. A discussion of some ways of dealing with ambiguous cases will be provided below.

Morphosyntactic properties of nouns fall into two groups: distributional (or configurational) and structural properties. Distributional properties have to do with how words are distributed in phrases, clauses, and texts. For example, nouns can serve as heads of noun phrases (see below), subjects and objects of clauses (see section 7.1), and topics of texts (see section 12.1.1). Structural properties have to do with the internal structure of the noun itself. For example, in some languages nouns exhibit case marking, number marking, gender marking, etc., whereas other grammatical categories tend not to exhibit these properties.

The **head** of a noun phrase is the one word within the phrase that refers to the same entity that the whole phrase refers to. For example, an

English phrase like *that computer man* refers to a time-stable concept, so we suspect it is a noun phrase. However, it also contains two words that also refer to time-stable concepts, *computer* and *man*. So the question arises as to which of the two nouns is the head of the noun phrase. The answer in this case is easy: the whole phrase refers to a man, not a computer, therefore the noun *man* is the head of the noun phrase. For languages that either have no grammatical category of adjective, or for which adjectives and nouns are very similar formally, the identification of the head of a noun phrase can be more difficult. In such a language, the words for *red* and *hen*, in an expression like *the red hen*, could equally refer to the entity that the whole phrase refers to. That is, the color terms and other descriptive terms can function just like nouns. For these languages, noun phrases such as *the red hen* are often considered to be examples of apposition, i.e., *the red one, the hen*. Doris Payne (1990) has proposed a method for determining headship even in this type of language. In her system, the head of a noun phrase in any given context is the element that **persists** in the discourse that follows. So when a participant in a story is mentioned in a phrase like *the red hen*, if it can subsequently be referred to as *the red one*, then *red* is the head. If, on the other hand, it can subsequently be referred to as *the hen*, then *hen* is the head. Doris Payne (1990) argues that in Yagua the ordering of elements in the noun phrase is sensitive to this notion of headship.

Probably every language has grammaticalized ways of adjusting the grammatical category or subcategory of a linguistic form, to make it either more or less noun-like. Such devices can be referred to as **derivational processes** (see section 2.0). For example, some forms function grammatically like nouns, but derive from roots that are semantically more verb-like. For such forms the time stability criterion is difficult, if not impossible, to apply. Therefore the only criteria available are the distributional and structural properties of the form.

English words suffixed with *-ing* illustrate how to determine the categorical status of a derived form. It is very difficult to think of a term such as *walking* as expressing a time-stable concept – the concept inherently involves motion and change, therefore the form is not a prototypical noun. However, let us look at the distributional and structural properties of this form to determine just how "noun-like" it is. First, can it distribute like a noun? Prototypical nouns can function as subjects and objects of clauses.

Can *walking* be the subject or object of a clause? The following examples show that *walking* passes this distributional test for nounhood:

(1) a. *Subject*: *Walking* is good for you.
     b. *Object*: I like *walking*.

Structural properties of prototypical nouns include: (1) the possibility of taking descriptive modifiers (*the **red** car*), and (2) the use of genitive case pronouns (***my** car*). Again, the form *walking* passes both of these tests:

(2) a. *Descriptive modifiers*:   slow walking
     b. *Genitive case pronouns*: his walking (*he walking)

Even though *walking* passes both of the major tests for nounhood, other tests reveal that it is not the best example of a noun. For example, ability to pluralize, to take determiners, and to take a wide range of descriptive modifiers are all properties of prototypical nouns in English. It is rare or odd-sounding for verbs with the *-ing* suffix to display these properties:

(3) a. *Pluralization*:   ?many walkings
     b. *Determiners*:   ?the walking to school
     c. *Descriptive modifiers*: ?red/little/pretty/fine walking

Also, verbs suffixed with *-ing* can sometimes take adverbial modifiers that noun cannot:

(4) a. ?I like slowly walking.
     b. I like walking slowly.
     c. *I like slowly cars.
     d. *I like cars slowly.

This morphosyntactic property makes the form *walking* seem a little more like a verb.

Solutions to the problem of which grammatical category *walking* belongs to vary from analysis to analysis. Such solutions include:

1 Taking some nominal properties as criterial. For instance, we could simply define noun for English as a form that can refer to its only argument with a genitive pronoun. In this case *walking* is a noun. However, if we decided

that ability to pluralize or take a wide range of descriptive modifiers were the criteria for nounhood, then *walking* would not be a noun. We would just have to make a somewhat arbitrary decision and stick to it consistently.

2 Making up a different grammatical category for each complex of nominal features instantiated by some form or forms in the language. In this case only those lexical items that have all nominal properties would be considered nouns. Forms such as *walking* would be considered something else, such as present participles (see below for a definition of the term "participle").

3 Acknowledging that the difference between nouns and verbs is a continuum, and that verbs with the *-ing* suffix fall somewhere in between the two extremes.

Solution 1 above is problematic because (a) it cannot be applied universally and (b) it ignores the obvious but inexact semantic basis for the grammatical category. Criterial definitions are inherently questionable for supposedly universal categories because there is always the possibility that some language may not display a particular criterion. We do not want to say that such languages lack universal categories (if so, the category is not universal, so our universal definition fails anyway). It is invariably the case that criterial definitions (even those found lurking in the pages of this book) are biased toward the well-known languages of the world. Some of the most interesting discussions in linguistics have been those involving languages in which important grammatical categories display different morphosyntactic properties than those of the well-studied languages.

Secondly, picking an arbitrary morphosyntactic feature as criterial, however closely that feature seems to correlate with intuitive notions of what the category should include, ignores the question of why the category exists in the first place. For example, to define nouns as all forms that refer to an argument with a genitive pronoun is like defining the class of human beings as all featherless bipeds. Though this "definition" may succeed in distinguishing to a large extent the category of human beings from all other animals, it focuses on incidental rather than definitional (or necessary) properties. In other words, it begs the question of why one would even consider featherless bipeds as a class apart from all other potentially arbitrary classes of items in the natural world, say red socks, or broken sticks. Certainly if we were to take a feathered biped and remove all of its feathers, it would not become a human being. On the other hand, if we dye a white sock red it does enter the category of red socks. Furthermore, we can conceive of a world in which human beings were not featherless bipeds, whereas it is correspondingly difficult to conceive of a world in which red socks were really green. This shows that the category "human" consists of more than merely the conjunction of the features "featherless" and "biped." Another way of saying this is that "featherless bipeds" is a sufficient but not a necessary definition of the category "human being."

The best criterial definitions are those which include both necessary and sufficient criteria. Unfortunately, such definitions are extremely uncommon in linguistics. If a criterial definition such as ability to take genitive case pronouns is suggested for the category of nouns, one should also ask: what is it about items that take genitive case pronouns that makes them cohere as a category? Why should they have *that* property, and not some other (say, high tone on the first syllable)?

Solution 2 is the approach traditionally taken in descriptive linguistics. It has the advantage of giving the analyst pigeon holes within which to place the various word types in the language. The basic problem with this approach is that, like solution 1, it is not universally applicable. The categories derived from various clusters of morphosyntactic properties are (a) not necessarily related to one another in any systematic way, and (b) not comparable from one language to the next. This situation makes for a grammatical description that is less readable to someone with no previous experience with the language. For example, the term **participle** is found in many grammar descriptions. Nevertheless, what constitutes a participle in language A may or may not have any commonality with what is called a participle in language B. Therefore someone who knows language B may be misled when reading the description of language A.

Solution 3 reflects most accurately the nature of linguistic categorization. This in itself is a point in favor of this approach. However, it also has its disadvantages to the field linguist attempting to present information about a language clearly and precisely in a grammar sketch. These disadvantages include:

1 There is no explicit way of determining exactly *where* on the continuum between noun and verb a particular category falls. One could conceivably count nominal properties and verbal properties, and assign items with more verbal properties to a position closer to the verb extreme and vice versa for nouns. However, this approach assumes that all properties are

weighted equally in terms of their effect on the category membership of the form. There is no *a priori* reason to accept this assumption. In fact, solution 1 above is based on precisely the opposite assumption, namely that there exists one and only one property that is important enough to distinguish the category, all the other properties being incidental. In any case, it is futile to try to rank morphosyntactic properties according to their importance.

2 It is often the case that a fieldworker just does not know what all of the relevant properties are for a given form. For example, some verbs with *-ing* might take plurals more easily than others: *his many failings* vs. ?*his many eatings*. This fact puts *failing* closer to the noun end of the continuum than *eating*. These subtle differences among the behaviors of various forms are probably not available to the fieldworker faced with thousands of forms, each potentially exhibiting a cluster of from zero to about ten nominal properties.

3 The point of a grammatical sketch is to help readers understand how particular constructions function within the grammatical system of the language. It is clear that a detailed ranking of structures according to their relative nounhood would be of limited use in accomplishing this task. Given the observation above that such a task would also potentially be of unlimited complexity, it is not likely that many field linguists would attempt such a ranking.

The recommended approach is to combine solutions 2 and 3 in something like the following manner: forms that are indeterminate as to their grammatical category membership (such as verbs with *-ing* suffixes in English) can be given strictly formal labels (e.g., "*-ing* participles"), with an explanation given of their characteristic functions and key morphosyntactic properties. In most cases it is just not worth the effort to be more explicit than this. The payoff in terms of clarity of description is too minuscule. **Participle** is a relatively widely understood term for verb forms that have reduced verbal properties, but which are not full nominalizations. Clauses formed with participial verbs are often referred to as **participial phrases**. However, languages normally have more than one such form and, as mentioned above, the term participle has no more specific universal definition. Therefore, it is important to clarify that the label is simply a shorthand way of referring to the formal class as a whole, and that it should not imply that the form is directly comparable to forms that have been called participles in other languages.

3.1.1   Types of nouns

Every language has certain grammatically defined subclasses of nouns. The following sections describe proper names, and the distinctions between possessable vs. non-possessable and count vs. mass nouns. These subclasses are probably universal. Many languages also have a **noun class system** that consists of many finer distinctions. If the language has a noun class system, it should be described separately (see section 5.7).

3.1.1.1   *Proper names*

Proper names are nouns that are used to address and identify particular persons or culturally significant personages or places. Proper names are used to refer to specific individuals both speaker and hearer can identify, therefore they do not usually appear with articles, modifiers, possessors, relative clauses, or other devices that render nouns more identifiable. For example, in English proper names are distinguished in that they do not (easily) take articles, quantifiers, or other modifiers:

(5)   *Proper names*   *Common nouns*
     Mt. Rushmore   car
     ?the Mt. Rushmore   the car
     ?several Mt. Rushmores   several cars
     ?an outlandish Mt. Rushmore   an outlandish car
     ?a Mt. Rushmore that has four   a car that has four presidents'
        presidents' faces carved in it   faces carved in it

All of the expressions preceded by ? above can be used in English, but the context must be such that the referents are taken as not automatically identifiable. This is an unusual circumstance for the use of proper names.

Proper names often differ from common nouns in other grammatical respects. For example, in many Austronesian languages special case markers are used with proper names. The following examples are from Cebuano, the major language of the southern Philippines. This language employs the prenominal case markers *ni* "actor" and *si* "patient" (or "absolutive" or "topic") for proper names only. For common names the markers *na* and *ang* respectively are used:

(6)   a.   Gibalhin na   tawo ang kaabaw.
        moved   ACT man PAT buffalo
        "The man moved the water buffalo."

b. Gibalhin ni   Doro ang kaabaw.
       ACT.PN   PAT
"Doro moved the water buffalo."

c. Gibalhin na tawo si   Doro.
       ACT   PAT.PN
"The man moved Doro."

This is only one respect in which proper names may be distinguished from common nouns grammatically.

3.1.1.2   *Possessability*

Many languages have one of the following distinctions:

type 1: possessable vs. unpossessable nouns;
type 2: inherently possessed vs. optionally possessed nouns;
type 3: alienably possessed vs. inalienably possessed nouns.

Maasai (Eastern Nilotic) employs a type 1 system. In Maasai many nouns cannot normally be grammatically possessed. Items that can be possessed include cows, houses, kin, goats, tools, wells, and money. Items that cannot easily be possessed include meat, water, rivers, mountains, land, rocks, wild animals, stars, etc. For example:

(7)   *Non-possessable*   *Possessable*
       ɛnkɔ́p   "land"/"dirt"   ɛnkɛ́rái   "child"
       ??ɛnkɔ́p áy "my land"   ɛnkɛ́ráy áy   "my child"

In many West African, Austronesian, and Amerindian languages there is a distinction between inherently possessed vs. non-inherently possessed nouns. In these languages, all nouns can be possessed, but some absolutely must be. Inherently possessed nouns normally include body parts and kinship terms. The following examples are from Seko Padang, a Western Austronesian language of South Sulawesi (examples courtesy of Tom Laskowske):

(8)   *Optionally possessed*   *Obligatorily possessed*
       kaya-ku "my shirt"   baki-ku   "my basketful"
       kaya-na "his/her shirt"   baki-na   "his/her basketful" or
                                                  "basketful"

       kaya   "shirt"   *baki   (no meaning)

Finally, in many other languages there are two grammatically distinct possession strategies. All nouns can be possessed, but each noun undergoes only one of the strategies. Usually the two kinds of possession are termed **alienable** vs. **inalienable** possession. Inalienable possession is used for roughly the same class of nouns that are possessable in type 1 languages like Maasai, and inherently possessed in type 2 languages like Seko Padang. Alienable, inalienable, and inherent possession are described in more detail in section 5.6. It is possible that a language might employ a combination of these types of systems.

3.1.1.3   *Count vs. mass nouns*

Languages often make a grammatical distinction between nouns that refer to things that can be counted (**count** nouns) and those that refer to substances, like water, sand, air, wood, etc. (**mass** nouns). In English, mass nouns do not pluralize (unless used in a special, count, sense). Furthermore, mass and count nouns take distinct, but partially overlapping, classes of articles and quantifiers:

(9)   *Mass nouns*   *Count nouns*
        sand   car
        ?many sands   many cars
        much sand   ?much car
        some sand   ?some car
        ?a sand   a car
        ?some sands   some cars

Notice that this distinction is semantically based, but evidence for its existence is formal properties. There is potentially an infinite number of "noun subclasses" based on semantic properties, but these subclasses are only significant for the grammar if they have some overt consequences. It is interesting to note how the grammaticalized formal properties can be used to produce special effects. For example, some of the expressions marked as questionable above may be used to accomplish specialized communicative tasks:

(10)   a. We'll have *three waters* please.   (Mass noun being used as a count noun to refer to a *bounded quantity* of the substance concept.)

        b. That's *a lot of car* you've got.   (Count noun being used as a mass noun to refer to a *quality* of the countable concept.)

3.1.2   The structure of the noun word

If the language is at all polysynthetic (see chapter 2), an overview of the structure of the noun word can be helpful. For English this may be the following:

(11)   STEM-PL

In other words, a noun consists of a stem plus an optional marker of plurality. For more polysynthetic languages, this diagram would be much more complex. For example, in Guaymí (a Chibchan language of Costa Rica and Panama) the noun diagram would be something like the following:

(12)   POSS-STEM-DIM/AUG-CL-PL

That is, a noun word consists of an optional possessive prefix, an obligatory stem, an optional diminutive or an augmentative suffix, an optional classifier, and an optional plural suffix. These diagrams are expository devices only; they are meant to help the reader of the grammar understand the general structure of nouns. They do not necessarily represent theoretical claims.

3.1.3   Pronouns and/or anaphoric clitics

For many languages it is difficult to distinguish **pronouns** from **agreement** (or concord) affixes. Here we will give strictly formal definitions, though it must be kept in mind that there is no direct correlation between the function of a particular device in one language and formally similar devices in other languages (though there are generalities that can be made – see section 12.1.1). For example, free pronouns in English function roughly like person marking does in Spanish. In standard English, verb agreement cannot constitute the only reference to a participant, e.g., *walks* is not a well-formed clause, even though the -*s* suffix in some sense "refers to" a third person singular subject. In Spanish, on the other hand, the third person singular form of the verb is sufficient to stand as a complete clause, e.g., *anda* "he/she walks." So we want to say that in Spanish, person marking on the verb is an **anaphoric device**, that is, it counts as the only reference to the subject of the verb. Person marking on verbs in English, on the other hand, merely "agrees with" the independently expressed subject of the verb.

Now, let us compare the pronouns. Spanish free pronouns are used very rarely in discourse, and are usually described as "emphatic" or "contrastive," whereas English pronouns are much more frequent. When we look at English pronouns more closely, however, we find that there are really two types – stressed and unstressed. Most pronouns in English discourse are unstressed. If they are stressed, they function very similarly to the Spanish pronouns, i.e., to signal contrastiveness of some sort (see section 10.1). So a Spanish clause with a pronoun, e.g., *ellos vinieron*, roughly corresponds in function to an English clause with a stressed pronoun, THEY *came* (as opposed to someone else). The Spanish clause without a pronoun, *vinieron*, corresponds more or less to the English clause with an unstressed pronoun, *they came*. Hence it appears that English and Spanish each have two anaphoric devices functioning within the domain of participant reference. Spanish person marking corresponds functionally to English unstressed pronouns while Spanish pronouns correspond to English stressed pronouns (roughly speaking). This illustrates the fact that devices that seem similar formally (e.g., pronouns in English and Spanish) can function very differently in discourse. Once the anaphoric devices are identified formally, the investigator must strive to understand how the various devices function within the system of participant reference.

Pronouns are free forms (as opposed to affixes) that function alone to fill the position of a noun phrase in a clause. They normally have all the distributional properties of noun phrases.

Anaphoric clitics are not free morphologically – they must attach (cliticize) to another word (see section 2.0 on clitics). However, like pronouns they are in complementary distribution with full noun phrases. That is, typically either a noun phrase or a clitic, but not both, can refer to an entity in a given clause. For example, in Yagua, a reference to a subject can be either a full noun phrase (ex. 13) or a proclitic (ex. 14), but not both (ex. 15):

(13)   Manungo murrą́ą́y
       M.   sing
       "Manungo sings."

(14)   sa-murrą́ą́y
       3SG-sing
       "He sings."

(15)   *Manungo sa-murrą́ą́y.

That *sa-* is not a pronoun is evidenced by the fact that it cannot stand alone. For example, you cannot answer a question like *Who's singing?* simply with the form *sa*; there is a distinct third person singular pronoun, *níí*, that is used in such contexts. Also, *sa-* can only appear immediately before the verb stem, whereas pronouns (such as *níí*) have the same distributional privileges as full noun phrases (i.e., they can occur pretty much anywhere in a clause). Furthermore, there is good morphological evidence that *sa-* is a clitic. With certain verb classes it enters into morphophonemic rules that do not cross word boundaries. For example, when the verb begins with the syllable *ha*, the *h* is lost, and a long nasalized vowel occurs:

(16)   sa "3sg" + hatu "drink" = sąątu "he drinks"

Example 17 shows that this process does not cross word boundaries. Notice that the final *a* of the first word and the initial *ha* of the second do not coalesce to *ąą*:

(17)   Estela hatu   *Esteląątu
        Estela drink
        "Estela drinks."

In summary, *sa-* in Yagua is an anaphoric clitic because it is morphologically bound, yet is in complementary distribution with noun phrases.

Accusative and dative "pronouns" in Romance languages fulfill this definition of anaphoric clitics because (a) they must be phonologically bound, and (b) they distribute differently than full noun phrases – the clitics occur before inflected verbs and after non-inflected verbs in most cases, whereas there are no such distributional restrictions on full noun phrases. One cannot answer a question such as *Whom did you see?* in Spanish simply with the form *la* "her;" rather, a full pronoun is required.

The following are distinctions likely to be relevant for the pronoun/anaphoric clitic paradigm. Not all of these will be applicable to all languages, and there may be more that are not mentioned here. Most of these will be discussed in more depth in the following paragraphs.

1 *Person.* "First person" refers to the speaker. "Second person" refers to the hearer. First and second persons are sometimes collectively referred to as **speech act participants**. "Third person" usually refers to any non-speech act participant.[1]

Table 3.1 The pronoun system of Samoan

	Singular	Dual	Plural
1st person: "I"	a'u		
"Emotional"	'ita		
"Inclusive"		'ita'ua ("just you and I")	'itatou ("you, I and he/she/they")
"Exclusive"		'ima'ua ("I and he/she")	'matou ("I and they")
2nd person: "you"	'oe	'oulua ("you two")	'outou ("you three or more")
3rd person	ia	'ila'ua ("they two")	'ilatou ("they three or more")

Many languages have an **inclusive/exclusive** distinction within the category of first person. First person inclusive includes speaker and hearer and may or may not include a non-speech act participant. Some languages have an "inclusive dual" form, even though dual may not be specified in any other part of the grammar. This form refers only to speaker and hearer and excludes a non-speech act participant. First person exclusive includes the speaker and a non-speech act participant, but excludes the hearer.

2 *Number*. Like nouns, pronouns and anaphoric clitics can vary for number. The most common number distinctions are singular vs. plural; less common are singular, dual, and plural. Systems with more number distinctions than these are rare, but do exist. For example, some Austronesian languages, particularly in Vanuatu, indicate singular, dual, trial, and plural. However, in these languages the entire range of distinctions is only available for animate referents.

Table 3.1 illustrates the system of free pronouns in Samoan (Polynesian, from Mosel and Hovdhaugen 1992). In addition to having inclusive/exclusive and singular/dual/plural distinctions, Samoan also has an "emotional" first person singular pronoun. This pronoun is used primarily to show that "the speaker is emotionally involved in the situation" (Mosel and Hovdhaugen 1992: 121).

3 *Gender, noun class*. Typical gender categories include masculine, feminine, and neuter or inanimate. Many languages provide a much richer

system for classifying nouns. This system often finds expression in the pronouns and/or anaphoric clitics (see section 5.7).

4 *Grammatical relations*. Subject, object, ergative, absolutive (see chapter 7).

5 *Semantic roles*. AGENT, PATIENT, etc. (see section 3.2.0).

6 *Definiteness/specificity*. In many languages different pronouns are used for non-specific and/or indefinite referents. For example, English employs the forms *whoever, whatever, wherever*, etc., as non-specific pronouns. Third person plural forms are often used to refer to non-specific or inde-finite referents (see section 8.2.2 under impersonal passives).

7 *Honorifics*. Very often different pronouns or anaphoric clitics are used depending on the relative social statuses of the speech act participants. In English, there are some unusual situations where special forms are used in place of the standard second person pronoun *you*. For example, when addressing a judge in a courtroom situation it is still customary to use the term *your honor*. Many other languages use honorifics on an everyday basis. For example, standard Spanish uses *tu* and *te* for the second person subject and object pronouns when speaking in a familiar manner. In a more formal situation *Usted* and *le* are more appropriate.

?
What are the distributional properties of nouns?
What are the structural properties of nouns?
What are the major formally distinct subcategories of nouns?
What is the basic structure of the noun word (for polysynthetic languages) and/or noun phrase (for more isolating languages)?
Does the language have free pronouns and/or anaphoric clitics? (These are distinct from grammatical agreement. Agreement will be discussed later. Also, the functions of pronouns and clitics will be discussed later.)
Give a chart of the free pronouns and/or anaphoric clitics.

References: Givón (1983a, 1984), Craig (1986), Mühlhäusler and Harré (1990), Weisemann (1986), Hopper and Thompson (1984), Schachter (1985).

3.2   Verbs

The class of **verbs** in any language is the grammatical category that includes lexemes which express the least time-stable concepts, e.g., events such as *die, run, break*, etc. (Givón 1984: 51, 55). As with nouns, the time-stability continuum only defines the prototypes. In determining whether a questionable form is a verb or not, one must determine how closely it follows the morphosyntactic pattern of prototypical verbs.

Morphosyntactic properties of verbs fall into two groups: distributional (or configurational) and structural. Distributional properties have to do with how words function in phrases, clauses, and texts. For example, verbs can serve as heads of verb phrases, predicates of clauses, and they code events in a text. Structural properties have to do with the internal structure of the verb itself. For example, in some languages verbs exhibit subject agreement, tense/aspect/mode marking, etc., whereas forms that belong to other grammatical categories do not.

The functions of some major verb or verb-phrase operations (e.g., tense/aspect/mode) will be discussed in depth in later sections. Here, the basic structure of the verbal word or verb phrase should be described.

3.2.0   Semantic roles

Before discussing the various types of verbs that may exist in a language (section 3.2.1), it is necessary to present a fuller discussion of the notion of semantic role. **Semantic roles** are conceptual relationships in the "message world" (see section 0.2.3). Though they influence the morphosyntax profoundly, they are not primarily morphosyntactic categories. They are part of the "content" of linguistic messages rather than categories of linguistic form. Ideally, semantic roles are the roles that participants play in message world situations, quite apart from the linguistic encoding of those situations. So, for example, if in some real or imagined situation, someone named John purposely hits someone named Bill, then John is the AGENT and Bill is the PATIENT of the hitting event, regardless of whether any observer ever utters a clause like "John hit Bill" to describe that event.

Often the term **argument** is used to refer to the participants and their semantic roles that are normally associated with a given verb. For example, a scene typically described by the verb *eat* in English has to have two participants – an "eater" and an "eaten" thing. Therefore the verb *eat* is said to have two arguments, at least conceptually (semantically).[2] Formally, however, speakers may adjust the content of their messages by overtly mentioning more or fewer than these two arguments, e.g.:

(18)   a. *Bonny* ate *beans* with her *knife*.   (three participants on stage)
        b. *George* already ate.   (one participant on stage)

Even in 18b we understand that George ate *something*; it just does not matter, for the purposes of this particular communicative act, what it was that he ate. However, *knife* in 18a does not have the same status; if *knife* is omitted we do not necessarily know that Bonny used an instrument at all. The instrument is not central to the definition of the concept of "eating" the way the eaten thing is, so *knife* is not an argument. We will use the term **oblique** to refer to optional participants such as *knife* in 18a. The arguments of a verb and their semantic roles must be specified in the lexical, or dictionary, entry for each verb. Sometimes this information is known as an **argument structure** or **case frame** of the verb.[3]

Recent works that have influenced linguists' thought on semantic roles most profoundly have been those within the framework of **Case Grammar** (Fillmore 1968, 1977, Anderson 1971, 1977, *inter alia*). A great many works build upon the insights in these core articles. In this section I will present the concepts of "classical" Case Grammar. Fieldworkers with interest in pursuing specific proposals for formulating the relationship between semantic roles and grammatical relations are heartily encouraged to consult the references provided.

In the tradition of Case Grammar, semantic roles are referred to as "cases" or **deep cases**. We will avoid this terminology as it conflicts with our notion of cases as being morphosyntactic rather than semantic categories of nominals (section 7.1). In the tradition of generative grammar they have come to be called **thematic roles** or simply **theta roles**. Unfortunately, this terminology conflicts with the term "thematic structure" that we will use in a very different sense in discussing the structure of discourse (section 12.1.2). The term "semantic role" is the most unambiguous and widely understood terminology available. Nevertheless, all fieldworkers should be aware of the alternate terminologies.

3.2.0.1 *Some common semantic roles*

Here we will describe some semantic roles most often expressed by the grammatical relations of subject, object, and indirect object in natural languages. These are AGENT, FORCE, INSTRUMENT, EXPERIENCER, RECIPIENT and PATIENT (Comrie 1989: 52–53). Others, e.g., LOCATION, DIRECTION, SETTING, PURPOSE, TIME, MANNER, etc. are more likely to be expressed in oblique phrases or adverbials, though even these can at times be expressed by subjects or objects, e.g., *He swam the channel* (*channel* = LOCATION of swimming), *We did Norway last summer* (*Norway* = SETTING), *This bed was slept in by Che Guevara* (*bed* = LOCATION).

An AGENT is "the typically animate perceived instigator of the action" (Fillmore 1968).[4] In scenes likely to be described by the following clauses, *Percival* would be the AGENT:

(19)   a. Percival ate beans.
     b. Percival ran around the block.
     c. That vase was broken by Percival.
     d. Whom did Percival kiss?
     e. It was Percival who deceived the president.

A prototypical AGENT is conscious, acts with **volition** (on purpose), and performs an action that has a physical, visible effect. It is a powerful controller of an event. According to this characterization, *Percival* in 19a and c is a near prototypical AGENT. In 19b, although Percival is conscious and presumably acts with volition, there is no visible change in the world that results from Percival's act. The same sort of observation can be made for 19d and e. Therefore, Percival is a less-than-prototypical AGENT in 19b, d and e.

A FORCE is an entity that instigates an action, but not consciously or voluntarily. For example, *the wind* is a FORCE in the following clauses:

(20)   a. The wind opened the door.
     b. The wind blew in through the open window.
     c. That vase was broken by the wind.
     d. What did the wind knock over?
     e. It was the wind that formed those rocks.

An INSTRUMENT is an entity that instigates an action indirectly. Normally an AGENT acts upon an INSTRUMENT and the INSTRUMENT affects the action. For example, in the following clauses, *a hammer* is an INSTRUMENT:

(21)   a. Prescott broke the window with a hammer.
     b. A hammer broke the window.

    c. That window was broken by a hammer.

    d. What did Prescott break with a hammer?

    e. It was a hammer that Prescott broke the window with.

An EXPERIENCER neither controls nor is visibly affected by an action. Normally an EXPERIENCER is an entity that receives a sensory impression, or in some other way is the locus of some event or activity that involves neither volition nor a change of state. For example, in the following English clauses, *Lucretia* is an EXPERIENCER:

(22)   a. Lucretia saw the bicycle.

      b. Lucretia broke out in a cold sweat.

      c. The explosion was heard by Lucretia.

      d. What did Lucretia feel?

      e. It was Lucretia who smelled smoke first.

Although FORCE, INSTRUMENT, and EXPERIENCER are clearly semantically distinct from AGENT, languages often treat them the same as AGENT for purposes of grammatical expression. For example, in English, all of these roles are fairly commonly expressed as subjects. However, this is not necessarily true for all languages. The examples from Guaymí and Gujarati cited below (section 3.2.0.2) show that sometimes EXPERIENCERS appear in a different morphological case than AGENTS. How any language expresses semantic roles and allows adjustment in the relationship between semantic roles and grammatical relations are important issues for linguistic theory and description. These issues are discussed in more detail in chapters 7 and 8.

A RECIPIENT is the typically animate destination of some moving object. The difference between RECIPIENT and DESTINATION is similar to, but more subtle than, the difference between AGENT and FORCE. Consequently, in many languages, the forms used for DESTINATIONS are similar to those used for RECIPIENTS. For example, English uses the preposition *to* to mark both roles:

(23)   a. I sent the book to Mary.   (Mary = RECIPIENT)

      b. I sent the book to France.   (France = DESTINATION)

PATIENT is the unmarked semantic role. If an entity does not act with volition, instigate an event, receive something, or experience a sensory impression, it is probably a PATIENT. In the following clauses, *Joaquin* is the PATIENT:

(24) a. Montezuma stabbed Joaquin.
      b. Joaquin fell from the third floor.
      c. Joaquin was amazed by the mosquito.
      d. Who wanted Joaquin?
      e. It was Joaquin that the republicans believed.

A prototypical PATIENT undergoes a physical, visible change in state. In 24a and b *Joaquin* is a fairly prototypical PATIENT. In 24c–e *Joaquin* does not undergo a change in physical state. English, however, treats these as "the same" as more prototypical PATIENTS.

3.2.0.2   *The linguistic encoding of semantic roles*

A central contribution of Case Grammar was to observe that semantic roles do not correspond directly to grammatical relations. For example, in the following clauses the formal category of subject (as manifested by preverbal position, pronominal form and potentially verb agreement in English) realizes three distinct semantic roles:

(25) a. I opened the door with the key.   subject = AGENT
      b. The key opened the door.   subject = INSTRUMENT
      c. The door opened.   subject = PATIENT

Furthermore, *the key* is an oblique phrase in the first example and subject in the second, even though it fills the same semantic role in both clauses. Similarly, *the door* is the direct object in 25a and b, but subject in c, even though it is the semantic PATIENT in all three clauses. The determination of which participant becomes subject, then, is a matter of **perspectivization** (Fillmore 1976). For example, clauses 25a, b, and c could all be descriptions of the same situation, but from different perspectives.

As field linguists we should not be surprised that semantic roles do not correspond directly to grammatical relations. This is because semantic roles are conceptual notions whereas grammatical relations are morphosyntactic. A principle often reiterated in this book is that morphosyntax "discretizes" (imposes discrete categories upon) conceptual space. This is because the human mind cannot function adequately with infinite variability (see the references cited for further discussion). From this point of view, a semantic role such as AGENT is not a discrete category; rather, it defines one extreme of a continuum. Any given participant in any given situation may be more or less AGENT-like. The following diagram illustrates this continuum (adapted from Givón 1984):

The relation between conceptual space and morphosyntactic expression

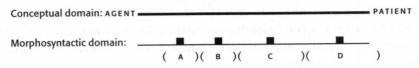

In this diagram, the dark squares indicate the "focal coding points" for four hypothetical morphosyntactic devices that function along the AGENT–PATIENT continuum. Parentheses indicate inexact boundaries. Concepts that occur right at the focal points are very "easy" to code. As concepts diverge from the focal point (or prototype) the choice of which coding device to use becomes less clear.

    In the broad tradition of Case Grammar, there have been several attempts to formulate a list of universal semantic roles that languages pay attention to morphosyntactically, e.g., the references cited below, Chafe (1970), Longacre (1976), among others. Such lists have consistently proven inadequate – as soon as a list is published, some language is argued to grammaticalize a new semantic role. The problem is that semantic roles are conceptual, hence infinitely variable. Languages reflect this variability in many, if not an unlimited number of, different ways. The question of determining a list of universal semantic roles, then, becomes one of how fine a level of analysis is appropriate. Ultimately, every semantic role played by every participant in every message world situation is subtly different from every other one. However, an infinitely long list of semantic roles is as useless as no list at all. The important question for descriptive linguists is how the morphosyntax of the language is sensitive to semantic roles. In other words, which grammatical relations express which semantic roles in which contexts?

    Some languages allow various case-marking patterns depending roughly on the semantic roles of the core nominals. So, for example, in Guaymí (a Chibchan language of Costa Rica and Panama), EXPERIENCERS appear in the dative case:

(26)   Davi-e   Dori gare.
         David-DAT Doris know:PRES
         "David knows Doris."

(27)   Toma-e Dori tïrï.
         Tom-DAT Doris remember:PRES
         "Tom remembers Doris."

(28)   Ti-e   ru   hatu-aba.
         1SG-DAT airplane see-PAST
         "I saw the airplane."

(29)   Ti-e   tïmëna nib-i.
         1SG-DAT thirst   feel-PRES
         "I feel thirst." ("I'm thirsty.")

Certain other verbs that describe involuntary actions place one central participant in a LOCATIVE case:

(30)   a. José-*biti* Maria köinigwit-ani-nggö.
          José-LOC Maria forget-PAST1-ASP
          "José forgot Maria."

       b. Köinigwit-ani-nggö ti-*biti*.
          forget-PAST1-ASP   I-LOC
          "I forgot it." (or "It was forgotten upon me.")

(31)   Davi-*bötö* Dori hurö rïb-aba.
         David-LOC Doris fear feel-PAST2
         "David was afraid of Doris."

(32)   Ti-*bötö* kö   nib-i   tibo.
         I-LOC   place feel-PRES cold
         "I'm cold."

In Gujarati (an Indo-Aryan language of India), AGENTIVE particip-ants are treated differently in the past tense (ex. 33a) than in the present tense (33b) (examples courtesy of Mridula Adenwala):

(33)   a. raju-e   kam kar-y-uN
          Raju-ERG work do-PAST-SG
          "Raju did work."

       b. raju kam kar-e ch-e
          Raju work do-SG AUX-SG
          "Raju does/is doing work."

Note that the AGENT, Raju, takes the "ergative" case marker *-e* in 33a but no case marker in 33b.[5] In 33a Raju is more AGENTIVE than in 33b in that a completed act describes an accomplished change of state in the world, whereas the result of the ongoing action represented in 33b is still not known. Since a prototypical AGENT engenders some concrete, visible change in the world, the AGENT of 33a is a "better" (or more prototypical) AGENT than the one in 33b.

Other languages express information concerning the semantic roles of the arguments of the clause via markers on the verb. Many Western Austronesian languages are famous for this. For example, in Tagalog (a major language of the Philippines), there are several verb forms depending on the semantic role of one of the nominal arguments:

(34)   a. *Humiram* ang babae ng pera   sa   bangko.
           A:borrow   woman   money OBL bank
           "The woman borrowed money from a bank."

       b. *Hiniram* ng babae ang pera   sa   bangko.
           P:borrow   woman   money OBL bank
           "The woman borrowed the money from a bank."

       c. *Hiniraman* ng babae   sa   pera   ang bangko.
           L:borrow   woman   OBL money   bank
           "The woman borrowed money from the bank."

Notice the different verb forms and prepositional case markers on the noun phrases in each of these clauses. The prepositional case marker *ang* occurs before "topic" nominals, and the verb inflects for the semantic role of this nominal. In 34a the verb form *humiram* says in effect "the nominal preceded by *ang* is the AGENT." The form *hiniram* says "the nominal preceded by *ang* is the PATIENT," while the form *hiniraman* says "the nominal preceded by *ang* is the LOCATION." Some verbs in Tagalog are said to have up to seven different forms that indicate seven different semantic roles. Many of these constructions may be insightfully analyzed as **applicatives** (section 8.1.2).

3.2.1   Verb classes

The following is a list of some semantically defined verb classes that might evoke distinct morphosyntactic treatment. Not every grammar will require a section dealing with each type. The point is to describe any distinctive morphosyntactic properties of any of these classes, e.g., un-expected case-marking patterns, restrictions on tense, aspect, or mode marking, etc. (see chapter 9). Other useful and more elaborate systems for semantic classification of verbs can be found in Chafe (1970), Dowty (1987), Foley and Van Valin (1984), among others.

Most languages employ various derivational operations that adjust the argument structure of a verb. These important and complex processes merit special treatment, such as described in chapters 8 and 9. The chapter on grammatical categories would probably be too long if all the information on how categories can be adjusted were included.

3.2.1.1   Weather verbs

To rain, *(be) wind(y)*, *(be) cold*, *(be) hot*, *to thunder*, *to flash* (*as lightning*), *(get) cloudy*, *(be) dark*, *(be) light*, *to dawn*.

3.2.1.2   States

These may very well be covered under predicate adjectives or predicate nominals (sections 6.1 and 6.2). This section is only for languages that have a class of **stative verbs**, e.g., *(be) hot/cold* (not weather), *broken, rotten, melted, skinned, dead, alive, born, unborn*.

3.2.1.3   Involuntary processes

These are one-argument verbs in which the argument:

(a) undergoes a change in state;
(b) does not act with volition;
(c) does not necessarily move through space;
(d) is not the source of some moving object.

For example, the intransitive senses of *grow, die, melt, wilt, dry up, explode, rot, tighten*, and *break* would belong to this class. These verbs answer the question, "What happened to X?," but less easily "What did X do?":

What happened to Sylvan?	He died.
What did Sylvan do?	??He died.
What happened to the mustard?	It dried up.
What did the mustard do?	??It dried up.

3.2.1.4   Bodily functions

These are like involuntary processes except they do not involve a change of state. Some languages may treat these in special ways morphosyntactically, often as onomatopoeic expressions. For example, *cough, sneeze, hiccup, burp, bleed, sweat, vomit, expectorate, urinate, defecate, sleep/awaken*(?), *cry*.

3.2.1.5   Motion

The basic, unmarked motion verb(s), *come/go*, may have different morphosyntactic properties from motion verbs that express a particular manner, like *swim, run, walk, crawl, fly, jump*, etc. Furthermore, while all motion verbs have an affected participant (the person or thing that moves), some attribute more control to that "affectee" than others do. The language may make a morphosyntactic distinction here. All the motion verbs listed so far describe voluntary activities. The following are possibly involuntary activities: *fall, drop, flow, spew, squirt*, etc.

Finally, many languages make a distinction between **locomotion**, i.e., change of place, and simple motion, e.g., spinning, jumping in place, running within an area as opposed to running out of one place and into another. For these languages, oddly enough, the locomotion verbs tend to behave more like stative verbs than do verbs that simply describe motion. For example, in Wappo (northern California) the locomotion verbs fall into the stative class. Examples 35a and b illustrate simple stative verbs with their characteristic suffix -*khi?*:

(35) a. mey-i   söy'iya-*khi?*
          water-NOM hot-STAT
          "The water is hot."

      b. lel-i   ceta wil-*khi?*
          rock-NOM there sit-STAT
          "The rock is over there."

For processes, *se?* contrasts with -*khi?*:

(36) a. cephi   hincatk:-se?
          3SG:NOM wake:up-DUR
          "She's waking up." (process)

      b. cephi   hincatel-*khi?*
          3SG:NOM wake:up-STAT
          "She's awake." (state)

But with verbs of locomotion, *khi?* also occurs, even though these express past punctual actions:

(37) a. ah   pawata? te-hew'i-*khi?*
          1SG:NOM once   DIR-jump-STAT
          "I jumped down once."

      b. met'e-t-i   me?a i-thu   nat'o?ah-*khi?*
          woman-PL-NOM many 1SG-DAT come-STAT
          "Many women came to me (i.e. to my house)."

      c. cephi   te-piyola-*khi?*
          3SG:NOM DIR-sneak-STAT
          "She sneaked in."

It is significant that all of these motion verbs that take the stative suffix describe *locomotion*, not simple motion. That is, each involves movement out of one **scene** and into another. A clause like *He ran into the kitchen* would be locomotive, whereas *He ran by* would not. It is very common for languages to treat predicates of locomotion as statives, even though other predicates of motion are active. This is because change in place is metaphorically similar to change in state. Even in English we can sometimes use the stative auxiliary *be* for the perfect aspect with concepts in which the subject changes place or state:

(38) a. He is/has grown.   change of state
      b. He is/has escaped/risen.   change of place
      c. He *is/has spoken.   no change of place or state

Other languages actually treat predicates of locomotion as nominal predicates (see section 6.3).

Some languages employ verbal operators that change a verb from one class to another. For example, many languages of the Americas employ verbal markers that transform a non-locomotion verb into a locomotion verb. In Yagua, the suffixes *-nuvïï*, *-nuvaa*, and a few others indicate that the action expressed by the verb they attach to describes a trajectory of motion grounded to a particular locational scene (T. Payne 1990a):

(39) a. Naani-ipeni-yąą
          3DL-dance-DIST
          "They dance all over the place." (non-locomotion)

   b. Naani-ipeni-yąą-*nuvɨ̈*
       3DL-dance-DIST-on:arrival1
       "They dance all over on arrival." (locomotion to current scene)

   c. Naani-núú-*ñuvee*
       3DL-look-on:arrival2
       "They look on arrival." (locomotion to new scene)

Both *-nuvɨ̈* and *-nuvaa* indicate that the action expressed by the verb occurs upon arrival on some scene. The opposition between the two is determined by whether that scene is the currently activated one or if it implies the activation of a new scene. The complex verb stem consisting of a verb root plus suffix then patterns just like a locomotion verb. For example, it has inflectional possibilities characteristic only of other verbs of motion. Other similar suffixes in Yagua include: *-rɨ̈* "passing by," *-ja* "moving horizontally, across water or land," *-jasúmiy* "moving upwards," *-siy* "departing."

     Some verbs of motion specify a portion of a trajectory of movement, rather than the whole trajectory. Such verbs include "depart" (specifies beginning of movement), "arrive" (specifies end of movement) and others. These may or may not be treated like other verbs of motion.

3.2.1.6   Position

     Verbs that describe the static position of an object, e.g., *stand, sit, crouch, kneel, lie, hang*, etc., tend to have morphosyntactic properties similar to verbs of motion. For example, in English, verbs of position and locomotion can appear in presentative constructions (see section 6.4). Other kinds of verbs cannot easily occur in such constructions:

(40)

Motion	*Position*	*Other*
Here comes my bus.	There sits my bus.	?There burns my bus.
Under the bed scurried the cat.	Under the bed crouched the cat.	?Under the bed died the cat.

3.2.1.7   Actions

     Verbs which describe voluntary acts, but which do not involve an overtly affected patient, e.g., *dance, sing, speak, sleep/rest, look* (*at*), *read, deceive, care for, carry*(?), can be said to express actions. Note that action verbs can be either **dynamic**, i.e., involve change (*dance, sing, speak*), non-dynamic (*rest, look at*) or somewhere in between. These may answer the question "What did X do?," but less easily "What happened to X?," unless a slightly ironic, sarcastic, or extended meaning is desired:

What did Lucretia do?	She danced the tango.
What happened to Lucretia?	??She danced the tango.
What happened to the tango?	??Lucretia danced it.
What did Wimple do?	She read *War and Peace*.
What happened to Wimple?	??She read *War and Peace*.
What happened to the book?	??Wimple read it.
What did Ashley do?	She cared for her mother.
What happened to Ashley?	??She cared for her mother.
What happened to Ashley?	??Her mother cared for her.

3.2.1.8   *Action-processes*

Action-processes are situations that involve both a voluntary actor and a distinct affected PATIENT, such as *kill, hit, stab, shoot, spear* (and other violent events), plus the transitive senses of *break, melt, smash, change*, etc. Verbs that express action-processes answer both of the questions "What did X do?" and "What happened to X?":

What did Michael do?	He melted the ice.
What happened to the ice?	Michael melted it.
What did Aileron do?	She broke Trevor's nose.
What happened to Trevor's nose?	Aileron broke it.

3.2.1.9   *Factives*

Factive verbs are those that describe the coming into existence of some entity, e.g., *build, ignite, form, create, make, gather* as in "a crowd gathered," etc.[6] Hopper (1986) suggests that factives may never be treated differently from plain action verbs.

3.2.1.10   *Cognition*

Verbs of cognition express such concepts as *know, think, understand, learn, remember*, and *forget*. In many languages all or many of these are based on the same root, often the name of an internal body part, e.g., heart, liver, stomach (see section 3.2.1.12 on emotion verbs below and section 3.2.0.2 on verbs with EXPERIENCERS as subject).

3.2.1.11 Sensation

Sensation (or "sensory impression") verbs express concepts involving the senses: *see, hear, feel, taste, sense, observe, smell,* and *perceive.* Again, these are verbs whose subjects are likely to be experiencers.

3.2.1.12 Emotion

Verbs that express concepts like *fear, like/love, be angry/sad/ mournful, be happy/joyful/pleased, grieve/mourn* represent another class that is often based on a nominal root that signifies an internal body part such as "heart." For example, in many Papuan languages, the center of thinking and feeling is the liver. Therefore, expressions of emotion and cognition are compounds based on the root for "liver." This example is from the Orya language of Irian Jaya, courtesy of Phil Fields:

(41)   Ano   en-lala-na   beya-na.
        1SG:GEN liver-liquid-TOP much-be
        "I am worried." (lit.: "My bile is much," or "I have much bile.")

In Kom, a Grassfields Bantu language of Cameroon, the source of worry is the stomach (example courtesy of Peter Yuh):

(42)   ïlvïà   wom luun kï tèyn na   Sâm nïn grï   wì
        stomach my   hot like this COMP Sam 1SG come not
        "I am worried that Sam may not come."

In Yagua there are two verbs that express cognitive processes: one, *dáátya,* signifies mental processes, like knowing or understanding; the other, *jaachipiy,* signifies more "emotional" or reflective processes, such as "ponder" or "meditate." The second is transparently related to the noun root *jaachiy* meaning "heart." The following is a single example that illustrates both the nominal and derived verbal uses of this root:

(43)   Naanajaachipíyąąnúúyanú   jíjeechitya.
        naana-jaachiy-píy-yãâ-núúy-janu   jíy-jaachiy-tà
        3DL-heart-VBLZR-DIST-IMPERF-PAST3   COR-heart-INST
        "She pondered in her heart."[7]

3.2.1.13 Utterance

Utterance verbs, such as *speak, talk, say, tell, ask, answer, shout, yell, whisper, call, assert, imply, state, affirm, declare, murmur, babble, converse, chat, discuss, sing,* and many others are often onomatopoeic expressions (section 12.3.2). As such they may exhibit irregular phonological and/or morphological properties.

3.2.1.14   Manipulation

Manipulation verbs express concepts that involve the use of physical or rhetorical force to get someone else to do something. Examples include *force, oblige, compel, urge, make, cause, let, allow,* and *permit. Forbid* and *prevent* are also manipulative, though they imply the use of force to *keep* someone from doing something (see section 8.1.1 on causatives).

3.2.2   Verb structure

In polysynthetic languages, the most complex words are usually the verbs. In a grammar sketch of such a language it is useful to provide a general overview of the structure of the verb word. As with the structure of the noun word (section 3.1.2), a simple diagram may be useful here. For example, the structure of an English verb might be represented as:

(44)   ROOT-TENSE/AGR

In other words, a verb consists of a root plus an optional tense marker (*-ed*) or agreement marker (*-s*).

In more polysynthetic languages, the diagram may be much more complex. For example, the diagram for Panare is the following:

(45)

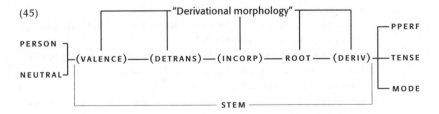

Even this diagram does not capture all of the complexity of the Panare verb. The details of this particular diagram are not important. The point is just to illustrate one feature of a grammar or grammar sketch that may help the reader begin to build a mental picture of how verbs in the language are put together.

The following is a list of operations that are likely to be expressed in the verb word in polysynthetic languages. In more isolating languages many of these may be expressed analytically, by particles or adverbs. In the following list, references are made to the sections in which these operations are discussed in more depth.

verb agreement/concord (7.1, 9.5)
semantic role markers (applicatives) (8.1.2)
valence increasing devices (8.1)
valence decreasing operations (8.2)
tense/aspect/mode (TAM) (9.3)
evidentials (9.6)
location and direction (9.4)
speech act markers (10.3)
verb(-phrase) negation (10.2)
subordination/nominalization (chapter 11, 9.1)
switch-reference (11.4)

?

What are the distributional properties of verbs?
What are the structural properties of verbs?
What are the major subclasses of verbs?
Describe the order of various verbal operators within the verbal word or verb phrase.
Give charts of the various paradigms, e.g., person marking, tense/aspect/mode etc. Indicate major allomorphic variants.
Are directional and/or locational notions expressed in the verb or verb phrase at all?
Questions to answer for all verbal operations:

(a) Is this operation obligatory, i.e., does one member of the paradigm have to occur in every finite verb or verb phrase?

(b) Is it productive, i.e., can the operation be specified for all verb stems, and does it have the same meaning with each one? (Nothing is fully productive, but some operations are more productive than others.)

(c) Is this operation primarily coded morphologically, analytically, or lexically? Are there any exceptions to the general case?

(d) Where in the verb phrase or verbal word is this operation likely to appear? Can it occur in more than one place?

References: Bybee (1985), Fillmore (1968, 1977), J. Anderson (1977), Dowty (1987), Vendler (1967), Schachter (1977, 1985), Foley and Van Valin (1984).

3.3   Modifiers

3.3.1   Descriptive adjectives

An **adjective** is a word that can be used in a noun phrase to specify some property of the head noun of the phrase. Adjectives are problematic in almost every language. Unlike nouns and verbs, adjectives cannot be characterized in terms of a prototype. This is because there is no semantically definable class of concepts that universally falls into a category that we would want to call adjectives; rather, adjectives stand "between" nouns and verbs, lexicalizing properties or characteristics that are indeterminate or variable in terms of time stability. Some languages have no formally distinct category of adjectives. In such languages, property concepts are expressed as either nouns or verbs. Many other languages can express property concepts either as nouns or as verbs depending on how they are used in discourse (Thompson 1988).

If a language has a morphosyntactically distinct class of adjectives, these adjectives will express at least the following properties:

> AGE (young, old, etc.)
> DIMENSION (big, little, tall, short, long, etc.)
> VALUE (good, bad)
> COLOR (black, white, red, etc.)

Other properties that may be expressed by adjectives include:

> PHYSICAL CHARACTERISTICS (hard, heavy, smooth, etc.)
> SHAPE (round, square, etc.)
> HUMAN PROPENSITY (jealous, happy, clever, wary, etc.)
> SPEED (fast, slow, quick, etc.)

An empirical study by Thompson (1988) has shown that the most common functions of words that express property concepts are (1) to predicate a property of some referent already on the discourse stage, and (2) to introduce new participants into the discourse. Here are some examples from English of each of these functions (most of these are from Thompson 1988):

(46)   *Function 1: Predication* (see section 6.2)
   a. And her parents weren't even that *wealthy*.
   b. That got me so *mad*.
   c. She's getting *good*.

(47)   *Function 2: Introduction of new referent*
   a. He had *black and white striped* sheets in his bedroom.
   b. That's a *great* car you've got.
   c. We're made for *Danish modern* apartments.

Function 1 is logically similar to the prototypical function of verbs as predicators, while function 2 is logically similar to the prototypical function of nouns as words that refer to entities. It is understandable, then, why languages tend to lump adjectives either with nouns or verbs.

Acehnese is a language in which property concepts are lexicalized as verbs. For example, when used as a predicate they may take verbal morphology, such as an "undergoer" suffix (ex. 48a). This is analogous to stative verbs (48b):

(48)   a. gopnyan saket-*geuh*.
          3   sick-UNDGOER
          "She's sick."

       b. gopnyan takot-*geuh*   keurimueng.
          3   fear-UNDGOER DAT tiger
          "She fears the tiger."

Also, any verb can be used as a modifier with no special morphology:

(49)   ureueng *pula* pade nyan.
       person   plant rice that
       "That person planting rice."

Finnish, on the other hand, is a language in which property concepts are lexicalized as nouns, whether they are used as predicates (ex. 50a) or as modifiers (50b):

(50)   a. Auto   on sininen.
          car:NOM is blue:NOM
          "The car is blue." (predicating function)

       b. iso-ssa auto-ssa
          big-LOC car-LOC
          "in the big car" (modifying function)

In 50a the word expressing the property "blue" appears in the nominative case, just like the noun *auto*. In 50b the property concept word *iso* carries the locative case marker, as does the head of the phrase.

In many languages words that express property concepts (or "adjectives") are treated formally as verbs when they are predicators and as nouns when they are modifiers. In Dutch, for example, predicate adjectives do not inflect while adjectives that modify nouns inflect like nouns. Other languages, e.g., Yoruba, are said to lexicalize some property concepts always as nouns and others always as verbs.

English fairly clearly has a distinct class of adjectives. For example, properties of verbs in English include: (1) ability to take past tense, and (2) agreement with a third person singular subject in the present tense. Properties of nouns include (1) ability to take a plural marking, and (2) ability to head noun phrases that take articles, modifiers, and quantifiers. Adjectives in English have none of these properties (except in those rare cases where an adjective is used as a noun, e.g., **The poor** *will always be with you* or in elliptical expressions, e.g., *Would you like to try the **white** or the **red**?*):

(51)   *He talls.
        *He talled.
        *They talls. / *three talls girls
        *a tall / *the tall

In summary, there are five major classes into which languages are known to fall with respect to their treatment of "property concepts:"

Typology of morphosyntactic treatment of property concepts (PCs)

1	PCs lexicalized as verbs.	Acehnese and other Austronesian languages
2	PCs lexicalized as nouns.	Finnish
3	PCs sometimes nouns and sometimes verbs depending on the demands of discourse.	Dutch
4	Some PCs lexicalized as nouns and others as verbs.	Yoruba
5	Distinct class of "adjectives."	English

3.3.2   Non-numeral quantifiers

Non-numeral quantifiers include such terms as *much, many, few, some, a lot of, a great deal of, tons of* (as in *There were tons of people at the concert*), etc.

3.3.3   Numerals

Some languages are reported to have number systems consisting of as few as four terms: *one, two, three,* and *many*. Other languages have native terms for the first few numbers (e.g., 1, 2, and 3) but then resort to terms borrowed from a trade language for the higher numbers. Still others have native terms that can be used to count almost infinitely. English uses native terms from one to 999,999. *Million* is a borrowing from French meaning "big thousand" (*billion, trillion,* etc. are backformations from *million*). In many parts of the world, different vocabulary is used to express numerical concepts depending on the context. For example, most Philippine languages have native terms for numbers into the thousands. These terms are used in most everyday situations. However, in the domains of money and time, Spanish terms are used. This is in spite of the fact that Spanish is no longer a trade language in the Philippines.

Different languages employ different number systems. Almost all natural number systems are either base five (quintenary) or base ten (decimal). A few are reported to be base twenty (vigesimal). This is probably because people universally keep track of quantities of items using their fingers and toes, and these are conveniently divisible by five, ten, and twenty. In many languages, the word for "five" is the same as or etymologically related to the word for "hand." "Ten" may be a compound related to "two hands." In languages of Papua New Guinea, it is common for the word for "twenty" to be a compound meaning literally "one person," i.e., the number of fingers and toes of a person. A base-five (quintenary) number system is one where the words for "six," "seven," "eight," and "nine" consist of the word for "five" plus the word for "one," "two," "three," and "four" respectively. There may be phonological reduction and/or some extra morphological trappings. For example, "six" may be expressed as "one on top of five," "seven" as "two on top of five" etc. "eleven," "twelve," etc. may then be expressed as "one on top of two fives," "two on top of two fives," etc.

Panare uses a quintenary number system. Not all Panare speakers use exactly the same system, but the variations are all based on units of five. The system is built around body-part terms, most fundamentally the roots *eña* "hand" and *pata* "foot." Numbers between multiples of five may involve expressions referring to digits of the foot: *yipun* "its head" or "its point" (referring to the toes) or *yipoj* "its covering" (an alternative expression for the toes). *E'ñapa* "person" enters into the numeral system for referring to multiples of one hundred, and not "twenty" as one might expect. For example, *asa' e'ñapa* (literally "two people") does not mean "forty," but "two hundred." When counting beyond twenty where the hands and feet of a single individual have been exhausted, *tyakope* "again, another" is added to indicate "another (person)."

When *toosen* (or *toose-jmën*) "big one" occurs in a numerical expression, its effect is to multiply whatever precedes it by five. Thus, *asa' patáipun toosen* (literally: "two foot:its:point big:one") translates as "two on a foot (=twelve) times five" or "sixty." *Na-patá-ipun toosen* "another-foot-its:point big:one" means "twenty times five" or "one hundred." This use of *toosen* derives from the colloquial Venezuelan Spanish expression *(un) fuerte* "strong (one)" for a five-Bolívar coin. The Panare calque is not surprising since a prime occasion for referring to quantities above twenty is when dealing with money, and prices in the rural economy are commonly quoted in *fuertes*. Table 3.2 illustrates many of the numbers of Panare, as used in the community of Guaniamo.

Table 3.2   The quintenary number system of Panare

English	Panare	Possible derivation and literal translation
one	tityasa	
two	asa'	
three	asoonwa	
four	asa'nan	
five	eeña katóme	"full hand"
six	tiisa natoityo	tityasa eeña katoityo "one from the other hand"
seven	asa'kye natoityo	asa' eeña katoityo "two from the other hand"
eight	asa'nan kíñe	
nine	asa'nan natoityo	asa'nan eeñakatoityo "four from the other hand"
ten	panaa ñípun	pana eeña y-ïpu-n toward hand GEN-head-POSS
eleven	tiisa patáipun	tityasa pata yïpun "one toe of the foot"
twelve	asa' patáipun	"two toes of the foot"
fifteen	pata katóme	"full foot"

Table 3.2 *continued*

English	Panare	Possible derivation and literal translation
sixteen	tiisa nakatoityo	
seventeen	asa'kya nakatoityo	
eighteen	asa'nan kiña katoityo	
nineteen	asa'nan eeña katoityo	
twenty	napatáipun	na-pata yïpun "another foot's toes"
twenty-one	napatáipun tiisa tyakópe	"one other toe of another (person)"
thirty	napatáipun nánipun tyakópe	"another foot's toes, and hands of another (person)"
thirty-two	napatáipun nánipun asa' tyakópe	"another foot's toes, and hands, plus two of another (person)"
forty	asa'nan kíña toosen	"eight big:one"
forty-three	asa'nan kíña toosen asoonwa	"eight big:one plus three"
fifty	asa'nan kíñe pana nípun tyakópe	"eight (big:one) plus hands of another (person)"
fifty-four	asa'nan kíñe pana nípun asa'nan tyakópe	"eight (big:one) plus hands, plus four of another (person)"
sixty	asa' patáipun toosen	
sixty-five	asa' patáipun toosen eeña katóme	
seventy	asa'nan patáipun toosen	
seventy-six	asa'nan patáipun toosen tiisa natoityo	
eighty	tiisa nakatoityo toosen	
eighty-seven	tiisa nakatoityo toosen asa'kye natoityo	
ninety	asa'nan kiña katoityo toosen	
one hundred	napataipun toosen	"the toes of another foot big:one"
two hundred	asa' e'ñapa	"two people"
one thousand	panaa ñípun e'ñapa toosen	"ten people big:one"

?

1 If you posit a morphosyntactic category of adjectives, give evidence for not grouping these forms with the verbs or nouns.
   What characterizes a form as being an adjective in this language?
2 How can you characterize semantically the class of concepts coded by this formal category?
3 Do adjectives agree with their heads (e.g., in number, case, and/or noun class)?
4 What kind of system does the language employ for counting? Decimal, quintenary?
5 How high can a fluent native speaker count without resorting either to words from another language or to a generic word like *many*? Exemplify the system up to this point.
6 Do numerals agree with their head nouns (e.g., in number, case, and/or noun class)?

3.4   Adverbs

Adverb is a "catch-all" category. Any word with semantic content (i.e., other than grammatical particles) that is not clearly a noun, a verb, or an adjective is often put into the class of adverb. Semantically, forms that have been called adverbs cover an extremely wide range of concepts. For this reason they cannot be identified in terms of time stability or any other well-defined semantic parameter. Also, they typically function on the clause or discourse level, i.e., their semantic effect (scope) is relevant to entire clauses or larger units rather than simply to phrases. As with adjectives, there are no prototypical adverbs. Formally, adverbs can be characterized primarily in terms of their distribution. They are typically the most unrestricted grammatical category in terms of their position in clauses (Givón 1984: 77). Some adverbs of English are signaled by the suffix *-ly*, e.g., *quickly, slowly, finally, adverbially*, etc. In the following subsections, English examples of various classes of adverbs are presented. Not every language exhibits all of these classes, and any language may have classes not represented here.

3.4.1   Manner

This is the largest subcategory of adverbs in every language: *quickly, slowly, patiently*, etc. In English, manner adverbs are often formed from adjectives by the addition of the suffix *-ly*.

3.4.2   Time

Yesterday, today, tomorrow, next/last year/week/month, early, late, etc. Yagua has an adverb *tą́ąriy,* which means something like *long time.* With a clause in the past tense it means "a long time ago;" in other clauses it means "for a long time" or "late in the afternoon."

3.4.3   Direction/location

Up/downriver, up/downhill, up/down(ward), north(ward), south-(ward), east(ward), west(ward), left(ward), right(ward), hither, thither, etc.

3.4.4   Evidential/epistemic

Evidential adverbs indicate the source of the information contained in the clause (e.g., hearsay, first-hand observation, second-hand observation, or pure conjecture). Epistemic adverbs indicate the degree to which the speaker is committed to the truth of the clause. English does not have a clear class of evidential adverbs. Instead it uses what appear to be verbs of utterance or perception to accomplish this function, e.g., *I understand, they say, I hear,* etc. That these are not really prototypical matrix verbs is evidenced by the fact that these locutions distribute like adverbs in a clause (see section 11.2 on matrix verbs). For example:

(52)   Democracy is, *I understand,* the best form of government.
        They are going to dedicate a new linguistics building, *I hear.*

In many languages that have lexicalized evidential adverbs, these can be traced etymologically to verbs of utterance or perception. English does have epistemic adverbs, e.g.: *possibly, definitely, clearly,* etc. English also uses erstwhile matrix verbs of cognition for this purpose, e.g., *I think, I know,* etc.

?

1   What characterizes a form as being an adverb in this language? If you posit a distinct class of adverbs, argue for why these forms should not be treated as nouns, verbs, or adjectives.
2   For each kind of adverb listed in this section, list a few members of the type, and specify whether there are any restrictions relative to that type, e.g., where they can come in a clause, any morphemes common to the type, etc.
3   Are any of these classes of adverbs related to older complement-taking (matrix) verbs?

---

4   Constituent order typology

4.0   Introduction

4.0.1   Historical and theoretical background

For many years linguists have noticed that discourse tends to be expressed in **clauses**. The notion of a clause seems so intuitive, so central to our conception of language that it is almost incomprehensible to imagine a theory of language, that did not include it. There is good reason for this intuition; a significant portion of cognition and reasoning in mature human beings is **propositional** (see section 8.0). That is, people mentally combine and manipulate concepts in chunks involving one or two conceptual entities and a relation, activity, or property concerning them. Communication tends to be multipropositional, consisting of groups of conceptual "chunks," each contributing some bit of information to the message to be communicated. The clause (or sometimes "sentence") is the linguistic expression of a proposition; a proposition is a conceptual notion, whereas a clause is its formal morphosyntactic instantiation.[1]

Even as propositions consist of entities and a property, activity, or relation, so clauses tend to consist of nouns and a predicating element, either a nominal/adjectival/stative element, or a verb. Given this characterization of propositions, there is no immediately obvious "natural" order in which the component parts of a proposition should be expressed. In fact we find that the order in which the predicating element (hereafter "verb" or simply "V" for short) and related nouns occur in clauses varies considerably from language to language, and even within the same language.

Descriptive linguists have long observed that individual languages structure their clauses in characteristic ways; some languages tend to place the verb at the end of a clause, others at the beginning, still others place it

Table 4.1   Summary of Greenberg's universals (from appendix 2 of Greenberg 1963)

Greenberg's universal	Parameter	Correlation	
1	main clauses	V-O	O-V
3, 4	adpositions	prepositions	postpositions
2	genitive (possessor) and head noun	N-G	G-N
17	head noun and modifier	N-M	M-N
24	relative clauses and head noun	N-RelCL	RelCL-N
22	comparatives	Adj-Mkr-Std	Std-Mkr-Adj
16	inflected auxiliaries	Aux-V	V-Aux
9	question particles	sentence-initial	sentence-final
12	question words	sentence-initial	sentence-initial or elsewhere
27	affixes	prefixes	suffixes

somewhere in the middle. Finally many languages seem to place the verb just about anywhere. Among the nominal (noun-like) constituents of a clause, an important distinction has traditionally been drawn between subject and object (S and O).[2] From this point of view there are six logically possible orders of constituents in a clause that contains a subject (S), an object (O), and a verb (V). These are: SOV, SVO, VSO, VOS, OSV, and OVS. Languages can often be categorized according to which of these orders is typical, or "basic." Though the assumption that subject and object are indeed the universal categories relevant to the ordering of nominal elements in a clause has been seriously questioned (see below and Doris Payne, 1986, 1992a, Mithun 1987, *inter alia*), this typology is often a useful starting point for conceptualizing the syntactic structure and investigating the functions of various orders in any language.

Greenberg (1963) observed that several syntactic characteristics tend to correlate with certain of the six basic constituent orders mentioned above. Table 4.1 summarizes the observations that Greenberg made for VO and OV languages. For example, if a language normally places the object after the verb in main clauses, then it tends to exhibit all the structural properties in the V-O column. Conversely, if a language normally places the object before the verb, then it will tend to exhibit the properties in the O-V column. The reader is encouraged to consult appendix 1 of Greenberg (1963) for a more inclusive summary of Greenberg's observations.

It is important to recognize that Greenberg simply observed certain correlations. He did not attempt to provide a reason for (i.e., to "motivate") those correlations, or even to test them for statistical significance. In this sense, Greenberg did not attempt to *predict* constituent orders in as yet unstudied languages. Nevertheless, Greenberg's work stimulated the field of typological linguistics and has continued to be very influential.

Much subsequent work on constituent order typology has focused on discovering motivations for the correlations observed by Greenberg, e.g., Lehmann (1973), Vennemann (1974), Hawkins (1983), and Dryer (1988). In order to "motivate" a correlation between two syntactic characteristics (e.g., SOV order and postpositions), the research paradigm has been first to show that the correlation between the characteristics is not random, and then to show that the correlation could not be otherwise, e.g., logically exclude the possibility that the correlation could have been other than the observed facts. In this sense, these subsequent studies attempted to make *predictions* of constituent orders. That is, they hoped that given certain key constituent orders, e.g., main declarative clause order and order of genitive and head in the noun phrase (Hawkins 1983), for any language they would be able to accurately guess (predict) what the other constituent orders would be.

Since 1963, much research has revealed problems with Greenberg's original six-way typology. Significant revisions, criticisms and extensions of Greenberg's work are found in Hawkins (1983, 1994), Doris Payne (1985a), Mithun (1987), and Dryer (1988). The three major problems with the original typology are: (1) the difficulty in identifying the basic constituent order for many languages of the world; (2) the fact that Greenberg's typology simply assumed that languages order their nominal elements according to the grammatical relations of subject and object; and (3) Greenberg did not even attempt to come up with a significantly large and random sample of languages.

The first two problems are probably due to a general Euro-centric bias among linguists. That is, since the European languages that many linguists speak order their main-clause elements according to status as subject and object, and since these categories are readily identifiable in most of these languages, it has been assumed, not just by Greenberg, that all languages must operate in the same way. However, subsequent research, much of which has been done by speakers of non-Indo-European languages, has revealed that in many languages grammatical relations just are not as clearly identifiable as they are in Indo-European. Furthermore, even when they are identifiable, it is often doubtful whether any significant correlations can be drawn between constituent orders and grammatical relations. While nouns themselves are relatively easy to identify universally, there are many different properties (sometimes "statuses" or "roles") that noun phrases have when they enter into syntactic constructions. The roles of subject and object are central in most Indo-European languages, but there is no *a priori* reason to expect that other characteristics, perhaps agent/patient, definite/indefinite, given/new, animate/inanimate, big/small, or abstract/concrete would not also affect the positions of nouns in clauses. Hence, it should be a matter of empirical observation, not *a priori* assumption, whether and to what extent constituent orders in a language can be stated in terms of S and O.

Languages that organize their constituent orders according to some principle other than grammatical relations are often called "free" or "flexible" constituent order languages. Sometimes they are called **non-configurational** languages (Hale 1983). More recently this typology has been refined, and the term **pronominal argument** languages has been used (Jelinek 1984, 1988). From the point of view of language as a symbolic system, we would expect that such an obvious and easily manipulable structural variable as the order of words in a clause would be exploited to express *some* important functional distinction. Indeed, discourse-based studies of "free" constituent order languages show that constituent order in such languages is far from random (see section 4.1.03 below and the references cited therein).

In spite of these problems with the Greenberg typology, it is still helpful to a reader of a grammar sketch to have some sense of the basic constituent order type the language represents. However, in this discussion we will replace the traditional two-way distinction between subject and object with a three-way distinction among what Dixon (1979) and Comrie (1978a) have called "semantico-syntactic roles." These are the most agent-like argument of a transitive clause, only argument of an intransitive clause and other argument of a transitive clause:

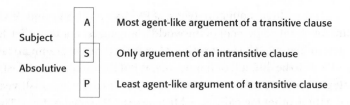

Within this framework, the **subject** category consists of the set of A together with S, while the **absolutive** category consists of the set of S together with P. These terms will be elaborated and given more substance in section 7.1. For purposes of constituent order typology, then, languages can be characterized in terms of A, S, P, and V rather than simply S, O, and V. This new terminology both provides for languages that treat the intransitive subject like a transitive object in terms of constituent ordering (e.g., Kuikúro, see section 7.1) and provides a bridge into the more detailed treatment of grammatical relations in chapter 7.

4.0.2   Distribution of constituent order types around the world

From studies that assume that subject and object are relevant for basic constituent order, it appears that APV/SV and AVP/SV are the most common constituent order types; they occur in virtually every area of the world in about equal proportions. Japanese is a nearly prototypical APV/SV language. English is a fairly consistent AVP/SV language, allowing alternatives such as PAV (*Beans I like*) and VS (*Here comes my bus*). However, these alternatives are clearly pragmatically marked, occurring rarely and only in very well-defined discourse environments. Together APV/SV and AVP/SV languages constitute approximately 70 percent of the world's languages.

The third most common constituent order type is VAP/VS. This type is well represented in Austronesian languages (Philippines, Pacific Islands, Madagascar, and the interior of Indonesia and Malaysia), and in many Nilo-Saharan and Semitic languages of eastern and northern Africa. It is also quite common in the Americas. Verb-initial languages tend to allow more flexibility of constituent orders than do verb-final or verb-medial languages. For this reason, if discourse in a given language contains many verb-initial clauses, it may be difficult to determine what the *basic* constituent order is.

These three common types, APV/SV, AVP/SV, and VAP/VS, account for about 85 percent of the world's languages. For the other 15 percent, determination of basic constituent order in terms of grammatical relations is likely to be difficult or impossible. What the three major constituent order types have in common is that the A precedes the P in transitive clauses. In the three other logically possible types, the P precedes the A. The tendency for A to precede P in basic, pragmatically neutral clauses is so overwhelming that it is extremely unlikely that it could have arisen by chance. This fact has led many researchers to reflect on possible cognitive motivations for the categories of A and P. That is, many have asked "What is it about nominals categorized as A and P that causes languages to practically always order A before P in basic clauses?" Some of this research is discussed in chapter 8.

As mentioned above, if a language employs verb-initial clauses quite frequently (approximately 25 percent or more) in discourse, it will probably be quite difficult to determine a "basic" order. This will be because of either or both of the following tendencies: (1) verb-initial languages often avoid the use of full noun phrases, preferring to rely on pronouns and/or anaphoric clitics; and (2) verb-initial languages often are less sensitive to grammatical relations than are other languages. That is, their basic clause structure can often be insightfully described as a verb followed by one or more noun phrases. The order of the noun phrases following the verb tends to be determined by pragmatic or semantic factors that are only indirectly characterizable in terms of grammatical relations. This is true for many Western Austronesian languages. It is also true of many verb-initial languages of the Americas, e.g., Mayan and other Meso-American languages.

4.1   Constituent order in main clauses

The following section is organized into three headings: (1) how to determine the "basic" constituent order of a language; (2) examples of "rigid" constituent order languages; and (3) examples of "flexible" constituent order languages.

4.1.01   How to determine the "basic" constituent order of a language

Most linguists would consider the "basic" constituent order of a language to be exhibited at least in pragmatically neutral clauses. However, identifying one clause type as "pragmatically neutral" may be problematic. It is especially difficult to find pragmatically neutral clauses that contain one or more full noun phrases. A general way to approach this problem is, first, to eliminate clause types that are known to exhibit variant constituent orders in some languages. These would include:

1 dependent clauses;
2 paragraph-initial clauses;
3 clauses that introduce participants;
4 questions;
5 negative clauses;
6 clearly contrastive clauses (e.g., clefts, answers to questions, etc.).

It is fairly certain that the clauses that remain are largely pragmatically neutral. If in these remaining clauses there are examples of transitive verbs with two full NPs and if there is consistency of order of those NPs with respect to the verb, then a basic constituent order can be identified. Unfortunately, this is a rare situation as pragmatically neutral clauses tend to have a verb and one or fewer noun phrases. Nevertheless, most languages can be classified as "verb-initial," "verb-medial," or "verb-final" even if the relative orders of A and P are indeterminate.

It is important to remember that the orders of elements in other construction types (e.g., noun or adpositional phrases) is not evidence for a particular order in main clauses. For example, Greenberg observed that languages with postpositions are always (in his sample) of the OV type. However, if we know the language has postpositions rather than prepositions, we cannot use Greenberg's observations to claim that the basic order in main clauses must be OV. Greenberg did not make predictions – only observations based on a very small sample. Languages are too often inconsistent for us to take non-main-clause orders as clues to main-clause order.

4.1.02 Characteristics of "rigid" constituent order languages

In the following examples, prototypical P arguments appear in bold type. There are many constituent types that function like the P argument in terms of order. These appear in italic type. They are not *prototypical* P arguments in that they do not necessarily refer to visible, concrete entities that undergo a change in state as a result of the action of the verb.

Nevertheless, they share at least the formal property of clause position with P arguments. Some of these constituent types are illustrated for each of the constituent orders exemplified below:

(1)   *English, AVP (SVO in the earlier system)*
  a. Dimaggio hit **the ball**.   direct object
  b. Bart went *to the bathroom*.   oblique
  c. The executioner knew *that she had lost her job*. object complement
  d. The woman wanted *to vomit*.   object complement
  e. They told the cat *to wait*.   object complement
  f. The coach was *ugly*.   predicate adjective
  g. The man was *a wretched ping-pong player*. predicate nominal

(2)   *Hindi, APV (SOV)*
  Raam-nee **khaanaa** khaa-yaa
  Ram-ERG food   eat-PAST
  "Ram ate food."

(3)   *Jacaltec (Mayan), VAP (VSO)* (examples from Craig 1977: 9)
  a. xa' ix te' **hum** *wet* an direct and indirect objects
    gave CL:she CL:the book to:me 1
    "She gave the book to me."

  b. xahtoj naj *yiban no'* *cheh* oblique object
    go:up CL:he on CL:the horse
    "He climbed on the horse."

(4)   *Malagasy, VPA (VOS)*
  a. manasa **lamba** Rasoa   direct object
    wash clothes Rasoa
    "Rasoa is washing clothes."

  b. nanome **vola** *an-Rabe* aho direct and indirect objects
    gave money to-Rabe I
    "I gave money to Rabe."

  c. manaiky *manasa ny zaza* Rasoa object complement
    agree wash the baby Rasoa
    "Rasoa agreed to wash the baby."

4.1.03   Characteristics of "flexible" constituent order languages

    So-called "flexible" or "free" constituent order languages are those in which some principle other than grammatical relations governs the order of nominals in a clause. For example, in Biblical Hebrew the order of noun phrases with respect to the verb is reported by Givón (1984: 208ff.) to be determined largely by pragmatic factors. In general, new, indefinite information occurs preverbally, whereas given, definite information occurs postverbally. The following passages from Biblical Hebrew illustrate this variation for S/A, P and oblique arguments:

(5)   *Biblical Hebrew, V-S/A vs. A/S-V order*

    a. *VS, already identified(definite)/identifiable subject*
       va-yavo'u **shney ha-mal'axim** Sdom-a   b-a-'erev
       and-came two   DEF-angels Sodom-LOC in-the-evening
       "So the two angels came to Sodom in the evening,"

    b. *SV, previously unidentified subject*
       vï-Lot   yoshev bï-shaʕar Sdom;
       and-Lot sitting at-gate of:Sodom
       "and Lot was sitting at the gate of Sodom;"

    c. *VA, already identified subject*
       va-yar' **Lot**
       and-saw Lot
       "and Lot saw (them)"

    d. *V-only, highly topical subject*
       va-yaqom . . .
       and-rose
       "and rose . . ." (Genesis 19: 1)

(6)   *Biblical Hebrew, VP vs. PV order*

    a. *VP, continuing, identifiable object*
       . . . va-yiqah 'elohim **'et-ha-'adam**
          and-took God   ACC-DEF-man
       ". . . and God took the man"

    b. *VP(PRO), continuing identifiable object*
       va-yanihe **hu** bï-gan   'eden
       and-put him in-garden:of Eden
       "and put him in the garden of Eden"

    c. *Anaphoric agreement (dependent clause)*
       lï-'ovd-**o** u-lï-shomr-**o**;
       to-work-it and-to-guard-it
       "to work and guard it;"

   d. *VP, continuing, identifiable object*
   va-yïsav   YHWH 'elohim 'al   **ha-'adam le**-'mor:
   and-ordered YHWH God   unto the-man to-say
   "and God ordered Adam, saying:"

   e. *PV, new object in contrast*
   "**mi-kol 'es ha-gan**   'axol to'xel,
   from-all tree the-garden eating you:eat
   "You may eat from all the trees in the garden,"

   f. *PV, new object in contrast*
   u-me- 'es   ha-da'at   **tov ve-ra'** lo' to'xel.
   and-from-tree the-knowledge:of good and-evil NEG you:eat
   "but from the tree of knowledge of good and evil you may not eat."
   (Genesis 2: 15–17)

Mithun (1987) questions the notion that every language should be describable in terms of a basic order of constituents determined by grammatical relations. She argues that in at least three languages, Cayuga (Iroquoian of Ontario), Ngandi (Australian of East Arnhem Land), and Coos (of Oregon), grammatical relations have no direct effect on constituent order. Instead, pragmatic status of the nominal constituents is the best determiner of the order of those constituents with respect to the verb. Here we will briefly summarize Mithun's data.

In all three languages some form of the following generalization summarizes constituent ordering:

> New, indefinite or otherwise "newsworthy" information is placed early in the clause.

In the following examples from Cayuga, we see PV order when the P refers to a non-specific, newly mentioned entity (7a), and VP order when the P refers to a specific identified item:

(7)   a.   P   V
            katsihwá' kihsa:s
            hammer I-seek
            "I am looking for a hammer." (said in a hardware store, with no particular hammer in mind)

      b.   V   P
            to: ti' nika:nô:' nê:kyê katsíhwa'?
            how then so-it-costs this   hammer
            "How much does this hammer cost?" (holding a specific hammer)

Ngandi (from Heath 1978: 206) follows a similar principle:

(8)   a.   S   V
      Načuweleñ-uŋ gu-jark-yuŋ   gu-ja-walk, . . .
      then-ABS   GU-water-ABS GU-now-go:through
      "Then water passes through, . . ." (first mention of water)

      b.   V   S
      Načuweleñ-uŋ gu-ja-geyk-da-ni   gu-jark-yuŋ
      then-ABS   GU-now-throw-AUG-PR GU-water-ABS
      "Then the water rushes through." (subsequent mention of water)

Coos (Frachtenberg 1913: 7) also follows this "indefinite first" principle:

(9)   a.   P   A   V
      TE tc!i'cil   yüL is   yö'qat . . .
      that matting we two split:it
      "Let's split this mat . . ." (first mention of mat)

      (they did so, and went down to examine the earth. The earth was still not
      solid, even . . .)

      b.   V   P
      i   lau tci   uxhi'touts   hE tc!icil.
      when that there they:two:put:it:down the matting
      "after they had put down the mat." (subsequent mention of mat)

   In these three languages, the positions of all nominal clause constituents (i.e., A, P, and oblique elements) are apparently determined to a
large extent by pragmatic factors. For some languages, one nominal element exhibits a fairly fixed position (variable only under extreme pragmatic pressures), while another is more variable. Some other languages that
operate in this way are:

       Guaymí (fixed PV, flexible A);
       Panare, Nadëb (fixed VA, flexible P);
       Apuriñą (fixed AV, flexible P).

   The areas of the world in which languages seem particularly sensitive to pragmatic ordering principles are the Americas, Australia, and
to a lesser extent Austronesia and South Asia. Not enough studies of constituent order in discourse have been conducted in Africa to allow generalizations regarding the sensitivity of African languages to pragmatic
principles in constituent ordering. The Slavic languages are apparently the

most pragmatically sensitive in the Indo-European family, though they do not approach the degree of pragmatic variability demonstrated by such languages as Cayuga (Mithun 1987: 309–10). It should be emphasized, however, that pragmatic factors influence constituent order in all languages to one degree or another. For some languages pragmatic factors are so dominant that it is difficult or impossible to describe the "basic" constituent order in terms of grammatical relations. On the other hand, even in languages in which pragmatics clearly dominates constituent order, grammatical relations may still have some correlation with particular clause positions.

It is interesting that all three of the languages discussed by Mithun share several morphosyntactic properties, besides pragmatically determined constituent order. Many of these properties also hold for other such languages (e.g., Panare, Papago, Ute). It remains to be seen whether these properties characterize a substantive linguistic type. Some of the morphosyntactic properties that correlate with pragmatic constituent ordering are:

1 Polysynthetic morphological typology (see chapter 2).
2 Agent and/or patient marking on the verb.
3 A tendency towards ergative case marking on NPs (see chapter 7).
4 "Loose" syntactic structure, i.e., nominal elements may occur under a different intonation contour than the verb, and adverbial, or other clause-level elements, may freely intervene between the verb and the nominal elements.
5 A tendency to avoid the use of full noun phrases in discourse. The occurrence of clauses with two or more noun phrases is rare.

One final caution: almost any language can be claimed to allow all possible orderings of A, P, and V if enough different kinds of constructions are included. The following are some examples from English:

(10)   a. Fred skins mules.   AVP
       b. It's mules that Fred skins.   PAV
       c. (There he sits,) skinning mules, that Fred.   VPA
       d. Skins 'em, Fred does to them mules.   VAP
       e. Fred's a mule skinner.   APV
       f. That mule skinner's Fred.   PVA

To determine "pragmatic ordering principles" that would account for this variation would amount to determining the discourse functions of all the various clause types represented (clefts, participial clauses, nominalizations, etc.). Such an enterprise is not necessarily unreasonable, as long as one understands that the variable being tested is not simply different orders of V, A, and P.

Care should be taken in conducting and evaluating studies of constituent order variation in any language. For one thing, linguists who conduct constituent order studies of languages for which they do not understand the basic clause types are particularly prone to bizarre analyses (as illustrated above). Second, grammatically marginal clauses such as 10d may be produced and accepted by consultants in preliterate or newly literate societies more readily than they would be by speakers who have more static perceptions of their language. Often the marginality of such clauses may be difficult for preliterate consultants to describe. Finally, and most importantly, the syntactic status of many clause types is often in a state of flux. For example, nominalizations such as 10e and f often function very much like verbal clauses with the nominalizer (-*er* in English) functioning as a tense, aspect, or mode marker (see, e.g., T. Payne 1990b). In fact, noun and verb morphology often overlap to such an extent that it is difficult to determine whether one is dealing with a verbal clause or a predicate nominal based on a nominalized verb. Whereas it is quite clear (to fully competent native speakers trained in linguistics) that 10a and e represent very different construction types, and that order is certainly not the only respect in which they differ, out of context these clauses seem to express very similar ideas. This sort of functional similarity leads in many languages to a reanalysis of the predicate nominal construction (as in 10e) as a kind of verbal predication. If the language under study is in the process of such a change (and even if it is not), the probability of mistakenly including predicate nominals in a study of constituent order in verbal clauses is quite high (especially if the language uses a zero copular element in predicate nominals; see section 6.1). On the other hand, if the language has already accomplished the reanalysis from predicate nominal to verbal clause (a process that is one of the major sources of ergative constructions; see, e.g., Gildea 1992), it would be fully appropriate to conduct a study to determine the discourse pragmatic functions of the two construction types. However, it would still be questionable to consider such a study to be simply one of determining the functions of variant constituent orders.

❷ ··
       General questions for all units of structure:
   (a) What is the neutral order of free elements in the unit?
   (b) Are there variations?
   (c) How do the variant orders function?
       Question specific to main clause constituent order: What is the
       pragmatically neutral order of constituents (A/S, P, and V) in basic clauses of
       the language?
   ··

4.2   Verb phrase

Auxiliaries are verbs in that they satisfy the morphosyntactic
definition of verbs (whatever that may be for the language), e.g., they occur
in the position of a verb and they carry at least some of the inflectional
information (subject/object "agreement" and tense/aspect/mode marking)
normally associated with verbs. However, they are auxiliary in that they do
not embody the major conceptual relation, state, or activity expressed by
the clause. They are often semantically "empty" (e.g., *do* in English *He does
go to school*), or they express "auxiliary" information such as tense, aspect,
or mode, e.g., *can* and *hæftə* in English.[3]

Auxiliaries normally derive from full verbs. The most likely verbs
to become auxiliaries are stative verbs such as *be*, *stand*, and *sit*. The next
most likely sources for auxiliaries are simple verbs of motion such as *go*
and *come*. Finally, complement-taking verbs such as *say*, *finish*, *start*, *permit*, *make*, *force*, and *want* also often become auxiliaries.

If a language has a verb-phrase element that displays at least some
of the inflectional information common to verbs but is distinct from the
verb that expresses the main lexical content of the clause, then this word
can be called an auxiliary. In a few languages such forms do not seem to
come from verbs at all, and the way in which they express the inflectional
information is not very much like the way verbs do, i.e., they may exhibit
irregular or completely distinct inflectional paradigms. For example, many
Uto-Aztecan languages employ a series of particles before the main verb.
The following examples are from Luiseño, a Uto-Aztecan language spoken
in southern California, as presented in Steele (1981: 23):

(11)   noo *n*   hunwuti patiq
         I   1SG bear   shoot:PRES
         "I am shooting the bear."

Here the particle *n* expresses the person of the subject of the clause, whereas the verb, *patiq*, is in a form that expresses the tense. In 12 there are two particles, *nu* and *po*, where *nu* is an allomorph of the 1SG subject marker and *po* expresses future tense:

(12)   noo *nu po* hunwuti patin
          I   1SG FUT bear   shoot:FUT
          "I will shoot the bear."

Finally, a third particle, *xu*, expressing modal information, can appear before both of the other two particles. Again, the inflection on the main verb changes:

(13)   noo xu   *n*   *po* hunwuti pati
          I   MOD 1SG FUT bear   shoot
          "I should shoot the bear."

Steele (1981) argues that this complex of particles that precedes the main verb forms a constituent that can be labeled AUX. Notice that there is no root for this auxiliary element. It is simply a "position" in the clause structure of Luiseño that can be filled by a number of different elements, all of which modify the concept expressed by the clause in various ways. All the utterances in 11–13 describe a scene in which someone shoots a bear. The contribution of the AUX element is to adjust the scene to express various nuances (see section 9.3 for a discussion of tense, aspect, and mode). For the purposes of a chapter on constituent order, it is sufficient to identify the position of such auxiliary elements with respect to the main verb. In Luiseño that would be AUX-V.

If a verb phrase element does not take any of the inflectional information associated with verbs, it may still be called an "auxiliary," although it cannot be properly termed an "inflected auxiliary" and therefore will not enter into the discussion of constituent order. For example, the forms *should, might, ought*, and *used* (as in *He used to eat beans*) do not inflect at all, although they are sometimes referred to as *modal auxiliaries*. In other languages it may be difficult or impossible to distinguish such forms from certain kinds of adverbs.

?
        Where do auxiliaries occur in relation to the semantically "main" verb?
        Where do verb-phrase adverbs occur with respect to the verb and
        auxiliaries?

4.3   **Noun phrase**

Noun phrase elements include determiners (section 5.5), numerals (section 3.3.3), genitives (possessors) (section 5.6), modifiers (i.e., attributive adjectives, section 3.3.1), relative clauses (section 11.5), noun classifiers (section 5.7), and the head noun. The head noun is the noun that is modified by all the other elements, e.g., *dogs*, in *those three big black dogs that are always barking at me*. It is the noun that refers to the same entity that the whole phrase refers to (see section 3.1).

Although Greenberg's original work suggested that the order of elements in the noun phrase correlates with the order of elements in the main clause, subsequent work by Dryer (1988) shows that this result was mistaken. Using a much larger sample, Dryer concludes that there is no statistically significant correlation. Nevertheless, it is still important to note the order of elements in the noun phrase.

?

Describe the order(s) of elements in the noun phrase.

4.4   **Adpositional phrases (prepositions and postpositions)**

The term **adposition** is a cover term for prepositions and postpositions. These are usually particles, though they may be clitics or substantives, i.e., nouns or verbs, that say something about the semantic role of an adjacent noun phrase in the clause. If a language has case markers (see section 7.1), the distinction between case markers and adpositions may be problematic. Section 5.4 provides a rule of thumb for making this determination. The following are examples of prepositions and postpositions:

(14)   *Prepositions: Spanish*
  a. *en* la mesa
     "*on* the table"
  b. *dentro de* la casa
     "*inside of* the house"
  c. *sobre* mi carro
     "*over* my car"
  d. *hasta* la tarde
     "*until* the afternoon"

(15)   *Postpositions: Japanese*
  a. biku *no* "*of/inside/near* the fishbasket"
  b. kookyu *ue* "*above* the palace"

Adpositions derive historically from nouns or verbs. For some languages, particularly languages that employ serial verbs extensively (section 11.1), it may be difficult to decide whether a given form is an adposition or a dependent verb. In the following example from Akan, the form *wɔ* is a perfectly good verb meaning "to be at" (16a). It also functions as a locative preposition (16b):

(16)   *Akan* (Ghana, courtesy of Kweku Osam)

    a. ɔ-**wɔ**   Eugene
       3sg-be:at
       "He is in Eugene."

    b. o   hun no **wɔ** Eugene
       1pl see 3pl in
       "We saw them in Eugene."

One indication that *wɔ* is a verb in 16a but not in 16b is that in predicate locative clauses like 16a *wɔ* can take verb agreement, whereas in 16b verb agreement is not possible. Such tests show that *wɔ* really does belong to different grammatical categories in these two examples.

In Ndjuká, an English-based creole language of Surinam, the verb *gi* "give" is also a locative, dative, or benefactive preposition (George Huttar, p.c.):

(17)   Boo gi   den gi   mi.
       blow give 3pl give 1sg
       "Honk at them for me."

Sometimes there are *no* formal properties to distinguish serial verbs from adpositions (see chapter 11 for more discussion of serial-verb constructions).

In other languages the adpositions come from nouns. For example, in English the phrase *on top of* is a complex preposition consisting partially of the noun *top*. For many languages adpositions come from body-part nouns, e.g., "back" for "behind," "face" for "in front," "head" for "up," and "foot" for "down" (Casad 1982, Heine and Re 1984). The set of basic adpositions in most languages is rather small, consisting of perhaps five or six forms. Other, more complex, relational notions are expressed by complex adpositions built up out of combinations of adpositions and nouns. English is unusually rich in basic prepositions. These include:

(18)   at, to, from, in, out, on, over, under, around, through, for, by, with, along, etc.

Other very common prepositions in English are compounds:

(19)   into, upon, toward (*to* + the directional suffix *ward*), on top of,
         underneath, behind, below, beneath, out of, next to, etc.

In some languages it may be difficult to distinguish adpositional phrases from possessed noun phrases. For example, in Yagua, the form that translates "in front of (someone)" is homophonous with "on (someone's) forehead":

(20)   sa-moo-mu
         3SG-forehead-LOC
         "in front of him/her" or "on his/her forehead"

In other languages, there may perhaps be no marker of the locational relation other than the noun. In such cases, the distinction between adpositions and nouns may be indeterminate. The following is an example from Swahili (Bantu, East Africa):

(21)   alikiweka **juu** ya meza.
         3SG:put:it top of table
         "He/she put it on the table."

In this example *juu* simply means "top." In Swahili there is apparently no way, or reason, to distinguish this form as a preposition rather than just a noun. One way to express this indeterminacy would be to say that *juu* is a noun root functioning as a preposition in this example.

?

Is the language dominantly prepositional or post-positional? Give examples. Do many adpositions come from nouns or verbs?

Additional references: Matisoff (1973), DeLancey (1991), Welmers (1973).

4.5   Comparatives

A **comparative** is a construction in which two items are compared according to some quality, e.g., *My daddy is bigger than your daddy*. Many languages do not have a syntactically distinct comparative construction. These languages express comparison by simply juxtaposing two (or more) clauses expressing the degree to which the compared entities exhibit the quality in question, e.g., to say "My daddy is bigger than your daddy," one would say something like "Your daddy is big. My daddy is very big." The crucial elements of a grammaticalized comparative construction are: (1) the known **standard** against which the subject of the clause is compared; (2) the **marker** that signals that the clause is a comparative construction; and (3) the **quality** by which the subject is compared with the standard. The standard is a noun phrase, the marker can be a special particle, an adposition, or an affix, and the quality is normally expressed through an adjective. For example:

(22)   *Japanese: standard–marker–quality*
        Inu ga   meko yori ookii.
        dog NOM cat   than big
                  STD   MKR QUAL
        "The dog is bigger than the cat."

"The dog" in this clause is the subject of the comparison: that is, it is the item whose size is being compared to that of a known standard. The position of the subject of a comparative construction is not as typologically significant as the relative positions of the standard, marker, and quality. STD–MKR–QUAL order is common in PV languages.

(23)   *Irish: quality–marker–standard*
        Tá an madadh nios -mó ná   an cat.
        is the dog   big -er than the cat
                          QUAL MKR   STD
        "The dog is bigger than the cat."

The order QUAL–MKR–STD is common in VP languages. Comparative constructions are often inconsistent with the general constituent order pattern of the language.

?
    Does the language have one or more grammaticalized comparative
    constructions?
    If so what is the order of the standard, the marker, and the quality by which an
    item is compared to the standard?

4.6   Question particles and question words

Question particles are discussed in section 10.3.1.1; question words are discussed in section 10.3.1.2. In this section, simply exemplify these elements, especially noting their positions with respect to other clause elements.

?

In yes/no questions, if there is a question particle, where does it occur?
In information questions, where does the question word occur?

4.7   Summary

Very few languages conform 100 percent to the general expectations provided by Greenberg (1963). As with morphological typology, there is no quantitative method for determining how close a particular language is to its "ideal" type. The chapter on constituent order typology in a grammar sketch should contain a summary of the constituent orders of the language in comparison to Greenberg's universals as outlined in table 4.1. The language can then be characterized impressionistically as a "very consistent," "fairly consistent," or "inconsistent" language of constituent order type X. For example, English is a fairly consistent AVP language, exhibiting inconsistency only in the placement of its descriptive modifiers in the NP, and in allowing both pre- and postnominal genitives ("John's house" alongside "the house of John"). Japanese is a very consistent APV language, Yagua is an inconsistent VPA language, etc.

It is important to note that particular orders within non-main-clause units are not evidence for any main-clause order. For example, a language may have the basic order of AVP in main clauses, but every other unit may have orders consistent for APV languages (e.g., postpositions, postverbal auxiliaries, prenominal modifiers, etc.). This is *not* evidence that the language has APV word order. It may indicate that APV is a diachronically older order for the language, but it is not an argument for a particular synchronic order. Greenberg's universals are simply correlations based on a sample of about thirty languages. They are not *predictions* of what one will find in any given language. Languages that deviate from Greenberg's ideal types do not "violate" Greenberg's universals. They are simply inconsistent with the ideal type. Since the majority of languages of the world are inconsistent, it may be more appropriate to dub a perfectly consistent language as a violation of expectations! Sometimes it may be appropriate to call a language a PV-type language, even though the basic constituent order in main clauses is VP, and vice versa. This point of view ascribes no particular importance to main-clause constituent order – it is simply one property among many. If a language has all the characteristics of a VP language except it has PV basic order in main clauses, it is still a fairly consistent "VP-type" language. It only deviates in one respect.

?

How does this language compare in its constituent orders to universal expectations, as represented by Greenberg (1963), Hawkins (1983), or some other well-known typology?

5 Noun and noun-phrase operations

To this point we have been viewing language from a fairly broad structural perspective. In chapter 2 I suggested a framework for describing the general morphological characteristics of a language without discussing in detail the meanings of the various morphemes. Chapter 3 presented ways of distinguishing the major grammatical categories of the language, including cataloging the morphosyntactic operations that are associated with each category. However, the precise communicative functions of each operation were not discussed. In chapter 4 we considered constituent order typology, again without treating the functions that alternate constituent orders might have.

Many of the categories, structures, and operations mentioned briefly from a "form-first" perspective in the previous three chapters will receive more detailed treatment in the following seven. The present chapter describes tasks, or functions, that tend to be associated with noun phrases, and presents further details concerning how morphosyntactic operations are expressed in noun phrases.

5.1   Compounding

A **compound** is a word that is formed from two or more different words. For example the word *windshield* is composed of the words *wind* and *shield*. Of course, not every sequence of words is a compound. Hence there must be an explicit way of distinguishing compounds from simple sequences of words. The criteria for calling something a compound fall into two groups: (1) formal criteria, and (2) semantic criteria. Compounds may exhibit any of the following formal properties. (1) A stress pattern

92

characteristic of a single word, as opposed to the pattern for two words, e.g., *bláckbird* (the species), has a different stress pattern than *black bird* (any bird that happens to be black), cf. also *líghthouse keeper* vs. *light hóusekeeper*. (2) Unusual word order, e.g., *housekeeper* consists of a noun plus a verb where the noun represents the object rather than the subject of the verb. Normally objects come after the verb in English. (3) Morphophonemic processes characteristic of single words, e.g., the word *roommate* can be pronounced with a single *m*, whereas normally if two *m*'s come together accidentally in a sentence both are pronounced, e.g., *some mice* will be understood as *some ice* if both *m*'s are not pronounced. (4) Morphology specific to compounds, e.g., the *-er* of *can-opener*. *To can open* is not a verb, **I can opened all evening*, but with the instrumental *-er* suffix the compound *can open* is treated exactly as though it were a verb stem, following the pattern of *slicer, grinder*, etc. In German, genitive case endings function as morphological "glue" in compounds when their use would be disallowed in the corresponding noun phrase:

(1)   *German* (from Anderson 1985a)
       Bischoff-s-konferenz
       bishop-GEN-conference
       "conference of bishops"

In this example the *-s* cannot be functioning as a genitive marker because it is a genitive *singular* marker, and the compound refers to a conference of many bishops. On the other hand, sometimes compounds are morphologically simpler than a corresponding noun phrase, e.g., English *spider web* as opposed to the phrase *spider's web*.

The dominant semantic property of compounds is that the meaning of a compound is either more specific or entirely different than the combined meanings of the words that make up the compound. For example, the term *windshield* cannot be used for any shield against wind, but only for those specific items made of transparent material used in vehicles of various sorts. So while a line of trees along a farmer's field could for the nonce be called a *wínd shíeld* (though the technical term is *shelter belt*), it cannot be called a *windshield*. Similarly, *blackbird* (the compound) is only appropriately used to refer to particular species of bird, though members of other species, such as crows, vultures, etc., can legitimately be called *black birds*. Some compounds contain one part which is not a real word, e.g., *huckleberry, cranberry*, etc. In fact, sometimes neither part is an independent word, at least not one that can be synchronically related to the meaning of the whole compound, e.g., *chipmunk, somersault, mushroom, blacksmith*.

Mandarin Chinese is a language which makes extensive use of compounds, but for which there are few, if any, formal criteria for identifying a compound. That is, there are no tone or morphological differences between compounds and the corresponding phrases. Some authors posit a stress difference between compounds and phrases, but this is not widely accepted. The following are a few of the thousands of compounds in Mandarin (from Li and Thompson 1981: 47):

(2)   fēng-liú   huā-shēng
         wind-flow   flower-born
         "amorous"   "peanut"

         máo-dùn   kāi-guān
         spear-shield   open-close
         "contradictory"   "switch"

         féi-zào   tiān-qì
         fat-black   heaven-breath
         "soap"   "weather"

?

Is there noun-noun compounding (e.g., *windshield*)?
How do you know it is compounding?
Is there noun–verb (or verb–noun) compounding that results in a noun (e.g., *pickpocket, scarecrow*)?
Are these processes productive (like noun-verb-*er* in English *can-opener*)?
How common is compounding?

5.2   Denominalization

A very common operation that applies to nouns is **denominalization**. The term **nominal** can be translated "noun-like;" so to **denominalize** something is to make it less noun-like, or turn it into a verb, adjective, or some other grammatical category. Sometimes operations that create verbs from nouns are called **verbalization** (Clark and Clark 1979). Perhaps the most common type of denominalization makes a possessive verb out of a noun. For example, the Yup'ik noun suffix *-ngqerr* means "to have N" where N is the noun to which the suffix is attached. The following examples (from Reed *et al.* 1977) illustrate some common nouns with their denominalized counterparts:

(3)   patu   "lid"   patungqerr   "to have a lid"
        qayar   "kayak"   qayangqerr   "to have a kayak"
        irniar "child"   irniangqerr   "to have children"
        enr   "bone"   enengqerr   "to have a bone"

Another common denominalization process takes a noun, N, and forms a verb that means "become N." These processes are called **inchoative** (we will distinguish inchoative as a nominal operation from **inceptive** as a verbal operation, though in the literature the term inchoative sometimes refers to a verbal aspect). For example in Panare the suffix -*ta* when applied to a noun usually means "to become N:" *i'yan* "healer," *i'yatan* "to become a healer."

The Eskimo languages are particularly rich in denominalization processes. The meanings of verbs formed by these suffixes include such concepts as the following (in these examples N refers to the noun to which the suffix attaches):

(4)   to go toward N
        to be N
        to be at N
        there is N/there lacks N
        to have plenty of N
        to be afflicted in one's N
        to have cold Ns
        to play with N
        to hunt for N
        to capture N
        to eat N

Denominalization processes (other than possessives and inchoatives mentioned above) tend to express culturally "institutionalized" activities (Mithun 1984). This is illustrated in the Eskimo examples, e.g., hunting, capturing, eating, playing, being cold, and being afflicted are undoubtedly concepts that are very common in the Eskimo context.

Some denominalizers have a "generic" function: that is, when attached to a noun, they form a verb that refers to whatever activity is

usually associated with that noun. The following examples are from Mapudugun (courtesy of María Catrileo):

(5)   kofke   "bread"   kofke-tu   "eat bread"
        kaweyu   "horse"   kaweyu-tu   "ride horse"

Sometimes it is difficult to distinguish denominalization from
noun–verb compounding (**noun incorporation**, see section 8.2.7). One
criterion is that if the denominalizer is independently used as a verb in
other contexts with substantially the same meaning, then it is incorporation. If the denominalizer is not attested as a verb (though it probably will
be related to a verb), then it is "true" denominalization. Some of the Eskimo
suffixes referred to above are clearly related to verbs, but they are distinct
enough in form and meaning from their corresponding verbs to cause us
to call them denominalizing suffixes.

> **?**
>
> Are there any processes (productive or not) that form a verb from a noun?
> An adjective from a noun?
> An adverb from a noun?

5.3   Number

Nouns and noun phrases are often marked for **number**. The most
common number distinction is between singular and plural. For example,
the singular/plural distinction is obligatorily marked for all English nouns
that refer to concepts that can be counted (those that consist of individually salient units), e.g., *dog* "singular" and *dogs* "plural." Other number distinctions are (1) singular vs. dual vs. plural, and (2) singular vs. dual
vs. trial vs. plural. Dual refers to two items only, while trial refers to three
items. The last type is very rare, and the singular, dual, plural type is fairly
rare, at least in systems of noun-phrase marking; it is more common in
participant reference marking on verbs (see section 9.5).

Many languages only mark number in noun phrases occasionally.
An interesting question for such languages (probably the majority of the
world's languages) is when to mark plurality and when not to mark it.
Some languages only mark certain classes of nouns, e.g., animate nouns,
for number, while other nouns are left unmarked, or are marked only
"optionally" (see below). Other languages only indicate plurality of nouns
that are highly "topical" (see section 10.0.3).

For languages that have morphological case marking on nouns, it is common for number to be intertwined with the case-marking system. That is, there may be different forms for the case markers, depending on whether the item is singular, (dual, trial) or plural. This is the case, for example, in Latin and many other Indo-European languages:

(6)   *Latin*

	Singular	Plural	Gloss
Nominative	porta	portae	"gate/s"
Genitive	portae	portārum	"of the gate/s"
Dative	portae	portīs	"to the gate/s"
Accusative	portam	portās	"gate/s"
Ablative	portā	portīs	"by/with the gate/s"

In most number-marking systems the singular is unmarked while the non-singulars are marked in some way. Some languages mark both singular and plural, e.g., Swahili (Bantu) *umu-ana* "child" vs. *aba-ana* "children." Another possibility is for the plural to be unmarked while the singular receives a mark of some kind, though this is rare. For example, in Desano, a Tucanoan language of Colombia, some nouns are unmarked in the plural but marked with a noun classifier when singular (see section 5.7 on noun classification):

(7)   su?ri   "clothes"   su?ri-ro   "one item of clothing"
        gasi   "canoes"   gasi-ru   "canoe"
        yukü   "trees"   yukü-gü   "tree"
        nome   "women"   nome-o   "woman"

In some varieties of Arabic, the singular of most nouns is morphologically more complex than the plural:

(8)   *Palestinian Arabic* (courtesy of Maher Awad)
        tufax   "apples"   tufaxa   "apple"

Some languages only require plurality to be marked on certain kinds of nouns, e.g., animate nouns. For example, in Mandarin Chinese, plural pronouns are marked with the suffix *-men* (ex. 9). Nouns referring to people may be marked for plurality with the same suffix (ex. 10). Other nouns cannot be directly marked for plurality; rather, plurality is expressed via separate quantifiers (ex. 11) (Li and Thompson 1981):

(9)   *plurality obligatorily marked for pronouns*

tā	"he/she"	tā-men	"they"
nǐ	"you (sg.)"	nǐ-men	"you (pl.)"
wǒ	"I"	wǒ-men	"we"

(10)   *Plurality optionally marked for human nouns*

háizi	"child"	háizi-men	"children"
kèren	"guest"	kèren-men	"guests"
péngyǒu	"friend"	péngyǒu-men	"friends"

(11)   *Plurality optionally expressed periphrastically for other nouns*

shū	"book/books"	shū yíxiē	"some books"
yèzi	"leaf/leaves"	yèzi xǔduō	"many leaves"

Number can be expressed by any of the usual morphosyntactic processes, e.g., prefixation (see Swahili above), suffixation (English, Arabic), infixation (Ifugao, see below), stem change (Endo), reduplication (Ifugao), suprasegmental modification, suppletion (Endo), or distinct particles (Tagalog). So far no language has been found to use word order to express plurality, e.g., there are no languages in which the possessor precedes singular nouns but follows plural nouns. The following examples will illustrate some of the more unusual number-marking systems.

In Ifugao, a group of closely related Philippine languages, plurality is indicated by reduplication of the first syllable or by infixation:

(12)   *Tuwali Ifugao* (courtesy of Lou Hohulin)

tagu	"person"	tatagu	"people" (reduplication of first syllable)
babai	"woman"	binabai	"women" (infixation of -*in*-)

In Ifugao reduplicative plural marking is "optional" when referring to plural entities. It is more common for an independent particle to occur in place of or in addition to the reduplication (see ex. 14 from Tagalog).

In Endo (Western Nilotic, Kenya), plurals are very complex. Most of them must be considered suppletive (13a, b), though there is regularity within certain classes of nouns (13c, d):

(13)   a. aráan   "goat"   no   "goats"
        b. árááwa   "moon," "month"   áró   "months"
        c. chemur   "breastbone"   chemurtiin   "breastbones"
        d. eya   "mother," "maternal aunt"   eyaatíín   "mothers," "maternal aunts"

Plurality in noun phrases is sometimes expressed by a special particle. This is especially common in Australian and Austronesian languages. The following are examples from Tagalog (Philippines):[1]

(14)   ang babae   "the woman"   ang *mga* babae   "the women"

In some languages there are noun markers that express the idea of "and company" or "*et al.*" This marker is often identical to the form that indicates accompaniment (the *with* of *I went **with** mother*). For example, Yagua employs a suffix *-ve* for this purpose:

(15)   a. sa-súúy   Manúngu
           3SG-sing M.
           "Manungu sings."

       b. ri-čúúy   Manúngu-ve
           3PL-sing M. -AC
           "Manungu and company sing."

This suffix is not properly termed "plural" since it does not mean there were many "Manungus" (a man's name). Rather, it means that there was a group of people, including one salient person named Manungu.

A similar operation is found in Ifugao. In Ifugao, the accompaniment marker is a prefix, *hin-*. When occurring on a noun referring to a person, it refers to that person and relatives, or "the clan" (examples from Tuwali Ifugao, courtesy of Lou Hohulin):

(16)   ama   "father"   hin-ama   "father and
                                              child/children"
        agi   "cousin"   hin-aagi   "a bunch of relatives"

When used with another noun, N, this prefix means "a quantity measured by N:"

(17)   basu   "cup"   him-basu   "a cup full" (e.g., a cup
                                                 and its contents)
        iduh   "spoon"   hin-iduh   "a spoon full"
        kalton "box"   hing-kalton   "a box full."

A more complex system is found in Dyirbal, an Australian language. In Dyirbal, animate nouns and pronouns can be marked as being members of a pair or a larger group (Dixon 1972: 51):

(18) a. Bayi Burbula miyandaɲu.
      CL B.   laughed
      "Burbula laughed."   (singular)

    b. Bayi Burbula-*gara* miyandaɲu.
      "Burbula and one other person laughed."   (dual)

    c. Bayi Burbula-*maŋgan* miyandaɲu.
      "Burbula and several other people laughed."   (plural)

In this section, number marking on nouns and noun phrases has been described. Numeral systems are discussed in section 3.3.3; number as a verbal inflection is discussed in section 9.5.

?

Is number expressed in the noun phrase?

Is the distinction between singular and non-singular obligatory, optional, or completely absent in the noun phrase?

If number marking is "optional," when does it tend to occur, and when does it tend not to occur?

If number marking is obligatory, is number overtly expressed for all noun phrases or only some subclasses of noun phrases, such as animates?

What non-singular distinctions are there?

5.4 Case

It is sometimes difficult to distinguish **case marking** from **adpositions** (the latter consist of **prepositions** and **postpositions**). This is undoubtedly because there is no necessary universal distinction between the two; like most structural distinctions, the two categories describe extremes of a continuum. The following is a rule that probably works 90 percent of the time. However, the distinction described by this rule is rather subtle, and so may not be obvious in early stages of language analysis. Furthermore, in any language there may be exceptions.

> *Rule of thumb.* Case marking is the morphosyntactic categorization of noun phrases that is imposed by the structure within which the noun phrase occurs. Adpositions are free of such configurational constraints.

So, for example, whether a noun phrase occurs in the dative or accusative case in some languages is determined by the grammatical requirements of the verb (or other case-**governing** element) with which that noun phrase is in some grammatical relationship. Whether a noun phrase occurs with a locative or benefactive adposition, however, probably depends purely on the communicative intent of the speaker – it is not imposed by some other grammatical element in the configuration.

In Latin, for example, verbs require that their objects occur in one of a few morphological cases. If the object occurs in some other case, either ungrammaticality or a different sense of the verb results. This is the sense in which Latin verbs **govern** the case of their objects (e.g., the verb *servire* governs the dative case, etc.). Prepositions in Latin also govern the case of their objects. So, e.g., *cum* governs the ablative case, while *contra* governs the accusative case. Prepositions in Latin are, however, not themselves governed by some other element in the configuration; so no verb requires that its object occur in a *cum* phrase, for example. Adpositional phrases are usually (though not always) "optional" sentence constituents. The following is an example from Yagua. In Yagua there is a pair of homophonous verb roots, *dííy*, meaning either "kill" or "see." The only grammatical difference between the two is that "kill" governs the accusative case (example 19a) while "see" governs the dative case (19b):[2]

(19)   a. sa-dííy nurutú-0
          3sg-kill alligator-ACC
          "He killed an alligator."

       b. sa-dííy nurutí-íva
          3sg-see alligator-DAT
          "He saw an alligator." (or "His vision rested on an alligator.")

Example 19b is evidence that *-íva* "dative" is in fact a case marker rather than a postposition. There are many postpositions in Yagua, such as *-imu* "locative" as in *nurutiimú* "to the alligator," but these are not governed by any verb. It is necessary to note that morphological binding does not distinguish case marking and adpositions. Case markers can be free or bound, prepositional or post-positional. The same is true for adpositions. It so happens that in the classical languages the case markers are phonologically as well as functionally distinct from the adpositions. In Yagua and many other languages, this is not the case. It is true that case markers (as defined above) tend to be more closely tied phonologically to their hosts than are adpositions, but this is not a defining property of case markers. Here we have given a definition based strictly on syntactic function.

The following is a short list of semantic roles that typically are grammaticalized as morphological cases. Keep in mind, however, that there is never a direct, one-to-one mapping between semantics and morphosyntax. This list simply characterizes general tendencies:

Semantic role	*Morphological case*
AGENT	nominative, ergative (section 7.1)
PATIENT	accusative, absolutive
RECIPIENT	dative
POSSESSOR	genitive

Formatives that instantiate other semantic roles can usually be given the same label as the semantic role, e.g., locative, benefactive, instrumental. Insofar as possible, cases and adpositions should be labeled according to their prototypical, or basic, function.

> **?**
>
> Do nouns exhibit morphological case?
> If so, what are the cases? (The functions of the cases will be elaborated in later sections.)

5.5   Articles, determiners, and demonstratives

Operators, whether bound or free, which directly express something about the identifiability and/or referentiality of a noun phrase are often called **articles** (see section 10.0.1 for definitions of identifiability, referentiality, and other pragmatic statuses). Articles, such as the English *the* and *a(n)*, are relatively rare in the world's languages. More common are **demonstratives** (or **demonstrative adjectives**), such as *this, that, these,* and *those*. Some linguists use the term **determiner** to refer to formatives like *the* and *a(n)*. This term usually also includes quantifiers (*some, many, a few, each, every*), numerals, possessors, as well as demonstratives. This broad category does not very often exhibit consistent syntactic behavior, e.g., few languages consistently place them all in the same position in the noun phrase. Therefore, "determiner" is not very viable as a universal natural class.

However, probably all languages have a clear class of demonstratives. These are normally free forms, and may precede or follow the noun they function with. Demonstratives may also be anaphoric on their own, as in *What is **that**?*, in which case they may be termed **demonstrative**

pronouns. Demonstratives imply "pointing to," or "demonstrating," the object they refer to, e.g., ***that*** *house* (said while pointing to a house), or *I'll take three of* ***those*** (said while pointing at some group of objects).

In addition to exhibiting the features common to the pronoun system of the language (number, gender, etc.), demonstratives often express distance, or orientation with respect to the speaker/hearer. For example, the English system has two degrees of distance, represented by the forms *this* and *that* (*these* and *those* in the plural). Other languages may have three degrees of distance. If there appear to be more than three degrees of distance, chances are there is some other parameter that the system is sensitive to in addition to the distance parameter. Some languages make a distinction between items close to the hearer, items close to the speaker, and items distant from both. Others code the difference between visible items and non-visible items. When two or more of these parameters interact within a single system, the results can be very complex.

Most operators that embody pragmatic or semantic information about a noun will tend to occur more often with nouns of particular grammatical relations (e.g., identifiers in English are more frequent in discourse on nouns that occur in the subject role). In many cases these tendencies have become grammaticalized. One common phenomenon is articles that mark identifiability only for direct objects. Farsi is one Indo-European language that does exhibit this property:

(20)   *Farsi* (courtesy of Jalleh Banishadr)
    a. Man dombale kitob hæsdæm.
       I   look:for book AUX
       "I'm looking for a book."

    b. Man dombale kitob-ro hæsdæm.
       I   look:for book-DEF AUX
       "I'm looking for the book."

This identifiability distinction in Farsi is not morphologically manifested for noun phrases in any other syntactic role.

In a few languages this grammaticalization has gone so far as to render it difficult to determine whether a given particle or affix is a noun-phrase or verb-phrase operator. For example, Panare (Carib, Venezuela) has a set of prenominal particles that function very much like articles in that they encode information about the identifiability/specificity as well as animacy and location of the noun that follows. However, they only occur before nouns that function as subject of the sentence, and then only subjects that come immediately after the verb, and then only in non-past tenses! Because these Panare particles have so many characteristics of verb-phrase operators (i.e., consistent position directly after the verb, occurring only in certain tenses) it is difficult to determine whether they should be regarded as functioning more closely with the verb to their left or with the subject nominal to their right.

> **?**
>
> Do noun phrases have articles?
>
> If so, are they obligatory or optional, and under what circumstances do they occur?
>
> Are they separate words, or bound morphemes?
>
> Is there a class or classes of demonstratives as distinct from articles?
>
> How many degrees of distance are there in the system of demonstratives?
>
> Are there other distinctions besides distance?

5.6   Possessors

Languages typically express many semantic relationships with the same formal construction used to express ownership. We will call such formal constructions **possessive constructions**, even though the semantic relationship is not always one of possession, e.g., the phrase *my professor* does not refer to a professor that I "possess" in the same way that *my clothes* refers to clothes that I possess.

It is important to distinguish possessive noun phrases from **possessive clauses**, discussed in section 6.5. A possessive noun phrase contains two elements: a possessor and a possessed item. Sometimes the possessor is referred to as the **genitive** (regardless of whether the language has a morphological genitive case). The possessed item is referred to as the **possessum** or the **possessee**:

(21)   Mary's   dog
        possessor possessee
        The love of my life
        possessee possessor

Some languages make a formal distinction based on the semantic difference between **alienable** and **inalienable** possession. Semantically, alienable possession is the kind of possession which can be terminated: e.g., I can transfer possession of my worldly goods to someone else, hence my relationship to my worldly goods is one of alienable possession. Inalienable possession is the kind of possession that cannot be terminated. Languages which distinguish inalienable possession always include kinship terms and body parts within the class of inalienably possessed items. My head will always be my head, and my brothers and sisters will always be my brothers and sisters. Apart from body parts and kinship terms, some languages include certain culturally important items within the class of inalienable possessions, such as cows, canoes, machetes, etc. Finally, there are usually a few items that semantically seem to go with one class, but which are grouped with the other class for no apparent reason: e.g., a language may treat rocks as inalienable and brothers as alienable.

The following sentence illustrates both inalienable and alienable possession in Ndjuká (Surinam Creole, example courtesy of George Huttar):

(22)   [A wagi   fu mi] de gi   mi baala.
        the vehicle for 1sg cop give 1sg brother
        "My car is for my brother."

The bracketed portion of this example illustrates the standard way of expressing alienable possession: a preposition intervenes between the possessed item and a pronoun referring to the possessor. The last NP, *mi baala*, illustrates the standard way of expressing inalienable possession. As is common in alienable/inalienable possessive constructions, alienable possession requires more morphosyntactic material (in this case the preposition *fu*) than does inalienable possession. This fact may be seen as an **icon** of the closer conceptual link between possessor and possessed item in inalienable possession.

Similar but not identical to inalienable possession is **inherent** possession. Certain items are inherently possessed, e.g., body parts, kinship terms, and items of personal adornment. Other items are not normally possessed, such as trees, the sky, etc. Some languages require that references to inherently possessed items include reference to a possessor. So in such languages you cannot say simply *brother* or *hand*. You have to say whose brother or whose hand. There may be inherent possession in a language without an alienable/inalienable distinction. A language with inherent possession may have just one kind of possessive construction, but simply require that some items be possessed, while imposing no such requirement on other items. In systems of alienable/inalienable possession there are two (or perhaps more) grammatically distinct kinds of possessor coding.

Mangga Buang, like many other Papuan languages, exhibits a combination alienable/inalienable and inherent/non-inherent distinction. When the possessed noun refers to one of the class of inalienably possessed items, it takes a possessive suffix (examples in 24). When the possessor of an inalienably possessed noun is third person singular, no pronoun or suffix is used (examples in 25). Alienable possession is expressed by a pronoun with the genitive suffix -*te*, plus the head noun with no suffix (examples in 26). Thus there are three structures:

(23) a. PRN NP-POSS   inalienable, non-third person singular possessor
      b. NP   inalienable, third person singular possessor
      c. PRN-te NP   alienable possession

Examples of each of these structures are provided below (courtesy of Joan Healey):

(24)   PRN N-POSS *(inalienable/inherent possession, non-third person singular possessor)*

      a. sa   nama-ngg
          1SG hand-1
          "my hand"

      b. o   nama-m
          2SG hand-2
          "your hand(s)"

      c. ham nama-m
          2PL hand-2
          "your (pl.) hands"

      d. sa   gaande-ngg
          1SG cousin-1
          "my cousin'

(25)   N only *(inalienable/inherent possession, third person singular possessor)*
      a. nama   "his/her hand"
      b. gaande   "his/her cousin"
      c. lava   "his/her speech/language"
      d. hali   "his brother/her sister"

(26)   PRN-*te* N (*alienable possession*)

    a. sa-te   voow
       1SG-POSS dog
       "my dog"

    b. yi-te   bayêên
       3SG-POSS village/house
       "his/her village/house"

In this language inalienable nouns are inherently possessed insofar as they are always understood as possessed even though the most common possessive affix is 0 for third person possessors. Alienable nouns are not understood as possessed unless they are preceded by the genitive pronoun. Compare the following with 26 above:

(27)   a. voow   "a dog" (*"his/her dog")
        b. bayêên "a village" (*"his/her village")

In some languages there is a class of "un-possessable" nouns. Some examples from Maasai are given in section 3.1.1.2.

❓

How are possessors expressed in the noun phrase?

Do nouns agree with their possessors? Do possessors agree with possessed nouns? Neither, or both?

Is there a distinction between alienable and inalienable possession?

Are there other types of possession?

When the possessor is a full noun, where does it usually come with respect to the possessed noun?

5.7   Class (including gender)

A **noun class**, **gender**, or **grammatical gender** system is the grammatical classification of nouns, pronouns, and other referential devices. Often such a system correlates with some extralinguistic grouping, such as human vs. non-human or female vs. male. However, gender for a linguist is a *grammatical* classification, which may be quite independent of any natural classification (see examples below).

If there is to be a distinction between gender and noun class systems, it is that noun class systems typically involve the presence of **classifiers**, i.e., special operators that are used in some or all noun phrases to directly express the class of the noun. For example, Yagua employs classifiers in noun phrases which involve numbers:

(28) a. tïn-kïï vaturµ
          1-CLS woman (married)
          "one married woman"

     b. tïn-see vaada
         1-CLS   egg
         "one egg"

Pure gender systems do not, generally, require classifiers; rather, the grammatical distinction is made via "agreement."

   If the language has a noun class system, it will almost certainly be well installed in the number system. If nothing else in the language agrees with nouns in terms of class, numeral expressions will. Sometimes noun classes correspond (with varying degrees of directness) to semantic classes such as biological gender, physical shape, sociocultural function, etc. In many Indo-European languages, nouns are "masculine," "feminine," or sometimes "neuter." For example, Spanish expresses the difference between masculine and feminine by a suffix -*o*/-*a*: *niño* "boy," *abogado* "male lawyer," *maestro* "male teacher," *niña* "girl," *abogada* "female lawyer," *maestra* "female teacher," etc. Most adjectives must reflect the class of their head nouns, e.g., *abogado bueno* "good male lawyer" vs. *abogada buena* "good female lawyer." The class that a particular noun falls into is fairly clear for items that have a biological gender, namely animates. However, all nouns in the language are subject to the class system, and non-animates are classified apparently arbitrarily as masculine or feminine (rather than neuter). Romance languages even differ from one another as to the class that particular lexical items fall into, e.g., Italian *il tavolo* (m.), French *la table* (f.) "the table/board;" Italian *il mare* (m.), French *la mer* (f.) "the sea." There is even at least one word in Italian which is masculine in the singular and feminine in the plural: *il uovo* "the egg" and *le uova* "the eggs." This is simply to show that noun class systems, even those that seem to have a firm natural basis, often exhibit a certain degree of irregularity.

   Other noun classification systems are based on other dimensions of reality than biological gender, e.g., shape (roundish objects, longish objects, stubby objects, etc.) or function (adornments, items associated

Table 5.1 Some Swahili noun classes

Class number	General content	Prefix	Example	Gloss
1	human, sg.	mu-	mwalimu	teacher
2	human, pl.	wa-	walimu	teachers
5	miscellaneous, sg.	ji-	jino	tooth
6	miscellaneous, pl.	ma-	meno	teeth
7	miscellaneous, sg.	˙ki-	kiazi	sweet potato
8	miscellaneous, pl.	vi-	viazi	sweet potatoes
10	everyday items, pl.	ny-	nyembe	razors
11	everyday items, sg.	u-/w-	wembe	razor

with procuring food, items associated with fighting, foods, people, etc.). In every case, however, there are items that seem as though they should belong in one class, but for some apparently idiosyncratic reason, are placed in another class. For example, in Yagua rocks and pineapples are classed as animates.

The most famous noun class systems are those found in the Niger-Kordofanian languages of Africa. Noun class systems also occur in Australia, Asia, and in the Americas. The examples in table 5.1 are from Swahili, a Bantu (Niger-Kordofanian) language of East Africa. In the Bantu languages, singulars and plurals generally fall into separate classes.

?

Is there a noun class system?

What are the classes, and how are they manifested in the noun phrase?

What dimension of reality is most central to the noun class system (e.g., animacy, shape, function, etc.)? What other dimensions are relevant?

Do the classifiers occur with numerals? Adjectives? Verbs?

What is their function in these contexts?

Additional references: Dixon (1968), Allen (1977), Adams and Conklin (1973), Craig (1986), Carlson and Payne (1989), Corbett (1991).

5.8   Diminution/augmentation

Most languages employ operators in the noun or noun phrase that indicate unusual sizes. The term for operations that express unusual smallness is **diminutive** while operations that express unusual largeness are **augmentatives**. For example, Yagua employs the diminutive suffix -*déé*:

(29)   quiváá̢ "fish"   quivąą̢déé "little fish"

This suffix is also used on adjectives to express the idea of "a little bit ADJ:"

(30)   já̢á̢mura "big"   já̢á̢muradéé "a little bit big"

It can also occur on almost any other kind of word to express an idea similar to "just" as in English "just over there," "just a dog," or "just a minute," etc.

Typically, diminutives also carry an endearing sense, e.g.:

(31)   English: sweet-y   lamb-kins
                 DIM   DIM

Correspondingly, augmentatives often carry negative or undesirable connotations:

(32)   *Spanish*
         durmi-lon
         sleep-AUG
         "sleepyhead/lazybones"

There is an apparently universal iconic tendency in diminutives and augmentatives: diminutives tend to contain high front vowels, whereas augmentatives tend to contain high back vowels.

?

Does the language employ diminutive and/or augmentative operators in the noun or noun phrase?

Questions to answer for all nominal operations:

(a) Is this operation obligatory, i.e., does one member of the paradigm have to occur in every full noun phrase?

(b) Is it productive, i.e., can the operation be specified for all full noun phrases and does it have the same meaning with each one? (Nothing is fully productive, but some operations are more so than others.)

(c) Is this operation primarily expressed lexically, morphologically, or analytically? Are there exceptions?

(d) Where in the noun phrase is this operation likely to be located? Can it occur in more than one place?

6 Predicate nominals and related constructions

....

Every language has clauses that express **proper inclusion, equation, attribution, location, existence,** and **possession** (defined below). Sometimes this "family" of constructions is collectively referred to as **predicate nominals**. However, in this book we will use this term in a more specific sense, reserving it for those clauses in which the semantic content of the predication is embodied in a noun. This definition distinguishes predicate nominals from similar constructions such as **predicate adjectives, predicate locatives,** and others. The following discussion will define this family of clause types using preliminary examples from English. Section 6.1 will describe each type in more detail, providing a typology of the various ways languages are known to form these clause types.

The following is an example of a predicate nominal clause in English:

(1)   Frieda is a teacher.

In this construction the predicate is *is a teacher*, and the main semantic content of this predicate is embodied in the noun *teacher*. The verb *is* (a form of *be*) simply specifies the relationship between *Frieda* and *teacher* and carries the tense/aspect and person/number information required of independent predications in English. Sometimes the noun phrase *a teacher* is called "the predicate nominal" or even "the nominal predicate" of the clause. In this discussion, the term predicate nominal will normally refer to the entire clause.

Predicate adjectives are clauses in which the main semantic content is expressed by an adjective. If the language lacks a grammatical

111

category of adjective, there will be no grammatically distinct predicate adjective construction (see section 3.3.1 on how to identify adjectives as a grammatical category). Semantically, these clause types can be described as **attributive** clauses:

(2)   John is tall.
       My car is green.

Existential constructions predicate the existence of some entity, usually in some specified location:

(3)   There is a bee in your bonnet.
       There is a book on the table.

Locational (or predicate locative) constructions predicate location:

(4)   The gift is in the horse's mouth.
       The book is on the table.

Possessive clauses predicate possession:

(5)   Sally has nineteen cats.
       The table has a book on it.
       The book is John's.

These construction types tend to be similar to one another grammatically in that they all tend to lack a **semantically rich** lexical verb. By semantically rich, we mean a verb that itself expresses the major semantic content of the predication. Verbs like *be* and *do* in English are not (normally) semantically rich in that they must be accompanied by some other lexical item, either a noun (for *be*) or a verb (for *do*) in order to form a predication. These kinds of verbs are sometimes termed **semantically empty**. They are also sometimes called **grammatical verbs** because they assume the grammatical trappings necessary to express predications in the language, though they contribute little to the lexical meaning.

Two of the predicate types included in the above list may not seem very similar to predicate nominals to native speakers of English. These are **existential** and **possessive** clauses. Many languages employ the same construction type for the entire family, whereas others, like English, employ

Table 6.1 Predicate types according to the likelihood of lacking a semantically rich lexical verb

Most likely to lack a semantically rich verb				*Not very likely to lack a semantically rich verb, but still may*
Predicate nominals (equative, proper inclusion)	> Predicate locatives, adjectives (attributive)	> Existentials	> Possessive clauses	> Locomotion clauses
←——————— Subject matter for this chapter ———————→				

one construction for a portion of the family only. Predicate types can probably be arranged along a continuum based on how likely they are to lack a semantically rich lexical verb. The continuum in table 6.1 represents an impression rather than an empirically proven fact about languages. In this chapter we will somewhat arbitrarily draw the line between possessive clauses and locomotion clauses.[1] In the corresponding section of any particular grammar, it may be appropriate to include more or fewer of these construction types in a chapter on predicate nominals and related constructions. For example, in English, possessive clauses are treated grammatically as transitive clauses; in Hopi, locomotion predicates structurally belong to the family headed by predicate nominals.

Predicate nominals and related constructions are worthy of description in their own right. However, they particularly merit detailed description because they constitute a useful grammatical template that adapts to serve many other functions in discourse. For example, predicate nominal morphosyntax often functions in domains variously termed "focus," "topicalization," etc. Many pragmatically marked structures such as clefts and passives tend to be based on the predicate nominal pattern (see section 10.1.3). These constructions in turn often become the source for new main-clause structures (e.g., the progressive aspect in English *He is walking* is a verbal clause type that derives from an earlier predicate locative pattern – see, e.g., Gildea 1992). Therefore, a good understanding of predicate nominal and related constructions in a language can provide important insights into the synchronic grammar of pragmatically marked structures, and the historical development of the central construction types.

6.1   Predicate nominals

Predicate nominal clauses typically express the notions of **proper inclusion** and **equation**.

Proper inclusion is when a specific entity is asserted to be among the class of items specified in the nominal predicate. For example *He is a teacher* might be paraphrased "he is a member of the class of items designated by the noun *teacher*." Usually the subject of a predicate nominal clause indicating proper inclusion is specific (*he*), and the nominal predicate is non-specific (*a teacher*).

Equative clauses are those which assert that a particular entity (the subject of the clause) is identical to the entity specified in the predicate nominal, e.g., *He is my father*. Sometimes it is difficult or impossible to determine which nominal is the predicate and which is the subject in equative clauses. Most languages make no grammatical distinction between proper inclusion and equative clauses, though they may.

In the following discussion we will provide a list of ways languages are known to accomplish proper inclusion and equation. Any given language will employ one or a combination of these strategies. If a language employs a strategy not mentioned here, it is worth a paper to describe it.

1 *NP NP juxtaposition.* The most common type of predicate nominal is one in which two noun phrases are juxtaposed with no copular element intervening (see below for a definition of the term "copular element" or "copula"):

(6)   *Cebuano* (Austronesian, Philippines)
       magyuyuta si   Juan
       farmer   ABS John
       "John is a farmer."

(7)   *Russian* (Slavic)
       Ivan uchít^j el^j.
       John teacher
       "John is a teacher."

2 *NP copula NP.* Predicate nominal constructions often employ a **copula**. For our purposes a copula is any morpheme (affix, particle, or verb) that joins, or "couples," two nominal elements in a predicate nominal construction. It marks the clause as a predicate nominal and often carries the tense/aspect and other information necessary for predications in the

language. The particle *si* that stands between the two NPs in the Cebuano example above is not a copula; rather, it is a case marker associated with the noun *Juan* and occurs in all types of clauses, not just predicate nominals. Also, it does not inflect for tense/aspect, etc.

In many languages a copula will only occur in past tenses and/or in otherwise semantically marked predicate nominal clauses. "Present tense" (i.e., the unmarked, neutral tense/aspect) predicate nominals are likely to consist simply of two juxtaposed noun phrases. In Russian a copula appears in tenses other than simple present:

(8)   Ivan bïl   uchít^jel^j
        John be:MASC teacher
        "John was a teacher."

In the following paragraphs we will describe six types of copular construction that are known to exist in the world's languages. Any given language may employ several or all of these under different circumstances. It may also exhibit copulas that stand "in between" some of the definitions given here, or it may exhibit a previously unattested copula type.

(a) *Copula is a verb.* For some languages the form that joins the two nominals in a predicate nominal construction has many or all of the morphosyntactic properties that characterize verbs in that language. For instance, the copula may inflect for tense, aspect, and/or mode, and it may occur in the normal verbal position in the clause, i.e., clause-initially, clause-finally, or clause-medially. Semantically, however, copular verbs are "empty." That is, they carry little or no semantic content other than whatever is involved in converting a noun phrase into a predicate. A good example of a copular verb is the English verb *be*:

(9)   a. Marty *is* a sports fan.
        b. They *are* Oregonians.
        c. She *was* my favorite teacher.
        d. You *are* fine students.

Although *be* is very irregular, it exhibits all the essential properties of verbs in English: (1) it varies for person (*he **is***, *you **are***); (2) it varies for tense (*I **am***, *I **was***); and (3) it most neutrally occurs in clause-medial position.

Mandarin is another verb-medial language that employs a copular verb (examples courtesy of Lynn Yang):

(10)   Wǒ de jiě-jiě   *shì* yī-ge lǎo-shī
        1SG GEN older: sister be one-CL teacher
        "My older sister is a teacher."

(11)   Wǒ de jiě-jiě   yǐ-qián *shì* yī-ge   lǎo-shī
        1SG GEN older: sister before be one-CL teacher
        "My older sister used to be a teacher."

In Mandarin the morphosyntactic properties of verbs are very limited. However, to the extent that verbs can be identfied grammatically, the copula *shì* in Mandarin can be considered a verb, i.e., it appears in clause-medial position, and it is not restricted to particular tense/aspects.

For verb-final languages, the copular verb normally comes at the end of the clause:

Japanese (courtesy of Mitsuyo Hamaya)
(12)   imooto-wa   sensei *desu*
        younger: sister-TOP teacher be:PRES
        "My younger sister is a teacher."

(13)   imooto-wa   sensei *deshita*
        younger: sister-TOP teacher be:PAST
        "My younger sister was a teacher."

The copular element has all the properties of verbs in Japanese. This is also true of Korean:

Korean (courtesy of Insun Park)
(14)   na-ïi   nuna-nïn   sʌnsæŋnim *i-ta*
        1SG-GEN elder: sister-TOP teacher   be-IND
        "My elder sister is a teacher."

(15)   na-ïi   nuna-nïn   sʌnsæŋnim *i-ʌt-ta*
        1SG-GEN elder:sister-TOP teacher   be-PAST-IND
        "My elder sister was a teacher."

For verb-initial languages, if there is a copular verb, it normally comes at the beginning of the clause:

(16)   *Maasai* (Tucker and Mpaayei 1955: 91)
     a. *í-rá* ol-Maasani
        2-be MASC-Maasai
        "You are a Maasai."

b. *á-rá* ol-Maasani
1-be MASC-Maasai
"I am a Maasai."

c. (*é-rá*) ol-Maasani   ninye
3-be MASC-Maasai 3SG
"He is a Maasai."

Characteristics of copular verbs. There are several properties that tend to characterize copular verbs universally:

(i)   Copular verbs tend to be very irregular. That is, they often exhibit unusual conjugational patterns as compared to the more "normal" verbs in the language. Paradigms of copular verbs tend to be suppletive and/or defective (see section 2.2).

(ii) Copular verbs belong to the same semantic class as very stative verbs, e.g., *stand, sit, live, exist, appear, seem, become,* etc. Often they derive from other stative verbs or occasionally from simple verbs of motion such as *go* or *come*.

(iii) Copular verbs tend to function as auxiliaries in other constructions (see section 4.2 on auxiliaries). In fact, when a language develops auxiliaries, the first verbs to become auxiliaries are the copular verbs. Second are the verbs of motion (Foley and Van Valin 1984).

(b) *Copula is a pronoun.* For some languages the form that joins two nominals in a predicate nominal construction is a pronoun. Normally the copular pronoun corresponds to the subject nominal:

(17)   *Hebrew*
ha-ish   *hu* av-í
DEF-man he father-my
"The man is my father."

(c) *Copula is an invariant particle.* Some languages use a special invariant particle to join two nominals in a predicate nominal construction. This particle may derive from a verb or a pronoun, but if it is invariant, i.e., if it remains the same regardless of the person/number/gender of the subject, or the tense/aspect of the clause, then it should be called a particle. For example (example from Carlson 1994):

(18)   *Sùpyìré*
wuu ɲe laklibii
we   COP students
"We are students."

That this form is not a verb is evidenced by the fact that it does not allow any of the tense or aspect marking common to verbs in Sùpyìré.

(d) *Copula is a derivational operation.* In a few languages, a predicate nominal clause is formed by taking the predicate noun and applying a derivational operation that forms a verb from that noun. The predicate nominal then becomes a verb grammatically, as evidenced by its position in the clause and the inflectional information it expresses (example from Fasold 1992b):

(19)   *Bella Coola* (Salishan, Canada)
          staltmx-aw wa-?imlk
          chief-INTR PROX-man
          "The man is a chief."

In this clause, the predicate noun is *staltmx* "chief." Evidence that it is functioning as a verb is that it takes the intransitive verbal suffix *-aw*.

3 *Copular morpheme or verb in non-present tenses.* Most languages that do not use a copula in simple, present tense predicate nominals, do use a copular verb or morpheme in certain tenses, aspects, or modes. Past and future tenses are common environments in which to find copular verbs or morphemes (20b and c):

(20)   *Yagua*
       a. máchituru ráy
          teacher   1SG
          "I am a teacher."

       b. ra-*vyicha*-núú-yanu máchituru
          1SG-be-CONT-PAST3 teacher
          "I used to be a teacher."

       c. rá̰-á̰   *vicha* máchituru
          1SG-FUT be   teacher
          "I'm going to be a teacher."

That the copular form is a verb in Yagua is evidenced by the fact that it takes verbal aspect (continuative, ex. 20b), tense (distant past, ex. 20b), and mode (future/irrealis, ex. 20c). It also inflects for person, and occurs in clause-initial position (ex. 20b).

Russian also employs a copular form in non-past tenses:

(21)   on *bïl* uchít^jel^j
       "He was a teacher."

(22)   aná   *bïl-á*   njánjə
       3SG:FEM be-FEM nurse:FEM
       "She was a nurse."

It stands to reason that some copular forms should stand "in between" verbs and invariant particles since copulas often derive historically from verbs. A defective verb is simply a verb that has lost some of its verbal properties, i.e., it is on its way to becoming an invariant particle but just has not got there yet. We will see that at least in existential constructions, the number distinction for the English verb *be* is neutralizing. In this sense, then, *be* is becoming defective in this environment.

Summary of the typology of predicate nominal constructions. The following simple formulas summarize the predicate nominal types discussed in this section. These "formulas" are not meant to represent constituent order:

1	no copula	NP NP
2	Copula	
(a)	copula is a verb	NP V NP
(b)	copula is a pronoun	NP PRO NP
(c)	copula is an invariant particle	NP COP NP
(d)	copula is a derivational operation	[NP]$_v$ NP
3	Copula only in non-present tenses	NP (COP) NP

The most common system is to not use a copula in the simplest predicate nominal constructions, i.e., present tense, and to use one of the above copula types in other tenses, aspects and/or modes.

?

How are proper inclusion and equative predicates formed?
What restrictions are there, if any, on the TAM marking of such clauses?

6.2   Predicate adjectives (attributive clauses)

Predicate adjectives (e.g., *He is tall*) are seldom distinct structurally from predicate nominals. Treat them separately only if they exhibit some distinctive formal property or properties. See section 3.3.1 for characteristics that may distinguish adjectives from nouns.

The morphosyntax of predicate adjectives is usually identical or similar to that of predicate nominals:

1	no copula	NP ADJ
2	Copula	
(a)	copula is a verb	NP V ADJ
(b)	copula is a pronoun	NP PRO ADJ
(c)	copula is an invariant particle	NP COP ADJ
(d)	copula is a derivational operation	[NP]$_v$ ADJ
3	Copula only in non-present tenses	NP (COP) ADJ

(23)   *English*
  a. Rick is a pacifist.   predicate nominal
  b. Rick is patient.   predicate adjective

Sometimes predicate adjectives use a different copula than predicate nominals do:

(24)   *Spanish*
  a. Ofelia *es* profesora.   "Ofelia is a teacher."
     *Ofelia *está* profesora.
  b. Ofelia *está* enferma.   "Ofelia is sick."
  c. Ofelia *es* enferma.   "Ofelia is a sick person/invalid."

As in many languages, there are few, if any, formal properties that distinguish nouns from adjectives in Spanish. Lexical items that embody properties, e.g., *red*, *sick*, *large*, etc. can function exactly like nouns, i.e., *la roja* "the red one," *la enferma* "the sick one," *la grande* "the large one," etc. Both nouns and adjectives normally inflect for gender and number. Students of Spanish learn that the language has two copular verbs. In order to decide which verb to use in a given instance, the rule of thumb is that if the property being predicated is permanent, then *ser* is used. If the property is temporary, *estar* is used. This rule probably works 80 percent of the time, and so is sufficient for most beginning students. However, advanced students also must memorize many exceptions. In fact the two copular verbs contrast in that *ser* is used for predicate nominals and *estar* for predicate adjectives and other states, such as locations:

(25)   El castillo *está* en el cerro.   "The castle is (*estar*) on the hill."
          *El castillo *es* en el cerro.   *ser*

For locations (as well as many other situations), *estar*, the copula for predicate adjectives, must be used even though the state can only be understood as permanent. This is because the relationship between subject and predicate in a locational construction is not one of class membership or identity. In most cases properties expressed by adjectives are temporary, whereas the relations of proper inclusion or identity (the semantic definition of a predicate nominal clause) are more permanent. For this reason the rule of thumb is of some use.

> **?**
> How are predicate adjectives formed? (Include a separate section on predicate adjectives only if they are structurally distinct from predicate nominals.)

6.3   Predicate locatives

Some languages, such as English, use the copular verb or morpheme in locational clauses. This is also true in Estonian (Finno-Ugric, Estonia):

(26)   raamat *on*   laual
          book   be:3sg table
          "The book is on the table."

There is a secondary type of locational construction in English that uses the verb *have*: "The table has a book on it." Notice the correlation between possessor and location – in English location is equivalent to an inanimate possessor. Hence this secondary means of forming predicate locatives is based on the model of possessive clauses. For many other languages, in particular Russian and Estonian, it is the other way around – possessive clauses are built on the model of locationals, but with an animate location.

Some languages use a special locative word. This word is often translated as "be at":

(27)   *Mandarin*
       shū *zài* zhuō-zi shàng
       book be:at table   on
       "The book is on the table."

In Mandarin, as in many languages, the locative word in a locational construction is the same as a locative adposition.

Other kinds of phrases can be formed in which the main semantic content of the predication is embodied in an adpositional phrase. These usually follow the pattern of predicate locatives:

Benefactive	This letter is for Melvin.
	Trix is for kids.
Accompaniment	Mary was with child.
	You were with me that day.
??	This award is for outstanding achievement.
	My stick is to teach you a lesson.

In a cross-linguistic typological survey, Clark (1978) compared about forty languages according to how they treat existential (E), possessive (P), and locational (L) clauses. Clark subsumed all of these under the heading of *locational* constructions because they all typically have a LOCATION word (LOC) and a NOMINAL (NOM) whose location is specified by the LOC. The following examples illustrate how NOM and LOC are distributed in E, P, and L constructions in English:

E: There is <u>a bee</u> <u>in your bonnet</u>.
         NOM LOC
P: <u>Lucretia</u> has <u>nineteen cats</u>.
    LOC   NOM
L: <u>The cat</u> is <u>under the bed</u>.
    NOM   LOC

It may seem odd that the *possessor* in a possessive clause is considered to be a *location*, but when you think about it, that is what possession is: when you possess something it is literally or figuratively located "on," "at," or "with" you. As illustrated in section 6.5, many languages pay attention grammatically to this cognitive similarity in that possessors are treated formally the same as locations.

However, word order usually distinguishes possessive clauses from locational clauses, even if no other formal property does. The following statistical tendencies on word order in E, P, and L constructions are from the findings of Clark (1978):

E: LOC before NOM (27 of 40 languages);
P: LOC before NOM (35 of 40 languages);
L: NOM before LOC (33 of 40 languages).

From these figures we see that the LOC is much more likely to precede the NOM in possessive and existential constructions than in locationals. In the following sections we will describe existential and possessive constructions, often making reference to Clark's study.

❓ How are locational clauses (or predicate locatives) formed?

6.4   Existentials

Existential constructions typically require a locational or temporal adjunct, e.g., *under the bed* in the clause:

(28)   There is a cat under the bed.

Many languages treat such clauses as "There is a God" morphosyntactically as existentials, even though there is no locational adjunct expressed. However, such "pure" existential clauses are not at all common in everyday discourse. Most languages use an intransitive verb form to express this sort of idea, e.g., "A God exists."

Existentials typically serve a **presentative** function, i.e., to introduce participants onto the discourse stage. Hence the nominal element (NOM in Clark's terminology) is almost always indefinite. Existential constructions in English tend to sound odd with definite nominals:

(29)   ??There are the lions in Africa.

Usually there is no or reduced evidence of grammatical relations in existential constructions, e.g., case marking, verb agreement, etc. This is true in colloquial English:

(30)   a. There's bears in the forest.
        b. There's ants in the syrup.
        c. There's lots of women in linguistics.

Though English teachers may shudder at these examples of verb agreement "errors," such expressions are extremely common and natural in spoken English. This indicates that the existential *be* is becoming a defective verb (see section 2.2), a very common property of existential constructions universally. In languages without a tradition of prescriptive grammar, speakers are freer to respond to this sort of functional naturalness.

Existential constructions commonly share features of predicate nominals, e.g., the copular morpheme, as in English. The following example is from Estonian:

(31)   laual *on* klaas piima
       table be glass milk
       "There is a glass of milk on the table."

Some languages do not use the copular morpheme in existentials even though they may have a perfectly good copula. The Mandarin clause below cannot mean "The book is on the table:"

(32)   *yǒu* shū yī-běn zài zhuōzi shàng
       EXIST book one-CL at table on
       "There is a book on the table."

In Mandarin the existential particle *yǒu* is clearly distinct from the copula *shì*.

Existentials often have special negation strategies, e.g., a verb meaning "to lack" as in Turkish and Russian:

(33)   *Turkish*
    a. *Affirmative existential*
       kösede   bir kahve *var*
       on:corner a   book EXIST
       "There is a book on the corner."

    b. *Negative existential*
       kösede   bir kahve *yok*
       on:corner a   book LACK
       "There isn't a book on the corner."

(34)   *Russian*
    a. *Affirmative existential*
       jest   kniga na stolʲé
       EXIST book on table:LOC
       "There is a book on the table."

b. *Negative existential*

n^{j}et   knigi   na stol^{j}é

NEG:EXIST book:GEN on table:LOC

"There isn't a book on the table."

Finally, like copular verbs and particles, existential particles often have extended functions. In particular, existential particles often play a role in "impersonal" or "circumstantial" voice constructions. A marginal example of this use of the existential in English is:

(35)   There'll be dancing in the streets.

This clause type is sometimes referred to as an "impersonal" construction, or an "impersonal passive" (see section 8.2.2). It expresses situations in which there is no need to mention any specific actor or actors. Other languages, e.g., Malagasy, use the existential particle much more often than English does to downplay the centrality of an actor (Keenan and Ochs 1979):

(36)   *Malagasy* (Austronesian, Madagascar)

    a. misy mi-tomany

        EXIST INTR-cry

        "There's crying" or "Someone's crying."

    b. misy mi-tady

        EXIST INTR-look:for

        "There's looking for" or "Someone is looking for something."

If a language employs the existential particle or particle for special purposes in non-existential constructions, those constructions would not necessarily be described in the chapter on existentials. For instance, the Malagasy examples in 36 would be treated in the chapter on voice or pragmatically marked structures. It may be helpful, however, to mention the extended uses in this chapter, and provide a pointer to where they are treated in more detail.

?

How are existential clauses formed? (Give examples in different tense/aspects, especially if there is significant variation.)

How are negative existentials formed?

Are there extended uses of existential morphology? (Provide pointers to other relevant sections of the grammar.)

6.5   Possessive clauses

Remember that possessive clauses (e.g., *I have a dollar*) are distinct from possessive noun phrases (*my dollar*). Languages usually employ existential and/or locational structures to express the notion of possession. Occasionally possessive clauses use a special verb like "to have." This verb often derives from the verb for "hold" or "carry." The more common situation, however, is for the possessive clause to use a copular verb or particle. Estonian uses the copular morpheme. To say "The child has milk" you say literally "Milk is at the child:"

(37)   *Estonian*
    a. lapsel   *on*   piima
       child:LOC be:3SG milk
       "The child has milk." (lit.: "Milk is at the child.")

    b. mul   *on*   tikku
       1SG:LOC be:3SG match
       "I have a match." (lit.: "A match is at me.")

This is reminiscent of such colloquial English expressions as *Got any money on you?*

Turkish uses the verb meaning "exist" that also occurs in the existential constructions. To say "The child has a father," you say literally "The child's father exists:"

(38)   *Turkish*
    cocugun babasi *var*
    child:GEN father exist
    "The child has a father."

Mandarin is similar to Turkish in this respect. To say "He has a book" you say something like "To him exists a book:"

(39)   *Mandarin*
    tā *yǒu* yī-běn shū
    3SG exist one-CL book
    "He/she has a book."

You can also say "To him is a book" in Mandarin, but this is less natural:

(40)   *Mandarin*
    ?tā *shì* shū
    3SG COP book
    "He/she has/is a book."

Table 6.2 **Summary of predicate nominals, E, P and L constructions**

Language	PRED NOM	*E*	*P*	*L*
English	be	be	be/have	be
French	est	a	a/est	est
Mandarin	shì	yǒu	yǒu	zài
Turkish	-im(etc.)	var	var	var
Russian	0/bïl	jest	jest	0/bïl
Estonian	on	on	on	on

In French the same verb that is used in existentials in an impersonal sense is also used in possessive clauses. Russian allows the same form for possessive clauses as in predicate locatives (like Estonian). To say "I have a book" you say "A book exists to me:"

(41)   *Russian*
u menja (jest) kniga
to me:GEN EXIST book
"I have a book."

?
How are possessive clauses formed?

6.6   Summary of predicate nominal and EPL relationships

Table 6.2 summarizes the morphological characteristics of predicate nominal, existential, locational, and possessive clauses in six languages mentioned in the above discussion.

E, P, and L constructions, while apparently serving logically distinct functions, are conceptually quite similar: they all embody a stative (i.e., non-eventive) situation in which the location or existence of one item (NOM) is specified with respect to some other item (LOC). According to Clark (1978), the main functional difference is the relative *animacy* and *definiteness*[2] of the two elements (referred to informally as NOM and LOC). As we might expect, however, the difference probably really lies in the notion of **topicality**. This is a notion which cannot be adequately identified on intuitive evidence alone. Rather, topicality can only be determined through rigorous investigation of texts. Definiteness and animacy are highly correlated with topicality, since human beings tend to select animate and definite (identifiable) entities as topics. However, definiteness does not in any way *define* topicality. See section 12.1.1 for further discussion of the notion of discourse topicality.

7   Grammatical relations

Grammatical relations (GRs) are often thought of as relations between **arguments** and **predicates** in a level of linguistic structure that is independent (or "autonomous") of semantic and pragmatic influences. For descriptive linguists it is important to recognize that GRs have universal functions in communication, while at the same time defining them in terms of language-specific formal properties.[1] The formal properties that most directly identify GRs are the following:

1 case marking;
2 participant reference marking on verbs;
3 constituent order.

Common terms used to refer to grammatical relations are **subject, direct object, indirect object, ergative**, and **absolutive**. The term **oblique** refers to nominals that lack a GR to some predicate. Explicit definitions and examples of these terms and the ways they are expressed will be given beginning in section 7.1 below. The following discussion will attempt to provide some background and justification for the notion of grammatical relations. This discussion is important to the reader who has serious questions about the "how" and "why" of grammatical relations, but may be skipped by those who want to just get down to the business of describing the system of GRs in a language.

Grammatical expression of semantic roles and pragmatic statuses (see chapters 3 and 10) is understandable in terms of the communicational function of language. However, it is much more difficult to explain GRs in this way. For example, it is intuitively obvious why a language should clearly and easily express the difference between the semantic roles of

129

AGENT and PATIENT – in many communication situations it is highly pertinent to distinguish entities that act from those that are acted upon. If a language did not make this distinction it would be difficult to communicate propositions like "John killed the lion" because there would be no way for the speaker to make it clear who killed whom.

Similarly, it is important for speakers to be able to easily communicate pragmatic statuses, such as topicality or identifiability (see chapter 10). As speakers, we structure messages so as to accurately identify important items or activities that we sense the hearer cannot identify on his/her own. And in the interests of efficiency, we refrain from overly identifying items that we judge to be either unimportant or easily identified by the hearer. This delicate balance between accuracy and efficiency is an important principle of human behavior in general and is apparent in many aspects of life (see Zipf 1949, Grice 1975, and other references on pragmatics). In summary, it makes sense that languages should have automated, well-oiled systems of expressing pragmatic statuses as well as semantic roles of nominals in discourse.

However, no such intuitive or pretheoretical justification for grammatical relations, as they are commonly thought of among linguists, is forthcoming. Why should a language pay particular attention to relations between arguments and predicates in an abstract level of structure that is not sensitive to semantics or pragmatics? What use is this kind of structure to speaker and hearer in communication? If GRs turn out to be a kind of representation or "mapping" of semantic roles and/or pragmatic statuses (and conceivably other functional roles as yet undiscovered), then their existence may be explained in terms of the communicational function of language. But simply as labels on nodes in the autonomous syntactic form of sentences, they have no obvious value. They clearly exist, and may even be universal; however, *why* they exist is not immediately evident.

There are severe problems, nonetheless, with asserting too quickly that grammatical relations are direct representations of semantic roles and/or pragmatic statuses. For example, as mentioned in section 3.2.0, there are many (potentially an unlimited number of) semantic roles and pragmatic statuses, whereas there are only about three GRs in any given language. How can three formal categories express infinite variability in the message world? In fact it is a common observation that a given GR in any language typically may express many different semantic roles, and that particular semantic roles may be expressed by several different GRs. For example, the grammatical subjects (underlined) of the following clauses each express a very different semantic role:

(1)   a.   George opened the door.   subject = AGENT
      b.   This key opened the door.   subject = INSTRUMENT
      c.   The wind opened the door.   subject = FORCE
      d.   The door was opened by the wind. subject = PATIENT

The fact that semantic roles do not map directly onto grammatical relations, at any conceivable level of abstraction, is *prima facie* evidence for some linguists (e.g., Rosen 1983) that GRs cannot derive from semantic roles. Therefore GRs must have independent status (be "autonomous") in any linguistic theory.

Attempts to derive grammatical relations from pragmatic statuses are similarly unproductive. For example, some linguists have proposed that the "subject" category in language is the linguistic manifestation of a pragmatic status such as "topic." Now topic is a term that is even more difficult to independently define than is AGENT (see section 10.0.3). However, most traditional definitions assume some form of the statement "the topic is what the sentence is about." If we try to apply this definition to real data, we run into similar problems as above. For example, in the following sentences it is hard to imagine a way of identifying the subject, *I*, as "what the sentence is about" independently of its status as grammatical subject:

(2)   a.   I just married the most beautiful woman in the world.
      b.   Now BEANS I like.
      c.   As for democracy, I think it's the best form of government.

These sorts of example make it clear that there is no direct "mapping" or "derivational" relationship from the intuitively significant notions of semantic role or pragmatic status to GRs. Nevertheless, languages do seem to have grammatical relations. GRs have proven useful to linguists for centuries, even though there has been much debate and little agreement as to why they should exist. They seem natural because languages do have them, but their functional status in language has been difficult to explain satisfactorily.

Modern functional linguists would take a different approach to the definition of grammatical relations. From a functional point of view, the obvious though inexact relationship between pragmatic statuses/ semantic roles and grammatical relations is motivated in terms of the notion of **prototype** plus grammaticalization (see the Introduction, section 0.2.2). For example, a noun phrase that is both a very good semantic AGENT and a very good pragmatic topic is likely to be expressed as a grammatical subject. A functionalist would say that such a noun phrase is a **prototypical** subject. It is the kind of noun phrase, in terms of pragmatic/semantic role, that provides the functional basis for the formal category of subject in the first place. It is a very *useful* category, therefore it makes sense that languages should have a highly automated (grammaticalized) way of expressing it.[2]

Now, what happens when a noun phrase refers to a slightly less prototypical AGENT, or a less prototypical topic? As mentioned above, languages tend to have only about three grammatical relations. This indicates that pragmatic or semantic deviation can be quite significant before a nominal must be excluded from a particular GR. It would seem unreasonable and inefficient to have a grammatical distinction for every conceivable nuance in semantic/pragmatic role. That would be like having an entirely different word for every conceivable shade of color in the spectrum. Therefore "clustering" of pragmatic/semantic roles occurs. Referents that are "close enough" to the prototype are expressed by noun phrases in the same GR as are more prototypical referents. Since this notion of "close enough" is a judgment call on the part of language users, there is variability from language to language (and even, in some languages, from situation to situation) as to how the roles cluster. For example, in the English sentence *John likes beans* the person who "likes" is treated the same grammatically as the AGENT of an agentive verb like *kill* or *eat*. In other languages, notably Spanish, the person who likes something is treated as an indirect object:

(3)   me   gusta   la   yuca
       1SG:DAT like:3SG ART manioc
       "I like manioc."

In this sentence the subject is *yuca*, as evidenced by third person verb agreement. The "liker" is referred to with the dative pronoun *me*. Hence it appears that in Spanish the experiencer of the sensation of "liking" is given the same grammatical relation as RECIPIENTS or PATIENTS of more agentive verbs, whereas in English the experiencer clusters grammatically with

AGENTS. In summary, GRs are automated (overlearned or institutional-ized) formal categories that allow languages to deal with an infinite range of variability in the realm of semantic roles and pragmatic statuses. This is not to say that languages have no way of communicating many degrees of agentivity or topicality. It is just that they do not have automated, well-oiled grammatical means of doing so.

It is an empirical observation that languages tend to have about three distinct core grammatical-relation categories (usually subject, object, and indirect object).[3] This probably reflects human cognitive limitations on keeping track of participant roles in a given situation and/or the number of participant roles necessary to express the kinds of messages human beings normally care to express. In other words there are two, and possibly three, categories necessary to keep participant roles distinct in normal human interaction without overburdening the mind.

7.1   Systems for grouping S, A, and P

In order to adequately define grammatical relations, it is conveni-ent to identify three basic semantico-syntactic roles, termed S, A, and P (Comrie 1978a). Similar terms are used by Dixon (1972, 1979, 1994) and Silverstein (1976). These terms, introduced briefly in section 4.0, presup-pose two prototypical clause types:

(4)   a. *Single argument*
          "Bob left."
             S   V (verb)

       b. *Multi-argument*
          "Bob greeted Aileron."
             A   V   P

The S is defined as the only nominal argument of a single-argument clause. Sometimes this type of clause is referred to as an **intransitive** clause (see chapter 8 for a discussion of different kinds of transitivity; see section 3.2.0 for a discussion of the term "argument"). The A is defined as the most AGENT-like argument of a multi-argument clause.[4] Sometimes this type of clause is referred to as a **transitive** clause. If there is no argument that is a very good AGENT, the A is the argument that is treated morphosyntact-ically in the same manner as prototypical AGENTS are treated. Usually there will be one argument in every verbal clause that exhibits this property, though there may not be. More complex systems are described below. P is the "most PATIENT-like" argument of a multi-argument clause. Again, if none of the arguments is very much like a PATIENT, then the argument that is treated like a prototypical PATIENT is considered to be the P.

The grammatical relation of **subject** can be defined as S together with A, while **direct object**, or simply "object," can be defined as P alone. Some languages pay more attention to this grouping than do others. In the following extended discussion, I will present the various systems for grouping S, A, and P and the morphosyntactic means languages employ to express these groupings.

Languages may treat S and A the same, and P differently. The following English examples illustrate this fact with pronominal case forms – one form, *he*, is used for third person singular masculine pronouns in both the S and the A roles. A different form, *him*, is used for third person masculine singular pronouns in the P role:

(5)   a. He left.
       b. He hit him.

The Quechuan languages (a group of languages spoken throughout the Andes mountains in South America) manifest this system in morphological case marking on free noun phrases. In the following examples the same case marker, 0 (zero), occurs on noun phrases in both the S (ex. 6a) and A (6b) roles. Another case marker, *-ta*, occurs on noun phrases in the P role (Weber 1989):

(6)   *Huánuco Quechua*
       a. Juan-0   aywan.   "Juan goes."
           Juan-<u>NOM</u> goes
                S

       b. Juan-0   Pedro-ta   maqan.   "Juan hits Pedro."
           Juan-<u>NOM</u> Pedro-<u>ACC</u> hits
                A   P

This system is often referred to as a **nominative/accusative** system. If any morphological case marks both S and A roles, it is called the **nominative** case, while the case that marks only the P role is the **accusative** case. This system seems very reasonable to speakers of Indo-European languages since most of these languages, to the extent that they have case marking at all, exhibit a nominative/accusative system.[5]

The following examples from Yup'ik Eskimo (Alaska) illustrate another system for grouping S, A, and P:

(7)   a. Doris-aq ayallruuq.   "Doris traveled."
           Doris-ABS traveled
                 S

       b. Tom-am Doris-aq cingallrua. "Tom greeted Doris."
           Tom-ERG Doris-ABS greeted
                A   P

In these examples the case marker *-aq* occurs on the S argument of an intransitive clause (7a) and the P argument of a transitive clause (7b). The case marker *-am* marks only the A of a transitive clause. If any morphological case marks A alone it can be called the **ergative case**. Similarly, any morphological case that marks both S and P can be termed the **absolutive case**:

ergative | absolutive

This system is known as an **ergative/absolutive** system, and it often seems unnatural to speakers of Indo-European languages since it is very rare in these languages. However, it is extremely common in other areas of the world. Ergativity occurs as a basic system for organizing grammatical relations in Australia, Central Asia, Basque, and in many languages of the Americas. It occurs as a partial case-marking system in South Asia (Nepal, Tibet, India, Pakistan, Bangladesh, Bhutan) and in many other languages of the Americas. Many Austronesian languages have also been claimed to exhibit this system.

In addition to morphological case marking on pronouns or free noun phrases, languages may manifest ergative/absolutive or nominative/accusative systems in other areas of the morphosyntax. First we will discuss person marking on verbs, then constituent order.

We have seen above that Quechua manifests a nominative/ accusative system in case marking of free noun phrases. Quechua also manifests a nominative/accusative system for organizing grammatical relations in person marking on verbs:

(8)　a.　Aywa-n.　　"He goes."
　　　　go-<u>3sg</u>
　　　　　S

　　b.　Aywa-a.　　"I go."
　　　　go-<u>1sg</u>
　　　　　S

　　c.　Maqa-ma-n.　"He hit me."
　　　　hit-1sg-<u>3sg</u>
　　　　　P　　A

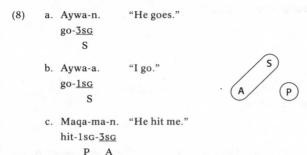

In example 8a the third person singular S of an intransitive verb is referred to by the suffix -*n*. In 8b the first person S argument is expressed by the suffix -*a* (actually length on the final vowel of the root). Example 8c shows that the suffix -*n* is also used for third person A arguments of transitive verbs. So A and S are treated morphologically "the same" by the person-marking system of Quechua. The fact that, in 8c, the first person suffix for P arguments is -*ma* rather than -*a* illustrates that P and S are treated as "different." This system of marking S and A alike and P differently has been defined as a nominative/accusative system.

As might be expected, languages can also manifest an ergative/ absolutive GR system in person marking on verbs. Yup'ik will again serve as our example of such a system:

(9)　　*Yup'ik*
　　a.　Ayallruu-nga.　"I traveled."
　　　　traveled-<u>1sg</u>
　　　　　S

　　b.　Ayallruu-q.　　"He traveled."
　　　　traveled-<u>3sg</u>
　　　　　S

　　c.　Cingallru-a-nga.　"He greeted me."
　　　　greeted-<u>3sg</u>-<u>1sg</u>
　　　　　A　　P

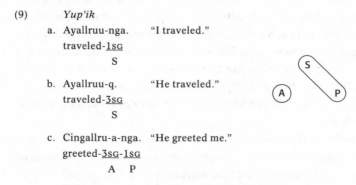

In example 9a the suffix -*nga* indicates a first person singular S argument of an intransitive verb. In 9b the suffix -*q* marks the third person S. In 9c the suffix *-nga* marks the first person P argument of a transitive clause. Since this is the same marker that is used for first person S arguments, this suffix groups S and P together morphologically into an absolutive category. The third person singular A argument of a transitive clause is expressed by a suffix *-a*. Since this suffix is different from the third person S suffix it can be said to identify ergative arguments. This treatment of S together with P as distinct from A is defined as an ergative/absolutive system.

Since constituent order is universally one major means of expressing grammatical relations, one might ask whether ergative/absolutive and/or nominative/accusative systems can be manifested in constituent order. Of course, the answer is "yes." English, consistent with its strong nominative/accusative orientation, treats S and A alike in that both subjects of intransitive verbs and subjects of transitive verbs most neutrally occur in preverbal position. Objects of transitive verbs, on the other hand, are treated differently in that they occur in postverbal position.

However, manifestation of constituent order nominativity or ergativity is rare for the following reason. Strictly speaking, constituent order ergativity would only be possible if the verb occurs in between its two core arguments (i.e., AVP or PVA languages). In all other logically possible constituent order types, both P and A occur most neutrally on the same side of the verb. Therefore either both are in the same position or both are in different positions from the intransitive S argument. Hence there can be no "grouping" of S with A against P or S with P against A.

Nevertheless, there are a few languages that exhibit an ergative/absolutive system in constituent ordering. Not surprisingly, these languages also have ergative/absolutive case marking. Furthermore, as with all languages, languages that exhibit constituent order ergativity also allow alternative orders. As pointed out by Dixon (1994: 52), it would be impertinent to characterize a language as "ergative" solely on the basis of constituent order.

The clearest examples of constituent order ergativity are in verb-medial languages. In these languages the verb and the P argument form a "tight" constituent in transitive clauses and the verb and the S argument form an analogous constituent in intransitive clauses. The A argument in transitive clauses tends to "float," i.e., may occur on either side of the tight verb plus P constituent.

In Kuikúro, a Cariban language of Brazil, SV (intransitive) and PV (transitive) are very rigid structures. The most neutral position for the A argument is following the PV complex (ex. 10b) (examples from Franchetto 1990):

(10)   a.   karaihá   kacun-tárâ
        non-Indian work-CONT
          S   V
        "The non-Indian is working."

      b.   kuk-aki-sâ   ta-lâígo léha karaihá-héke
         1INC-word-POSS hear-FUT ASP non:Indian-ERG
          P   V   A
        "The non-Indian will hear our words."

In 10a the S argument of an intransitive verb occurs in preverbal position; in 10b the P argument of a transitive verb occurs in preverbal position, and the A argument occurs in postverbal position. Since both S and P occur in the same position, we can say that this language manifests an ergative/ absolutive system in constituent order. This pattern is reported to occur in other lowland South American languages and in Päri, a Western Nilotic language of Sudan (Anderson 1988, reported in Dixon 1994: 50–51). The "mirror-image" of this pattern, in which VS and VP form tight constituents, is reported for Huastec (Mayan, Mexico; Edmundson 1988) and Paumarí (Arawá, Brazil; Chapman and Derbyshire 1991).

    One language, Sanuma (a variety of Yanomamï spoken in Brazil and Venezuela), is a verb-final language that is reported to exhibit constituent order ergativity. In this language, SV and PV form tight constituents. In transitive clauses A precedes P and V, but if there is any other constituent, call it X, it must occur after A. Thus the orders are AXPV and XSV (Borgman 1990, as reported in Dixon 1994: 52). Since A is treated distinctly by being separable from the PV complex, this pattern can be considered to be a kind of ergativity.

    Many languages have what might be considered "discourse-based constituent order ergativity." For example, Ochs (1988) shows that in Samoan the most neutral clause structure in discourse is a verb followed by a single noun phrase (NP). If the verb is intransitive, that NP is the S; if the verb is transitive, the single NP is the P. Thus the NP that follows the verb is almost always an absolutive nominal. Ochs describes the basic constituent order of Samoan as V NP_{abs}. This pattern of VS, VP (subsumed under the

notation V NP$_{abs}$) is extremely common in discourse, whereas VA and VAP
are extremely uncommon. In this sense the category "absolutive NP" (S
and P) coheres as a category to the exclusion of A, thus defining an ergative
system.

Many other languages, e.g., Kamaiurá of Brazil, commonly exhibit
the mirror image of the Samoan system, namely NP$_{abs}$V constituent order
in discourse (Seki 1990):

(11)   a.   wararuwijaw-a o-jaró
            dog-ABS   3-bark
            "The dogs are barking."

       b.   h-etymakaŋ-a w-e'yj
            3POSS-leg-ABS 3-scratch
            "He scratches his leg."

Example 11a is an intransitive clause in which the S argument precedes
the verb; example 11b is a transitive clause in which the P argument precedes the verb, and the A argument is expressed only in verb agreement. It
is rare for the A argument to be expressed as a full NP in transitive clauses
in discourse.

When we say constituent order ergativity in these languages is
"discourse-based" we mean that it is not a strict grammatical requirement.
Under a strictly formal grammatical conception of basic constituent order,
Samoan and Kamaiurá would probably be considered to exhibit VAP and
APV constituent order respectively.

7.2   Functional explanations for groupings of S, A, and P

We have seen that languages can organize their systems of grammatical relations in at least two distinct ways. In this section we will see
that in fact there are three other logically possible ways, but that all three
of these are far less common than the ergative/absolutive or nominative/
accusative systems. This observation leads us to investigate possible functional motivations for the various patterns.

Figure 7.1 illustrates the five logically possible ways in which languages could conceivably group S, A, and P in terms of case marking on
noun phrases or agreement/concord on verbs. Above each type an informal

Figure 7.1 Logically possible systems for organizing S, A, and P

estimate of the relative number of languages that instantiate each type is given, based on Tomlin (1986).

The question that immediately comes to mind for the functional linguist is, why should so many languages employ systems I and II, while so few employ systems III, IV, and V?[6] Could it not have been simply random which system a given language would "choose"? The answer to this question stems from the **discriminatory** and **identifying** functions of grammatical relations. GRs tend to distinguish nominal clause elements that have very different functions and unite those that have similar functions. First we will discuss the discriminatory, or differentiating, function.

The most important distinction to make among A, S, and P is between A and P. This is because A and P are the only arguments (among these three) that are instantiated in the same clause, and it is very important from the point of view of communication to identify which argument is acting upon which other argument. On the other hand, the two other distinctions, S vs. A and S vs. P, are communicationally irrelevant. This is because by definition these combinations of roles never occur in the same clause, therefore there is no possibility that they would ever be confused. Systems I and II are equally efficient from this point of view. They both make the important distinction between A and P, and do not unnecessarily distinguish S.

All of the other systems, however, are dysfunctional in one way or another. In particular, system IV ignores the important distinction between A and P and makes a useless one between S on the one hand and A and P on the other. System V ignores all distinctions, while III overdistinguishes them. From the point of view of the discriminatory function of grammatical relations, then, it is understandable why systems I and II should be about equally common, and systems III, IV, and V should be far less common.

In addition to the discriminatory function, however, grammatical-relation assignment also has an **identifying function**. That is, in addition to keeping nominal elements that have different roles distinct, GRs also serve to unite nominal elements whose roles are similar. This is a manifestation of the general principle that formal similarity (or **isomorphism**) results from functional similarity (Haiman 1980). From this point of view the treatment of S and A as "the same" in system I leads us to expect some functional similarity between these roles. Similarly, the treatment of S and P as "the same" in system II would suggest some functional commonality to these two roles.

There are semantic and discourse-pragmatic factors that may motivate S and A isomorphism or S and P isomorphism. First we will discuss the semantic factors.

The semantic similarity between S and A is agentivity: if a clause has an AGENT, it will be the S or the A argument, depending on whether the clause is transitive or intransitive.

(12)   a. Jorge stalked out of the room.   S is agentive.
       b. Wimple embraced the Duchess.   A is agentive.

The semantic similarity between S and P is change of state. If any argument in a clause changes state, it will be either the S or the P:

(13)   a. The bomb exploded.   S changes state.
       b. Lucretia broke the vase.   P changes state.

It is very difficult to conceive of a transitive clause in which the A changes state independently of the P. Possible examples are quite marginal, e.g., *John underwent surgery, Paul received a blow to the head,* etc.

The discourse-pragmatic similarity between A and S is topicality (Comrie 1989). A and S are the roles in which highly topical information is likely to be expressed. This observation is related to the fact, mentioned above, that A and S tend to be agentive insofar as people tend to select AGENTS as topics. Nevertheless, agentivity and topicality are logically independent variables. For example, sentences like *John underwent surgery* and *Paul received a blow to the head* represent situations in which the topicality of the human participants overrides their lack of agentivity. Humans are so much more likely to be selected as topics than such entities as "surgery" and "a blow to the head" that they are treated as A, even though they are arguably less agentive than the non-human entities in these particular situations.

The discourse-pragmatic similarity between S and P is that these are the roles in which "new" or "asserted" information is overwhelmingly expressed (Du Bois 1987). New participants are hardly ever introduced into discourse in the A role. This fact has been observed in empirical studies of discourse in many languages and is probably a universal. For example, in English it is possible to introduce a participant onto the discourse stage in the A role of a transitive clause (ex. 14b), but this is highly unusual in actual discourse:

(14) a. I was watching Ashley cross the street when
      b. suddenly <u>a big ferocious dog</u> nipped her leg.

A much more "natural" way of expressing this kind of idea is to introduce the new participant in an S or P role, then express the transitive event. Examples 15a and b are more natural as follow-up utterances to example 14a:

(15) a. . . . suddenly <u>a big ferocious dog</u> ran up and nipped her leg.
                     S

      b. . . . suddenly I saw <u>a big ferocious dog</u> nip her leg.
                              P

We have seen that there are semantic and pragmatic commonalities that may motivate formal similarity between S and A or between S and P. However, there is very little functional commonality between A and P. A arguments tend to be agentive, topical, and represent old information. P arguments, on the other hand, tend strongly to be patientive and to represent new information about 50 percent of the time. Therefore it makes sense that a large number of languages treat S and P or S and A alike morphosyntactically, but treat A and P differently.

The GR system of any given language will apparently center on one or a combination of these semantic or pragmatic principles. Grammatical-relation assignment in ergative languages can be thought of as paying more attention to change of state and/or new information, whereas grammatical-relation assignment in nominative/accusative languages pays more attention to topicality and/or agentivity. The less common systems (systems III and V) may represent GR systems in transition.

At this point we are prepared to provide a broader characterization of ergativity. The broadest possible definition of ergativity is the following:

> An ergative/absolutive system is any morphosyntactic system which unites
> S and P as opposed to A.

This definition refers to *systems* (i.e., case marking, verb agreement, etc.),
not languages. The term "ergative language" is simply an informal term that
refers to languages that have an ergative case-marking system on full noun
phrases in basic clauses (e.g. Eskimo languages), or exhibit an ergative system of verb agreement and no case marking on noun phrases (e.g., Mayan
languages). Ergativity itself is merely a convenient way of conceptualizing
some aspects of the clause structure of some languages. It is not a holistic
typology that necessarily makes a wide range of predictions concerning
other aspects of a language's grammatical structure.

In view of this broad definition, we may ask the question whether
English has any ergativity. The following examples illustrate some marginal evidence of ergativity in English:

(16)   a. escap-ee
            S

       b. employ-er   c. employ-ee
            A   P

The suffix *-ee* (a reflex of the French past participle) forms a nominalization
that refers to the S of an intransitive verb (ex. 16a) and the P of a transitive
verb (16c). A morphologically distinct suffix, *-er*, must be employed to form
a nominalization that refers to the A of a transitive verb (16b). In this
respect, then, S and P are treated alike, while A is treated differently.

Another marginal example of ergativity in English is noun incorporation (see section 9.2). When an argument is incorporated into
the present participle of the verb in English, it is either the S of an intransitive verb (17a) or the P of a transitive verb (17b) that is incorporated.

(17)   a. bird-chirping
            S

       b. fox-hunting   c. *doctor-recommending
            P   A

Although English does allow marginal incorporation of A arguments (*this
medicine is **doctor-recommended***), this type of incorporation is not available for present participles (**I went **doctor-recommending** aspirin last*

*evening, *I heard **doctor-recommending** outside my window*). This is further illustrated by the fact that *fox-hunting* cannot mean "hunting that foxes do;" rather, it must mean "hunting with foxes as the object."

These facts illustrate some processes in English that might be said to operate on an ergative/absolutive basis. In many other languages ergativity spreads much farther through the grammatical system. However, very few, if any, languages can be said to be "purely" ergative while many languages are (close to) purely nominative. In the following section we will describe various ways in which languages are known to manifest a partially nominative/accusative and partially ergative/absolutive system for organizing GRs.

7.3   Split systems

Some languages exhibit more than one system of organizing grammatical relations. In most such "split" systems the distinction between one subsystem and the other is related either to the semantics/pragmatics of intransitive clauses (**split intransitivity**, section 7.3.1) or to the semantics/pragmatics of transitive clauses (**split ergativity**, sections 7.3.2 and 7.3.3). Further information on split intransitivity can be found in Merlan (1985) and Mithun (1991); further information on split ergativity can be found in Silverstein (1976), DeLancey (1982), and the references on ergativity cited above.

7.3.1   Split intransitivity

Some languages express S arguments of intransitive verbs in two or more morphologically distinct ways. Such languages are sometimes said to exhibit **split intransitivity**. The most common split intransitive systems express some S arguments in the same way as transitive A arguments and others in the same way as transitive P arguments. Other terms that have been used for such systems include **stative/active**, **active**, **split-S** and **fluid-S** systems, among others. To illustrate this phenomenon, we will imagine that English exhibited a split intransitive system. Subjects of certain intransitive verbs (probably those that are active or agentive) would take the pronouns common to subjects of transitive verbs (18a), whereas subjects of other intransitive verbs (probably those that are stative or non-agentive) would take objective pronouns (18b):

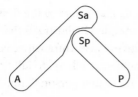

Figure 7.2 Split intransitive systems for organizing GRs

(18)   a. He went.
       b. Him died.

This type of system does not fit the five-way typology illustrated in figure 7.1. Instead the diagram in figure 7.2 may be helpful. S_a arguments are those intransitive subjects that are treated grammatically like transitive A arguments, while S_p arguments are those intransitive subjects that are treated like transitive P arguments. Perlmutter (1980) and many other linguists use the term **unaccusative** to refer to intransitive predicates that treat their S argument like a transitive P argument.

Usually there is a fairly obvious semantic basis for the distinction between the two types of S arguments, though the basis is apparently not the same for every language (Mithun 1991). For example, in modern colloquial Guaraní (Paraguay) intransitive verbs that describe dynamic events fall into the S_a class, while those that describe states fall into the S_p class. In Lakhota (a Siouan language of the upper Midwestern United States), intransitive verbs in which the S is an AGENT take S_a subjects, while those in which the S is a PATIENT take S_p subjects. Examples 19a, b, and c illustrate transitive clauses in Lakhota (examples quoted in Mithun 1991, or provided by Walter and Delores Taken Alive of Little Eagle, South Dakota):

(19)   a. a-ma-ya-phe
           DIR-1SG-2SG-hit
           "You hit me."

       b. wa-0-ktékte
           1SG-3SG-kill
           "I kill him."

       c. 0-ma-ktékte
           3SG-1SG-kill
           "He kills me."

Examples 19a and c illustrate that the prefix *ma-* refers to the first person singular P argument of a transitive clause. Example 19b illustrates that the prefix *wa-* refers to the first person A of a transitive clause. Intransitive verbs that do not involve volition on the part of the subject, such as "to fall," "to die," and "to shiver," take the P prefix *ma-* to refer to first person S arguments:

(20)   a.   ma-hîxpaye
            1SG-fall
            "I fall"

       b.   ma-t'e'
            1SG-die
            "I die"

       c.   ma-č'ăča
            1SG-shiver
            "I shiver"

Intransitive verbs that are normally carried out agentively, e.g., "to play," "to swim," and "to sing," take the A prefix, *wa-*, for first person S arguments:

(21)   a.   wa-škate
            1SG-play
            "I play"

       b.   wa-nûwe
            1SG-swim
            "I swim"

       c.   wa-lowâ
            1SG-sing
            "I sing"

Guaymí, a Chibchan language of Costa Rica and Panama, illustrates a complex split-S system of case marking of free noun phrases. Example 22 illustrates a transitive clause in which the A is marked with the suffix *-gwe* and the P is left unmarked (examples from Rafael Bejarano Palacios, Coto Brus, Costa Rica):

(22)   Toma-gwe Dori d″ma-ini.
           Tom-ERG Doris greet-PAST1
           "Tom greeted Doris."

Subjects of intransitive verbs that involve volition can also take this *-gwe* suffix:

(23)   Dori-gwe blit-ani.
        Doris-ERG speak-PAST1
        "Doris spoke."

Subjects of verbs that do not involve volition may not take the *gwe-* suffix:

(24)   Nu   ŋat-ani.
        dog:ABS die-PAST1
        (*Nu-gwe ŋat-ani.)
        "The dog died."

We will see in section 7.3.2 that the split-S system in Guaymí only operates in the past tenses. Nevertheless, these examples do show that a split
intransitive system for organizing grammatical relations can be manifested
in nominal case marking as well as in verb agreement.

There are no languages for which subjects of non-agentive or
stative intransitive verbs are treated like A arguments while subjects of
agentive or active intransitive verbs are treated like P arguments. This universal makes sense in terms of the identifying function of GRs (see above).
Agentive intransitive subjects are functionally more like prototypical A
arguments, in that both act with volition and control. Similarly, non-
agentive intransitive subjects are functionally more like prototypical P
arguments in that both receive or undergo the action expressed by the
verb. It would be dysfunctional for agentive intransitive subjects to share
morphology with transitive patients, while non-agentive intransitive subjects shared morphology with transitive agents.

Some languages can treat the intransitive subject of certain verbs
as either A or P depending on the semantics desired. For example, the concept expressed in English as *to fall* can either be conceived as something
the subject *does* or as something that the subject *undergoes*. In some languages this distinction is grammaticalized in the way the subject argument
is expressed. In Chickasaw, a Muskogean language of the southeastern
United States, the subject of some verbs can be expressed in any of three
ways, depending on the semantics. For example, the root *chokma* "good,"
can be inflected for A when the subject acts volitionally (25a), for P when
goodness is a property exhibited by the subject (25b) and for a dative
participant when goodness is a feeling experienced by the subject (25c)
(examples from Catherine Wilmond):

(25) a. Chokma-li.   "I act good." (volitional)
          good   -1sgA
                  S

      b. Sa-chokma.   "I am good." (non-volitional)
          1sgP-good
          S

      c. An-chokma.   "I feel good." (experiential)
          1sgD-good
          S

As with split-S systems, there are no fluid-S systems that treat
agentive subjects of intransitive verbs like P arguments, while treating
non-agentive intransitive subjects like A arguments. That is, there are no
systems that exhibit the following sort of pattern:

(26) a. He hit him.
      b. Him fell (on purpose).
      c. He fell (accidentally).

As might be expected, split-S and fluid-S languages do not constitute two mutually exclusive language types. Typically, a given language will
have some intransitive verbs that require S_a subjects, others that require S_p
subjects, and still others that allow either S_a or S_p subjects.

A few languages have been shown to exhibit split intransitivity
based on discourse pragmatics. For example, in Yagua, intransitive verbs of
locomotion can take S_a or S_p subjects depending on the discourse context:

(27) a. Muuy sii-myaa-si-ñíí.
          there run-COMPL-out-3:P
          "There he rushed out."

      b. Sa-sii-myaa-síy.
          3:A-run-COMPL-out
          "He rushed out."

In example 27 the subject is expressed as an enclitic -*ñíí*. This is the form
that is used for P arguments of transitive verbs. In 27b the subject is expressed with a prefix *sa-*. This is the form used for A arguments of transitive verbs. It is clear that this distinction is not based on semantics since the
S arguments of both clauses are understood to be equally agentive, volitional, etc. An empirical study of narrative text shows that S_p subjects occur

at scene changes and episodic climaxes (27a), whereas S_a subjects occur elsewhere (27b) (T. Payne 1992).

Similar observations have been made for Pajonal Campa (Heitzman 1982) and Asheninca Campa (J. Payne and D. Payne 1991). These languages are both areally but not genetically related to Yagua.

7.3.2   Split ergativity
7.3.2.1   *Split ergativity based on relative topic-worthiness of A and P*

Some languages rely partly or completely on inference to distinguish A from P in most circumstances.[7] Imagine a language for which none of case marking, person marking, or constituent order distinguished A from P in transitive clauses. In such a language, how could speakers express and hearers understand the crucial information concerning who acts upon whom? The answer to this question is that in the vast majority of transitive situations, one of the participants is pragmatically more likely to be the A than the other one. The pragmatically more probable A argument can automatically be assumed to be the A, unless specific cues to the contrary are provided. When a language provides such cues in certain circumstances but not others, a "split" system may result.

Before exemplifying this principle, let us examine the simplest case using hypothetical data. In most situations involving humans and non-humans, the humans are more likely to be the controlling actors than are the non-humans. (In the following examples, we will imagine a verb-initial language that happens to have the same vocabulary as English.)

(28)   a. Ate <u>Anna food</u>.
          A   P

    b. Ate <u>food Anna</u>.
          P   A

If the situation involves "eating" and one argument is a person and the other argument is food, the chances of food being the AGENT and the person being the PATIENT are nil – people eat food but food does not eat people. Pragmatic knowledge of the world is sufficient to allow hearers to infer which of the arguments is the A and which is the P. Therefore no special marking, either verb agreement, nominal case marking, or constituent order, is necessary to express this fact. Sierra Popoluca is just such a language (all Sierra Popoluca examples are courtesy of Ben Elson):

(29)   a. i-ku't-pa   xiwan wi'kkuy
           3P3A-eat-PERF Juan   food
           "Juan ate food."

       b. i-ku't-pa   wi'kkuy xiwan
           3P3A-eat-PERF food   Juan
           "Juan ate food."

       c. xiwan wi'kkuy iku'tpa   "Juan ate food."
       d. xiwan iku'tpa wi'kkuy   "Juan ate food."
       e. wi'kkuy iku'tpa xiwan   "Juan ate food."

These examples illustrate that some kinds of entities are inherently more likely to be agents than are others. We can say that humans are more **agent-worthy**, i.e., more likely to be agents, than are non-humans. But of course the real situation is not a simple dichotomy. In fact, entities, or rather grammatical devices that refer to entities, can be characterized along a hierarchy of **agent-worthiness** (or by extension **topic-worthiness**, discussed below):

$$1 > 2 > 3 > 1 > 2 > 3 > \text{proper names} > \text{humans} > \genfrac{}{}{0pt}{}{\text{non-human}}{\text{animates}} > \text{inanimates}$$

agreement > pronouns

definite   >   indefinite

This entire hierarchy is not grammaticalized in any given language, but neither is it a theoretical model based on a pre-empirical notion of "agent-worthiness." Rather, it derives from a survey of languages that rely, at least partially, on pragmatics to distinguish A from P in some subset of their transitive clauses. In all such languages, the argument further to the left on the hierarchy will automatically be understood as AGENT, unless some specific marker signifies otherwise.[8] What is crucial about this hierarchy is that the arrows always (in languages studied to date) go from left to right. That is, there is no language for which an argument lower on the hierarchy will automatically be understood as acting upon an argument higher on the hierarchy. Morphological or grammatical signals must always be employed to express such a situation.

Sometimes, this hierarchy (and other similar ones) has been called an **agentivity hierarchy** or an **animacy hierarchy**. These are not really very accurate terms, as many of the elements have nothing to do with animacy or agentivity in the usual sense. For example, verb agreement, pronouns, and proper names can refer to biologically animate or inanimate, agentive or non-agentive entities. The reality that this hierarchy reflects is the fact that certain kinds of entities, namely things that move, have power, and initiate action, are more likely to be selected as topics of conversation than are others. Also, certain grammatical forms, such as agreement and pronouns, are more likely to refer to highly topical entities (see section 12.1.1). The notion of **inherent topic-worthiness** will be elaborated and clarified at several points throughout this book. For now, let us describe the connection between agentivity and topicality in terms of the notion of **empathy** (Kuno 1976). According to Kuno, there is an **empathy principle** of human communication that can be expressed as follows:

> Human beings tend to select as topics entities with whom they empathize, first of all themselves, then the person they are speaking to, then other human beings, then non-human animate beings, and finally the inanimate world. Therefore, morphosyntactic expressions whose function is to refer to topical entities indirectly tend to refer to entities that speakers empathize with.

A less technical way of expressing this fact is to say that people identify with and like to talk about things that act, move, control events, and have power. Therefore utterances in communication tend to make AGENTS highly topical, and action tends to flow from the highly topic-worthy, agentive, entities to less topic-worthy entities. This is not to say that action *always* flows from highly topic-worthy and agentive arguments to less topic-worthy and patientive arguments. In fact, the ways in which languages deal with deviations from the natural flow of action are some of the more fascinating aspects of linguistic structure. It is just that the normal, or most common, situation is for people to choose powerful, dynamic, and controlling entities as topics of communication.

Let us make these notions concrete with some actual examples. What about a situation where both arguments of a transitive clause are equally likely to be agentive? Then true ambiguity may result, as is the case in Sierra Popoluca:

(30)   i-ko'ts-pa   xiwan petoj
         3P-3A-hit-PERF John   Pedro
         "Juan hit Pedro" or "Pedro hit Juan."

Even these types of clause are normally ambiguous only when divorced from their contexts. For example, imagine the sentence in 31 occurring in two stories involving Juan and Pedro:

(31)   a.   *Context 1*
Pedro sat quietly as he listened to that braggart Juan go on and on. Everyone could tell that Pedro was getting angry. Still he remained silent. Then, suddenly, Juan said something that Pedro couldn't ignore. Pedro jumped up and . . . (example 30).

   b.   *Context 2*
Juan sat quietly as he listened to that braggart Pedro go on and on. Everyone could tell that Juan was getting angry. Still he remained silent. Then, suddenly, Pedro said something that Juan couldn't ignore. Juan jumped up and . . . (example 30).

In both of these oversimplistic contrived situations the context makes it clear which of the two participants is the A and which is the P. This is what might be called **context-imparted topic-worthiness**. In fact, there are really relatively few potential situations in communication where determination of A and P cannot be made either by inherent or by context-imparted topic-worthiness. Some languages rely on context-imparted topic-worthiness more than others. In Sierra Popoluca, if there is any doubt, an intransitive clause will follow the ambiguous one:

(32)   a.   ko'tstap petoj
"Pedro is hit."

   b.   ko'tso'ypa xiwan
"Juan hits or does hitting."

Having presented the concept of a topic-worthiness hierarchy, we can now relate that hierarchy to the topic of split ergativity. In any given transitive clause, one argument will probably be inherently more topic-worthy than the other. The "neutral" or "natural" state of affairs (according to the empathy principle stated above) is for the argument that is the most topic-worthy to be the A. As discussed above, some languages employ no overt coding of A or P status when this natural flow of action from high to low topic-worthiness is adhered to. However, some of those languages do use a special case marker on either the A or the P of a transitive clause only in those unusual circumstances when the P is high in topic-worthiness, or when the A is low in topic-worthiness.

As an example of this phenomenon, we might suppose Sierra Popoluca employed a case-marking system to render sentences such as 30 less ambiguous. There would be two possible case-marking solutions to the ambiguity problem. One would be to mark the A with a special case marker (33a) and the other would be to mark the P (33b):

(33)   *Hypothetical data based on Sierra Populuca*
    a. itko'tspa xiwan pҽtoj-a   "Pedro hit Juan."
                        -A
           P   A

    b. itko'tspa xiwan-p pҽtoj   "Pedro hit Juan."
                 -P
           P   A

Assuming that intransitive subjects remain unmarked, the solution represented in 33a results in an ergative/absolutive case-marking system with -*a* functioning as the ergative case marker. The solution represented in 33b results in a nominative/accusative case-marking system, with -*p* functioning as the accusative case marker. Each of these solutions is equally efficient in accomplishing the task of distinguishing A and P arguments. Theoretically (and occasionally in reality) both solutions may be used. This results in a **tripartite** system of organizing grammatical relations:

(34)   a. Vomited George-0.   "George vomited."
                  S

    b. Hit <u>George</u>-p <u>Bill</u>-a   "Bill hit George."
              P   A

When the flow of action is in the normal, expected direction from high to low on the topic-worthiness hierarchy, no special marking is needed to make A and P explicit. The pragmatics of the situation make it easy to infer who is acting on what. However, when P is unexpectedly high on the hierarchy, it may need to be specially marked. Similarly, when A is unexpectedly low on the hierarchy, it may need to be marked. Placing a special marker on P results in a nominative/accusative system. Therefore, the nominative/accusative solution (ex. 33b) is likely to be employed when direct objects are high on the topic-worthiness hierarchy. The ergative/absolutive system is likely to be used for A arguments that are low on the topic-worthiness hierarchy. In fact, this is a universal of split-ergativity based on semantic/pragmatic content of the noun phrases in transitive clauses. This universal can be expressed as follows:

(35)   *Universal*

> If a language exhibits split ergativity based on the topic-worthiness of the noun phrases in the transitive clause, it is always the case that the nominative/accusative system will be manifested for nominal arguments that are high in topic-worthiness and the ergative/absolutive system will be manifested for nominal arguments that are low in topic-worthiness.

In other words, when split ergativity is based on the semantic and/or pragmatic characteristics of the noun phrases, it will always be the case that noun phrases higher (to the left) on the topic-worthiness hierarchy will trigger a nominative/accusative subsystem, while noun phrases lower (to the right) on the hierarchy will trigger an ergative/absolutive subsystem. This hierarchy will be repeated here for convenience:

$$1 > 2 > 3 > 1 > 2 > 3 > \text{proper names} > \text{humans} > \genfrac{}{}{0pt}{}{\text{non-human}}{\text{animates}} > \text{inanimates}$$

agreement > pronouns

definite   >   indefinite

The actual location of the split on the hierarchy varies from language to language, but the general arrangement of high = nominative/accusative and low = ergative/absolutive is invariant.

Now we turn to some examples of this universal. Managalasi, a highland language of Papua New Guinea, employs an ergative/absolutive case-marking system for pronouns and a nominative/accusative system for person marking on verbs (examples courtesy of Judy Parlier):

(36) a. a   va?-ena
          2SG go-FUT:2SG
          "You will go."

      b. na va?-ejo
          1SG go-FUT:1SG
          "I will go."

      c. nara a   an-a?-ejo
          1SG 2SG hit-2SG-FUT:1SG
          "I will hit you."

      d. ara na an-i?-ena
          2SG 1SG hit-1SG-FUT:2SG
          "You will hit me."

In examples 36c and d -*ra* marks the pronominal A of the transitive clauses while 0 marks the P. In 36a and b 0 marks the S of the intransitive clauses. This grouping of S with P as opposed to A illustrates a classic ergative/absolutive system of pronominal case marking. Verb agreement, however, operates on a nominative/accusative system: -*ena* agrees with second person singular S and A arguments (37a and d), and -*ejo* agrees with first person singular S and A arguments (36b and c). The agreement markers for P arguments are *a?* (2SG, ex. 36c) and *i?* (1SG, ex. 36d). Thus in verb agreement S and A are treated alike and P is treated differently.

In Dyirbal, an Aboriginal language of Australia, first and second person pronouns operate on a nominative/accusative basis (37):

(37)   *Dyirbal* (Dixon 1972)
   a. ngana-0 banaga-nʸu   "We returned."
      1PL-NOM returned-NONFUT
      S

   b. nyura-0 banaga-nʸu   "You all returned."
      2PL-NOM returned-NONFUT
      S

   c. nyura-0 ngana-na bura-n   "You all saw us."
      2PL-NOM 1PL-ACC   saw-NONFUT
      A   P

   d. ngana-0 nyura-na bura-n   "We saw you."
      1PL-NOM 2PL-ACC   saw-NONFUT
      A   P

Third person pronouns and all other noun phrases in Dyirbal, however, operate on an ergative/absolutive basis. Notice that the A argument, *yabu* "mother," in 38c carries the ergative case marker -*ŋgu*:

(38)   a. ŋuma-0   banaga-nʸu
         father-ABS return-NONFUT
         "Father returned."

       b. yabu-0   banaga-nʸu
          mother-ABS return-NONFUT
          "Mother returned."

       c. ŋuma-0   yabu-*ŋgu*   bura-n
          father-ABS mother-ERG see-NONFUT
          "Mother saw father."

Table 7.1 Dyirbal case marking

	S	A	P	
1, 2 pronoun	-0	-0	-na	nominative/accusative
3 pronoun	-0	-ŋgu	-0	ergative/absolutive
Names	-0	-ŋgu	-0	ergative/absolutive
Common NPs	-0	-ŋgu	-0	ergative/absolutive

Table 7.2 Cashinawa

	S	A	P	
1, 2 pronoun	-0	-0	-a	nominative/accusative
3 pronoun	-0	-˜	-a	tripartite
Full NPs	-0	-˜	-0	ergative/absolutive

Table 7.1 summarizes the case-marking system of Dyirbal in terms of semantico-syntactic roles and type of noun.

Cashinawa, a Panoan language of Peru, exhibits a nominative/accusative system for case marking of first and second person pronouns, a tripartite system (system V of figure 7.1 above) for third person pronouns and an ergative/absolutive system for all other noun phrases. These data are summarized in table 7.2 (courtesy of Eugene Loos). The fact that the system for marking third person pronouns is tripartite can be seen as the intersection of the nominative/accusative and the ergative/absolutive systems. That is, a tripartite system marks *both* the A *and* the P in order to maximally distinguish them (see example 34). In particular, Cashinawa employs nasalization from the ergative/absolutive system to mark the A and a vowel *-a* from the nominative/accusative system to mark the P in the redundantly marked tripartite system for third person pronouns.

Even languages that do not exhibit an ergative/absolutive system can support or refute the universal in 35. For example, in Spanish most clausal arguments that are referred to with full noun phrases are not case-marked. However, direct objects that refer to specific, human participants take an accusative case marker:

Table 7.3 Spanish

	S	A	P	
1, 2, 3 person marking	a,-o, etc.	-a, -o,etc.	lo/le, te, me, etc.	nominative/accusative
Pronouns	0	0	a	
Definite human NPs	0	0	a	
Definite non-human NPs	0	0	0	neutral
Indefinite NPs	0	0	0	

(39) a. Estoy buscando una empleada.
          be:1SG looking:for INDEF housekeeper
          "I'm looking for a housekeeper (don't have one in mind)."

      b. Estoy buscando **a** una empleada.
          be:1SG looking:for CM DEF housekeeper
          "I'm looking for a housekeeper (have a specific one in mind)."

In other words, the case marker *a* is used only when a specific and human direct object is mentioned. All other nominal direct objects are not case-marked. Therefore case marking for specific human direct objects manifests a nominative/accusative system, but case marking for all other classes of full noun phrases is neutral. It so happens that verb agreement and pronominal case marking also operate on a nominative/accusative basis. Therefore, Spanish is nominative/accusative in the highest ranges of the topic-worthiness hierarchy right up to the point of non-specific human direct objects. Then it becomes neutral. These data are illustrated in table 7.3. Again, if the *a* case marker happened to occur on non-human or non-specific direct objects, the universal expressed in 35 would be violated.

Many languages case-mark direct objects only when they are "definite" or identifiable. Turkish, Hebrew, and Farsi are well-known examples of such languages. Following are some examples from Farsi (the Indo-European national language of Iran – examples courtesy of Jalleh Banishadr):

(40) a. Man dombale kitob hæsdæm.
          I   look:for book AUX
          "I'm looking for a book."

Table 7.4   Summary of split ergativity based on semantic/pragmatic characteristics of NPs

	Agreement	1/2 pronoun	3 pronoun	Definite human	Def NPs	Other NPs
Managalasi	nom./acc.	erg./abs.	erg./abs.	–	–	–
Dyirbal	none	nom./acc.	erg./abs.	erg./abs.	erg./abs.	erg./abs.
Cashinawa	nom./acc.	nom./acc.	nom./acc. erg./abs.	erg./abs.	erg./abs.	erg./abs.
Spanish	nom./acc.	nom./acc.	nom./acc.	nom./acc.	–	–
Farsi	nom./acc.	nom./acc.	nom./acc.	nom./acc.	nom./acc.	–
nom./acc. (*erg./abs.						erg./abs. *nom./acc.)

    b.   Man dombale kitob-ro   hæsdæm.
       I   look:for book-CM AUX
       "I'm looking for the book."

In these examples the suffix -*ro* appears only on direct objects, and only on direct objects that are identifiable. Again this fact is consistent with the universal stated in 35.

    Table 7.4 summarizes and compares the data presented so far. In every case, the nominative/accusative system extends from the left of the topic-worthiness hierarchy and the ergative/absolutive or neutral system (indicated by –) extends from the right of the hierarchy. No language has been documented to date that violates this pattern. Cashinawa is particularly interesting in that it illustrates a system when the ergative/absolutive and nominative/accusative systems actually overlap.

7.3.2.2   *Split ergativity based on tense–aspect*

    Some languages manifest a nominative/accusative system in one tense–aspect category and an ergative/absolutive system in another. In all such languages, the ergative/absolutive system occurs in the past tense or perfective aspect, while the nominative/accusative system occurs in the non-past tense(s) or imperfective aspect (DeLancey 1982). To date, no clear exceptions to this universal have been attested. The following example is from Georgian, the national language of the Republic of Georgia:

(41)   *Georgian* (from Comrie 1989)

   a. Student-i   midis.
         -NOM goes
      "The student goes."

   b. Student-i   ceril-s   cers.
         -NOM letter-ACC writes
      "The student writes the letter."

   c. Student-i   mivida.
         -ABS went
      "The student went."

   d. Student-ma ceril-i   dacera.
         -ERG letter-ABS wrote
      "The student wrote the letter."

In these examples, the case marker -*i* marks S and A nominals in the "present" tense (examples 41a and b). Therefore, it is appropriate to refer to this case marker as marking nominative case. The same operator, however, marks S and P nominals in the "past" tense (examples 41c and d). In these clauses, then, it is appropriate to describe -*i* as an absolutive case marker.

DeLancey (1982, 1990) proposes functional explanations for this universal phenomenon based on the notion of starting point vs. endpoint perspective. We have already noted that an ergative/absolutive system for organizing GRs can be thought of as being "patient-oriented." Similarly, a nominative/accusative system can be thought of as agent-oriented. Now, past tense and perfective aspect provide ways of expressing situations as completed events. The result of a completed transitive event is likely to be recorded in the patient. In fact, for DeLancey, the definition of PATIENT as a semantic role has more to do with its status as the endpoint of an action, rather than as the participant most likely to undergo a change in physical state. Therefore, the past tense and perfective aspect are more patient-oriented than are non-past tense and/or imperfective aspect.

Perhaps the best way of illustrating this principle is through example. Example 42 is a past tense, perfective aspect clause of English:

(42)   George hit (has hit) Bill.

If true, this statement describes the event from the point of view of a completed act, perhaps with Bill lying on the floor with a bloody nose. Bill is definitely and wholly involved in the action from this point of view. Example 37, on the other hand, is in the future tense:

(43)   George will hit Bill.

This statement can be construed as saying more about George than about Bill. That is, from this point of view, Bill is not yet involved in the event, though George is very much involved. George is probably angry, and may be storming down the hall ready to do violence, while Bill is still going happily about his everyday business. The clause is presented from the perspective of its (potential) inception, and the event begins with George. Therefore, we can say that the future is agent-oriented. Similarly, though less obviously, the imperfective aspect presents the situation as ongoing, and therefore still under the control of the initiator, with the end result still unknown. This is one way of conceptualizing the commonality between non-past tenses, non-perfective aspects, and agentivity.

Before leaving the topic of split ergativity, we will present one more example of a combination split ergative case-marking system. This is from the Guaymí language of Panama and Costa Rica. As illustrated earlier, Guaymí has a straightforward split-S case-marking system in both of the two past tenses. This is illustrated in 44a, b, and e. The ergative case marker -*gwe* can only occur on the A arguments of transitive verbs or agentive intransitive verbs in one of the past tenses:

(44)   a. Dori-gwe blit-ani.
            Doris-ERG speak-PAST1
            "Doris spoke."

        b. Nu ŋat-ani.
            dog die-PAST1
            "The dog died."

        c. Toma-gwe Dori dəma-ini.
            Tom-ERG   Doris greet-PAST1
            "Tom greeted Doris."

        d. Dori blit-e.
            Doris speak-PRES
            "Doris is speaking."

        e. Toma Dori dəma-e.
            Tom Doris greet-PRES
            "Tom is greeting Doris."

f. Nu ŋat-e.
    dog die-PRES
    "The dog is dying."

In the non-past tenses, however, the ergative marker never occurs, regardless of the semantics or transitivity of the verb (44c, d, and f). One could say that Guaymí has two quite distinct case-marking systems, one for the past tenses and one for the present. Consistent with the universal expressed at the beginning of this section, the only system that contains even a trace of ergativity is that which is used in the past tenses:

Past   Present

S_a	S_p		S
A	P	A	P

7.3.3   Summary of split systems for organizing grammatical relations

There are three respects in which languages can exhibit split systems for organizing their grammatical relations. Individual languages may be sensitive to one or a combination of these types of split systems. These systems have been described as split intransitivity and split ergativity based on relative topic-worthiness of the arguments in transitive clauses and split ergativity based on tense–aspect in transitive clauses.

A split intransitive system is one in which the only argument of intransitive clauses can be expressed either as an A argument of a transitive clause or as a P argument of a transitive clause. It is always the case, in such systems, that agentive, active, volitional intransitive subjects take A-like morphosyntax while non-agentive, stative, non-volitional intransitive subjects take P-like morphosyntax.

Split ergativity based on topic-worthiness depends on a hierarchy of animacy, empathy, potential of agency, etc. of the arguments in transitive clauses. In such systems, arguments that are higher on this hierarchy will condition the nominative/accusative system and arguments that are lower on the hierarchy will condition the ergative/absolutive system.

Languages may also have split ergativity based on tense–aspect. If so, then a nominative/accusative system will be used in non-past tense and/or non-perfective aspects, while an ergative/absolutive system will be used in past tense and/or perfective aspects.

7.4   "Syntactic" ergativity

A syntactic process is said to operate on an ergative/absolutive basis if in some way it responds to S and P as "the same" and A differently. For example, as mentioned earlier, noun–verb incorporation in many languages, including English, might be said to operate on an ergative/absolutive basis because S and P can be incorporated but A less easily:

(45)   a.   bird-chirping   incorporation of S
       b.   fox-hunting   incorporation of P
       c.   *doctor-recommending   incorporation of A

This might be considered to be a case of **syntactic ergativity** in English. Of course, noun–verb incorporation is a very marginal syntactic process in English, but there are a few languages in the world for which processes that are more central to the morphosyntax do seem to operate on an ergative/absolutive basis.

In order to understand what it means for a syntactic process to respond to S and P as "the same," it may be helpful to illustrate some processes in some familiar languages that respond to S and A as the same. "Complement subject omission" is a process that is sensitive to S and A as a category in all languages investigated to date. For example, in English one may say:

(46)   a.   Bob wants *to leave*.   intransitive complement
       b.   Bob wants *to kiss Aileron*. transitive complement

(47)   a.   Bob wants *Aileron to leave*.   intransitive complement
       b.   Bob wants *Aileron to kiss him*.   transitive complement

In 46a the S argument of the intransitive complement clause (see section 11.2) *X leave* is understood to be the same as the subject of *want*. In 46b the A of the transitive complement clause *X kiss Aileron* is also understood to be the same as the subject of *want*. Under these conditions, the S or the A of the complement clause may be omitted in English. In 47a and b, however, the subject of each complement clause is different from the subject of *want*, therefore the subject of the complement clause cannot be omitted. The important fact is that the *object* of 47b cannot be omitted either:

(48)   *Bob wants Aileron to kiss.   "Bob$_i$ wants Aileron to kiss Bob$_i$."

By allowing omission of S and A arguments of the complement clause when coreferential with an argument (for the verb *want* it is the subject) of the matrix clause, but not allowing omission of P arguments under the same conditions, this syntactic process treats S and A alike and P differently. Therefore it manifests a nominative/accusative system.

Is it possible for a language to have a similar process that is sensitive to the ergative/absolutive distinction? Certainly, it is logically possible, but to date no clear examples have been documented. In order to illustrate such a system, we will have to call the process "complement argument omission" so as not to prejudice the issue toward the familiar subject-based systems. If complement argument omission in English were sensitive to the ergative/absolutive distinction, 49a and b would be grammatical, but 49c would be ungrammatical:

(49)   *Hypothetical data based on English*
    a. Bob wants to leave.   "Bob$_i$ wants Bob$_i$ to leave."
    b. Bob wants Aileron to kiss. "Bob$_i$ wants Aileron to kiss Bob$_i$."
    c. *Bob wants to kiss Aileron. "Bob$_i$ wants Bob$_i$ to kiss Aileron."

To date no languages have been documented that exhibit such a system.

However, some syntactic processes may manifest a nominative/accusative system in some languages and an ergative/absolutive system in others. For example, Dyirbal (Australia) is a language in which the syntactic processes of relativization and clause coordination are sensitive to the ergative/absolutive distinction (Dixon 1994, ch. 6).The following is a summary of Dixon's discussion of relativization in Dyirbal.

Examples 50 and 51 illustrate simple intransitive and transitive clauses. The form *ŋuma* "father" is in the absolutive case, as indicated by the fact that it takes no case marker (S in example 50 and P in example 51), while *-ŋgu* marks the ergative case on *yabu* "mother" in (51):

(50)   ŋuma-0   banaga-n^{y}u   (ABS = S)
          father-ABS return-NONFUT
          "Father returned."

(51) ŋuma-0   yabu-ŋgu   bura-n   (ABS = P)
      father-ABS mother-ERG see-NONFUT
      "Mother saw father."

In Dyirbal, only absolutive arguments can undergo relativization (see section 11.5 on relative clauses). That is, only an absolutive argument can be the relativized NP within a relative clause. This is illustrated for intransitive relative clauses in 52 and 53, and transitive relative clauses in 54. In all of these examples the relative clause appears in brackets.

In 52 the head of the relative clause (RC) is "father," and this NP is omitted ("gapped") from the relative clause itself (indicated by X). The "zero" absolutive case marker that appears on the head and the clause itself refers to the role of "father" in the main clause. In this example, however, the role of "father" in the relative clause also happens to be absolutive:

(52) ŋuma-0 [X   banaga-ŋu-]-0 yabu-ŋgu   bura-n
      father-ABS (father) return-REL-ABS mother-ERG see-NONFUT
      "Mother saw father who was returning."

In 53 the head of the intransitive RC is *yabu* "mother." This too is then omitted from the relative clause. In this example, however, the role of "mother" is different in the relative clause than in the main clause. Since the relative clause is intransitive, the role of its only argument must be absolutive. But the role of the complex noun phrase that is modified by the relative clause is ergative with respect to the main clause verb "see:"

(53) ŋuma-0   yabu-ŋgu [X   banaga-ŋu-]-rru bura-n
      father-ABS mother-ERG (mother) return-REL-ERG see-NONFUT
      "Mother, who was returning, saw father."

In example 54 the head of the transitive relative clause is *yabu* "mother." *Yabu* is also missing from the relative clause itself. However, this example is unacceptable because *yabu* is the *ergative* nominal in the relative clause, i.e., she is the one who does the seeing:

(54) *yabu-0   [ŋuma-0   X   bura-ŋu]-0 banaga-nʸu
      mother-ABS father-ABS (mother) see-REL-ABS return-NONFUT
      ("Mother, who saw father, was returning.")

In order to say something like "Mother, who saw father, was returning" in Dyirbal, a special intransitive construction called an **antipassive** (see section 8.2.5) must be employed in the relative clause. This construction changes the case of "mother" to absolutive, thus rendering it eligible to be relativized. This restriction that relativization apply only to absolutive nominals occurs in several other Australian languages as well as other languages that have an absolutive case. Languages that do not have a morphologically defined absolutive case do not have this restriction.

Another syntactic process that is sensitive to the ergative/absolutive distinction in some languages is "conjunction reduction." This is the process whereby one element of a conjoined clause can be omitted when coreferential to an element in the previous clause. For example, in English, an argument of the second of a conjoined pair of clauses can be omitted when it is coreferential with an element of the first clause:

(55)   a. George greeted Barbara and coughed.
        b. George grabbed Barbara and slapped him.

In 55a, we understand that George is the person who coughed. If we want to specify that Barbara coughed, we must mention her explicitly:

(56)   George greeted Barbara and she coughed.

With no further specification, 55a must be interpreted such that George, and not Barbara, coughed. In 55b we again understand that George is the omitted element of the second of the conjoined pair of clauses and *him* refers to an unnamed third participant. Even though it would be pragmatically quite plausible for someone named Barbara to slap someone who might grab her, it is virtually impossible to infer from this clause that Barbara is the subject and George the object of the second conjoined clause. Since the omitted element, *George*, is the S (55a) or the A (55b) argument, and cannot be the P argument, we can say that conjunction reduction in English is sensitive to the nominative/accusative distinction.

Consistent with its morphological and syntactic ergative character, Dyirbal is a language in which the "pivot" (in Dixon's terminology) for conjunction reduction is the absolutive nominal (1994: 160–69). The same is true in Yup'ik, another morphologically ergative language:

(57)   Tom-am Doris-aq cinga-llru-a   tua-llu quyi-llru-u-q.
        Tom-ERG Doris-ABS greet-PAST-3 > 3 then-and cough-PAST-INTR-3
        "Tom greeted Doris and (she) coughed."

Table 7.5 Syntactic processes sensitive to the ergative/absolutive system, the nominative/accusative system or neither in the surveyed languages

	NOM/ACC	ERG/ABS	Neither
Complement-argument omission	x		
Reflexivization	x	x	
Relativization	x	x	
Conjunction reduction	x	x	x

In this example the second clause is only specified for a third person singular subject. Nevertheless, the only possible understanding is that Doris is the one who coughed. This must be because Doris in the first conjunct is in the absolutive case. Thus we can say that conjunction reduction in Yup'ik is sensitive to the category absolutive.

In summary, certain syntactic processes (such as complement argument omission) appear to be universally sensitive to the nominative/accusative distinction. Other syntactic processes are sensitive to the ergative/absolutive distinction in some languages, and the nominative/accusative distinction in others. Still other processes that respond to subject and object arguments are not sensitive to either of the major distinctions. There are apparently no processes that are universally sensitive to the ergative/absolutive distinction.[9] Table 7.5 illustrates this pattern.

7.5   Summary

Figure 7.3 summarizes the definitions of the terms S, A, P, nominative, accusative, ergative, and absolutive as we have presented them in this chapter.

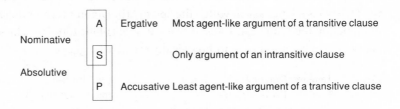

Figure 7.3 Semantico-syntactic roles (Comrie 1978a)

Languages can manifest a nominative/accusative or an ergative/absolutive system in any one or more of the following areas of the morphosyntax:

1 case marking of full noun phrases;
2 pronominals;
3 person marking on verbs (agreement or anaphoric clitics);
4 constituent order;
5 syntactic processes (complement subject omission, reflexivization, conjunction reduction, relativizability etc.).

If a language consistently manifests an ergative/absolutive system in case marking of full noun phrases, it is likely to be called an "ergative language." Mayan languages do not have case marking of full noun phrases, yet they are widely considered to be "ergative" because their person-marking systems are solidly organized on an ergative/absolutive basis. Such "ergative" languages always (as attested to date) manifest a nominative/accusative system in one or more of the other areas mentioned above. Therefore "ergative" vs. "non-ergative" is not a holistic typology that can necessarily be applied to whole languages; rather, it can only be applied to certain systems within languages. Nevertheless, the fact that some syntactic processes can be sensitive to the ergative/absolutive distinction, e.g., relativization in Dyirbal, conjunction reduction in Yup'ik, illustrates that ergativity need not necessarily be merely a surface morphological phenomenon.

?

Exemplify some simple intransitive, transitive, and ditransitive clauses. Three-argument clauses may not unequivocally exist.
What are the grammatical relations of this language? Give morphosyntactic evidence for each one that you propose.

(a) Subject?
(b) Ergative?
(c) Absolutive?
(d) Direct object?
(e) Indirect object?

There are basically four possible sources of evidence for grammatical relations:

(a) morphological case on NPs;
(b) person marking on verbs;
(c) constituent order;
(d) some pragmatic hierarchy.

Is the system of grammatical relations in basic (affirmative, declarative) clauses organized according to a nominative/accusative, ergative/absolutive, tripartite, or some other system?
Is there a split system for organizing grammatical relations? If so, what determines the split?

(a) Is there split intransitivity? If so, what semantic or discourse/pragmatic factor conditions the split?

(b) Does the system for pronouns and/or person marking on verbs operate on the same basis as that of full NPs?

(c) Are there different grammatical-relation systems depending on the clause type (e.g., main vs. dependent clauses, affirmative vs. negative clauses)?

(d) Are there different grammatical-relation assignment systems depending on the tense and/or aspect of the clause?

(e) Are there any syntactic processes (e.g., conjunction reduction, relativization) that operate on an ergative/absolutive basis?

Additional reading: Dixon (1994), Plank (1979, 1984).

8 Voice and valence adjusting operations

Every language has operations that adjust the relationship between semantic roles and grammatical relations in clauses. Such devices are sometimes referred to as alternative **voices**. For example, the passive operation in English when applied to most transitive verbs places the PATIENT in the subject role and the AGENT in an oblique role. The more normal arrangement for transitive verbs is for the AGENT to bear the subject relation and the PATIENT the object relation:

(1) a. *Active*
         Orna baked these cookies.   AGENT = subject
                                            PATIENT = object

     b. *Passive*
         These cookies were baked by Orna. PATIENT = subject
                                            AGENT = oblique

In this chapter we will discuss a range of structures that adjust the relationship between grammatical relations and semantic roles in terms of **valence**. Not all of these would be considered in traditional grammar under the heading of "voice," but because of their functional similarity and because many languages treat them in structurally comparable ways, it is often convenient to group some or all of these operations together in a single chapter of a grammar or grammar sketch.

Valence can be thought of as a semantic notion, a syntactic notion, or a combination of the two. **Semantic valence** refers to the number of participants that must be "on stage" (see section 0.2.3) in the scene expressed by the verb. For example, the verb *eat* in English has a semantic valence of two, since for any given event of eating there must be at least an

169

eater and an eaten thing. In terms of predicate calculus, the concept EAT is a relation between two variables, x and y, where x is a thing that eats and y is a thing that undergoes eating. This semantic relationship would be represented in predicate calculus notation as EAT(x, y) (see below).

Grammatical valence (or **syntactic valence**) refers to the number of arguments present in any given clause. A syntactic **argument** of a verb is a nominal element (including possibly zero, if this is a referential device in the language) that bears a grammatical relation to the verb (see chapter 7). So, for example, a given instance of the verb *eat* in English may have a syntactic valence of one or two. In a sentence like *Have you eaten yet?* there is no direct object, so the only argument of the verb is the eater. Similarly, in *She ate away at the bone* there is only one argument of the verb. *Bone* does not bear a grammatical relation to the verb. When we talk about "valence adjusting operations," we mean morphosyntactic operations that adjust the grammatical valence of a clause.

There is an important difference between the omission of a verbal argument in a sentence like *John already ate* and a zero pronoun as in *John came in and 0 sat down*. Object omission is a valence adjusting operation, whereas zero pronominalization is not. In the first, the lack of a direct object is due to the unimportance of the identity of the eaten thing. This claim is easily demonstrated by observation of English speakers in action: in the overwhelming majority of instances when a verb with a semantic valence of two occurs with no reference to the second argument, the situation is one in which the identity of the item that fills that second argument role has not been established and need not be established in order for the speaker to achieve his/her communicative goal. On the other hand, the "zero pronoun" in the example *John came in and 0 sat down* functions in exactly the opposite kind of situation, namely when the identity of the referent is so well and recently established that confusion with some other entity is impossible. One would hardly ask "Who sat down?," or even entertain the possibility that it was anyone other than "John" after someone utters the above sentence. On the other hand, one could very naturally ask "What did he eat?" after someone says *John already ate*.

In many languages zero pronominalization (or zero anaphora) is much more prevalent than it is in English. In such languages (sometimes called **pro-drop** languages) it may be difficult to distinguish constructions with reduced syntactic valence from those with zero pronouns. In the extreme case of languages with no morphological means of expressing grammatical relations, and few restrictions on zero anaphora, the only way to decide is to examine the discourse context. But then, for such languages (e.g., the Chinese languages, Thai), it is largely a moot point whether a particular construction constitutes reduced valence or not. The concept of syntactic valence is valuable insofar as it leads to an understanding of alternative arrangements of grammatical relations (e.g., alternative case-marking patterns, verbal affixation, or constituent order). If the language provides few such alternatives, then syntactic valence is not much of an issue for the descriptive linguist.

The notion of valence is closely aligned with the traditional idea of **transitivity**, i.e., a **transitive** verb is one that describes a relation between two participants such that one of the participants acts toward or upon the other. An **intransitive** verb is one that describes a property, state, or situation involving only one participant. Sometimes intransitive verbs, e.g., *run* in *I run*, are called "univalent," i.e., they have a semantic valence of one. Similarly, transitive verbs such as *kill* in *He killed a bear* are called "divalent." Trivalent verbs are those that have three core participants, e.g., *give* in "He gave Mary a book." Sometimes such verbs are perhaps confusingly called "bitransitive." Although recent studies (principally Hopper and Thompson 1980) have taken the term "transitivity" to mean the degree to which an event "carries over" from an active, volitional AGENT to a PATIENT, still it is common to find the term used in the traditional way.

Unfortunately, in the past linguists have not always been careful to distinguish semantic transitivity from grammatical transitivity. So, for example, there are some who would say *eat* is always a transitive verb. These linguists use the term transitive in the sense we use the term "semantically transitive." Others would say *eat* is sometimes transitive and sometimes intransitive. These linguists are most likely referring to syntactic transitivity. Still others would say that there are two related verbs *eat* in the lexicon of English, one of which is transitive and the other intransitive.

As always, in this discussion we will consider semantic properties to be properties of the conceptual representation of things and events in the message world, and syntactic properties to be properties of linguistic elements in sentences. From this perspective, the semantic valence of a verb, V, refers to the number of necessary *participants* in the scene expressed by V. Syntactic valence, then, is the number of verbal *arguments* in a clause in which V is the main predicator. Languages typically have various ways of adjusting, i.e., increasing, decreasing, or rearranging the syntactic valence of clauses. The semantic/pragmatic (i.e., conceptual) effect of increasing syntactic valence can be characterized most generally as upgrading a peripheral participant to center stage, whereas the effect of decreasing valence is to downplay a normally center-stage participant to peripheral status, or eliminating it from the scene altogether. Furthermore, the participants brought onto or taken off center stage can be **controllers**, i.e., agents or agent-like participants, **affected** or patient-like participants or they may be recipients, instruments, or benefactees. Thus we can identify a typology of valence adjusting operations as follows:

Valence increasing devices

Those that add a controlling participant:	causatives
Those that upgrade a peripheral participant:	applicatives[1]
	possessor raising

Valence decreasing devices

Those that "merge" controlling and affected participants:	reflexives
	reciprocals
	middles
Those that downplay a controlling participant:	subject omission
	passives
	inverses[2]
Those that downplay an affected participant:	object omission
	antipassives
	object demotion
	object incorporation

Sections 8.1 and 8.2 systematically describe and exemplify valence adjusting operations according to this typology.

Valence adjusting operators are very common in verbal morphology. Ninety percent of the languages investigated by Bybee (1985) have morphological manifestation of valence marked on the verb. This is the most common category of verbal morphology, even surpassing tense, aspect, and subject agreement. In 84 percent of the languages, valence is a derivational operation, while in 6 percent it is inflectional. So, while tense, aspect, and subject agreement are more common *inflectional* operations, valence is more common overall.

As derivational operators, valence adjusting morphemes often appear in different "areas" of the verbal word or verb phrase from the tense/aspect/mode (TAM) operators (see section 9.3). For example, in Panare TAM operators are exclusively suffixal, but valence decreasing operators are prefixal:

(2)   wë-s-amaika-yaj   chu
         1-DETRANS-put/store-PAST 1SG
         "I sat down."

In this sentence *amaika* is a semantically transitive root meaning "to put," "to store," or "to keep" something. The derivational prefix *s-* changes this root into an intransitive stem that means "to sit." All tense, aspect, and mode operators are suffixal, as illustrated here with the past tense operator *-yaj*.

In Yagua, another language in which TAM morphology is suffixal, valence increasing and decreasing operators are also suffixal. However, the valence adjusting suffixes are consistently closer to the verb root than the TAM suffixes:

(3)   sa-suuta-*táni*-ñúú-yanu-níí-ra
         3-wash-CAUS-CONT-PAST3-3-INAN
         "He made him wash it long ago."

In this example the suffix *-tániy* is the morphological causative operator (see section 8.1.1). It and a few other morphological valence adjusting operators always appear closer to the verb root than do the inflectional operators.

Valence adjusting operators tend to derive from free verb roots that, at an earlier stage of the language, formed analytic constructions. Occasionally, however, valence adjusting operators derive from inflectional operators such as participant reference forms (pronouns or anaphoric clitics). Morphological reflexives are one example of valence adjusting operators that often are best categorized as inflectional (i.e., languages often have a reflexive operator that participates in the verbal paradigm for person and number – see section 8.2.1). Furthermore, there is a distinct tendency for passive voice and perfect aspect markers to be related synchronically and/or etymologically (see section 9.3).

8.0   Valence and predicate calculus

It may be useful to think of valence in terms of **predicate calculus**. At various points in the discussion of valence increasing and decreasing operations, concepts and notation from predicate calculus will be employed. Also, it is common to find this notation used in the linguistic literature. It is a good idea for anyone involved in linguistic analysis to be comfortable with the notational system and terminology of predicate calculus. The following are definitions of a few important terms:

> **Term** designation for a thing, as opposed to a property of things or a relation between things (see **variable** and **constant** below).
>
> **Variable** a term that has no specific reference, e.g., "x," "y," etc.
>
> **Constant** a term that does have specific reference in the message world, e.g., *Yankee stadium, Socrates, Montezuma, the unicorn in my garden, the number 3*, etc.
>
> **Argument** a place within a predicate to be filled by a term or a proposition.
>
> **Predicate/function** a property that can be applied to a term or a relation between terms, e.g., "be human," "be mortal," "die," "eat," "laugh," etc.
>
> **Propositional function** a predicate applied to a variable or set of variables, e.g., "x is human," "some unspecified thing ate some unspecified thing," "some unspecified person laughed," etc.
>
> **Proposition** a predicate applied to a constant or set of constants, e.g., "Socrates is human," "Montezuma laughed," "Barbara kissed George," etc.

$f(x)$ is pronounced "a function of x." This notation refers to some property or activity that might hold true for the variable x. For example $f(x)$ = RED is a way of expressing the idea that "x is red," while $f(x)$ = LAUGH would express the idea that "x laughs." Linguists commonly abbreviate this predicate calculus notation by substituting the property or activity directly for the f, e.g., RED(x) and LAUGH(x).

LAUGH(Montezuma) is a proposition. It is one possible **instantiation** of the propositional function LAUGH(x). *Montezuma laughed* is one possible English instantiation of the proposition LAUGH(Montezuma).

So far we have been concerned with one-place functions. Often functions have more than one argument. $f(x, y)$ is pronounced "a function from x to y." Sometimes this can be restated as "a relation between x and y." EAT(x, y) is one possible relation between two entities x and y. By convention we normally express the initiating argument first. We will call this convention the **linearity convention**. So EAT(x, y) can be thought of as referring to the relationship of "eating" that holds between some as yet unspecified eater (x) and some as yet unspecified eaten thing (y). EAT(Cortez, possum) is one proposition that instantiates the propositional function EAT(x, y). *Cortez ate possum* is one English instantiation of the proposition EAT(Cortez, possum). *The possum ate Cortez* is *not* an instantiation of this proposition because of the linearity convention.

Propositions can also be arguments of functions. This is why argument and term are not the same thing. Capital letters (P, Q, R, etc.) are usually used as abbreviations for propositions. These can fill argument slots in other propositional functions, e.g., if P = LAUGH(Montezuma), then TRUE(P) = TRUE(LAUGH(Montezuma)) = the English expression *It is true that Montezuma laughed.*

Usually English words in capital letters designate semantic predicates, while words in lower case indicate lexemes in actual languages. This distinction is meant to distinguish between concepts (in capital letters) that are independent of linguistic expression, and the actual expressions in languages. One way of saying this is that English is the **meta-language** used to represent the semantic notions that are expressed by sentences in the actual language being described. This, admittedly, can be confusing, especially when the actual language and the meta-language are the same. Also, when the two are different, care must be taken not to bias one's analysis of the semantics of an expression in the actual language by superimposing the semantics of the meta-language on it. This is an inherent difficulty with predicate calculus-based approaches to semantics.

The following illustrates a two-place proposition filling an argument slot of another propositional function:

> P = KISS(x, y) = Xavier kisses Yolanda.
> P' = WANT(x, P) = Xavier wants to kiss Yolanda.
> Alternatively: WANT(Xavier, (KISS(Xavier, Yolanda)))

This notation may be useful in conceptualizing the various valence adjusting devices discussed in the following sections.

8.1   Valence increasing operations

8.1.1   Causatives

Linguists and philosophers have always been interested in causation. Causative constructions (or **causatives**) are the linguistic instantiations of the conceptual notion of causation. Causatives can be divided into three types: lexical, morphological, and periphrastic/analytic. A morphological causative is one kind of "valence increasing" operation.

> *Definition*: a causative is a linguistic expression that contains in semantic/logical structure a predicate of cause, one argument of which is a predicate expressing an effect.

> A causative construction can be symbolized as:
> CAUSE(x, P) = x causes P

One possible English instantiation of this predicate calculus statement is the following:

> CAUSE(Montezuma, EAT(Cortez, possum)) = Montezuma caused Cortez to eat possum.

The definitions of the predicates in a causative construction are:

> **Predicate of cause** the predicate that contains the notion of causation, e.g., CAUSE(x, P). Sometimes the predicate of cause is referred to as a **matrix** predicate (or matrix clause) because the predicate of effect is embedded within the predicate of cause (see section 11.2).
> **Predicate of effect** the predicate that expresses the effect of the causative situation, e.g., EAT(Cortez, possum). Sometimes it is said that the predicate of effect is **embedded** in the predicate of cause.

The definitions of the core arguments of a causative construction are:

> **Causee** AGENT of the caused event. Sometimes the causee is referred to as the **coerced endpoint** (Croft 1990: 241).
> **Causer** AGENT of the predicate of cause and so normally also of the causative situation. Sometimes the causer is referred to as the **agent of cause**.

Causative constructions can be formed on the basis of intransitive or transitive caused events. Causative predicates always involve one more argument than the caused predicate. Therefore if the caused event is intransitive, the causative is transitive. If the caused event is transitive, the causative is bitransitive, etc. For example:

> *Intransitive caused event*
> Cortez made [Montezuma laugh].
>   1   2

Transitive caused event

Montezuma made [Cortez eat possum].
    1   2   3

Other concepts that add one participant to a scene are also sometimes encoded by a valence increasing operation. Sometimes these operations are identical to the causative operation or operations. For example:

Believe:	Montezuma believes Cortez ate	possum. BELIEVE(m, P)	
Say:	Montezuma says	Cortez ate	possum. SAY(m, P)

Want:	Montezuma wants	Cortez to eat possum. WANT(m, P)
Ask:	Montezuma asked	Cortez to eat possum. ASK(m, P)
Permission:	Montezuma let	Cortez eat possum. LET(m, P)
(failure to prevent)		

The last three semantic notions often employ *exactly the same* morphosyntax as "pure" causatives, especially when they are expressed morphologically (see below).

Lexical causatives. Most, if not all, languages have some lexical causatives.
There are at least three subtypes of what we will term lexical causatives.
The unifying factor behind all of these types is the fact that in each case the
notion of cause is wrapped up in the lexical meaning of the verb itself. It is
not expressed by any additional operator. The three types are:

1 *No change in verb*
   Non-causative: *The vase broke.*
   Causative: *MacBeth broke the vase* (i.e., MacBeth caused the vase to
   break).
2 *Some idiosyncratic change in verb*
   Non-causative: *The tree fell.* (verb = "to fall")
   Causative: *Bunyan felled the tree.* (verb = "to fell")
3 *Different verb*
   Non-causative: *Stephanie ate beans.*
   Causative: *Gilligan fed Stephanie beans.*
   Non-causative: *Lucretia died.*
   Causative: *Gloucester killed Lucretia.*
   see/show, etc.

Morphological causatives. Morphological causatives involve a productive
change in the form of the verb. The verb *to fell* in English does not qualify

as a morphological causative because it is not derived by a rule that can be applied to many other verbs in the language. The only other candidate is *lay* [ley] as a causative of *lie* [lay]. If this *a* ɸ *e* stem change were at all productive, then this could be considered a morphological causative.

Turkish (Altaic) has two very productive morphological causatives. The suffix *-dIr* (the vowel varies depending on the context) can be applied to virtually any intransitive verb to form a causative of that verb (Comrie 1989):

(4) a. Hasan öl-dü
     H.   die-PAST
     "Hasan died." (intransitive, non-causative)

     b. Ali Hasan-t   öl-*dür*-dü
         A. H.   -ACC die-CAUS-PAST
         "Ali killed Hasan." (causative of intransitive verb)

To form a causative of a transitive verb, the suffix *-t* is used:

(5) a. Müdür mektub-ü imzala-dı
         director letter-ACC sign-PAST
         "The director signed the letter." (transitive, non-causative)

     b. Dišçi   mektub-ü müdür-e   imzala-*t*-tI
         dentist letter-ACC director-DAT sign-CAUS-PAST
         "The dentist made the director sign the letter."

Most morphological causatives express at least causation and permission. Georgian exhibits one such construction (from Comrie 1978a: 164):

(6) Mama shvil-s ceril-s   a-cer-*ineb*-s.
     father son-DAT letter-ACC PREF-write-CAUS-3SG
     "Father makes/helps/lets his son write the letter."

Many morphological causatives are restricted to use with intransitive stems (like Turkish *-dür* above). The following examples from Yup'ik Eskimo illustrate a typical range of functions often associated with morphological causative operators that are restricted to intransitive roots (Reed, *et al*. 1977: 177):

Root			*Stem*	
tuqu-	"die"		tuqute-	"kill"
tai-	"come"		taite-	"bring"

uita-	"stay"	uitate-	"let stay/leave alone"
tatame-	"be startled"	tamate-	"startle"
ane-	"go out"	ante-	"put outside"
itr-	"go in"	iterte-	"put in/insert"
atrar-	"go down"	atrarte-	"take down"
mayur-	"go up"	mayurte-	"put up"

However, Yup'ik also has other causative operators that function with transitive or intransitive roots:

(7)   *Intransitive root (go up)*
Qetunra-ni   tage-*vkar*-aa.
SON-ABS:POSS go:up-CAUS-3SG > 3SG
"He makes/lets his own son go up."

(8)   *Transitive root (eat)*
Arnam   irnia-mi-nun   neqerrlu-ut   nere-*vkar*-ai.
woman-ERG child-POSS-OBL dryfish-ABS:PL eat-CAUS-3SG > 3PL
"The woman makes/lets her child eat the dryfish."

(9)   *Intransitive root (go)*
Ayag-*cess*-gu.
go-CAUS-IMP:SG > 3SG
"Make/let him go."

(10)   *Transitive root (dry)*
Nukalpia-m   aana-mi-nun   kenir-*cet*-aa   kemek.
young:man-ERG mother-PASS-OBL dry-CAUS-3SG > 3SG meat:ABS
"The young man made/let his own mother dry the meat."

Quechua uses the same morphological causative for both intransitive (ex. 11b) and transitive (12b) stems. However, even in Quechua it is more common to use a periphrastic causative when the caused event is transitive:

(11)   *Intransitive root (sleep)*
a. noqa puñu-:
1SG   sleep-1SG
"I sleep." (non-causative)

b. noqa-ta puñu-*chi*-ma-n
1SG-ACC sleep-CAUS-1SG-3SG
"It makes me sleep."

(12)   *Transitive root (hit)*

   a. qam noqa-ta maqa-ma-nki
      2SG 1SG-ACC hit-1SG-2SG
      "You hit me." (non-causative)

   b. pay qam-wan noqa-ta maqa-*chi*-ma-n
      3SG 2SG-COM 1SG-ACC hit-CAUS-1SG-3SG
      "He makes you hit me."

The above examples illustrate a very common pattern with morphological causatives of lexically transitive verbs: the causee goes into an oblique case. In Turkish and Georgian, this is the "dative," in Yup'ik it is the "terminalis" (a kind of directional locative, abbreviated simply as OBL) and in Quechua it is the "comitative." The P of the verb stem remains in the accusative or, in Yup'ik, the absolutive case. Another possibility is for the causative of a transitive verb to allow two accusatives. The following examples are from Sanskrit (Comrie 1974: 16):

(13)   a. Rama-m veda-m adhyapa-yate.
       Rama-ACC Veda-ACC learn-CAUS
       "He teaches Rama the Veda."

     b. Batu-m odana-m bhoja-yati
       boy-ACC food-ACC eat-CAUS
       "He makes the boy eat food."

The Panjabi morphological causative borders on being lexical because the rule that derives a causative verb from a non-causative is very hard to formulate explicitly (examples courtesy of Lynn Conver):

(14)   *Panjabi* (Indo-European)

   a. *Non-causative*: k'ad
       o-ne   k'aNa k'ad-a
       3SG-ERG food eat-PAST:MSG
       "He ate food."

   b. *Causative*: k'lay
       timi-ne   o-nu   k'aNa k'lay-a
       woman-ERG 3SG-DAT food eat:CAUS-PAST:MSG
       "The woman made him eat food."

   c. *Non-causative*: dore
       Ram dore-a
       Ram run-PAST:MSG
       "Ram ran."

d. *Causative*: dəray

munci-ne   Ram-nu dəray-a

teacher-ERG Ram-DAT run:CAUS-PAST:MSG

"The coach made Ram run."

Analytic causatives. Most causatives in English are analytic in that they involve a separate causative verb, e.g., *make, cause, force, compel*, etc.

(15)   He made me do it.

Gloucester caused Lucretia to die.

Melinda forced her hairdresser to relinquish his position.

Marie compelled Taroo to dance with her.

Analytic causatives are not normally considered to be valence increasing operations, even though semantically they can be interpreted as such. Rather, in most cases they consist of a matrix verb (expressing the notion of CAUSE) whose sentential complement refers to the caused event (see section 11.2 on matrix verbs and complements). We will continue to include analytic causatives in this section because of the interesting functional generalizations that can be made across the three causative types. In a grammar sketch it is not a bad idea to include all causative types in one section.

Now we will discuss the relationship between **structural integration** and **conceptual integration** between cause and effect. Conceptual integration refers to how integrated or "close" the cause and effect are in the message world. Structural integration refers to how integrated the element expressing the cause and the element expressing the effect are in the causative construction. Conceptual integration is commonly described in terms of the distinction between **direct** and **indirect causation**.

Direct causation is where the causer is directly, instantly, and probably physically responsible for the effect. For example, the verb *kill* in English is a lexical causative that expresses direct causation, whereas *cause to die* is an analytic causative that expresses indirect causation. A clause like *Jesse killed the gunfighter* is likely to describe a situation in which Jesse is portrayed as directly and physically responsible for the gunfighter's death. The clause *Jesse caused the gunfighter to die*, on the other hand, might describe a situation in which the act that resulted in the gunfighter's death is removed physically and/or temporally from the act of his dying, e.g., Jesse may have tampered with the gunfighter's gun, or distracted him during a gunfight.

The relationship between structural integration and conceptual integration between cause and effect is instantiated in at least three different ways in the known languages of the world (from Givón 1984).

1 *Structural distance*: the number of syllables, or segments, involved in the causative operation is iconically related to the amount of conceptual distance between the cause and the effect (Haiman 1983a).
2 *Finite vs. non-finite verb forms*: if cause and effect are the same in terms of tense/aspect/modality/evidentiality and/or location, one of the verbs can be non-finite (i.e., not marked for tense/aspect etc., see section 9.3).
3 *Morphological case of the causee*: if the causee retains a high degree of control over the caused event, it will appear in a case normally associated with AGENTS, e.g., the nominative or ergative case. If it retains little or no control (i.e., it is completely manipulated by the causer), it will appear in a case normally associated with patients, e.g., the accusative or absolutive case.

These three "coding principles of causatives" will be discussed and exemplified below.

Coding principle of causatives 1: structural distance. For languages that have more than one formal kind of causative the "smaller" one (i.e., the one in which cause and effect are most closely united formally) will be used for more direct causation, while the "larger" one (i.e., the one in which morphosyntactic size of the causative construction is greater) will be used for less direct causation.

This principle is illustrated by Haiman (1983a) in terms of an "iconicity pyramid." In this pyramid the pinnacle is the construction in which cause and effect are expressed by a single lexical form. This is what we would term a "lexical causative" (see above). Morphological and finally analytic causatives are found at lower levels of the pyramid. These are construction types in which the cause is increasingly more distant morphosyntactically from the effect. This increased morphosyntactic distance is correlated with greater conceptual distance.

(16)

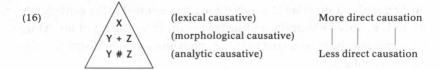

X	(lexical causative)	More direct causation
Y + Z	(morphological causative)	│ │ │
Y # Z	(analytic causative)	Less direct causation

Haiman's pyramid makes no claims as to the semantics of lexical vs. analytic causatives in different languages, but only within those languages that have more than one causative construction to express essentially the same idea. The following discussion, including the examples, is largely a summary of Haiman's important article.

Longer linguistic distance (according to Haiman's pyramid) is always correlated with greater conceptual distance. For this reason analytic causatives often "require" an animate causee. The greater conceptual distance implied by the longer analytic causatives signifies that the causer does not have direct physical control over the causee; rather, the causee retains some degree of control over the caused event. Such control is incongruous with an inanimate causee.

In English there is no grammatical constraint that the causee in an analytic causative be animate. However, if the causee is not animate (or for some other reason has no control over the caused event), the analytic causative sounds strange:

(17)   I caused the tree to fall.
            the chicken to die.
            the cup to rise to my lips.

All of these seem to imply magical powers because of the conceptual distance between cause and effect. This is not the case with corresponding lexical causatives.

(18)   I felled the tree.
         I killed the chicken.
         I raised the cup to my lips.

These imply a close connection between cause and effect, e.g., direct physical contact and complete control of the causer over the causee.

Japanese allows a morphological causative when the causee retains some control over the event (19a), but requires a lexical causative for inanimate causees (19b, c):

(19)   a. Taroo-wa Ryoko-o ori-*sase*-ta.
            T.-TOP   R.-ACC   descend-CAUS-PAST
            "Taroo made Ryoko come down."

         b. Taroo-wa nimotu-o   oros-ta.
            T.-TOP   baggage-ACC bring:down-PAST
            "Taroo brought the baggage down."

   c. *Taroo-wa nimotu-o   ori-*sase*-ta.

        T.-TOP   baggage-ACC descend-CAUS-PAST

Amharic illustrates this principle even within one type of causative. Amharic has two morphological causatives, one signaled by the prefix *a*- and the other by the prefix *as*-. The shorter of these is used for direct causation, while the longer one, *as*-, is always used for indirect causation:

(20)   a. Abbat lëgun sëga *a*-bälla

          father boy   meat CAUS-eat

          "The father fed the boy the meat." (direct physical control)

      b. Abbat lëgun sëga *as*-bälla

          father boy   meat CAUS-eat

          "The father forced the boy to eat the meat." (indirect control, e.g., by threat)

Korean illustrates this principle in morphological and analytic causatives:

(21)   a. ip-*hi*-ta   "to dress someone"

      b. ip-*key ha*-ta "persuade someone to dress"

(22)   a. ket-*I*-ta   "force to walk"

      b. ket-*key ha*-ta "enable to walk"

In each of these examples the first clause involves direct, physical action on the part of the causer, while the second clause involves more removed, less direct causation. These examples also illustrate that indirect causation often has additional semantic overtones, e.g., "enable," "permit," "persuade," "tell," etc.

Finally, Miztec also illustrates the principle that morphosyntactic distance correlates with conceptual distance in morphological and analytic causatives:

(23)   a. *s*-kée

          CAUS-eat(potential) (= put food in his mouth)

          "Feed him."

      b. *sá:à* hà nà kee

          CAUS NOM OPT eat   (= prepare food for him to eat)

          "Make him eat."

Coding principle of causatives 2: finite vs. non-finite verb forms. The more distant the cause from the effect in time or space, the more finite the verb that expresses the effect will be. For example, in Spanish direct causation is expressed via the verb *hacer,* "make/do/cause," and a non-finite verb form (24a). More indirect causation is expressed with a finite (though subjunctive) verb form (24b):

(24) a. Moctezuma hizo   *comer* pan   a   Cortez.
         M.   CAUS:3SG:PERF eat:INF bread DAT C.
         "Montezuma made Cortez eat bread."

      b. Moctezuma hizo   que Cortez *comiera*   pan.
         M.   CAUS:3SG:PERF that C.   eat:3SG:SUB bread
         "Montezuma made Cortez eat bread."

      c. Moctezuma se hizo comer pan.
         "Montezuma made himself eat bread."

      d. *Moctezuma se hizo que comiera pan.

In 24a the implication is that Montezuma directly and physically made Cortez eat bread, while 24b implies that Montezuma arranged for Cortez to eat bread, e.g., by killing all the cattle. In this case the distance in time and space between the cause (killing the cattle) and the effect (Cortez eating bread) is greater in 24b than in 24a. If the causer and the causee are identical, the finite verb form cannot be used for the effect (24d). In this case, identity of participants in the cause and the effect requires a non-finite verb form.

Coding principle of causatives 3: case of the causee. If the causee retains a high degree of control over the caused event, it will appear in a case normally associated with AGENTS, e.g., the nominative or ergative case. If it retains little or no control (i.e., it is completely manipulated by the causer), it will appear in a case normally associated with patients, e.g., the accusative or absolutive case. For example, when the causee retains some degree of freedom of action, it appears in the nominative case in English:

(25) a. I asked that he   leave.   (Request, causee retains right to say no.)
                      NOM

      b. I asked him to leave.   (Command, less likelihood that causee has the
               ACC   option to say no.)

c. I made him leave.   (No control retained by causee. Causee appears in
   ACC   accusative case, and complement lacks *to*. Effect
            very closely integrated to the predicate of cause.)

In Hungarian, the causee appears in the accusative case when the causee retains no control over the event (26), but in the instrumental case when it retains some control (27):

(26) En köhogtettem   a gyerek-<u>et</u>.
    I caused:to:cough the child-ACC
    "I made the child cough." (e.g., by slapping him/her on the back)

(27) En köhogtettem   a gyerek-<u>kel</u>.
    I caused:to:cough the child-INST
    "I got the child to cough." (e.g., by asking him/her to do so)

?

How are causatives formed in this language? There are basically three possible answers to this question:

(a) lexical   kill
(b) morphological   die + cause
(c) analytic/periphrastic cause to die

Give examples of both causatives of intransitive verbs (e.g., *He made Shin Jaa laugh*), and of transitive verbs (e.g., *He made Shin Jaa wash the dishes*). What happens to the causee in each type of causative?

Does the causative morphosyntax also serve other functions (e.g., permissive, applicative, benefactive, instrumental, etc.)?

Are there any other interesting or unusual facts about causatives in the language?

Further references: Comrie (1989, ch. 8), Givón (1984), Haiman (1983a).

8.1.2 Applicatives

Some languages have operations whereby a verb is marked for the semantic role of a direct object. Here we will refer to such operations as **applicatives**, though they are also called "advancements" or "promotions" to direct object. In most cases, an applicative can be insightfully described as a valence increasing operation that brings a peripheral participant onto center stage by making it into a direct object. The "new" direct object is sometimes referred to as the **applied** object. For verbs that already have one direct object, the applicative either results in a three-argument (ditransitive) verb, or the "original" direct object ceases to be expressed. In the latter case, the applicative cannot be considered a valence increasing device, since the original and the resulting verb have the same number of arguments; rather, the applicative simply ascribes a new, formerly peripheral, semantic role to the direct object.

Yagua has an applicative that does increase valence. The applicative suffix -*ta* indicates that a locative or instrumental participant is in direct object position:

(28) a. sa-duu   rá-viimú
          3SG-blow INAN-into
          "He blows into it." (valence = 1)

      b. sa-duu-*tá*-ra
          3SG-blow-TA-INAN:OBJ
          "He blows it." (valence = 2)

The same suffix -*ta* can be used with transitive verbs, in which case it increases valence from two to three:

(29) a. sį-įchití-rya   javanu quiichi-*tya*
          3SG-poke-INAN:OBJ meat   knife-INST
          "He poked the meat with the/a knife." (valence = 2)

      b. sį-įchití-*tya*-ra   quiichiy
          3SG-poke-TA-INAN:OBJ knife
          "He poked something with the knife." (valence = 3)

In 29a, the postposition that marks a nominal as having the semantic role of INSTRUMENT is the same form as the applicative verbal suffix (-*tya* and -*rya* are phonologically conditioned allomorphs of -*tá* and -*ra* respectively). In Yagua, transitive verbs that have the applicative suffix have all the grammatical properties of three-argument verbs, such as those meaning "give" or "send."

Kinyarwanda, a Bantu language of Rwanda (examples from Kimenyi 1980), has several applicative operators, depending on the precise role of the "applied" direct object:

(30) a. Umugóre a-ra-kor-*er*-a   umuhuungu igitabo.
          woman   she-PRES-read-BEN-ASP boy   book
          "The woman is reading the boy the book." (valence = 3,
          boy = BENEFACTIVE)

b. Umwáalimu y-oohere-jé-*ho*   ishuuri igitabo.
   teacher   he-send-ASP-LOC school book
   "The teacher sent the book to the school." (valence = 3, school = LOCATIVE)

In example 30a the suffix -*er* indicates that the first object after the verb has the semantic role of BENEFACTIVE. In example 30b, the suffix -*ho* indicates that the first object is a LOCATIVE. There are syntactic tests in Kinyarwanda that show that these elements really are syntactic direct objects of the verb (Kimenyi 1980). The verbal suffix indicates the semantic role of the object.

In Nomatsiguenga, a Pre-Andine Maipuran Arawakan language of the Eastern Peruvian foothills, a much more complicated system is found. In this language there are at least nine applicative suffixes that express a variety of semantic roles. Examples 31 and 32 show that direct objects of ordinary transitive verbs are referred to by verbal suffixes: -*ro* for feminine and -*ri* for masculine direct objects (all Nomatsiguenga examples are from Wise 1971):

(31)   Pablo i-niake-*ro* inato
       Paul   he-see-her mother
       "Paul saw mother."

(32)   Pablo i-pë-*ri*   Ariberito kireki
       Paul   he-give-him Albert   money
       "Paul gave Albert money."

Example 33b shows that there are two ways of expressing directional locatives (at least with the verb *areeka*, "arrive"): first, they can be expressed in a post-positional phrase (33a); second, they can be expressed as a direct object (33b). That *Siointi* is the direct object of 33b is evidenced by the fact that it appears with the agreement suffix -*ri*:

(33)   a. n-areeka Siointi-kë
           I-arrive S.   -LOC
           "I arrived at Shointi's."

       b. n-areeka-ri Siointi
           I-arrive-him S.
           "I arrived at Shointi's."

Since in 33b the verb *areeka* has a direct object, it is now grammatically transitive and we can say that its valence has increased. However, there is no special morphology on the verb to indicate this fact. For oblique elements of other semantic roles to advance to direct object status, applicative suffixes are needed. For example, in 34 the suffix *-te* indicates that the direct object has the semantic role of ablative (a location that is the goal of some locationally directed action).

(34)   LOCATIVE-1
         Pablo i-hoka-*te*-ta-be-ka-ri   Ariberito i-gotsirote
             he-throw-*toward*-E-FRUST-REFL-him Albert   his-knife
         "Paul threw his knife toward Albert."

That the form *Aribertito* is in fact the syntactic direct object of 34 is confirmed by the facts that (a) it occurs directly after the verb, and (b) it is preceded by the 3SG direct object enclitic *-ri*. The same arguments hold for the direct objects of verbs with the other applicative suffixes illustrated in 35–42:

(35)   LOCATIVE-2
         Pablo i-kenga-*mo*-ta-h-i-ri   Arberto
             he-narrate-*in:presence:of*-E-FRUST-REFL-him Albert
         "Paul narrated it in Albert's presence."

(36)   INSTRUMENT
         ora pi-nets-*an*-ti-ma-ri   hitatsia negativo
         that you-look:at-*INST*-FUT-FUT:REFL-him name   negative
         "Look at it (the sun during an eclipse) with that which is called a negative."

(37)   ASSOCIATIVE
         Juan i-komota-*ka*-ke-ri   Pablo otsegoha
             he-dam:stream-*ASSOC*-PAST-him Paul   river:branch
         "John dammed the river branch with Paul."

(38)   PURPOSE
     a. Pablo i-ata-*si*-ke-ri   Ariberito
             he-go-*PURP*-PAST-him Albert
         "Paul went with Albert in mind (e.g., to see him)."

     b. ni-ganta-*si*-t-ë-ri   hompiki
         I-send-*PURP*-E-TENSE-him pills
         "I sent him for pills."

(39)   REASON
     a. Pablo i-kisa-*biri*-ke-ri   Juan
             he-be:angry-*REASON*-PAST-him John
         "Paul was angry on account of John."

b. Pablo i-atage-*biri*-ke-ri   Juan
   he-go-REASON-PAST-him
   "John was the reason for Paul's going."

(40)   BENEFACTIVE
        Pablo i-pë-*ne*-ri   Ariberito tiapa   singi
        he-give-BEN-him Albert   chicken corn
        "Paul gave the chickens corn for Albert."

Nomatsiguenga and the other Campa languages probably have the most highly developed systems of morphologically distinct applicative operations on earth. There are two applicative suffixes that Wise (1971) analyzes as meaning "included" and "with respect to." These appear to indicate that the direct object has some unspecified relationship to the activity expressed in the verb:

(41)   *Included* (with reference to)
        a. Pablo i-samë-*ko*-ke-ro   i-gisere
           he-sleep-INC-PAST-it his-comb
           "Paul went to sleep with reference to his comb." (e.g., he was making it and dropped it)

        b. Pablo i-komoto-*ko*-ke-ri   pabati otsegoha
           he-dam:stream-INC-PAST-him father river:branch
           "Paul dammed the river branch with reference to father." (cf. 37 above)

(42)   *With reference to*
        a. Pablo i-pëna-*ben*-ta-h-i-ri   yaniri   kireki
           he-pay-WRT-E-FRUST-REFL-him howler:monkey money
           "Paul paid money for the howler monkey."

        b. pi-ngaki-*ben*-kima-ri   yaniri
           you-stay:awake-WRT-IMPER-him howler:monkey
           "Stay awake with reference to the howler monkey (e.g., because of him)."

In some languages the instrumental applicative can also be construed as a causative. For example, in Kinyarwanda, the causative and the applicative are the same morpheme, -*iiš*. The functional basis for this isomorphism is apparent in the following pair of examples (Kimenyi 1980: 164):

(43)   a. Umugabo a-ra-andik-*iiš*-a   umugabo íbárúwa.
           man   3SG-PRES-write-CAUS-ASP man   letter
           "The man is making the man write a letter."

b. Umugabo a-ra-andik-*iiš*-a   íkárámu íbárúwa.
    man   3SG-PRES-write-APL-ASP pen   letter
    "The man is writing a letter with a pen."

The only real difference between these two clauses is the animacy of the "causee." In both cases a causer acts on something or someone to accomplish some action. In 43a the thing he acts on is another human, whereas in 43b the thing he acts on is a pen. Other languages in which the same kind of isomorphism obtains are Yagua (see ex. 29 above), Malay, and Dyirbal (Croft 1990: 242). In many other languages the causative and instrumental applicatives are different morphemes. Nevertheless, the fact that they are often formally similar underscores the conceptual similarity between these apparently distinct functional types.

In Seko Padang, a Western Austronesian language, the suffix -*ing* has an applicative function when used with transitive verbs (44b), but a causative function when used with certain intransitive verbs (45b) (examples courtesy of Tom Laskowske):

(44)   a.   Yeni   mang-ala kin-anne:
            Jenny TRANS-get NOM-eat
            "Jenny is getting rice."

         b.   Yeni   mang-ala-*ing* kin-anne: adi-nna
            Jenny TRANS-get-APL NOM-eat   brother-3:POSS
            "Jenny is getting rice for her brother."

(45)   a.   jambu mi-rène'
            guava INTR-fall
            "Guava fell."

         b.   Matius   mar-rène'-*ing* jambu
            Matthew TRNS-fall-APL guava
            "Matthew dropped guava."

?

Are there any operations by which a participant which has a semantic role normally expressed in an "oblique" phrase can "advance" to direct object status?
What semantic roles are subject to these operations and how common are these constructions?

8.1.3   Dative shift

Many languages have two alternative morphosyntactic means of expressing a trivalent proposition. Trivalent propositions normally involve an AGENT, a PATIENT (usually an item conveyed from one person to another), and a RECIPIENT. Some English verbs that express trivalent propositions are *show*, *give*, and *send*. For each of these verbs the RECIPIENT (or EXPERIENCER in the case of *show*) occurs sometimes in the dative case, marked by the preposition *to*, and sometimes with no case marker. The construction in which the RECIPIENT does not take a preposition is termed a **dative shift** construction:

(46)   a. *Normal*
            Prudence gave her greatcoat to the curator.

        b. *Dative shift*
            Prudence gave the curator her greatcoat.

We consider dative shift to be a valence increasing operation because it is a means of bringing participants with peripheral semantic roles, e.g., RECIPIENT and BENEFACTIVE, onto "center stage" in addition to whatever participants may already be on stage. If there are other non-subject arguments in the clause, they acquire status as the "second object." In this position they may or may not retain morphosyntactic properties of direct objects.

There are two rather subtle differences between applicative and dative-shift constructions. These are: (1) applicatives involve some marking on the verb whereas dative-shift constructions do not; and (2) dative-shift constructions typically allow only RECIPIENTS and BENEFACTIVES to become direct objects whereas applicative constructions normally advance INSTRUMENTS and perhaps other obliques.

?
Is there a dative-shift construction?
What semantic roles can be "dative-shifted?"
Is dative shift obligatory?

8.1.4   Dative of interest

Some languages allow a participant that is associated with the event in some grammatically unspecified way to be referred to with a dative pronoun. Spanish is one well-known example:

(47)   Se   me quemó   la   cena.
        REFL 1SG burn:3SG:PAST DEF:FEM:SG dinner
        "Dinner burned on me." (valence = 2)

This clause might be translated "Dinner burned with respect to me" or "Dinner burned for me." Dative-of-interest constructions are distinct from applicatives and dative-shift constructions in that the argument that is added to the proposition is instantiated as a "dative" participant, i.e., as the third argument in a trivalent construction. With applicatives and dative-shift constructions, the additional argument appears as a direct object. With transitive verbs, the dative of interest can indicate that the participant referred to with a dative pronoun is the *possessor* of the direct object:

(48)   Le   cortó el   pelo.
        3DAT cut   the hair
        "She cut the hair (with respect to/on/for) him." (i.e., "She cut *his* hair.")

This last construction is sometimes called **possessor raising, possessor ascension**, or **external possession** (Haspelmath, to appear). However, all of these terms assume that the dative participant is at some deep level a syntactic possessor of the direct object, as in the English translation equivalent. But there is no particular reason to make this assumption for Spanish in light of the fact that Spanish has a fully productive "dative-of-interest" construction type. In fact, in most varieties of Spanish, it is possible, though less common, for the object in an example like 49 to remain possessed:

(49)   Me   cortó mi pelo.
        1DAT cut   my hair
        "She cut my hair (on/to/for me)."

Example 49 shows that the dative pronoun is not a "raised" possessor, since the possessor remains in place as part of the noun phrase *mi pelo*. The *me* in this example is just a "dative of interest" as in example 45. In other languages, however, there may be formal evidence that a grammatical "possessor" has been upgraded to status as a subject, direct object, or dative argument. Section 8.1.4 discusses more prototypical possessor raising constructions.

Chickasaw and Choctaw (Western Muskogean languages) have an unusual construction whereby a dative argument can optionally be "raised" to subject status. For example, 50a is a clause which contains a subject, marked by -*at* and a dative argument. The dative argument carries no case marker, but the verb takes a "III" prefix, which indicates that the un-casemarked noun is to be understood as a dative. In 50b, *hattak* "man" has been raised to subject status. This is evidenced by the fact that it appears initially in the clause (Chickasaw is an APV language), takes the -*at* subject case marker, and has all other properties of subjects (Munro 1984):

(50)   a.   Chihoow-*at* hattak im-oktani-tok
             God-SUB   man   III-appear-PAST
             "God appeared to the man."

       b.   Hattak-at Chihoow-*at* im-oktani-tok
             man-SUB God-SUB   III-appear-PAST
             "God appeared to the man."

What is uncommon about the construction in 50b is that it creates a "new" subject out of what would normally be a peripheral participant. Normally dative-of-interest constructions only advance peripheral participants to object status. However, in addition to these "double-subject" constructions, Chickasaw and Choctaw also allow more prototypical dative shift, dative of interest, and possessor raising constructions that raise a peripheral participant to object status. The possessor-raising constructions will be discussed in the following section.

8.1.5   "Possessor raising" or external possession

       In some languages possessor raising may in fact be a distinct process from dative of interest or other valence increasing devices in the language. For example, in Chickasaw and Choctaw, the possessor of the object of a clause can be "raised" to be the object. The verb then takes the dative prefix (glossed "III") discussed in the previous section:

Choctaw
(51)   a.   Naahollo i-tobi-ya   apa-li-tok   no possessor raising
             Anglo   III-bean-NS eat-1SG-PAST
             "I ate the white man's beans." ("white man's beans" = green peas)

       b.   Naahollo-ya tobi im-apa-li-tok   possessor raised
             Anglo-NS   bean III-eat-1SG-PAST
             "I ate the white man's beans."

(52) a. Tali i̱-hina-ya̱   ayska-li-tok   no possessor raising
          rock III-road-NS fix-1SG-PAST
          "I fixed the railroad track."

      b. Tali-ya̱   hina im-ayska-li-tok   possessor raised
          rock-NS road III-fix-1SG-PAST
          "I fixed the railroad track."

In 51a, *naahollo i̱tobiya̱* is a noun phrase meaning literally "white man's beans," with *naahollo* as the possessor, and the whole noun phrase marked with the non-subject suffix *-ya̱*. In 51b *nahollo* has been "raised" from its status as possessor of the object NP to being the object itself, as evidenced by the fact that it takes the *-ya̱* suffix. *Tobi*, "beans," in 51b is now without the III prefix, showing that it is no longer the head of a possessed noun phrase. The verb now takes the III prefix indicating that it has a "new" dative argument. If this were a dative-of-interest construction comparable to 47 above in Spanish, one would expect that it could be interpreted to mean "I ate beans for the white man." However, this meaning is not possible. The noun phrase "white man's beans" is an idiomatic expression that means "green peas," even when the possessor is raised to direct-object status, as in 51b. The fact that this meaning is still in force, even when it is no longer expressed by a possessed noun phrase, indicates that *nahollo* is still at some "deeper" level a possessor. Examples 52a and b are completely parallel to 51a and b but with the idiomatic expression "rock's road" meaning "railroad track." Example 52b could not conceivably mean "I fixed the road for the rock." Munro (1984) includes other arguments that show that possessor raising in Chickasaw and Choctaw must be distinct from a more generic "dative-of-interest" construction.

Maasai (a Nilotic language of Kenya and Tanzania) allows several kinds of possessor raising. The following examples illustrate a transitive clause with a possessed object (53a), and a corresponding clause in which the possessor of the object has been "raised" to object status (53b) (examples from Barshi and Payne 1996):

(53) a. N-é-ypid-óki   ɔltúŋání emúrt ây.
          CN-3-jump-DAT person neck my
          "A person jumped on my neck."

      b. N-áa-ypid-óki   ɔltúŋání emúrt.
          CN-3 > 1-jump-DAT person   neck
          "A person jumped on my neck."

The verb in 53a is marked with a prefix é- that indicates a third person acting on another third person participant. In 53b the prefix áa- indicates a third person acting on a first person. Also, the object noun phrase *emúrt* "neck" in 53b is not followed by the possessive pronoun *ây*. Thus a literal meaning for 53b might be "A person jumped on me the neck."

The following is an example of an intransitive verb with a possessed subject becoming a transitive verb with the possessor as the object:

(54)   áa-bʋak-ʌtá   ɔldía
        3 > 1-bark-PROG dog:NOM
        "My dog is barking."

In this example the inherently intransitive verb *bʋak*, "bark," takes the transitive prefix that indicates a third person acting on a first person argument. In other words, one might conceive of this clause as literally saying "The dog is barking me." However, the only possible actual meaning is "My dog is barking."

8.2   Valence decreasing operations

Languages can have morphological, lexical, and periphrastic/analytic means of reducing the valence of a verb. The most common morphological valence decreasing operations are reflexives, reciprocals, passives, and antipassives. These will be discussed in the following three subsections. Here we will introduce valence decreasing operations with an illustration from Panare, a Cariban language of Venezuela.

Cariban languages are famous for valence decreasing operations. In fact, in Panare most intransitive verbs in the lexicon are derived from transitives, though there are some semantically determined exceptions. Mayan languages also employ extensive detransitivization.

In Panare each transitive verb only occurs with a particular detransitivizing prefix. That is, no verb can sometimes occur with one detransitivizing prefix and at other times with another. This is not, however, a general characteristic of valence adjusting operations universally. Table 8.1 lists samples of typical Panare transitive verbs and their detransitivized counterparts grouped according to the detransitivizing prefix employed.

The meaning component contributed by the valence decreasing prefix varies from verb to verb, e.g., the conceptual difference between

Table 8.1 **Panare detransitivizing prefixes**

Prefix	Transitive		Detransitive	
ch-/s-	incha	"beware of"	chinchama	"think"/"fear"
	ipa	"feed"	chipa	"overeat"
	ireema	"feed"	chireema	"eat"
	irepa	"touch (tr.)"	chirepa	"touch (intr.)"
	amaika	"keep/put"	samaika	"sit"
	an	"take"	san	"ascend"
	ap-	"begin" (nominal O)	sap-	"begin" (clause complement)
	awa	"hit"	sawa	"hit oneself"
	-wachíka	"make sneeze"	s-wachíka	"sneeze"
	awant-	"endure X"	sawant-	"be sick"/"die"
	e'ka'	"bring"	se'ka'	"come"
	ï'nampa	"adorn X"	sï'nampa	"adorn self"
	ïnampa	"fight X"	sïnampa	"fight each other"
	m-nka	"finish X"	s-m-nka	"arrive"/"finish"
	o'koma	"raise"	so'koma	"rise"
	o'nama	"move X"	so'nama	"move self"
	o'renka	"dampen"	so'renka	"dampen self"
	ono	"mock"	sono	"laugh"
	uka'	"kill"	suka'	"die"
	ukinka	"paint X"	sukinka	"paint self"
	uru	"gripe at"	suru	"worry"
	etc.			
t-	-ka	"fatten"	t-ka	"be fat"
	ani'	"fill X"	taani'	"fill" (as a river rising)
	aru'ma	"cause to swing"	taru'ma	"swing"
	-sa	"straighten"	t-sa	"be straight"
	aweika	"wake X"	saweika	"awaken"
	ayapa	"make shout"	tayapa	"shout"/"make noise"
	ïn	"charge"	tïn	"cost"
	ïnaan	"hide X"	tïnaan	"hide self"
	iñan	"raise"	tiñan	"rise"
	u'	"give (tr.)"	tu'	"give (intr.)"
w-	marapa	"chase"	wï'marapa	"escape"/"become lost"
	muku	"close X"	wumuku	"close" (intr.)
	utu'	"break X"	wutu'	"break" (intr.)

"beware of" and "think" is very distinct from the conceptual difference between "to feed" and "to eat." In the first pair the subject of both verbs is the primary actor, i.e., the one that experiences a particular mental state. In the second, on the other hand, the subject of the derived intransitive verb is the participant that eats something, whereas the subject of the basic transitive verb is the one that causes someone else to eat. The object of the transitive verb is the participant that engages in eating.

Though there do seem to be some general semantic principles that underlie these detransitivizing prefixes (e.g., reflexive for *ch-/s-*, "anti-causative" for *t-*), there are numerous exceptions and none of the prefixes is fully productive. The only semantic commonality among them is that they all reduce the *valence* of the verb by one argument. In the following subsections we will discuss several different kinds of valence decreasing operations.

8.2.1   Reflexives and reciprocals

A prototypical **reflexive** construction is one in which subject and object are the same entity, e.g., English *She saw herself*. Reflexive operations reduce the semantic valence of a transitive clause by specifying that there are not two separate entities involved; rather, one entity fulfills two semantic roles and/or grammatical relations. As with many functional operations, reflexives can be expressed lexically, morphologically, or analytically. With lexical and morphological reflexives, the reduction in semantic valence is reflected in a corresponding reduction in grammatical valence.

A **lexical reflexive** is one which is tied to the lexical meaning of a particular verb. For example, the English verbs *to get dressed, wash, put on, shave*, etc. all normally imply that the AGENT and PATIENT are the same entity, e.g.:

(55)   Edward shaved, washed, and got dressed.

This clause implies that Edward shaved himself, washed himself, and dressed himself. If some other object is intended, it must be explicitly mentioned, e.g.:

(56)   Edward washed Claire.

Certain actions are highly likely to be accomplished reflexively, primarily "grooming" activities such as *wash, shave,* and *dress*. These concepts are typically expressed with the simplest (i.e., phonologically smallest, and least complex) kind of reflexive operation available in the language. Often this is the lexical reflexive.

A **morphological reflexive** is expressed by one of the morphological processes discussed in section 2.2. English has no morphological reflexives. The most well-known examples of morphological reflexives are probably those of Romance languages. However, the writing systems of these languages tend to obscure the fact that the reflexive morphemes are actually bound clitics rather than free words. For example, in Spanish a reflexive is formed from a transitive verb by the addition of the pro-clitic *se*:

(57)   *Non-reflexive*
         Matilde quemó la cena.   "Matilde burned dinner."

(58)   *Reflexive*
         Matilde se-quemó.   "Matilde burned herself."

All semantically transitive verbs must take the reflexive prefix to be understood as reflexive in Spanish. There are no lexical reflexives of the English variety:

(59)   a. Matilde lavó el carro.   "Matilde washed the car."
             Matilde se-lavó.   "Matilde washed (herself)."
             *Matilde lavó.

         b. Matilde afeitó el tigre.   "Matilde shaved the tiger."
             Matilde se-afeitó.   "Matilde shaved (herself)."
             *Matilde afeitó.

         c. Matilde vistió al niño.   "Matilde dressed the boy."
             Matilde se-vistió.   "Matilde got dressed."
             *Matilde vistió.

Russian offers additional examples of morphological reflexives. In Russian, a reflexive is formed by the addition of a suffix *-sja*:

(60)   a. *Non-reflexive*
            Boris umïvátʲ dʲetʲ-oj.
            Boris wash   child-PL:ACC
            "Boris washes the children."

         b. *Reflexive*
            Natáša umïvát-sja.
            Natasha wash-REFL
            "Natasha washes (herself)."

English has **analytic reflexives**. These are signaled by the "reflexive pronouns," i.e., *myself, yourself, himself, herself, ourselves, yourselves, themselves*, and *itself*, e.g.

(61)   McGovern burned himself.

This is an analytic reflexive because the presence of the reflexive operation is expressed via a lexical word that is distinct from the verb. From a purely syntactic point of view, the analytic reflexive operation of English is not a valence decreasing device. This is because there are still two syntactic arguments – *McGovern* and *himself*. We may want to say, however, that this clause is "semantically intransitive" because the two syntactic arguments refer to a single entity in the message world.

Abkhaz, a Caucasian language spoken in Georgia (Hewitt 1979), has a morphological and an analytic reflexive. Verbs that describe "inherently reflexive" activities take the morphological reflexive (62), while others take the analytic reflexive (63):

(62)   l-çə-l-kᵒabe-yt'
        3FSG-REFL-3FSG:ERG-wash-ASP
        "She washed (herself)."

Transitive verbs that describe activities that are not so commonly done reflexively use an analytic reflexive based on the word for "head:"

(63)   a-sark'a-ç'ə   s-xə   z-be-yt'
        DET-mirror-LOC 1:POSS-head 1:ERG-see-ASP
        "I saw myself in the mirror."

A literal translation of example 63 might be "I saw my head in the mirror." However, this is the standard way of saying "I saw myself in the mirror" in Abkhaz. The fact that inherently reflexive activities are expressed morphologically while other reflexives are expressed analytically is consistent with the iconicity principle, alluded to earlier, that "smaller" coding tends to express more inherent reflexivization.

The Abkhaz data also illustrate another common property of reflexives. Analytic reflexives are often based on body parts, usually "head" as in Abkhaz, but also "soul/self" or other parts, as in the following from sports or military English:

(64)   Get your butt over here!

A **reciprocal** clause is very similar conceptually to a reflexive. For this reason, reciprocals and reflexives are often expressed identically. A prototypical reciprocal clause is one in which two participants equally act upon each other, i.e., both are equally AGENT and PATIENT. For example, *They saw each other* is a reciprocal in English. Reciprocals are conceptually similar to reflexives in that both indicate that AGENT and PATIENT are coreferential, though for different reasons.

Lexical reciprocals are verbs for which reciprocity is a built-in component of their semantics. Some lexically reciprocal verbs in English are *kiss*, *meet*, and *shake hands*, e.g., *Matilde and Mary kissed* usually means "Matilde and Mary kissed each other." If some other situation is to be communicated, the object must be explicitly mentioned, e.g., *Matilde and Mary kissed Grandma*.

Many languages that have morphological reflexives also have **morphological reciprocals**. These languages typically express reflexives and reciprocals with the same morphological operators. Here we will provide examples from Spanish and Yagua.

Spanish

(65)   Matilde se-quemó.
        M.   REFL-burn:3SG:PAST
        "Matilde burned herself."

(66)   Matilde y   María se-conocieron   en Lima.
        M.   and M.   REFL-meet:3PL:PAST in Lima
        "Matilde and Maria met (each other) in Lima."

(67)   Matilde y   María se-quemaron.
        M.   and M.   REFL-burn:3PL:PAST
        "Matilde and Maria burned themselves" or "Matilde and Maria burned each other."

Often such constructions are technically ambiguous, e.g., examples 66 and 67 above. However, there are some ways of resolving the ambiguity. When the subject is singular, the reflexive reading is demanded (e.g., ex. 65). However, when the subject is plural, both reflexive and reciprocal readings are possible. In such cases, the context disambiguates. So example 66 would probably not mean "Matilde and Maria met themselves," as this represents a pragmatically bizarre interpretation, whereas 67 is truly ambiguous out of context.

Yagua is another language in which morphological reflexives and reciprocals are isomorphic (i.e., they have the same form). In Yagua the reflexive/reciprocal enclitic is *-yu*:

(68)   Suunumívachiy*u*.
        sa-junumívay-sìy-yù
        3SG-paint-PAST1-REFL
        "He painted himself."

(69)   Ruuvañúúyanúy*u*.
        riy-juvay-núúy-janú-yù
        3PL-kill-CONT-PAST3-REFL
        "They were killing each other."

In Seko Padang, reflexives are analytic (ex. 70), but reciprocals are expressed via a verb prefix *si-* (71):

(70)   *Reflexive*
        na-kale mang-kakoang-i
        3-body TRANS-call-APL
        "He called himself."

(71)   *Reciprocal*
        si-kakoang-i
        RECIP-call-APL
        "They called each other."

In English, reflexives and reciprocals are both analytic, but are not isomorphic. Reflexives use the reflexive pronouns, whereas reciprocals use the special anaphoric operator *each other*:

(72)   *Reciprocal*
        Melinda and Stephanie saw each other.

In some languages, especially those that have morphological reflexives, the reflexive/reciprocal morphology also occurs in noun phrases to indicate coreference between the possessor of the noun and an argument of the verb. Yup'ik Eskimo provides a ready example of this phenomenon (Reed, *et al.* 1977: 105):

(73)   Cenir-ta-a   maurlu-*ni*.
        visit-TRANS-3SG grandmother-REFL
        "He is visiting his own grandmother."

Yagua provides an example of a related phenomenon:

(74)   Suumutyǫ jíita naandaanúyu.
        sa-jumutyǫ jíita naana-daa-nú-yù
        3SG-answer JIITA 3DL-little-person-REFL
        "Her$_i$ son answered her$_i$."

In this example, the reflexive marker *-yu* indicates coreference between the object of the clause and the possessor of the subject noun phrase. If the son belongs to some other person, the regular third person object enclitic is used. There is no direct analog to this phenomenon in English. In the clause:

(75)   Her own son answered her.

the reflexive marker *own* goes with the *possessor* (as does the *-ni* in Eskimo). In Yagua it goes with the *object*. That is, it would be as if in English we could say:

(76)   *Her son answered herself.

This use of reflexive morphology does *not* decrease the valence of the clause. This is because its primary function is to express coreference between a possessor and a core clausal argument. It does not reduce the number of core arguments in the clause.

Another common "extended" usage of reflexive/reciprocal morphosyntax is to indicate a special kind of **emphasis**. For example, in English and many other languages, reflexive pronouns are used to emphasize that a reference is to a particular participant alone:

(77)   Edsel washed the car *himself*.
        Porsche *herself* washed the car.
        Mercedes washed the car all by *herself*.

(78)   The car *itself* is worth $10,000.
        Celica paid $10,000 for the car *itself*.

?
        How are reflexives expressed?
   (a) Lexically?
   (b) Morphologically?
   (c) Analytically?
        Are reflexives and reciprocals formally identical?
        Are there any "unusual" uses of reflexive/reciprocal morphosyntax? For example, does a reflexive marker appear in a noun phrase to indicate that the possessor of the noun phrase is the same as the subject of the clause?
        Does reflexive/reciprocal morphology ever indicate interclausal coreference?
        Are there other "extended" uses of reflexive or reciprocal morphosyntax?

8.2.2   Passives

The definition of a **passive** clause to be employed here is based on a prototype (Comrie 1989, Givón 1984: 164, Shibatani 1985). A prototypical passive clause is characterized both morphosyntactically and in terms of its discourse function. Morphosyntactically a passive is a semantically transitive (two-participant) clause for which the following three properties hold:

> 1 The AGENT (or most AGENT-like participant) is either omitted (*not* "zero-pronominalized," see the introduction to this chapter) or demoted to an oblique role.
> 2 The other core participant (the "P") possesses all properties of subjects relevant for the language as a whole.
> 3 The verb possesses any and all language-specific formal properties of intransitive verbs.

In terms of discourse function a prototypical passive is used in contexts where the A is relatively low in topicality with respect to the P. This is not a criterial definition; rather, it defines a prototype against which passive-like constructions can be compared. A construction may exhibit many or few of the morphosyntactic properties. Similarly, a passive-like construction may sometimes be used in contexts where a passive would be unexpected, given the above characterization. However, it is the case that constructions that possess the morphosyntactic properties of passives also generally exhibit the discourse-functional property mentioned above. Givón (1982b, 1984: 164, and 1990) provides a relatively comprehensive typology of various passive-like phenomena according to a definition similar to the one given here. In the following subsection we will discuss personal and impersonal passives. Under personal passives we will provide examples of lexical, morphological, and analytic passives.

8.2.2.1   Kinds of passive

Personal passives are constructions for which some specific agent is implied, but either is not expressed or is expressed in an oblique role. Personal passives can be lexical, morphological, or periphrastic/analytic. Examples of each type are provided below.

A **lexical passive** is any clause headed by a verb that is inherently passive in character. To be inherently passive, the verb must express a scene that includes the presence of a causing AGENT, but the PATIENT must be the grammatical subject. A verb such as *break* in English is not a lexical passive because when used intransitively it does not automatically embody a scene in which some AGENT acts upon some PATIENT, e.g., *The window broke.* The verb *bááryị* in Yagua, on the other hand, does specifically assert that the subject was the object of killing on the part of a conscious AGENT:

(79)   Sa-bááryị-máá.
        3SG-be:killed:in:battle-PERF
        "He was killed in battle."

If we imagine an English verb such as *murder* falling into the same class as *break* in English we would have some idea of the sense of this Yagua verb, i.e., *he murdered* would mean "he was murdered." True lexical passives are apparently quite rare.

Morphological passives are very common. They often employ the same or similar morphology as does perfect aspect (see the introduction to this chapter). Passive morphemes are also sometimes derived from copulas or affixes/particles that form nominalizations on the PATIENT of a verb. For example:

Kera (Afroasiatic, Chadic)

(80)   *Transitive*
        Hùlúm   gà-ng   hàrgá-ng gìdè   hiúw-a.
        man:DEF put-PAST goat-DEF womb pen-LOC
        "The man put the goat in the pen."

(81)   *Passive*
        Hàrgá-ng *dè*-gà-gè   gìdè   hiúw-a (kás hùlúm-a).
        goat-DEF PASS-put-REDUP womb pen-LOC hand man-LOC
        "The goat was put in the pen (by the man)."

Ute (agent of passive may not be expressed)

(82)   *Transitive*
        Ta'wóci tûpẹyci tïráabi-kya.
        man   rock   throw-PAST
        "The man threw the rock."

(83)   *Passive*
        Tûpẹyci tïráabi-*ta*-xa.
        rock   throw-PASS-PAST
        "The rock was thrown" or "Someone threw the rock."

English has **analytic passives**. In English passives a copular verb plus the "past participle" (a PATIENT nominalization) of the active verb is used:

(84)   The city was destroy-ed (by the enemy).
        COP   -NOM

Impersonal passives. The function of **impersonal passives** is essentially the same as that of basic passives: they downplay the centrality of an AGENT. One difference between personal and impersonal passives, however, is that impersonal passives can be formed from intransitive as well as transitive verbs. For example, in an intransitive impersonal passive clause like the German "Yesterday there was dancing," the identity of the participants in the dance is not central to the speaker's communicative goal; only the fact that dancing took place. The following English examples are close functional approximations of impersonal passive constructions in languages that have them. However, the English examples are based on other clause patterns, namely a "normal" active verb with a third person plural subject for 85a and an existential construction in 85b:

(85)   a. *They* say that by 2000 there will be no more trains in America.
        b. *There* will be dancing in the streets.

Some other languages, e.g., German and Lithuanian, employ passive morphology when the AGENT is unspecified:

(86)   *German*
        Es wird hier ge-tanzt.
        it be   here PASS-dance
        "Dancing takes place here."

(87)   *Lithuanian* (indicates uncertainty, doubt, etc.)
        Jo   čia per griovį šokta.
        3SG:GEN here over ditch jumped
        "(Evidently) he jumped over the ditch here." (lit.: By him here the ditch was jumped over.)

Spanish uses reflexive morphology in one kind of impersonal passives:

(88)   *Spanish*
        Se caen mucho acá.   "They fall a lot here."

We know of no languages that employ specific morphology just for impersonal passives. This is not particularly surprising, as the same statement is almost true for personal passives as well. As mentioned above, both morphological and analytic personal passives tend to employ formal structures, either bound morphemes or free words as the case may be, whose "basic" function is one of the following: (1) perfect aspect markers, (2) copulas, (3) PATIENT nominalizers. Similarly, impersonal passives tend to employ morphology common to (1) reflexive/reciprocal constructions, (2) existential constructions, and (3) third person plural markers. The following is an example of a third person plural subject marker functioning as an impersonal passive in Maasai (examples courtesy of Jonathan Ololoso):

(89)   a.   *Transitive*
            é-bol-í
            3-open-PL
            "It will be opened."

       b.   *Intransitive*
            ɛ-tɔ́n-ɪ
            3-sit-PL
            "People are sitting/staying."

That these are impersonal constructions and not just plain active clauses is evidenced by the fact that a free-standing AGENT cannot be expressed.

Other kinds of passives. Many languages possess more than one passive construction. For example, English has the common *be* passive (see above) and the less common *get* passive:

(90)   John *got* hit by a car.

The difference in meaning between these two passives is difficult to define satisfactorily. In other languages the different passives have less subtle functional differences. For example, Yup'ik has at least three morphological passives. These are illustrated below (Reed *et al.* 1977):

(91)   *Adversative*
            tuntuva-k nere-*sciu*-llru-u-q   (carayag-mun)
            moose-ABS eat-PASS-PAST-INTRNS-3SG bear-OBL
            "The moose was eaten (by a bear)."

(92)   *Abilitative*
         keme-k   ner-*narq*-u-q   (yug-nun)
         meat-ABS eat-PASS-INTRNS-3SG person-OBL
         "Meat can be eaten by people."

(93)   *Negative abilitative*
         tauna   ner-*nait*-u-q   (yug-nun)
         this:ABS eat-PASS-INTRNS-3SG person-OBL
         "This one cannot be eaten (by people)."

The adversative passive (example 91) expresses an event that happens to the detriment of the subject argument. In this case, being eaten is definitely something detrimental to the moose.

Japanese and a few other languages allow passive morphology to appear on semantically intransitive verbs. The result of this operation is termed "adversative" in Japanese grammar, although it is typologically very different from the Yup'ik adversative passive. Example 94b illustrates the normal morphological passive, expressed by the morpheme *-rare*:

(94)   a. *Transitive*
          Taro-ga   Hanako-o   nagut-ta
          Taro-NOM Hanako-ACC hit-PAST
          "Taro hit Hanako."

       b. *Passive*
          Hanako-ga (Taro-ni) nagu-*rare*-ta
                     -OBL hit-PASS-PAST
          "Hanako was hit by Taro."

Example 95b illustrates that with an intransitive verb, *-rare* indicates that the event occurred to the detriment of the subject, and the agent of the detrimental action is expressed in an oblique case, just like the agent of a normal passive clause:

(95)   a. *Intransitive*
          Tomodachi-ga ki-ta
          friend-NOM   come-PAST
          "His friend came."

       b. *Passive*
          Taro-ga   tomodachi-ni   ki-*rare*-ta
                     friend-OBL
          "Taro was arrived by his friend (to Taro's disadvantage)"

In Finnish, a P argument may remain in the accusative case when the verb occurs in the passive. In this type of passive the A cannot be expressed. Sometimes this kind of passive is called a **non-promotional passive**, because the P argument is not "promoted" to subject status, as evidenced by the fact that it remains in the accusative case (examples courtesy of Kari Valkama):

(96)   a. *Transitive*
       Maija   jätti   hän-et   kotiin
       Maija:NOM leave:PAST 3SG-ACC home:LOC
       "Maija left him at home."

       b. *Passive*
       Hän-et jätettiin   kotiin
       3SG-ACC leave:PASS home:LOC
       "He was left at home."

Finnish also has a more prototypical passive in which the P is promoted to the nominative case and the A appears in an oblique role.

?

Which type(s) of passive construction does the language have? Exemplify each type, and describe its function or functions.
(a) Lexical?
(b) Morphological?
(c) Analytic?
Are there "impersonal" passives, i.e., passives of intransitive verbs, or passives where there is not necessarily an AGENT implied?
Is a passive construction obligatory in any particular environment, e.g., when a PATIENT outranks an AGENT on some pragmatically defined hierarchy?
Are there other types of passives?

8.2.3   Inverses

Inverse constructions are technically valence "rearranging" devices, since they do not add or remove arguments from the clause. Rather, they "invert" the normal (or "direct") alignment between semantic roles and grammatical expression of those roles in a transitive clause, leaving the clause with the same number of arguments (usually two) as the corresponding direct construction. The semantic effect of a prototypical inverse construction is to downplay the centrality of the agentive participant with respect to the more patient-like participant. Therefore, inverses operate in the functional domain of valence reduction.

Here is a preliminary example from Nocte (also known as Naga, a Tibeto-Burman language of India). Examples of various types of inverses will follow:

(97)   a. nga-ma ate hetho-ang
            1-ERG   3   teach-1SG
            "I will teach him."

        b. ate-ma nga-nang hetho-*h*-ang
            3-ERG 1-ACC   teach-INV-1SG
            "He will teach me."

Example 97a is a normal, or "direct" clause based on the verb *hetho*, "teach." In this example the verb carries a suffix -*ang* that refers to the first person AGENT, "I." In example 97b the verb still carries the -*ang* that refers to the first person argument, but now the first person argument is a PATIENT rather than an AGENT. To make this rearrangement of semantic roles and grammatical expression explicit, the verb takes a special "inverse" suffix -*h*. This suffix essentially says "Beware! The argument that this verb agrees with is a PATIENT rather than an AGENT!"

One might wonder whether 97b could just be a kind of morphological passive construction. Evidence that 97b is not a passive is that the AGENT, "he" in example 97b, appears in the ergative case. This shows that the AGENT in the inverse construction is still an argument of the verb. Recall that in passives, the AGENT is either omitted or assigned to an oblique role.

Givón (1994) argues strongly that inverse is primarily a functional notion. This argument follows from Givón's general claim that the only insightful way of approaching a typology of voice phenomena is first to define voice in terms of functions, then determine how the functions are accomplished grammatically in any given language. "Inverse voice," from this perspective, is a reduction in centrality of the AGENT with respect to the PATIENT, but a less extreme reduction than passive voice. Not all languages have grammaticalized this particular function, but all of them accomplish it in one way or another, sometimes with a structure that is a more direct expression of a passive or some other functional voice. The studies in Givón (ed.) 1994 provide detailed information on how several languages deal grammatically with the concept of a **functional inverse**.

Nevertheless, there are clear examples of grammatically distinct inverse constructions. In this section we will describe the types of **grammatical inverse** constructions that are known to exist in the world's languages. Not every language will have one or more of these construction types, but all languages, at least according to those who define voice primarily in terms of function, have some construction that accomplishes the task of downplaying, but not eliminating, the centrality of the A argument with respect to the P.

Inverse constructions can be obligatory under certain syntactic conditions, or they can be a true pragmatic option. Gildea (1994), using terminology from Harris (1990), notes that if an inverse construction is obligatory, it cannot be considered a voice, since voice typically refers to constructions that are "optional," depending on factors such as relative topicality or other discourse considerations. In Harris' terminology, obligatory inverses are more reasonably compared to "alignment" systems, such as "ergative/absolutive" or "nominative/accusative" systems for organizing grammatical relations. However, if the inverse is an optional, pragmatically conditioned variant, it may be insightfully characterized as a voice.

8.2.3.1   *Both direct and inverse explicitly marked*

The first type of grammatical inverse construction we will discuss is the type that gave rise to the concept of inverse in the first place (Howse 1844). In this type, both "direct" and "inverse" verb forms are explicitly marked. This type of inverse construction is found in Algonquian (North American) languages:

(98)   *Plains Cree* (Algonquian, from Dahlstrom 1991)
    a. ni-se:kih-*a*-wak
       1SG-frighten-DIRECT-3PL
       "I frighten them." (direct)

    b. ni-se:kih-*ik*-wak
       1SG-frighten-INVERSE-3PL
       "They frighten me." (inverse)

In example 98a, the prefix *ni-* refers to the first person AGENT and the suffix *-wak* refers to the third person plural PATIENT. In example 98b the same prefix and suffix are used, but now they refer to a first person PATIENT and third person plural AGENT. The alignment between semantic roles (AGENT, PATIENT) and grammatical expression (*ni-*, *-wak*) has been reversed. The only overt expression of this reversal is the presence of the "direct" suffix *-a* in 98a vs. the "inverse" suffix *-ik* in 98b.

In Cree, the alternation between direct and inverse forms is determined by the following hierarchy:

second person > first person > third person proximate > third person obviative

When the AGENT in a transitive clause is higher (farther to the left) on this hierarchy than the PATIENT, the direct construction in required. When the AGENT is lower on the hierarchy than the PATIENT, the inverse is required. In 98a, the AGENT is first person, and the PATIENT is third person, therefore the direct construction is used. In 98b the AGENT is third person and the PATIENT is first person, therefore the inverse is used. If it helps, you might think of this system as requiring that the higher-ranked argument, according to this hierarchy, be referenced with a prefix, regardless of its semantic role. The inverse/direct suffixes then simply make the direction of the action explicit.

The terms **proximate** and **obviative** refer to two grammatically distinct categories of noun phrase. In Cree, obviative nouns are marked with a suffix *-ah*, while proximate nouns are unmarked. The functional difference between these categories is that proximate nouns tend to be more topical in discourse than obviative nouns. First and second persons always outrank third persons. But when two third persons interact, one of them must be proximate and the other one obviative. If the proximate, i.e., more topical one acts upon the obviative one, the direct verb form is used (99a). If an obviative argument acts on a proximate one, the inverse is used (99b):

(99)   a.   piyisk mihce:t nipah-*e:*-wak   ya:hciyiniw-*ah*
            finally many   kill-DIRECT-3PL Blackfoot-OBV
            "At last they had killed many Blackfoot."

       b.   ta:pwe: mac-a:yi:siyiniwe:sah nipah-*ik*-0   o:hi   ihkw-*ah*
            truly   bad-person   kill-INVERSE-3SG this:OBV louse-OBV
            "Truly the louse killed the evil man."

In 99a the word *ya:hciyiniw* "Blackfoot" is marked as obviative with the suffix *-ah*, just as the word *ihkw* "louse" is in 99b. However, in 99a the obviative noun is PATIENT while in 99b the obviative noun is AGENT. The only way to tell that 99b does not mean "Truly the evil man killed this louse" is the inverse marker -*ik* in the verb.

     In these circumstances, the Algonquian system may be character-ized as a "voice," since the determination of which participant to express as obviative and which to express as proximate is a pragmatic option based on the speaker's (unconscious) assessment of which participant is more topical. This is the same kind of decision as speakers have to make when choosing whether to use an active or a passive construction.[3] In Algonquian, however, this choice is not available when a first or second person argument is present. In that circumstance, the relative topicality of the arguments is fixed, and whether to use a direct or inverse construction is not a choice but is a 100 percent grammaticalized rule.

8.2.3.2 *Marked inverse*

     Some languages mark the inverse but not the direct construction. We saw an example of that in Nocte (example 97). Another example is from Jiarong, a Tibeto-Burman language of China:

(100) a. nga mə nasno-ng
        1   3   scold-1SG
        "I will scold him."

        b. mə-kə nga *u*-nasno-ng
            3-ERG 1   INV-scold-1SG
            "He will scold me."

In the direct construction, 100a, the verb expresses the first person AGENT with the suffix -*ng*. No other morphology occurs in the verb. In 100b, the verb agrees with the first person PATIENT with the same -*ng* suffix, but an inverse prefix *u*- appears on the verb.

     Finally, Kutenai, a language isolate of eastern British Columbia, Montana, and Idaho (Dryer 1994), is a marked inverse language that also employs a proximate/obviative distinction similar to what is found in Algonquian languages (see above):

(101) a. wu:kat-i palkiy-s   titqat'
          see-IND woman-OBV man
          "The man saw the woman." (direct)

b. wu:kat-*aps*-i titqat'-s palkiy
   see-INV-IND man-OBV woman
   "The woman saw the man." (inverse)

In Kutenai, the inverse construction is marked with the verbal suffix -*aps*, whereas the direct construction is unmarked. Furthermore, nouns are marked with an -*s* suffix when they are obviative, but are not marked when they are proximate. A major difference between the Kutenai and Algonquian systems is that in Kutenai the inverse is not used when first or second persons are involved. Therefore, inverse in Kutenai is always a pragmatically influenced option, and as such can be unhesitatingly considered a voice.

8.2.3.3 Special verb agreement markers for inverse situations

Quite a different sort of inverse construction is found in some languages of South America, and perhaps elsewhere. These languages incorporate inverse marking into their participant reference paradigms. When a language employs this strategy, special markings on the verb are not needed. For example, in Wayampi, a Tupí-Guaraní language of Brazil (examples courtesy of Cheryl Jensen), a single prefix is used to refer to both AGENT and PATIENT. Different prefixes are used in direct and inverse situations.

(102)   *Direct*   *Inverse*
        a-pota   "I like him."   e-pota   "He likes me."
        oro-pota "We like him."   ore-pota "He likes us."
        ere-pota "You like him."   ne-pota   "He likes you."

Similarly, Panare, an unrelated Cariban language of Venezuela, employs a special set of inverse prefixes, but only in past-perfective aspects:

(103)   *Direct*   *Inverse*
        tamayaj chu   yámayaj kën
             1SG   3SG
        "I knocked it down."   "He/she knocked me down."

        mamayaj amën   ayamayaj kën
             2SG   "He/she knocked you down."
        "You knocked it down"

What makes the Wayampi and Panare systems characterizable as inverses is that the verb varies for the argument that is higher on a person hierarchy, similar to what we have seen in Algonquian and elsewhere, regardless of whether that argument is AGENT or PATIENT. In both the Tupí-Guaraní and Cariban families, the hierarchy is the following:

$$\begin{matrix} 1 \\ 2 \end{matrix} > 3$$

When first and second persons interact in these languages, typically special **portmanteau** forms are used that vary for both arguments. Therefore, like Kutenai, the inverse systems of these languages only function when a third person is involved. These languages do not have a grammatically marked proximate/obviative distinction among third persons. However, it can be argued for Panare, at least, something like a proximate/obviative distinction is expressed via word order, with preverbal arguments being proximate and postverbal arguments being obviative (see below for a discussion of word order inverses).

8.2.3.4 *Word order ("functional" inverse)*

Sometimes constituent order variation can be thought of as a kind of "functional inverse" (Givón 1994). For example, in Cebuano goal–focus (or ergative) constructions can appear with VAP (ex. 104a) or VPA (104b) constituent orders:

(104)   *Cebuano* (Western Austronesian, Philippines)
   a. gi-higugma niya   ang bata
       GF-loved   3:ERG ABS child
       "She loved the child." (A > P)

   b. gi-higugma kini   niya
       GF-loved   this:one:ABS 3:ERG
       "She loved this one."   (P > A)

       (passive – for comparison)
   c. gi-laylay   siya sa usa ka sakit
       GF-afflicted 3:ABS OBL one LNK sickness
       "She was afflicted by illness." (P > > A)

A study of the use of these constructions in discourse (Payne 1994) shows that the VAP construction (104a) is used when the A is higher in topicality than the P. This is the normal discourse function of active, transitive clauses. The VPA construction (104b), on the other hand, is used when the P is slightly higher in topicality than the A. This is a discourse environment where an inverse is often used in languages that have a grammatically distinct inverse voice. Notice, however, that there is no marking on the verb that distinguishes the direct from the inverse construction. The only formal distinction is in the order of arguments following the verb.

Example 104c is included to show that the same "goal–focus" verb form occurs when the P is much more topical than the A. This is a discourse situation commonly associated with passive clauses (see section 8.2.2). This functional passive in Cebuano is grammatically distinct from the inverse in that AGENT is either omitted or assigned to an oblique role, marked by *sa*. Thus inverse and passive constructions can be identified in Cebuano, but not by any explicit marking on the verb.

> **?**   Does the language have a grammatically instantiated inverse construction?
>   If so, what type is it?

8.2.4   Middle constructions

The term **middle** or **middle voice** has been used in a variety of ways in different language traditions. What all such constructions have in common is that they involve detransitivization. The motivation for the term is that these constructions are neither passive nor active – they are in between, or "middle." We will consider a middle construction to be one that expresses a semantically transitive situation in terms of a process undergone by the PATIENT, rather than as an action carried out by an AGENT. Middle constructions are not to be confused with "medial clauses" or "medial verbs" (see section 11.4).

A prototypical middle construction is one which is signaled by some overt, usually morphological, operator (see examples below). However, most languages have verbs that can be used in a middle sense without any overt operator. We will use the term **middle verb** simply to capture the functional similarity between intransitive constructions formed with these verbs and morphological "middle" constructions in other languages. The verb *break* in English is a good example of a middle verb. Sometimes verbs of this class are called **labile verbs**. Used transitively *break* is a standard transitive verb. When used intransitively, however, the PATIENT rather than the AGENT is the subject, and the situation is expressed as a process (in terms of Chafe 1970) rather than as an action, e.g.:

(105)   *Transitive*
The workers broke the vase.

(106)   *Middle voice*
The vase broke (*by the workers).

This property distinguishes verbs such as *break* from other verbs that can be either transitive or intransitive (probably the majority of verbs in English), e.g.:

(107)   *Transitive*
I hit the vase.

(108)   *"Middle"*
*The vase hit.

The only difference between the function of a passive and the function of a middle construction is that a passive treats the situation as an action carried out by an agent but with the identity of the agent downplayed. A middle construction, on the other hand, treats the situation as a process, i.e., it ignores the role of the agent. Because passive and middle functions are so similar, many languages use the same morphology to express both. In Greek, for example, middle and passive constructions are the same in all tense/aspects except aorist:

(109)   *Koiné Greek*
"loose" (*present*)
Active: lúo   "I let (someone) loose"
Passive: lúomai   "I am let loose (by someone)"
Middle: lúomai   "I become loose"/"I let myself loose"

"loose" (*aorist*)
Active: élusa   "I let (someone) loose"
Passive: elúθen   "I was let loose (by someone)"
Middle: elusámen "I became loose"/"I let myself loose"

Mayan and Cariban languages, however, consistently treat middle constructions as distinct from passives:

(110)   *K'iche' Mayan* (England 1988: 74)
"hit"
Active: ch'ay   "hit"
Passive: xch'aay   "be hit (by someone)"
Middle: xch'aayik   "become hit"

(111)   *Panare* (Cariban)
         "keep"
         Active: amaika   "keep"
         Passive: amaikasa'   "be kept"
         Middle: samaika   "stay/sit/remain"

Frequently, middle constructions express the notion that the subject is both the controller and the affected participant. However, this characterization provides no way of distinguishing the function of middle constructions from the function of reflexives. Indeed, in many languages reflexives and middles are expressed by the same morphosyntax, but not always. In order to consistently distinguish middle and reflexive functions, we must employ the notion of **process** vs. **action**. Middle constructions express the scene as a process whereas reflexives and passives express the situation as an action.

Sometimes morphological middle constructions are called **anticausatives**. This is because they are the logical opposite of causative constructions. Instead of starting with a non-causative verb and adding a morpheme to make it causative, a middle construction starts with a causative verb and results in a non-causative verb. Consider the following Yagua examples:

(112) a. Sa-supatá-ra.
           3SG-pull:out-INAN
           "He yanked it out."

       b. Rá-supáta-y.
           INAN-pull:out-MID
           "It came out."

The simple verb stem (112a) contains the notion of CAUSE as part of its lexical entry, i.e., the gloss can be paraphrased "cause to come out." The morphological middle construction (112b) adds a morpheme which effectively *subtracts* the notion of cause from the lexical meaning of the verb. Similar observations can be made for the other middle constructions illustrated above.

?

Are there grammatically instantiated middle constructions?
Additional reading: Kemmer 1993

8.2.5   Antipassives

Like passive, **antipassive** is a valence decreasing operation. That is, it downplays the centrality of one participant in a scene by downgrading the syntactic status of the verbal argument that refers to that participant. Unlike passives, however, antipassives downplay the centrality of a PATIENT or "P" argument rather than an AGENT or "A" argument. Prototypical antipassives have the following formal characteristics:

1   The P argument is omitted or appears in an oblique case, often the INSTRUMENTAL case.
2   The verb or verb phrase contains some overt marker of intransitivity (e.g., it may take an explicit marker of intransitivity, inflect like an intransitive verb, etc., depending on the formal characteristics of intransitive verbs in that language).
3   The "A" appears in the ABSOLUTIVE case.

The following examples are from Yup'ik, an Eskimo language of Central Alaska:

(113)   *Transitive*
Yero-m   keme-q   nerre-llru-a.
Y.   -ERG meat-ABS eat-PAST-3SG/3SG
"Yero ate the meat."

(114)   *Antipassive*
Yero-q   (kemer-meng)   nerre-llru-u-q.
Y.   -ABS meat-INST   eat-PAST-INTRNS-3SG
"Yero ate (meat)."

In the example 114, the patient *kemermeng*, "meat," appears in the instrumental case, the verb takes the intransitive suffix *-u*, and the subject goes into the absolutive case.

The clearest examples of antipassives are found in morphologically ergative languages, i.e., those that have a morphologically defined absolutive case. In non-ergative languages, object demotion or omission (see below) serves essentially the same function as antipassive does in morphologically ergative languages. The crucial difference, if it is necessary to draw a distinction between object demotion/omission and antipassive (e.g., if a given language has both), is that in antipassives the verb takes some specific marker of antipassivization or intransitivity, whereas in object demotion/omission no such verbal marker occurs.

?

> Are there any grammatical structures that specifically function as antipassives?
> Is some other structure used to express transitive concepts when the P is
> very low in topicality?

8.2.6   Object demotion and omission

Like antipassive, **object demotion** is an operation that downplays
the centrality of a P argument. In fact, some linguists (e.g., Heath 1976)
have treated object demotion and object omission as types of antipassivization. Object demotion sometimes indicates "less involvement" of the P in
the event expressed by the verb. For example:

Bzhedukh (northwest Caucasian language)

(115)   *Transitive*
čʔaalya-m čʔəgʷo-ər ya-žʷoa
boy-ERG   field-ABS   3SG-plows
"The boy plows the field."

(116)   *Object demotion*
čʔaalya-r čʔəgʷo-əm ya-žʷoa
boy-ABS   field-OBL   3SG-plows
"The boy is trying to plow the field."

In 115 the interpretation is that the field is in fact being plowed, whereas
in 116 the field may or may not actually be affected by the action of the
boy. So we can say that the P is "less involved" with the activity of plowing
in example 116 than in example 115. The only reason we would probably
not want to call 116 an antipassive is that the verb does not contain any
overt representation of detransitivization.

Object demotion and omission also occur in non-ergative languages. For example:

(117)   *Transitive*
The hunter shot the deer.

(118)   *Object demotion*
The hunter shot at the deer.

(119)   *Object omission*
The hunter shot.

Like the Caucasian languages cited above, the object demotion construction in English tends to express a situation in which the P participant is less

involved in or less affected by the action of the verb. Similarly, object omission suggests that the identity of the P argument is totally irrelevant.

8.2.7   Object incorporation

Noun incorporation is where a core argument (subject or object) of a clause becomes "attached to" or "incorporated into" the verb. Incorporation exhibits all the characteristics of compounding discussed in section 5.1, namely (1) a stress pattern characteristic of words rather than phrases, (2) possibly unusual word order, (3) morphophonemic processes characteristic of words rather than phrases, (4) possibly special morphology, and (5) meanings that are more specific than the meanings of the individual parts.

Object incorporation is far more common than subject incorporation. In English both are possible, but not very productive. Incorporated forms in English are either lexicalized expressions such as *babysit,* or they are severely restricted with respect to their syntactic possibilities, e.g., *fox-hunt* can only be used in the progressive aspect: *We went fox-hunting,* not *I fox-hunted all morning* or *I fox-hunt for a living.* However, just about all transitive verbs that describe customary activities can incorporate a direct object in the progressive aspect, e.g., *girl-watching, car-washing,* etc. Occasionally one will hear an example of subject incorporation, e.g., *This medicine is doctor-recommended.* This construction is, like non-lexicalized examples of object incorporation, highly restricted, occurring only in the passive voice, cf. *He went doctor-recommending last week* or *She doctor-recommended aspirin for my headache.* In this case English reflects a universal tendency for object incorporation to be more common than subject incorporation.

Formally, object incorporation is a valence decreasing operation, since the object ceases to function as an independent argument and becomes part of a formally intransitive verb. Object incorporation is common in many parts of the world, in particular in Amerindian and Siberian languages. For example:

Chukchee (Siberia)
(120)   *Transitive*
         Tumg-e   na-ntəwat-ən kupre-n.
         friends-ERG 3SG-set-TRANS net-ABS
         "The friends set the net."

(121)   *Incorporated*
Tumg-ət   kupra-ntəwat-g'at.
friends-NOM net-set-INTRNS
"The friends set nets."

Object incorporation of various types occurs in the languages of
the Americas, and elsewhere. In Panare, the most common type of object
incorporation is only used for verbs that involve severing or removing parts
of things. The incorporated constructions differ from the non-incorporated
counterparts in that the incorporated versions imply that the item was
totally removed:

(122)   *Panare* (Cariban, Venezuela)
    a. y-ipu-n   yï-kïti-ñe   amën   *Unincorporated*
       3-head-POSS TRNS-cut-NONPERF:TRNS 2SG
       "You cut its head."

    b. y-u'-kïti-ñe   amën   *Incorporated*
       3-head-cut-NONPERF:TRNS 2SG
       "You cut off its head." (lit.: You head-cut it.)

In 121b the incorporated form, *u'*, bears little resemblance to the unincor-
porated form, *ipu*, but they are related by regular morphophonemic processes. The following illustrate additional Panare examples:

(123)   t-ipo-kïti-yaj   chu   *Incorporated*
        1 > 3-feather-cut-PPERF1 1SG
        "I cut off his feathers/body hair."

(124)   n-u'-pétyaka-yaj   kën   *Incorporated*
        3DIR-head-split-PPERF1 AN:INVIS
        "He$_i$ split his$_j$ head." (i.e., divided it into two separate pieces)

One might argue that object incorporation is just one instance of
a broader category of noun incorporation. Some additional examples of
noun incorporation are found in section 5.1.

?

Does the language have object demotion or omission constructions (as distinct
from antipassives)?
References: Sapir (1911), Green (1981), Mithun (1984), Sadock (1986).

9 Other verb and verb-phrase operations

In this chapter we will discuss a collection of operations likely to be expressed in verbs or verb phrases, but not covered in other chapters. The first two, nominalization and compounding, are typically derivational (see section 2.0). The other four – (1) tense/aspect/mode (TAM), (2) location/direction, (3) participant reference, and (4) evidentiality – are typically inflectional. Many of these operations are likely to be indistinct from each other in any given language. However, because there is a long tradition of describing them separately, it will be convenient to treat them that way in this chapter. It should be kept in mind, however, that in most cases there is significant semantic and morphosyntactic overlap within and among these families of morphosyntactic operations.

9.1 Nominalization

Every language has ways of adjusting the grammatical category of a root. For example, a noun can become a verb by a process of verbalization (see section 5.2). Of interest to this section are operations that allow a verb to function as a noun. Such operations are called **nominalizations**, and can be described with a simple formula:

$$V \rightarrow [V]_N$$

Or simply:

$$V \rightarrow N$$

A noun may be related to a verb in any number of different ways. For example, one noun may refer to the agent of the action described by the verb, while another refers to the result of the action described by the verb. Typically, a language will employ various nominalization operations that differ functionally according to the resulting noun's semantic relationship to the original verb. In the following sections the major types of nominalizations will be described and exemplified.

9.1.1   Action nominalization

An action nominalization refers to the action, usually in the abstract, expressed by the verb root. Action nominalizations can be formulated as:

$$V \rightarrow N_{\text{ACTION designated by V}}$$

English is particularly rich in action nominalization strategies. For example, one can argue that the root *walk* is basically a verb:

(1)   I *walk* to school.

However, there are various ways to form an action nominalization from this verb. The simplest way is with a "zero" operator. As in other sections of this book, zero derivation can be considered to be a lexical process:

(2)   Let's go for a *walk*.

In this example, the root *walk* is being used as a noun that refers to a specific instance of walking.

Occasionally, in English a verb plus a preposition can form a lexical nominalization:

(3)   That was a significant *breakthrough*. (< break through)
       He has a *hangup*. (< hang up)
       She gave him a *talking to*. (< talk to)
       They gave her a *makeover*. (< make over)

In addition to lexical strategies with zero operators, action nominalizations can be formed morphologically in English:

(4)   *Walking* is good for you.
       I'm looking for *employment*. (< employ)
       He worked in *construction*. (< construct)
       That's a new *procedure*. (< proceed)
       The *process* wore me out. (< proceed)
       Economic *growth* is down. (< grow)

All of these morphological strategies are lexically restricted. For example, even a strategy as common as -*ing* is not normally used with some verbs:

(5)   *Employing* is good for you.
        *I like the water's *spewing*.

Other strategies, e.g., -*ess*, -*th*, and -*ure*, are not very productive as verb-based nominalizers; therefore they come close to qualifying as lexical nominalization processes.

Samoan has a morphological nominalizer -*ga* that can function as an action nominalizer:

(6)   *Samoan* (Polynesian; examples from Mosel and Hovdhaugen 1992: 84)
        galue "to work" (verb)   galue-ga "some work"
        fai   "to do"   fai-ga   "action"

Nominalization may also be analytic. For example, Mandarin Chinese employs the particle *de* to form many kinds of nominalizations, including action nominalizations (example from Li and Thompson 1981):

(7)   wǒmen *hézuò*   *de*   wèntí   hěn jiǎndān
        we   cooperate NOM problem very simple
        "The problem concerning our cooperation is very simple."

This use of an analytic nominalization strategy is consistent with the analytic morphological typology of Mandarin. In the following sections the different kinds of Mandarin nominalizations formed with *de* will be illustrated.

9.1.2   Participant nominalizations

A participant nominalization is a verb-based nominalization strategy that results in a noun that refers to one of the participants of a verb root:

$$V \rightarrow N_{\text{PARTICIPANT of V}}$$

Languages typically employ various participant nominalization strategies. Often, but not always, the functional differences among the various participant nominalization strategies have to do with which participant is referred to, e.g., one strategy forms nominalizations that refer to the AGENT of the verb while another forms nominalizations that refer to the PATIENT. The following subsections provide a rough typology of participant nominalization.

9.1.2.1   Agent nominalizations

A nominalization that refers to the AGENT of the nominalized verb
is an **agent nominalization**:

$$V \rightarrow N_{\text{AGENT of V}}$$

Lexical agent nominalization is rather idiosyncratic (i.e., it does not apply
to all verbs) in English:

(8)   a *pickpocket* (< someone who picks pockets)
       a *scarecrow* (< something that scares crows)
       It was a *flop*. (< something that flopped)
       Left turn yield to oncoming traffic. (< drivers who plan to turn left)

One function of the suffix *-er/-or* in English is as a morphological
agent nominalizer:

(9)   employer (< employ) = someone who employs
       tax collector (< tax collect) = someone who collects taxes

In English, agent nominalizations generally refer to things with
reference to characteristic activities, rather than specific events. For example, the nominalization *builder* normally refers to someone who builds
things for a living, not to someone who happens to be building something,
perhaps for the first time. However, in many other languages, agent nominalizations are used to refer to specific activities:

(10)   *Yagua*
       dapųú-*ñu*
       hunt-NOM
       "hunter/one who is hunting"

In this example, the nominalization refers to anyone who happens to be
hunting at the moment, and not necessarily to one who characteristically
hunts.

Mandarin employs the particle *de* to form analytic agent nominalizations (Li and Thompson 1981):

(11)   *zhòng shuǐguǒ de*   hěn nán   guòhuó
       grow fruit   NOM very difficult make:living
       "It is difficult for fruit-growers to make a living."

(12)   *mài qìchē de*   dàbàn   dōu shì hǎo rén.
        sell car   NOM majority all be good person
        "Car sellers are mostly good people."

9.1.2.2   *Patient nominalizations*

A nominalization that refers to the patient of the nominalized verb
is a **patient nominalization**.

$$V \rightarrow N_{\text{PATIENT of V}}$$

Like agent nominalization, lexical patient nominalization is marginal in English, functioning mostly with the modifiers *good* and *bad*:

(13)   This book is a good *read*.
        That's a bad *buy*.

Sometimes morphological patient nominalizations are called **past
participles**. The *-ee* suffix in English is a patient nominalizer that comes
from the French past participle:

(14)   He is a new *employee*. (< employ)
        He is a Vietnam *returnee*. (< return)
        a *retiree*
        a *divorcee*
        an *escapee*

Panare has two patient nominalizers. The suffix *-sa'* forms a true
"past participle" in that the derived nominal refers to an entity according to
some event that that entity was involved in in the past:

(15)   yï-petyu'ma-*sa'*
        TRNS-hit-PAST:PART
        "The hit one."

There is also a "future participle," expressed by the suffix *-se'ña*. These nominalizations refer to an entity according to some event it is "destined" to be
involved in in the future:

(16)   ejke mën   y-onpa-*se'ña*   wï-ch-ireemë-në-to'
        NEG INAN:DIST TRNS-eat-FUT:PART INTR-DETRANS-feed-INC-PURP
        "There is no food for us to eat." (lit: there is no food destined to be eaten)

(17)   Mo   ka   n-aj   y-apanawa-*se'ña*?
        EXIST QM 3SG-AUX TRNS-rub-FUT:PART
        "Do you have something to rub on it?"

Mandarin Chinese employs the particle *de* to form analytic patient nominalizations. Because nominalizations with *de* are so common in Mandarin, sometimes only the context determines which kind of nominalization is meant:

(18)   zhèi zhǒng zhíwù kěyǐ dāng-zuò *chī de*
        this type   plant can take-be   eat NOM
        "(One) can take this type of plant as food." (*chi de* "food")

(19)   *wǒ mài de*   shì Zhōngguó huò
        I   sell NOM be China   product
        "What I sell is Chinese merchandise."

9.1.2.3   Instrument nominalizations

An **instrument nominalization** is a noun formed from a verb in which the noun refers to an instrument used to accomplish the act represented by the verb:

$$V \rightarrow N_{\text{INSTRUMENT for V}}$$

Instrument nominalizations are often formally identical to agent nominalizations. This is true for English, where the *-er* suffix is used for both AGENT and INSTRUMENT nominalizations:

(20)   coffee grinder, can opener, etc.

Spanish employs a productive compounding strategy to form instrument nominalizations of transitive verbs:

(21)   para-brisa-s
        stop-wind-PL
        "windshield"

        abre-lata-s
        open-can-PL
        "can-opener"

        saca-punta-s
        take:out-point-PL
        "pencil-sharpener"

9.1.2.4   Location nominalization

Many languages have strategies that form nominalizations that refer in a general way to some entity associated with the verb root. Often these nominalizations refer to a location where the activity described by the verb tends to occur:

(22)   *Yup'ik* -vik
        cali-vik
        work-NOM
        "workshop"

        ner-vik
        eat-NOM
        "restaurant, eating place"

        kumarr-vik
        burn-NOM
        "fireplace"

        mis-vik
        alight-NOM
        "landing strip"

(23)   *Yagua* -jo
        músá-jo
        descend-NOM
        "port" (place where one descends to the river to get water)

        jasúmiy-jo
        ascend-NOM
        "ladder, stairway"

Another function of the *-ga* nominalizer we saw earlier in Samoan is to form a location nominalization:

(24)   moe "to sleep"   moe-ga   "bed"
        a'o "to learn"   a'o-ga   "school"

9.1.2.5   Product nominalizations

English has lexical and morphological means of forming nouns that refer to the product or result of an event described by a verb root:

(25)   *Lexical*
        It's only a *scratch*.

Here the nominalization *a scratch* refers to something that resulted from an event of scratching. This is a lexical strategy because the nominalization is not signaled by any overt morphology.

(26)   *Morphological*
        We had to buy a *pérmit*.
        This donut is a *réject*.
        He is a recent *cónvert*.
        He has a *growth* on his neck.

The first three of these are morphological nominalizations because they are each related to their verb root by a leftward stress shift. *Growth* is derived from *grow* by a somewhat productive process that usually forms nouns from adjectives, e.g., *width*, *length*, *strength*, etc.

Product nominalizations are not the same as patient nominalizations. For example, something is a *growth* not because it underwent growing, but because it is a result of an event of growing. One would not refer to a child as a *growth* because she had undergone a lot of growing. Similarly, a *pérmit* exists because of an event of permission. It is not something that is permitted, i.e., that undergoes permission.

9.1.2.6   *Manner nominalizations*

The following are examples of lexical manner nominalizations in English:

(27)   a.   He has a mean *slice*.
        b.   I can't hit his *curve*.

In these examples, the nominalization is based on a verb that refers to the kind of act described, e.g., 27b refers to a kind of pitch in baseball that curves. This kind of nominalization appears to be uncommon among the world's languages.

❓
        Describe the processes (productive or not) that form a noun from a verb.
        Include at least:
    (a)   action nominalizations
    (b)   agent nominalizations
    (c)   patient nominalizations
        Is there a distinction between agent nominalizations that refer to characteristic activities (e.g., *teacher*) and those that refer to specific events (e.g., *the one who is teaching*)?

Describe any other participant nominalization strategies (e.g., instrument, location, product, or manner nominalizations).

Additional reading: Comrie and Thompson (1985).

....

9.2   Compounding (including incorporation)

Noun incorporation is where a noun becomes attached to the verb. Incorporation may exhibit all the characteristics of compounding discussed in section 5.1, namely (1) a stress pattern characteristic of words rather than phrases, (2) unusual word order, (3) morphophonemic processes, (4) special morphology or lack thereof, and (5) meanings that are more specific than the meanings of the individual parts. The most common type of noun incorporation is object incorporation. Example 28b illustrates object incorporation in Samoan, a Polynesian language:

(28)   *Samoan* (Mosel and Hovdhaugen 1992)
    a. Na fa'atau e   le   tama le   pua'a
        PAST sell   ERG ART boy   ART pig
        "The boy sold the pig."

    b. Na fa'atau-pua'a le   tama
        PAST sell-pig   ART boy
        "The boy sold pigs."

Example 28a illustrates a straightforward transitive clause in Samoan based on the verb *fa'atau* "to sell." In 28b the noun *pua'a* "pig" has been incorporated into the verb. A literal, though awkward, translation of 28b might be "the boy pig-sold." Evidence that incorporation has taken place is that the clause is formally intransitive, as shown by the fact that the agent does not take the ergative case marker *e*. Also, the verb–noun complex *fa'ataupua'a* is pronounced as a single word rather than as two separate words.

Many different grammatical elements can be incorporated into a verb to adjust the verb's meaning. Direct objects may be just one, albeit common, participant type to enter into such a construction. The following are some English examples of compound verbs formed with incorporated elements other than direct objects:

(29)   a. You must pay the amount to the service desk within the next thirty days or
       you will be *pay-deducted*.

b. Jeremy *kick-started* his motorcycle.
c. After pinning the pattern, *feather-cut* along the indicated lines.
d. Node A is *Chomsky-adjoined* to node B.

The distinctive syntactic and semantic properties of object incorporation are discussed in section 8.2.7.

Verb–verb incorporation. Sometimes verb roots combine to form more complex stems. Verbs of motion commonly enter into such compounds. For example, in Yagua the verb *jasúmiy* means "to go up." This verb can be compounded with just about any other verb in the language to indicate action accomplished in a rising direction:

(30)   Sa-súúy-*asúmiy*
        3SG-shout-rise
        "He shouts rising."

Baka, a central Sudanic language of Eastern Zaïre, employs similar verb–verb compounding (examples courtesy of Douglas Sampson):

(31)   a. ndá'ba "to go back" + ógu "to come" → ndá'baógu "to come back"
        b. óto "to put" + ómo "to leave" + lígi (no independent meaning) →
            ótoómolígi "to forget"

Verbs that freely enter into such compounds (often motion verbs) typically lose their verbal character and ultimately become derivational affixes. For example, in Quechua at the time of the Inca empire there was a verb -*kacha* that meant "to go about doing." In modern Huallaga Quechua (Weber 1989: 150) there is a verb suffix -*ykacha* that means "iterative" or "vacillating aimlessly." The *y* component is the old infinitive marker that would have appeared on the preceding verb:

(32)   kuyu-*ykacha*:-chi-shun
        move-ITER-CAUS-3PL:IMPER
        "Let's make it move (back and forth)."

The earlier meaning of this example would have been "Let's go about moving it."

At times it can be difficult or even impossible to objectively distinguish compound verbs from a series of distinct verbs (see section 11.1 on serial verbs), verbs plus a complement (section 11.2), auxiliary verbs plus main verbs, or verbs with derivational suffixes. In general the following rules of thumb may be of some use in selecting appropriate terminology:

1 If one of the roots in the suspect structure is not a contemporary verb in its own right, then you have a verb plus a derivational affix.

2 If the form of one of the roots is *substantially* distinct from its form as an independent verb, *and* if the meaning of that verb root is "bleached," i.e., less specific than the meaning of the same root as an independent form, then you may consider calling it a derivational affix.

3 If both roots can function as independent verbs, and if anything can come in between the two roots (e.g., inflectional morphology or object nominals), then you have serial verbs or complementation. See sections 11.1 and 11.2 for further information.

4 If both roots are recognizable verbs in their own right, but nothing can come in between them, *and* the meaning of the whole structure is "bleached," i.e., slightly different from the combination of the lexical meanings of the two roots, then you probably have verb–verb compounding.

These rules of thumb would identify the Yagua example to be verb–verb compounding, since *jasúmiy* is still a viable verb in the language; but would identify Quechua *-ykacha* to be a derivational suffix since *-kacha* no longer functions as an independent verb.

Of course, since some derivational affixes arise by continuous diachronic development from verbs, there is no absolute dividing line between compounding and affixation. However, in most cases a reasonable judgment can be made based on the above suggestions.

?

Can subject, object, and/or other nouns be incorporated into the verb?
Are there verb–verb compounding processes that result in a verb?

Additional reading: Sapir (1911), Green (1981), Mithun (1984, 1986), Sadock (1986).

9.3   Tense/aspect/mode

Tense, aspect, and **mode** (TAM for short) are operations that anchor or ground the information expressed in a clause according to its sequential, temporal, or epistemological orientation. Tense is associated with the

sequence of events in real time, aspect with the internal temporal "structure" of a situation, while mode relates the speaker's attitude toward the
situation or the speaker's commitment to the probability that the situation
is true. After valence (see chapter 8), aspect is the most common operation
associated with verbs. Bybee (1985: 31) finds that 74 percent of the languages in her randomized sample have morphological manifestation of aspect
in the verb. Mode is the third most common verbal inflectional operation,
occurring in 68 percent of the languages. Tense is seventh, occurring in
only 50 percent of the languages surveyed. TAM differs from valence, however, in that all are much more likely to be inflectional. Only 6 percent of
the languages in Bybee's sample have inflectional manifestation of valence.
Thus, though valence is more common overall, TAM constitute the most
common inflectional operations.

Tense, aspect, and mode are sometimes difficult to tease apart. In
fact, it may be that linguists have thought of these three categories as distinct only because they are somewhat distinct in the classical languages
and in Indo-European generally. Operators that occur in the TAM areas
of the verb or verb phrase are likely to have indistinct semantic ranges;
their meanings may seem to vary depending on the verb they are attached
to, or the case-marking or other characteristics of the core NPs (subject
and object) in the clause. TAM formatives may seem to combine tense,
aspect, modal, evidential (section 3.4.4), and/or locational/directional concepts (section 3.4.3). Some languages pay more attention to tense (e.g.,
English), others to aspect (e.g., Austronesian and African generally), others
to mode (Eskimo), and still others to location and direction (many American, Australian, and Papuan languages). Furthermore, some verb stems
may not allow certain operations while favoring others. Finally, certain
combinations of TAM operators may cooccur with greater than chance
frequency, whereas other logically possible combinations may seldom or
never occur. Groups (usually pairs) of operators that commonly cluster
together are some-times referred to as **hypermorphemes**.

Because of the interrelatedness and indeterminacy of many TAM
operations, beware of too quickly and confidently giving a TAM operation
a gloss. For example, in elicitation it may be common for a particular TAM
operator to occur in responses to English past tense prompts. It is tempting
to gloss such an operator with the label "past tense" without investigating its semantics in relation to other TAM operators in the system. Many

languages have been analyzed as having a tense system when in fact aspect is the more relevant parameter.

It is not uncommon for the tense/aspect/mode system of a language to interact in a significant way with other seemingly distinct subsystems such as nominal case marking or participant reference. For example, many languages use a nominative/accusative system of case marking and/or person marking on verbs in present tense and non-perfective aspects, but an ergative/absolutive system in clauses with perfective aspect or past tense (see section 7.1 for discussion of these terms and for examples). In other languages tense, aspect, and/or mode markers may be fused with the person markers. Such is the case in Seko Padang, a Western Austronesian language (examples courtesy of Tom Laskowske):

(33) a. ha-ni-aka-e:-da
      NEG-PASS-do-FUT:1INC–1INC:VER
      "Nothing will happen to us."

   b. ha-ni-aka-o:-do
      NEG-PASS-FUT:2-2VER
      "Nothing will happen to you."

Examples 33a and b illustrate that the future tense marker in Seko Padang varies for the person of the object.

Seko Padang also has a set of "veridical" mode markers (see section 9.3.3 on mode). These are "optional" second-position clitics (see section 2.2 on clitics) and have something of the semantic effect of *really* used as an adverb in English. Examples 33a and b also illustrate two of the veridical markers, *-da* in 33a and *-do* in 33b. Examples 34a and b illustrate two others:

(34) a. mi-pana'-*da*   ti-ampe-ku
      INTR-sick-3VER   T-grandparent-1SG
      "My grandparent is really sick."

   b. ku-boro-mo-*ko*
      1SG-swollen-PERF-1SG:VER
      "I am really full."

Beyond the clause-level syntax of the language, TAM marking is often deployed in interesting ways in the discourse (see section 12.1.3 on action continuity). For example, so-called "present tense" is often used to make a narrative describing past events more vivid: *Then he says to me* . . .

In the following sections, the concepts of tense, aspect, and mode will be discussed in more detail, and a few additional examples will be presented.

9.3.1   Tense

Tense is the grammatical expression of the relation of the time of an event to some reference point in time, usually the moment the clause is uttered. If we think of time as a line, with "now" represented by a point moving from left to right, we can conceptualize tense in terms of the following diagram:

Languages divide up this conceptual notion for purposes of grammatical marking in many different ways. One common tense system is past, present, and future:

Probably more common, however, are two-way distinctions, either past/non-past or future/non-future:

Another possibility that is rumored to occur is a two-way distinction between present and non-present. In such a system "past" and "future" actions would be coded with a single form:

Some languages make many tense distinctions. Though some languages are reported to have as many as five tense distinctions in the future, it appears that there are never more distinctions in the future than in the past. Yagua allows five tense distinctions in the past and two in the future:

Distant past	one year ago	one month ago	one week ago	today/ yesterday	"now"	immediate future	future

Now we will discuss some of the different ways in which languages express tense. All TAM operations are most often associated with the verbal word (for polysynthetic languages) or verb phrase (for more isolating languages). Just within English, tense can be expressed lexically, morphologically, or analytically:

(35)   is   > was   past: lexical (suppletion)
         walk > walked   past: morphological
         see > will see   future: analytic

Spanish has lexical and morphological manifestations of tense:

(36)   ir   > fue   "go"   > "went"   past: lexical
         hablar > habló   "speak" > "spoke"   past: morphological

Future tense markers often derive historically from free verbs meaning "want," "come," or "go:"

(37)   *Swahili* (Bantu, East Africa)
    a. a-taka ku-ja
       3-want INF-come
       "He/she wants to come."

    b. a-taka-ye   ku-ja
       3-want-REL INF-come
       "he/she who will come"

    c. a-ta-ku-ja
       3-FUT-INF-come
       "He/she will come."

Example 37a illustrates a clause with the form *taka* functioning as a free verb meaning "want." In relative clauses, the form is still *taka*, but it no longer means "want" (37b); rather, it expresses a simple future tense. Example 37c illustrates the fully grammaticalized form *ta-* functioning as a tense prefix on a main verb. The *ku-* no longer functions as the infinitive marker, but is simply a reflex of the older multiclausal structure.

In Bambara, and many other languages, the future tense marker is the same as the verb meaning "come:"

(38)   *Bambara* (Niger-Congo, West Africa)

    a. a   bɛ   na
        3sg PRES come
        "He/she is coming." ("come" as a free verb)

    b. a   na   taa
        3sg come go
        "He/she will go."

    c. a   na   na
        3sg come come
        "He/she will come."

Example 38a illustrates a simple clause headed by the verb *na* meaning "come." Example 38b illustrates *na* functioning as a future tense marker. That it has really lost the meaning "come" is evidenced by the fact that it collocates with the semantically incompatible verb *taa* meaning "go." Example 38c illustrates both the tense marker and main-verb functions of *na*.

In English and many other languages, the verb meaning "go" is grammaticalized as a future tense marker or auxiliary. Example 39b illustrates the Spanish verb *ir* (third person, singular, present tense form *va*) functioning as a future auxiliary:

(39)   a.   Fernando se   va   a   Corvallis.
        F.   REFL go:3sg DIR C.
        "Fernando is going to Corvallis." ("go" as main verb)

      b.   Fernando va   a   venir.
        F.   go:3sg DIR come
        "Fernando is going to come." ("go" as future auxiliary)

9.3.2   Aspect

Aspect describes the internal temporal shape of events or states. The following diagrams and English examples may help conceptualize some of the more common aspectual distinctions languages make. Keep in mind, however, that no language necessarily grammaticalizes any of these aspects, and that the aspectual operations grammaticalized in any given language may not line up exactly with these notions. In particular, English does not grammaticalize many aspectual notions. This does not mean that English clauses "have no aspect." It just means that there are few well-oiled grammatical means of expressing aspectual variation. For example, completion and inception are not fully grammaticalized in English.[1] They are expressed by analytic structures involving a matrix verb and a participial complement: *I finished working, I started working.*

    In the diagrams below, the following notation is used: > = unbounded time, | = a temporal boundary,] = completion, [= inception, x = a punctual event, i.e., an event that occurs instantaneously and therefore has no internal temporal structure.

(a) *Perfective.* In perfective aspect the situation is viewed in its entirety, independent of tense. The terms "preterit" and "aorist" usually refer to past tense plus perfective aspect. The main events of a narrative are normally recounted in perfective aspect, whereas collateral, explanatory, descriptive material occurs in various non-perfective aspects (e.g., imperfective, progressive, habitual):

        [———] He wrote a letter.

    The clause *he wrote* could be perfective, habitual, iterative, or almost any other aspect. The verb form simply encodes tense, leaving the aspectual distinctions to be disambiguated by the context. For example, *He wrote a letter* is not likely to be habitual or iterative, therefore perfective aspect is much more likely, though there is no specific marker of perfective aspect in the clause. On the other hand, *He wrote letters* is probably iterative (though it could be habitual) even though the verb form is the same as that in the previous example. Therefore we can say that English does not always grammaticalize aspect. This is different from saying that these clauses in English "have no aspect."

(b) *Imperfective.* In imperfective aspect the situation is viewed from "inside," as an ongoing process. Habitual and progressive aspects are subtypes of imperfective. See below and Comrie (1978b) for more details.

        ←————————————→ He writes letters.

(c) *Perfect.* Perfect aspect normally describes a currently relevant state brought about by the situation (normally an event) expressed by the verb.

        ————| x He has come from Aqaba.

He has come probably implies "he is here now," whereas *he came* does not. He may be here now or he may have come and left again. There is no direct implication of current relevance inherent in the simple past tense of English. Perfect aspect is not the same as completive. *He has finished working* (perfect completive) implies "he is not working now," whereas the perfective completive, *He finished working*, does not carry this implication: for example, it is pragmatically acceptable to say *He finished working at 12:00 and began again at 2:00*. In the perfect, however, this sounds strange: ??*He has finished working at 12:00 and began again at 2:00*. The similarity between the terms perfect and perfective is unfortunate, as these refer to very different aspectual categories. Nevertheless, these terms are very standard in the literature, and they must not be confused.

(d) *Pluperfect.* Pluperfect, like "preterit," refers to a combination of an aspect and a tense. Pluperfect combines perfect aspect and past tense. The effect of this combination is to shift the deictic centre (DC) from "now" to some point in the past. That is, the state that results from an event is presented as occurring at some point in the past:

⎯⎯⎯| DC ⎯⎯⎯ (now) I had entered a congested zone.

(e) *Completive.* Completive aspect expresses the completion of an event. Sometimes completive and inceptive aspects are called phasal aspects, because they refer to different "phases" of the event described by the verb:

>⎯⎯⎯⎯⎯⎯⎯| She finished working.

(f) *Inceptive.* Similarly, inceptive aspect expresses the starting point of an event:

[⎯⎯⎯⎯⎯⎯⎯> She began working.

(g) *Continuative/progressive.* Continuative or progressive aspect implies an ongoing, dynamic process. This is opposed to stative aspect, which implies no change over time. Continuous or progressive aspect is distinguished from habitual in that continuative or progressive refers to actual events, whereas habitual expresses the general truth that some event takes place from time to time. Habitual does not refer to any specific events.

The auxiliary *be* plus the present participle of the verb is a grammaticalized progressive aspect construction in English.

> ─────────────→ He is writing letters.

(h) *Punctual.* Punctual events are those which have no internal temporal structure because they occur in an instant in time. Sometimes this aspect is referred to as instantaneous.

x He sneezed.

(i) *Iterative.* Iterative aspect is where a punctual event takes place several times in succession.

 > -x-x-x-x-x-x-x-x-x-x- > He is coughing.

With inherently punctual verbs like *cough*, the progressive implies iterativity. With "non-punctual" (durative) verbs like *run* the progressive implies continuity. The progressive is often not appropriate with stative verbs like *know*, e.g., **Rudyard was knowing the answer.*

(j) *Habitual.* As mentioned above under continuative/progressive, habitual aspect expresses an assertion that a certain type of event, such as Rudyard walking to school, regularly takes place (i.e., is instantiated by actual events) from time to time. It does not imply that an instance of the event is taking place "now."

←─────────────→ He drinks.

The simple "present tense" verb forms in English do not indicate present tense, as defined here, for dynamic verbs. That is, the present tense forms in English do not anchor dynamic events (events that involve change over time) as occurring at the same time as the time of speaking ("now"). A clause such as *He walks to school* either means (a) habitual ("he walks to school every day"), (b) "historical present" (*So he gets out of bed, gets dressed, and has breakfast. Then he walks to school, see?*), which actually anchors the event at some point in the past, or (c) "future" (*Tomorrow he walks to school; I refuse to take him anymore*). Since *walk* describes a dynamic event, in order to anchor it to the moment of speaking, a progressive form is required: *He is walking to school.* "Static" or stative situations do not involve change over time. Verbs of sensation and mental state typically describe static situations, e.g., *She knows the answer, He sees a bear, I wonder what happened to Jane*, etc. For such verbs, the present tense form actually does anchor the event at the time of utterance. These also, in their normal senses, do not often occur in the progressive aspect: *?She is remembering his name.*

Aspect is not a morphological operator on verbs in English; rather, it is expressed analytically by predicate combining:

(40)   He has gone. (perfect)
        I am going. (progressive)
        I used to walk to school. (imperfective)
        I finished working. (completive)

There is a morphological component to these expressions of aspect in English in that the participles take a special morphological form (past participle of *go = gone*, present participle of *work = working*, etc.).

Spanish, as well as many other languages, expresses perfective and imperfective aspects morphologically, and perfect aspect with a morphological/analytic combination:

(41)   habló > hablaba "spoke" > "was speaking" perfective > imperfective
        haber hablado "have spoken" perfect: morphological/analytic

Mandarin expresses perfective aspect strictly analytically:

(42)   Zéi   pâo le
        thief run PERFECTIVE
        "The thief ran away."

Aspect marking frequently is located in various positions in the clause. For example, in Ewe aspect markers occur as a verbal suffix (43a), a prefix (43b), a clause-final particle (43c), and an auxiliary combined with a word order change (43d):

(43)   *Ewe* (Kwa, Niger-Congo)
        a. é-du-*a*   mɔ́li.
            3-eat-HAB rice
            "He/she eats rice."

        b. é-*ga*-du   mɔ́li.
            3-REP-eat rice
            "He/she repeatedly ate rice."

c. é-du mɔ́li *vɔ*.
   3-eat rice COMPL
   "He/she finished eating rice."

d. é-*le*   mɔ́li du-*m*.
   3-be:at rice eat-LOC
   "He/she is eating rice."

Example 43d also illustrates the common fact that progressive aspect constructions often derive historically from locational structures. In Ewe the auxiliary used for progressive aspect is the same form used in locational clauses (see chapter 6). The verb then takes a locational postposition. Literally, this clause could be translated "He/she is at rice-eating." This development is also apparent in English progressive aspect:

(44)   Stage 1: She is at walking.
        Stage 2: She is a-walking. (still heard in some dialects)
        Stage 3: She is walking.

Nominal marking sometimes affects the aspect of a clause (less often the tense or mode). For example, in English the difference between a generic and a specific direct object can convey the difference between habitual and perfective aspect:

(45)   I built houses. (past tense / habitual aspect)
        I built a house. (past tense / perfective aspect)

In Finnish, the difference between an accusative and a partitive direct object often expresses the distinction between perfective and progressive aspect:

(46) a. Han luki kirjan.
          he   read book:ACC
          "He read the book." (past perfective)

      b. Han luki kirjaa.
          he   read book:PART
          "He was reading the book." (past progressive)

For this reason, case markers can be mistaken for TAM markers. For example, in Guaymí the ergative case marker -*gwe* only occurs in perfective aspect clauses:

(47) a. Dorí-gwe ti   dëma-íni
          Doris-ERG 1SG greet-PERF
          "Doris greeted me."

      b. Dori ti   dëma-e
          Doris 1SG greet-PRES
          "Doris greets me."

The original grammatical description of Guaymí analyzed -*gwe* as a "tense marker" since it only occurred in what the author analyzed as past tense.

Location and aspect. It is worth mentioning here that there is often a synchronic and/or historical connection between aspect marking and location/direction marking (see section 9.4). A few examples from English will suffice to illustrate this point, though similar observations could be made for many other languages:

(48)   I *came* to see . . .   *come* = inceptive
          He cut *away* at the log.   *away* = imperfective
          Tom drank the Pisco sour *down*.   *down* = perfective
          I ate *up* all the ugali.   *up* = perfective
          They were *at* eating.   *at* = progressive (archaic)

9.3.3   Mode

Mode describes the speaker's attitude toward a situation, including the speaker's belief in its reality, or likelihood. It sometimes describes the speaker's estimation of the relevance of the situation to him/herself. The terms mode, mood, and modality are often used interchangeably, though some linguists make distinctions among these terms. The highest-level distinction in modal operations is between realis and irrealis, though like most conceptual distinctions these terms describe a continuum. A prototypical realis mode strongly asserts that a specific event or state of affairs has actually happened, or actually holds true. A prototypical irrealis mode makes no such assertion whatsoever. Irrealis mode does not necessarily assert that an event did not take place or will not take place. It simply makes no claims with respect to the actuality of the event or situation described. Negative clauses do assert that events or situations do not hold, but these are subject to the same realis–irrealis continuum as are affirmative clauses. For example, I can assert the reality of the statement *He did not clean the kitchen* just as weakly or strongly as I can assert the reality of its affirmative counterpart (see section 10.2 on negative assertions). Some languages, however, treat all negative clauses as irrealis.

Mode interacts significantly with aspect and tense (Wallace 1982). For example, habitual aspect clauses are less realis than perfective aspect clauses since habitual aspect describes an event type that is instantiated from time to time by actual events. Similarly, mode interacts with the referentiality and definiteness of the noun phrases associated with the verb. For example, entities under a highly realis mode assertion are more likely to be referential than those under an irrealis assertion:

(49)   Rudyard ate the Cheerios that were in the cupboard.

However, a less realis mode with a specific referential object sounds odd:

(50)   ??Rudyard always eats the Cheerios that were in the cupboard.

A less realis mode with a generic (non-referential) object sounds better:

(51)   Rudyard always eats Cheerios for breakfast.

Irrealis mode can refer to an event/situation which is presented as occurring in a contingent world. For example:

(52)   *If you eat Wheaties*, you'll be like the big boys.

In this clause the condition, *if you eat Wheaties*, is irrealis. Interrogative and imperative clauses are likely to be irrealis, since they do not assert that X did happen, but order it to come about, or question whether it will or did come about. So if a language grammaticalizes the notion of irrealis, chances are that interrogative and/or imperative clauses will fall into the irrealis category. Interrogative and imperative, however, are not themselves modes (see section 10.3). Terms that have been used for various kinds of assertions that are close to the irrealis end of the realis–irrealis continuum are the following: subjunctive, optative (wishes), potential (might, ability to), hypothetical/imaginary, conditional (if), probability, deontic (should, must, have to). For example:

(53)   *Subjunctive* (Spanish)
Si no hubiera   sido por Anita, mi reloj sería   perdido.
if NEG have:SUBJ been for Anita my watch would:be lost
"If it had not been for Anita, my watch would be lost."

(54)   *Optative*
I wish I had a million dollars.
I want to earn a million dollars.

(55)   *Potential*
I might earn a million dollars.
I can/am able to earn a million dollars.

(56)   *Hypothetical*
Let's suppose that I had a million dollars . . .
Now if it were possible to earn a million dollars as a college professor . . .
If you had eaten your Cheerios as a child, you would be doing better in school today.

(57)   *Conditional*
If you eat your Cheerios, you will be strong.
If you come home before six, we can go to the movie.

(58)   *Deontic* (obligation)
I have to earn a million dollars this year.
We should send out a Christmas letter.
There ought to be a law.
They must have dinner with us.

The term "deontic" comes from the same root as the English word *debt*. Deontic mode expresses the subject's duty or obligation to perform the irrealis act expressed by the verb. There are sometimes several deontic operators that express different degrees of strength of obligation, e.g., *must* is stronger than *should* in English. Sometimes what I have called "potential" mode is treated as part of the deontic continuum expressing very weak obligation.

(59)   *Epistemic* (probability)
They must have left already. (I infer from the time, or some other evidence.)
They will have left already.
They should have left by now.
They might have left by now.

"Epistemic" has to do with the speaker's degree of commitment to the truth of the proposition. Examples 58 and 59 show that *must* and *should* in English have both an epistemic and a deontic sense. The auxiliaries *might* and *will* also have multiple functions, depending mostly on the aspect of the clause. Often epistemic categories such as evidentiality and validationality are part of the modal system of the language. If so, they should be treated in the same section of a descriptive grammar. Nevertheless, because these are often distinct from mode, we will discuss them in a separate section of this outline (section 9.6).

TAM marking also often interacts with person marking on verbs. For example, languages sometimes employ an ergative/absolutive system for organizing grammatical relations in perfective aspect and a nominative/accusative system in imperfective aspect (see section 7.3.2.2). Seko Padang grammaticalizes the distinction between realis and irrealis mode simply by the use of a different set of person markers. Examples 60a and 61a illustrate declarative mode clauses, while 60b and 61b illustrate the corresponding irrealis mode:

(60)   a. *ku*-mu-tole'
            1SG-INTR-smoke
            "I smoke."   realis

       b. ha-mu-tole'-*ka*'
            NEG-INTR-smoke-1SG
            "I don't smoke."   irrealis (negative)

(61)   a. *0*-mammu-lao
            3-INTR-go
            "He walks."   realis

       b. i-mammu-lao-*i*
            COND-INTR-go-3
            "If he walks . . ."   irrealis (conditional)

In addition to having grammaticalized tense, aspect, and modal systems, languages often code temporal and modal notions periphrastically. Temporal adverbs are periphrastic indicators of temporal relations. These do not constitute part of the tense or aspect system. For example,

(62)   "I see the doctor tomorrow."   ("tense:" future)
       "I see the doctor every day."   ("aspect:" habitual)

It is obvious to us that *tomorrow* and *every day* are not tense markers in English, but that may be only because we have another marker whose function is clearly to indicate tense (-*ed*). In other languages, this may not be so clear. Indonesian, for example, along with many other languages of Insular and Mainland Southeast Asia, grammaticalizes very few aspectual and no tense distinctions. The only way of making temporal grounding explicit is via adverbials or extraclausal periphrastic devices.

?

> Is there a tense system? How does it operate? Future/non-future, past/
> non-past, past/present/future, or other? (You may want to treat these
> separately or group them, depending on how the language works.)
> How is aspect expressed?
> Is there a clear dividing line between tense/aspect and mode (probably not)?
> What are the modes?
> Is the case-marking pattern influenced at all by TAM?

Additional reading: DeLancey (1982), Givón (1984), Hopper (1979, 1982), Hopper and Thompson (1980).

9.4   Location/direction

Even as tense grounds a situation in time, location and directional marking ground situations in space. Spatial grounding has not been given as much prominence as tense, aspect, and mode in the linguistic literature. This is possibly because Greek, Latin, and other European languages do not have verbal operations expressing spatial grounding. However, many other languages do grammaticalize spatial grounding. In fact, for some languages, spatial deixis is more central to the verbal system than temporal deixis. Directional formatives are often related etymologically to the basic verbs of motion ("go," "come," and perhaps "arrive," "return," "depart," "go up," and "go down"). Some languages have only one basic verb of motion, and rely on directional formatives to distinguish whether the motion is away from a point of reference ("thither") or toward a point of reference ("hither"). This is true of Lahu and many other Tibeto-Burman languages (Matisoff 1973).

The system of verbal locational marking is often sensitive to the culture and/or environment of the people who speak the language. For example, many of the Quechuan languages, spoken in the Andes Mountains of South America, have verbal locational suffixes indicating action "uphill," "downhill," and "at the same altitude." Yagua, a language spoken along the rivers of lowland Peru, has similar suffixes that prototypically mean action done upriver or downriver:

(63)   Sąąna-a suuti-*imu*-níí.
         2DL-IRR wash-DR-3SG
         "Wash him/her downriver."

(64)   Sị-ịryi-*chá*-ra.
         3SG-get-UR-INAN
         "She/he gets it upriver."

Many Papuan languages (Papua New Guinea and Irian Jaya) have elaborate systems of locational marking on verbs. The following is an example from Orya (Tor-Lake Plain stock, Irian Jaya; example courtesy of Phil Fields):

(65)   esek-gul-bla-*in-hal-za*
         slide-NOM:SG > ACC:F-DAT:MASC-down-away-to:here
         "Slide it down and away to me."

In Yagua, the suffixes *-nuvïï*, *-nuvaa*, and a few others designate that the action expressed by the verb they attach to occurs relative to a particular locational scene and trajectory of movement (T. Payne 1992):

(66)   a.   Naani-ipeni-yąą-*nuvïï*.
            3DL-dance-DIST-on:arrival1
            "They dance all over on arrival." (current scene)

       b.   Naani-núú-*ñuvaa*.
            3DL-look-on:arrival2
            "They look on arrival." (new scene)

Both *-nuvïï* and *-nuvaa* indicate that the action expressed by the verb occurs upon arrival on some scene. The opposition between the two is determined by whether that scene is the currently activated one or if it implies the activation of a new scene. Other similar locational suffixes in Yagua include *-rïï* "passing by," *-ja* "moving horizontally, across water or land," *-jasúmiy* "moving upwards," *-siy* "departing."

In Otomí (Otomanguean, Mexico), the verb phrase contains an auxiliary element that inflects for person and number of the subject, for aspect, and for whether the action is away from a designated deictic center (exocentric) or toward a designated deictic center (centric). The deictic center is usually, but not necessarily, the location of the speaker at the time of speaking (examples courtesy of Henrietta Andrews):

(67)   ʔbü   x-*tí*   tzon   nìr   ngû
         when FUT1–2:EXO   arrive your house
         "When you arrive at your house (over there) . . ."

(68)   ngû g-*rí*   ʔúni
        as   FUT-2:CENT give
        "As you give (it) (here) . . ."

?

Does the language employ verbal affixes or verb-phrase grammatical functors that specify the spatial orientation or grounding of the situation?

References: Matisoff (1973), T. Payne (1984).

9.5   Participant reference

If participant reference marking on verbs is particularly complex, you may want to just describe the paradigm for main, declarative, perfective aspect clauses here and provide pointers to where the other paradigms are described. Then be sure to describe the other paradigms in the sections that pertain to their use. For example, it may be helpful to describe the paradigm for subjunctive mode in the section on mode, and the paradigm for negatives in the section on negatives, etc.

Participant reference on verbs is sometimes called **cross-reference, verb agreement, verb coding,** or **concord**. The last term is especially common among linguists who specialize in African languages. What all of the various systems described by these terms have in common is that they all ground the situation described by the verb in terms of the main participants in the situation. Participant reference can be either **anaphoric** or **grammatical**. Verbal participant reference is anaphoric when it can constitute the only reference to an argument in the clause (see above and section 3.1.3). For example, the word *hablo* in Spanish is a fully grammatical clause meaning "I speak." The *-o* suffix in itself constitutes an adequate reference to the subject argument. So we say that *-o* (and verbal participant reference generally in Spanish) is anaphoric. Sometimes languages, like Spanish, that have anaphoric verb agreement are called **pro-drop** languages, or **pronominal argument** languages (Jelinek 1988). In English, on the other hand, a verb form like *am* is not a fully grammatical clause even though it does make reference to a first person singular subject. In English, verbal participant reference must be accompanied by a free-form reference to the subject participant, e.g., I *am*. Sometimes non-anaphoric participant reference is called **grammatical agreement**, or simply **verb agreement**. Languages that employ non-anaphoric agreement extensively are sometimes called **lexical argument** languages (Jelinek 1988).

Arguments represented by person marking on the verb are said to have a **grammatical relation** to the verb (see chapter 7), but not all arguments that have a grammatical relation are necessarily represented on the verb. Participant reference (whether anaphoric or not) can be expressed by any of the morphological processes mentioned in section 2.2, e.g., prefixing, suffixing, stem changes, etc. Participant reference, both anaphoric and grammatical, almost always arises from a diachronic process extending from free pronouns, through anaphoric clitics, to grammatical agreement. For this reason, participant reference markers are often similar in form to the free pronouns (see section 3.1.3).

Occasionally verbs will be marked for the plurality of the *addressee* of a clause rather than of any of the grammatical arguments of the clause. Such is the case in Seko Padang:

(69)   ku-luma-a-ko-sse,   na?
        1SG-go-FUT-1SG:VER-PL OK
        "I'm really going to go, OK?" (plural addressee)

In this example, the plural marker, *-sse*, appears because the speaker is speaking to more than one person. Plurality is always an optional category in Seko Padang verbs, but in other contexts it can mean plurality of a verbal argument.

?
         Does the language mark the person and/or number of verbal arguments or
         speech act participants on the verb?
         Provide charts of the various paradigms.

9.6   Evidentiality, validationality, and mirativity

Evidentiality has to do with how languages express relative certainty of truth. It has been called "the linguistic coding of epistemology" (Chafe and Nichols 1986). **Epistemology** refers to how people obtain and evaluate knowledge. People have different attitudes toward knowledge partially because they obtain knowledge from different sources. For example, I am more certain of things I have experienced directly or have reliable evidence for; I am less certain of things I have heard second-hand, or have ambiguous evidence for. Languages typically provide morphosyntactic devices for expressing a range of attitudes toward knowledge. For example, an utterance like *It's raining* presents information as unquestionably true. In English, adverbs are often used to express something about the reliability of the information, or the probability of its truth, e.g., *It's probably raining* or *Maybe it's raining*. Inference from indirect evidence may be expressed with a modal auxiliary: *It must be raining*. Or the specific kind of evidence on which an inference is based may be indicated with a separate verb: *It sounds like it's raining* (Chafe and Nichols 1986).

These kinds of example show that, in English, evidentiality is not grammaticalized; rather, it tends to be expressed periphrastically by clause combining or adverbial expressions. Other languages may make evidential and other epistemic distinctions in the verb morphology. In such languages the evidential system is almost always linked to the tense/aspect/mode (TAM) system.

Some linguists (e.g., Weber 1986) make a distinction between **evidential force** and **validational** or **veridical force**. In this view evidential marking is strictly limited to indicating the source of the information expressed in the clause, whereas validational or veridical marking indicates the degree of commitment the speaker makes as to the truth of the assertion. Naturally, these two parameters parallel one another, since people are likely to be strongly convinced of the truth of information gained from direct experience and less convinced of the truth of information gained indirectly. Nevertheless, Weber shows that, at least for Quechua, even if the speaker is absolutely convinced of the truth of a proposition he has not directly witnessed, he may not use the direct evidence evidential. For example, in Quechua I cannot without hedging say "my mother's grandfather's name was Henderson" unless I have personally met my mother's grandfather.

It should be clear also that evidentiality is closely tied to tense, aspect, and mode. We are more likely to be sure of past events than future events, the completion of perfective events than of events still in process, realis assertions than irrealis assertions. As with location and direction marking, evidentiality and validationality are often difficult to tease apart from the TAM system, and there may be complex diachronic and synchronic relationships.

The most common type of evidential marker in language seems to be a **hearsay** particle. Yup'ik provides a straightforward example (Reed, *et al.* 1977):

(70)   Tua-llu-*gguq* nunaa-t   uku-t   uita-lri-it
       then-and-HSY village-ABS DEM-ABS be-PAST-3
       "And then there was this village, they say."

Without -*gguq* this clause would imply that the speaker has direct experience of the village described.

    Yup'ik also possesses an **inferential** evidential enclitic that contrasts with -*gguq* "hearsay" and -0 "direct." The inferential enclitic is -*ggem*:

(71)   Ak'a-*ggem*   ayag-llru-uq
       already-INFER leave-PAST-3
       "It seems he already left."

Example 71 would be used in a situation where the speaker did not personally see the person leave, nor was told about his leaving by someone else. Instead, the speaker has inferred that the subject has left, perhaps from noticing that he is no longer present.

    In Yup'ik (and the Eskimo and Iñupiat languages generally) the evidential particles are "second position enclitics" (see section 2.2). It is often the case that evidentials and validationals operate on the clause, rather than at verb-phrase level.

    Huallaga Quechua has three enclitics that are clearly evidential. These enclitics follow the clausal element that conveys new, or asserted, information (Weber 1986: 419ff.). It stands to reason that the evidentials should be associated with the new information in a clause, since one is more likely to question the source and status of new information than of given information. These enclitics are -*mi* "direct evidence," -*shi* "hearsay," and -*chi* "inference:"

(72)   Qam-pis maqa-ma-shka-nki   a. -*mi*
                             b. -*shi*
                             c. -*chi*
       you-also hit-1-PERF-2
       "You also hit me."
    a. I saw/felt you hit me and I was conscious.
    b. I was drunk, and someone informed me that you hit me.
    c. A group of people beat me up, and I think you may have been one of them.

In the future or other irrealis contexts, the evidentials express more validational, modal or rhetorical force:

(73)   Noqa a. -*mi* chaya-:-man   aywa-r-qa
          b. -*shi*
          c. -*chi*

1SG   arrive-1-COND go-ADV-TOP
"I would (-*mi*)/could (-*shi*)/might (-*chi*) arrive, if I were to go."

Like TAM marking, evidential and validational marking can be coded as verbal affixes, clause combining, or adverbial elements. In English we use matrix verbs to indicate both validational and modal concepts, e.g., *I think, I believe, I know* are validational whereas *I must, I should, I might* are modal. Other matrix verbs are evidential, e.g., *they say, it seems,* and *I see.*

Panare illustrates the interaction of evidentiality with tense and aspect. The immediate past perfective suffix, -*yaj*, tends to express **first-hand evidentiality**. In this respect it contrasts with the non-specific aspect markers:

(74)   a. Ti-yaj   kën   Kamána-pana
          go-PPERF1 AN:INVIS Camana-toward
          "He left for Camana (and I saw him go)."

      b. Y-u-të-n   kën   Kamána-yaka
          3-INTRNS-go-NON:SPEC AN:INVIS Camana-to
          "He went to Camana (at some unspecified time; I may not know when because I didn't see him go)."

Also, there are two perfect aspect suffixes. One of these, -*sa'*, typically expresses first-hand evidentiality whereas the other, -*jpë*, expresses inferential evidentiality:

(75)   a. wë-të-*sa'*   këj   kën
          INTRNS-go-PERF1 AN:PROX AN:INVIS
          "He has left (I saw him go)."

      b. wë-të-*jpë*   këj   kën
          INTRNS-go-PERF2 AN:PROX AN:INVIS
          "He must have left (e.g., all his clothes are gone)."

Some languages have what have been called **veridical** markers. Technically, veridical marking (or "verity") is the same as validationality. However, some languages distinguish a mode that expresses an increased intensity of the truth of the proposition, something like the adverbial use of *really* in English. This is the function of veridicals in Seko Padang, a western Austronesian language:

(76) a. mi-pana'-*da*   tiampe-ku
          INTR-sick-3VER grandparent-1SG
          "My grandparent is really sick."

      b. ku-boro-mo-*ko*
          1SG-swollen-PERF-1SG:VER
          "I am really full."

      c. ha-ni-aka-e:-*da*
          NEG-PASS-do-FUT:1INC-1INC:VER
          "Nothing will really happen to us."

      d. ha-ni-aka-o:-*do*
          NEG-PASS-do-FUT:2-2VER
          "Nothing will really happen to you."

Finally, some languages have grammaticalized ways of expressing how well a piece of information is integrated into the speaker's store of previous knowledge. This kind of attitude toward knowledge has been termed **mirativity** by Scott DeLancey (p.c.).

For example, in many languages there is a distinction between the expression of information that is surprising versus that which is unsurprising or expected. The form that means "surprising" can be glossed as "mirative:"

(77)   *Turkish*

        a. Kemal gel-di.
            "Kemal came."

        b. Kemal gel-mIš.
                     MIR
            "Kemal, surprisingly, came."

(78)   *Lhasa Tibetan*

        a. ngar   dngul   tog = tsam yod
            1SG:DAT money some   EXIST
            "I have some money." (expected)

        b. ngar dngul tog = tsam 'dug
                             EXIST:MIR
            "I have some money!" (unexpected)

The difference between 78a and 78b is that in the former the speaker is informing the hearer that the speaker has money, whereas 78b would be the kind of expression one would use if the speaker were to reach into her bag and unexpectedly discover that she had some money. A similar kind of distinction is found in Panare:

(79)   a. y-anï-ñe   këj mëj
           TRANS-bite-TENSE SPEC 3SG
           "It bites." (I inform you)

      b. anï-në mëj
           bite-INF 3SG
           "It bites!" (I just found out)

To summarize this discussion of evidentiality, validationality, and mirativity, I will present some examples from Tuyuca, a Tucanoan language of Colombia. This language has one of the most complex systems of evidentiality I have seen. It has the added complication of having evidentiality interwoven with the verbal participant reference system and the tense system. The relevant distinctions for Tuyuca seem to be whether the situation was witnessed by the speaker or not, whether it is general knowledge, inferred, or only hearsay (data from Barnes 1990).

(80)   a. kiti-gï   tii-gí
           chop:trees-MSG AUX-NONVISIBLE:PRESENT:3MSG
           "He is chopping trees." (I hear him)

      b. kiti-gï   tii-í
           chop:trees-MSG AUX-VISIBLE:PRESENT:3MSG
           "He is chopping trees." (I see him)

      c. kiti-gï   tii-hɔi
           chop:trees-MSG AUX-INFERRED:PRESENT:3MSG
           "Apparently he's chopping trees." (I can't really tell what he's doing)

      d. kiti-gï   tii-tí
           chop:trees-MSG AUX-NONVISIBLE:PAST:3MSG
           "He was chopping trees." (I heard him)

      e. kiti-gï   tii-yigï
           chop:trees-MSG AUX-HEARSAY:PAST:3MSG
           "They say he chopped trees."

The entire evidential paradigm for Tuyuca is given in table 9.1.

Table 9.1   Tuyuca evidential paradigm

	Visible	–Visible	Inferred	Hearsay	General knowledge
Past					
1/2	-wï	-tï	-yu	-yiro	-hɔyu
3Msg	-wi	-ti	-yi	-yigï	-hiyi
3Fsg	-wo	-to	-yo	-yigo	-hïyo
3pl	-wa	-ta	-ya	-yira	-hɔya
Present					
1/2	-a	-ga	–	–	-ku
3Msg	-i	-gi	hɔi	–	-ki
3Fsg	-yo	-go	-hɔo	–	-ko
3pl	-ya	-ga	-hɔra	–	-kua

?

Are there any grammaticalized indicators of evidentiality, validationality, or mirativity?

9.7   Miscellaneous

Some typical miscellaneous verb or verb-phrase operations include:

(a) Lexical time reference (as opposed to tense), e.g., *yesterday, tomorrow*. For example, Koyukon employs a verbal prefix *ee-* that means the action is performed "once only." The Yagua verb suffixes *-jásiy* "earlier today" and *-jay* "yesterday" have been called degrees of "tense" (section 9.4.1, D. Payne and T. Payne 1990), but may be analyzed as miscellaneous derivational morphemes, because (1) they are not required at all by the verb system, (2) it appears (though no statistical study has been done) that *-jay* is about as common as time adverbials such as *yesterday* in English, and (3) the information these suffixes express is very specific, i.e., their meanings are more characteristic of lexical items than of grammatical morphemes.

(b) Distributive, i.e., "all over the place," "with a back-and-forth motion."

(c) Environmental, e.g., "at night," "over water" (on motion verbs).

(d) Speaker attitude, e.g., "complaining," "frustration," "disgust."

Mapudugun (also known as Araucanian or Mapuche), of Chile, has some interesting verbal operations that indicate speaker attitude. In the following examples, the first sentence is the unmarked form, while the second and third represent "complaining" and "disgust" respectively (examples courtesy of María Catrileo):

(81)   a. θalílaenew   "He/she didn't greet me."
       b. talílaenew   "Poor me; he/she didn't greet me."
       c. ṭalílaeṇew   "That fool didn't greet me."

(82)   a. al^ykátulay "He/she didn't listen."
       b. alkátulay   "Oh dear; he/she didn't listen."
       c. aḷkátuḷay   "That fool didn't listen."

Athabaskan languages are particularly rich in what we can only describe as "miscellaneous" verbal operators. They are miscellaneous not only because they express semantic notions not embodied in the verbal morphology of languages familiar to most linguists, but also because their functions are variable and difficult to describe with a single inclusive statement. Perhaps further research will help elucidate a more explicit function for these forms. The presence of, or choice between, such morphemes typically is dependent on a complex of factors including verb semantics, verb stem shape, and syntactic valence. Such operations do exist in other language families of the world as well. Furthermore, most (if not all) verb morphology exhibits a certain degree of randomness and variability; it is just that Athabaskan languages seem to have taken this characteristic to an extreme. Therefore, a brief presentation of one Athabaskan system is in order here. The following data on Koyukon come exclusively from Thompson (1989).

Some verb morphemes or verb-phrase particles may have no clear or productive semantic effect. They may simply be required for certain roughly defined classes of verbs, e.g., verbs of motion, verbs of manipulation, transitive verbs, etc. Athabaskan languages are famous for their "verb classifiers." Koyukon has four verb classifier morphemes: 0-, *ł*-, *di*-, and *li*-. In the following examples the choice of classifier is not predictable from the semantics or phonological shape of the verb stems:

(83)   na-ghonh
       2S:SUB-make:PL [0 classifier]
       "You are making them."

(84)   ni-*ł*-tsee
       2S:SUB-CL-make:SG
       "You are making it."

(85)   *di*-bits
       CL-wide
       "It is wide."

(86)   *li*-ts'u*ł*
    CL-clean
    "It is clean."

Sometimes a given verb root can occur with more than one of these operators, in which case the operator "derives" a verb from one subclass to another. In Koyukon there is a tendency for the *ł*- classifier to be used with transitive verbs, and any intransitive verb can be made transitive by changing any classifier to *ł*-:

(87)   a.   atsah
      cry [0 classifier]
      "He/she is crying."

     b.   ni-*ł*-tsah
      2S:SUB-CL-cry
      "You are making him/her cry."

The verb classifiers of Koyukon (and Athabaskan languages generally) operate within many of the functional systems described in earlier sections, such as causation (87b), passive (ex. 88b and 89b), and applicative (ex. 90b):

(88)   a.   *Active*
      y-ee-to-ts'iyh
      3S:DO-once-FUT-pinch [0 classifier]
      "He/she will pinch him/her once."

     b.   *Passive*
      ee-to-*di*-ts'iyh
      once-FUT-CL-pinch
      "He/she will be pinched once."

(89)   a.   *Active*
      n-ee-to-*ł*-dzis
      2S:DO-once-FUT-CL-hit
      "He/she will hit you once."

     b.   *Passive*
      ee-ta-gh-ee-*l*-dzis
      once-FUT-PROG-2S:SUB-CL-hit [*li*- classifier]
      "You will be hit once."

(90)   a. *Normal transitive*
          li-*tł*-baats
          PERF-1SG:SUB:CL-boil
          "I boiled it."

       b. *Applicative ("Self-benefactive")*
          daa-l-*gi*-baats
          THM-PERF–1SG:SUB:CL-boil
          "I boiled it for myself."

These examples also illustrate what have been called the "theme" morphemes of Athabaskan. These are morphemes that are simply required for certain stems.

?

Does the language have any other "miscellaneous" verb or verb-phrase operations?

For any such miscellaneous operations, argue for why you have not treated them as TAM or location/direction marking.

10   Pragmatically marked structures

10.0   Pragmatic statuses

Pragmatics is the practice of utterance interpretation (Levinson 1983). Utterances are actual instances of language in use, therefore they always occur in a context and their interpretations always affect and are affected by the context. What we will call **pragmatic statuses** have to do with choices speakers make about how to efficiently adapt their utterances to the context, including the addressee's presumed "mental state." Like semantic roles, pragmatic statuses are usually, though not always, thought of as characteristics of nominal elements. However, semantic roles are features of the *content* of the discourse (see section 3.2.0), while pragmatic statuses relate the content to the *context*. Labels that have been used to describe various pragmatic statuses include: **given, new, presupposed, focus, topic, identifiable** (or **definite**), and **referential**. These terms will be described in the following subsections. But first we will sketch the conceptual background to these pragmatic notions.

People are constantly surrounded by sensory impressions, only a very small portion of which can be attended to at any given moment. Therefore, we have to be selective about which impressions to attend to, and which to ignore. When communicating with other people, we as speakers constantly (1) assess our audience's present mental state, e.g., what they already know, what they are currently attending to, what they are interested in, etc., and (2) construct our message so as to help the audience revise their mental state in the direction we would like it to go. For example, we may highlight items that we want someone to pay attention to, and which we sense he/she is not already paying attention to. Also, we may spend little communicative energy on information which we sense the audience is already thinking about or attending to. The study of how these kinds of highlighting and downplaying tasks affect the structure of linguistic communication is commonly referred to as pragmatics.

It should be pointed out that grammatical relations are one major means of expressing pragmatic information about nominal elements in discourse (see chapter 7). For example, in languages that have a well-grammaticalized subject category, subjects tend to be identifiable, given and already available in memory. Direct objects are either given or new in about equal proportions. Obliques (nominal clause elements that bear no grammatical relation to the verb) tend to express new information and/or information that is not central to the ongoing development of the discourse (Givón 1983b, Thompson to appear). Also, the pragmatic status of a nominal is influenced by many factors, including semantic roles. So, for example, people are likely to choose AGENTS as the main topics of their discourses. This is because there is a human tendency to pay attention to things that exercise power and control rather than things that do not.

In addition to the grammaticalized pragmatic statuses accorded to nominal elements in clauses by grammatical relations, languages typically express a vast range of pragmatic statuses via special morphosyntactic devices. Some such devices are commonly referred to as "focus" or "emphatic" devices. However, linguistic researchers should *not* use these terms unless they are defined very explicitly. These are probably the most overused and misused terms in linguistics. Instead, we will use the nontechnical term "pragmatic statuses." There are two reasons for this choice of terminology: (1) there is little standardization of terms within this domain (e.g., the terms "focus" and "topic" are antonyms in some traditions and synonyms in others!), and (2) a particular device may act differently in different languages. The devices described in section 10.1, however, are united in that they typically ascribe some sort of unusual pragmatic status to a clause element. Which particular status that is may vary from language to language.

In the remainder of this introductory section, various terms often used to refer to pragmatic statuses will be briefly described. The ways in which languages deal with these distinctions will be presented, beginning in section 10.1.

10.0.1   Identifiability and referentiality

Two pragmatic statuses that play a significant role in the grammars of most languages are **identifiability** and **referentiality**. Certain noun phrases refer to entities that the speaker judges should be **identifiable** by the addressee. The particle *the* is one means of expressing identifiability in English:

(1)   **The** Duke of Wimple trod on **the** princess' toe.

The use of *the* in this example instructs the addressee that there is a unique Duke of Wimple and princess that the speaker is referring to. Furthermore, if this were a real communication situation, the speaker would probably assume that the addressee knows who the Duke of Wimple and the princess are. That is, the speaker treats the participants in question as *identifiable* given the information the speaker assumes the addressee has available. If the particle *a* were used in place of *the*, the effect would be that there is not a unique referent for each of these terms. That is, there may be many Dukes of Wimple and many princesses that the addressee might identify and it is unknown or just does not matter which specific ones were involved in the action. In traditional English grammar the term **definite** has been used to describe the status we will refer to as identifiable.

Noun phrases can be **identified** (i.e., made identifiable) in several ways. The use of a proper noun normally implies that the speaker assumes the addressee can identify the referent:

(2)   George embraced Saddam.

Here the speaker assumes that there is no need to say "There was this guy named George . . . ," or "Do you remember that George guy we met at the party last weekend? . . ." to establish the identity of the participant referred to as *George*. Similarly, upon hearing a clause like 2, any addressee will assume the speaker is referring to some identifiable referent, and will quickly attach the name to a referent if at all possible. If a plausible referent is not identified, the addressee is likely to protest: "Hey wait a minute. Who's George?"

Often a noun phrase is identified by its association with some other already identified noun phrase. For example:

(3)   George's wife embraced Saddam.

In this clause the referent of the noun *wife* is established via its association with the proper name *George*. Since George is identifiable, and since presumably George has only one wife, then his wife should also be identifiable. So, NPs that are grammatically possessed by identifiable NPs are also identifiable.

Identifiability is not necessarily explicit. Identifiability in real language is always significant only in relation to the communication situation. That is, something is treated as identifiable if its referent is *explicit enough* for the speaker's current purposes. For example, consider the following clause:

(4)   I got mad at Hosni for writing on the living room wall.

Here the phrase *the living room wall* is treated as identifiable even though most living rooms would have more than one wall. It is just not relevant for the speaker's purpose in this case to distinguish *which* living room wall is being referred to (see Du Bois 1980 for further discussion). Similarly, even *George's wife* in 3 may not in itself identify a specific message world entity (i.e., in a situation in which George is known to have more than one wife). However, a clause such as 3 would still be acceptable if either (a) it just did not matter which wife were involved, or (b) the particular wife were identified in terms of the context, e.g., only one of George's wives visited Saddam, therefore it could only plausibly be that wife who embraced Saddam.

Referentiality is similar, but not identical, to identifiability. Here I will briefly contrast two approaches to the notion of referentiality: the first approach I will term **objective referentiality**; the second is **discourse referentiality** (Givón 1979, Du Bois 1980).

An entity is objectively referential if it exists as a bounded, individuated entity in the message world. Sometimes referentiality in this sense is referred to as **specificity**. The italicized noun phrases in the following clauses refer to objectively referential participants:

(5)   *Those men* are ridiculous.
        Someday I'd like to buy *your cabin* by the seashore.

This definition excludes the following:

(6)   *Generics*
         All men are ridiculous.
         Non-specifics
         Someday I'd like to buy *a cabin* by the seashore.

Notice that objective referentiality is not the same as identifiability. A generic referent can be identifiable in the sense that the speaker assumes the addressee can identify the genera (e.g., *all men* in example 6), though there is no specific individual being referred to. This fact is reflected in English grammar in that the particle *the* can mark generic noun phrases:

(7)   *The elephant* is a huge mammal.

Here the speaker instructs the addressee to identify the generic class referred to by *elephant* but not necessarily to single out any individual (objectively referential) elephant.

Similarly, non-identifiable entities need not be non-referential. For example:

(8)   Arlyne would like to marry a Norwegian.

This clause is ambiguous in English. It could mean that Arlyne would like to marry anyone that happens to be a Norwegian; or it could mean that Arlyne has a specific Norwegian in mind but the speaker just does not assume that the addressee can identify that Norwegian. In either case the Norwegian is treated as non-identifiable (as expressed by the particle *a*). In the first case it is non-referential (or non-specific), whereas in the second case it is objectively referential (or specific).

Spanish grammaticalizes the referentiality distinction for human direct objects. Referential human direct objects take the preposition *a* (example 9a), whereas non-referential human direct objects take no preposition (example 9b):

(9)   a. Estoy buscando *a*   una empleada.
            be:1sg look:for REF one housekeeper
            "I'm looking for a (specific) housekeeper."

        b. Estoy buscando una empleada.
            be:1sg look:for one housekeeper
            "I'm looking for a (any) housekeeper."

In contrast to objective referentiality, discourse referentiality has to do with continuing importance over a portion of text (Du Bois 1980). In general this is a more restrictive concept than is objective referentiality. That is, it is common for objectively referential entities to not be discourse referential, but it is difficult to conceive of discourse referential entities that are not also objectively referential. For example, any prop in a story might be objectively referential, as in the following:

(10)   She came in through *the bathroom window*.

In this clause *the bathroom window* is treated as objectively existing in the scene established in the discourse. However, if the window is never mentioned again, it would not be discourse referential, in terms of Du Bois (1980), because it would not have continuing presence on the discourse stage.

Many languages have been shown to be more sensitive to this notion of referentiality than to the notion of objective referentiality. For example, in Papago, items that are introduced into the discourse for the first time appear before the verb if they are "destined" to figure prominently in the following text (discourse referential), but appear after the verb if they are only transitory (Doris Payne 1992a). This is independent of the objective referentiality of the items. Wright and Givón (1987) have shown that the demonstrative *this* in spoken English is, among other things, an indicator of discourse referentiality. In spoken narratives, items introduced with *this* are much more likely to persist, i.e., be mentioned repeatedly, than are items introduced with either *the* or *a*:

(11)   I was just sitting there minding my own business when *this guy* walks up.

In 11 the speaker is very likely to continue talking about the referent of the expression *this guy*. In this sense *this* is a marker of discourse referentiality. Other terms that have been used for this concept are **deployability** (Jaggar 1984), **manipulability** (Hopper and Thompson 1984), and **importance** (Givón 1990). However, the important fact to remember is that natural languages tend to be more sensitive to this status, whatever it may be called, than to objective referentiality as defined within classical philosophy.

10.0.2   Focus

The following is a brief overview of ways in which the term "focus" (and various expansions of that term) have been used in the recent linguistic literature. This typology is adapted from Chafe (1976), Watters (1979), and Dik (1981).

There are three general approaches to the term focus. These are:

1 "Focus" is a term applied to some morphosyntactic operation or category whose function has not been adequately analyzed.
2 "Focus" is a term applied to one element of every clause. In this approach, focus can pretty much be equated with "new information" or "asserted information."
3 "Focus" describes a condition of some pragmatically marked clauses. Other clauses can be "focus-neutral" or "unfocused."

The first approach to the term focus will not be discussed at length here. It is evident in such locutions as "word order varies for focusing purposes." What this probably means is the writer does not understand the functions of the various word orders in the language being described.

The second approach to focus stems from the work of the **Functional Sentence Perspective** linguists of the **Prague School** (e.g., Mathesius 1939). According to these scholars, every sentence ("clause" in our terminology) has two parts; the part that refers to what the addressee is presumed to already have in mind, and the part that adds some new information. Some clauses may consist entirely of new material. Although the early Prague School linguists did not use the term "focus," they are to be credited with the *concept* of focus as the part of the clause that expresses new information. Other terms that are applied to this notion are **rheme**, **assertion**, and **new information**.

One heuristic for determining which part of a clause is focused in this conceptualization is to imagine the clause as an answer to an information question (see section 10.3.1.2 on information questions). The focus is the part of the answer that fills in the information requested in the prompting question:

What happened?   Billy pushed Johnny off the porch. (whole clause)
What did Billy do?   He pushed Johnny off the porch. (predicate focus)
Who pushed Johnny off the porch?   Billy pushed Johnny off the porch.
(subject focus)
Who did Billy push off the porch?   He pushed Johnny off the porch.
(object focus)
Where did Billy push Johnny?   He pushed him off the porch. (location
focus)

The third conception of the term focus is the view that takes focus to be a special pragmatic status that is not evident in all clauses. Sometimes this conception of focus is termed **marked focus**. Clauses that are "focused," or have a "focused constituent" in this sense, are **pragmatically marked**. That is, they deviate in their pragmatic nuances from most other clause types in the language. Many authors (e.g., Chafe 1976, Givón 1979) use the term **contrast** to describe this pragmatic function.

The major distinction in the typology of marked focus falls under the heading of "scope of focus." The scope of focus of a clause is either the truth value of the entire clause (for those clauses that have a truth value) or a constituent of the clause:

> *Scope of focus*
> entire clause = truth-value focus (TVF)
> a particular constituent = constituent focus (CF)

Truth-value focus counters the assumed presupposition that the truth value of the entire clause is in question. Bahasa Indonesia grammaticalizes TVF with the existential particle *ada* (data from Dik 1981):

(12) a. Ali pergi ke pasar
          Ali go   to market
          "Ali went to the market."

      b. Ali ada   pergi ke pasar
          Ali EXIST go   to market
          "Ali DID go to the market."

Example 12a is a focus-neutral clause in Indonesian, while 12b is a clause in which the truth value is focused. Notice that in the English translations, the same function is accomplished with the semantically empty auxiliary verb *do* and a non-finite main verb. Presumably, 12b would be uttered in a situation where the speaker had reason to believe the addressee believed that Ali did not go to the market. That is, 12b is an assertion in **contrast** to the presupposition of its negative. Sometimes TVF is called **polar focus**.

French has a special affirmation particle that is used only in contrast to a previous negative assertion:

(13)   Speaker A: Il n'a pas mangé la pomme.   "He didn't eat the apple."
        Speaker B: **Si**,   il l'-a   mangé.   "Yes he DID eat it."
                   CONTR 3 it-AUX eat

The non-contrastive affirmation particle in French is, of course, *oui*.

If the scope of focus for a particular clause is a constituent of the clause (CF), then it can be any one of the following focus types:

(a) *Assertive focus.* S believes H has no knowledge of the information:

(14)   They brought me a bowl of *this thick, green, mushy stuff.*

(b) *Counter-presuppositional focus.* This focus type comes closest to contrastive focus (see below) in the tradition of Chafe (1976) and Givón (1979). T. Payne (1987) calls this "exclusive contrast:"

(15)   Sally and Robert came over last night, but SHE got drunk.
         (presupposition: You thought Robert might have, but he didn't.)

(c) *Exhaustive listing focus.* That information which S asserts is unique in that the rest of the clause is true only with respect to it and false with respect to all other possible information:

(16)   I drank only Pepsi at the party.

Aghem, a Bantoid language of Cameroon, employs a complex system including constituent order and particles to express all of these focus types, and a few others (Watters 1979). See section 10.1.1 for a brief presentation of the Aghem data.

Another term that has been used to describe focus-like phenomena is **contrast** or **contrastive focus.** Here we will provide a characterization of contrastive focus as discussed by Chafe (1976).

A prototypical contrastive focus clause presupposes:

(a) a particular event E (taken loosely to mean any state of affairs) occurred;
(b) there is a group of entities that might have had a role, R, in E;
(c) the addressee "incorrectly" (in the eyes of the speaker) believes that one of the entities did in fact have the role R.

The contrastive focus clause then asserts:

(a) the "correct" identity of the entity involved, according to the perception of the speaker;
(b) the proposition that the entity the addressee thought had the role R in fact *did not.*

So for example, the English clause SALLY *made the salad* (with stress on *Sally*) implies that:

(a) there was a group of people, perhaps just Sally and Harry, that might have
      made the salad;
(b) the speaker has reason to believe that the addressee incorrectly thinks
      Harry made the salad.

By uttering this clause, then, the speaker asserts that:

(a) Sally was the person who made the salad, and
(b) Harry did not make the salad.

Not every instance of contrastive focus will have all of these
characteristics, but this is the prototype. Typically, languages will use exag-
gerated stress and some kind of **cleft** construction to signal contrastive
focus. Beginning with section 10.1, these various morphosyntactic structures will be described.

10.0.3   Topic
Like the term "focus," the term "topic" has been characterized
according to several broad approaches:

1 The topic is a dislocated clause constituent (see section 10.1.1 on left- and
   right-dislocation). Sometimes such elements are termed "topicalized," and
   the pragmatically marked structures that encode them "topicalization."
2 The topic is a clause-level notion that can be paraphrased "what the clause
   is about." Every (or almost every) clause has a topic in this sense (Reinhart
   1982).
3 The topic is a discourse-level notion that can be paraphrased "what the
   discourse is about." Not every clause in a discourse may mention the topic
   in this sense.
4 The topic is "the [conceptual or referential] frame within which the rest of
   the predication holds" (Li and Thompson 1976).
5 Topicality is a scalar discourse notion. Every nominal participant is topical
   to a certain degree. Relative topicality is inferred in terms of how often
   various participants are mentioned over a span of text (Givón 1983a).

Left- and right-dislocation are formal devices and therefore may
serve different functions in different languages. Since we are attempting to
define the term "topic" as a pragmatic notion, it would be confusing to use
such a closely related term as "topicalization" to refer to a formal device.
Therefore this usage will not be discussed further here.

The notion of topic as a clause-level pragmatic notion probably stems from the work of the Prague School linguists (see above). Like the term focus, the term topic was not used by these early linguists. Nevertheless, they came up with the *concept* that part of every (or almost every) clause is old, given, or known information. This part of the clause was called the **theme** by the Prague School linguists. It was defined in contrast to the **rheme**, i.e., that part of the clause that expresses new or asserted information (see section 10.0.2 above). This conceptual distinction is what eventually evolved into the clause-level topic/focus distinction.

10.1   The morphosyntax of focus, contrast, and "topicalization'

Probably the most common way of adjusting the pragmatic status of particular pieces of information is **intonation**. For example, we draw special attention to parts of our utterances by pronouncing those parts more loudly and/or at a higher pitch. Other common means of adjusting pragmatic status are word order, morphosyntactic operators (affixes or particles), and various **cleft** constructions. Each of these devices will be described and exemplified in the following sections.

The use of intonation is fairly self-evident – speakers adjust the pragmatic status of parts of their clauses by pronouncing them with varying degrees of loudness and levels of pitch. Occasionally tempo or vocalization type are used for pragmatic purposes. For example, slow staccato speech can suggest an intensive assertion in English: *We . . . have . . . no . . . more . . . money*! Screaming and whispering are obvious ways of achieving special pragmatic effects via vocalization type.

We will have nothing further to say about intonation or vocalization type here. In the following sections we will provide examples of constituent order, formatives, and cleft constructions.

10.1.1   Constituent order

The first step in determining what constituent orders are used to express pragmatic statuses is to decide whether the language has a basic constituent order based on grammatical relations (see section 4.1). If basic constituent order does not depend on grammatical relations, then order is probably directly sensitive to pragmatic statuses such as discourse referentiality or identifiability (see sections 10.0.1 and 12.1.1).

If constituent order is based primarily on grammatical relations, then unusual orders of nominals with respect to the verb can be very powerful signals of marked pragmatic statuses. For example, since English is an AVP language, clause-initial position and immediately preverbal position are candidates for pragmatically marked P arguments. English appropriates only clause-initial position for this purpose:

(17)   a.   Beans I like.
       b.   *I beans like.

Since immediately postverbal is the normal position for P arguments, this position does not attribute any special pragmatic status to P arguments beyond that of objects in general. Similarly, immediately preverbal is the normal position for A arguments in English, therefore that position does not attribute special pragmatic status beyond that of subjects in general. Other logically possible positions are simply not utilized in English:

(18)   a.   *Like I beans.
       b.   *Like beans I.
       c.   *Beans like I.

Aghem (a Niger Congo language of Cameroon) employs both positions adjacent to the verb (before and after) for expressing various kinds of pragmatic status. Like many languages of West Africa, Aghem exhibits the basic constituent order A AUX V P. The function of the immediately postverbal position in Aghem is to express focus as asserted or new information (characterization 2 of the typology of focus outlined in section 10.0.2):

(19)   Question: "Who ran?"
       Answer: à mɔ̀ ñíŋ *éná?*   "INAH ran."
                  it AUX run Inah

(20)   Question: fíl   á   mɔ̀ zí *kwɔ̀*   "What did the friends eat?"
                  friend SM AUX eat what
       Answer: fíl   á   mɔ̀ zí *kí-bé*   "The friends ate FUFU."
                  friend SM AUX eat fufu

(21)   Question: fíl á mɔ̀ zí *ghé*   bɛ́-'kɔ́   "Where did the friends eat fufu?"
                                where fufu
       Answer: fíl á mɔ̀ zí *án 'sóm* bɛ́-'kɔ́   "The friends ate fufu on the farm."
                               on farm

(22)   Question: fíl á mɔ̀ zí *zín* bɛ́-'kɔ́   "When did the friends eat fufu?"
                              when
         Answer: fíl á mɔ̀ zí *á'zɔ́ɔ*   bɛ́-'kɔ́   "The friends ate fufu yesterday."
                              yesterday

In all of these examples, including the questions, the focused constituent comes immediately after the verb. Intransitive subjects normally precede the verb, but in 19 the focused subject follows. Similarly, in the rest of the examples, the element that corresponds to the question word in the question appears in the immediately postverbal position.

The position immediately before the verb is employed for contrastive (or counter-presuppositional) focus in Aghem (under characterization 3 of the typology of focus in section 10.0.2):

(23)   "The friends ate fufu . . .
        fíl á mɔ̀ bɛ́-'kí *án 'sóm* zí   in the farm (not the house)."
                          á'zɔ́ɔ   yesterday (not two days ago)."
                          áŋ 'wó   with hands (not spoons)."

Dislocation (left and right) refers to the placing of a clause element outside the syntactic boundaries of the clause. Sometimes dislocation is referred to as **extraposition**. Left-dislocation is sometimes referred to as **preposing** and right-dislocation as **postposing**. The term **topicalization** refers to left-dislocation in the tradition of generative grammar and other autonomous approaches to syntax. Right-dislocation is sometimes referred to as **afterthought topicalization**. All of these terms assume that the leftward nominal in left-dislocation occupies a constituent structure position that stands outside the clause but is still adjoined to the clause at a higher level. In the generative tradition, that position is often referred to as the TOPIC position. In generative notation this is often displayed in the following way:

(24)   S' → TOPIC S

Here S' is pronounced "S prime" or "S bar" and refers to a grammatical structure that is larger than a clause ("sentence" in the generative tradition). S refers to a simple clause, while TOPIC refers to a structural position that is outside S, but still grammatically associated with it.

The TOPIC position, then, serves as a site for various elements to be "copied" out of S:

(25)   a. My father, he likes Beethoven.
        b. Beethoven, now I enjoy his music.

This notion of topic is strictly structural. Whatever functional (i.e., communicative) properties may be associated with topicalization constructions in this tradition are tangential to their structural status. In other words, questions of why speakers would want to "copy" a constituent into the TOPIC position, or why languages might have a TOPIC position at all, are not addressed in this framework.

Apparently all languages employ left-dislocation as a grammaticalized construction. Some also employ right-dislocation. It may be difficult to distinguish left-dislocation from (1) **apposition** of a free noun phrase to the clause, (2) **fronting** of an element within the clause, and (3) **clefting** (see section 10.1.3). The corresponding difficulty may also obtain for right-dislocation; however, the following discussion will be couched exclusively in terms of left-dislocation. The issue is whether the element to the left of the main predication is grammatically a part of the predication or not. That is, there are three possible grammatical statuses of a pragmatically prominent noun phrase that is in clause-initial position. These statuses can be schematized as follows:

(26)   a. [NP] [S]   apposition
        b. [NP S]$_{s'}$ left-dislocation
        c. [NP . . .]$_s$ fronting (if NP is not initial in the neutral constituent order)

In other words, noun phrases that are placed in clause-initial position can be grammatically separate from the following clause (26a), grammatically adjoined to the clause but not an integral part of it (26b), or an integral part of the clause (26c).[1]

In addition to these grammatical statuses, an NP may also be clefted. The grammatical structure of a cleft construction may be schematized as follows:

(27)   [NP$_i$] (COP) [. . . NP$_i$ . . .]$_S$

Cleft constructions will be discussed in more detail in section 10.1.3.

The following rules of thumb will help determine what kind of construction one is dealing with (these rules are ordered):

    1 If the construction normally falls under a single intonation contour, i.e., there is typically no pause or "comma" intonation after the initial NP, *and*

there is no special particle between the initial NP and the rest of the clause, *and* there is no reference to the initial nominal within the clause (other than grammatical agreement), it is fronting.

2 If the initial NP is recapitulated within S by a free referring form (i.e., anything besides grammatical agreement) *and* a pause or a special particle (other than the copula) can naturally intervene between the initial NP and S, then it is probably left-dislocation.

3 If the initial NP has no role in S, and/or adverbial elements can intervene between the initial NP and S, then it is probably apposition (sometimes referred to as **juxtaposition**).

4 If the element that intervenes between the initial NP and the rest of the clause is a form of the copula (e.g., *be*; see section 6.1) *and/or* the main predication has the form of a relative clause, then it is a cleft.

Examples:

(28)   Fronting: Beans I like.
        Left-dislocation: Beans, I like them.
                            As for beans, I think they're great.
        Apposition: Beans. Why do we always have leftovers?
        Clefts: Beans are what I like.
                            What I like is beans.
                            The ones I like are beans.

The special particles that many languages employ in dislocation constructions often derive historically from older copular forms. This fact illustrates that the distinction between clefting and dislocation is continuous rather than absolute. For expository purposes, however, it is convenient to draw the line at the point where the particle that sets off the left-dislocated element ceases to function as a copula in predicate nominal constructions. The following are examples of languages that employ special particles to set off dislocated noun phrases:

(29)   *Tagalog*
        Ang babae *ay* humiram ng pera   sa bangko.
        ABS woman LD A:borrow OBL money OBL bank
        "The woman, she borrowed money from a bank."

In Tagalog the particle *ay* functions like comma intonation does in other languages. It does not occur in predicate nominal constructions (unless the subject of the predicate nominal is left-dislocated). There is also a fronting construction that does not employ *ay*, and a distinct cleft construction (see section 10.1.3). Other languages that employ special particles in left-dislocation constructions include Malagasy (Austronesian) and Akan (Kwa, Niger-Congo):

(30)   *Malagasy*
         izahay *no* tia   anao.
         we   LD love you
         "WE love you."

(31)   *Akan*
         kòfí *nà* ɔ́wɔ́ Engìrési.
         Kofi LD be:in England
         "KOFI is in England."

10.1.2   Formatives

Some languages employ affixes or particles to ascribe special pragmatic status to noun phrases in clauses. There is a functional continuum between morphological case markers (see section 5.4) and markers of pragmatic status. This continuum can be roughly divided as follows:

Pragmatic status markers	English articles, Aghem focus particles, etc.
Overlay systems	Japanese and Korean "topic marking"
Case markers	Latin, Eskimo, Russian, Quechua, etc.

It must be kept in mind throughout this discussion that these structure types really represent a continuous scale. It is in principle very difficult to tease apart grammatical relations, semantic roles, and pragmatic statuses since they all influence one another to a great extent. However, generalizations can be made concerning the commonest, or most prototypical, functions of certain structure types. Prototypically, case markers are those grammatical devices that most directly express grammatical relations, i.e., grammaticalized semantic roles and pragmatic statuses (see chapter 7 on grammatical relations). The articles of English are good examples of pragmatic status markers. Typically, pragmatic status markers partially correlate with grammatical relations. For example, noun phrases that have the grammatical relation of *subject* are also likely to have the pragmatic status of *identifiable* in English. If this statistical correlation were to become a 100 percent generalization (not a very imminent possibility for English), then the pragmatic status marker *the* would become a subject case marker.

(See Shibatani 1991 for discussion of how pragmatic categories can become grammaticalized as grammatical relations.)

Aghem uses verb morphology and a focus particle to express various pragmatic nuances. For example, there is a special form of the auxiliary verb that is used for clauses that express truth-value focus (TVF) in the perfective aspect. Example 32a illustrates a neutral perfective aspect clause, while 32b illustrates a TVF perfective aspect clause:

(32) a. éná? *mɔ̀* fúo kí-bɛ́ â fín-ghɔ́
          Inah AUX give fufu to friends
          "Inah gave fufu to his friends."

      b. éná? *má'á*   fúo kí-bɛ́ â fín-ghɔ́
          Inah AUX:FOC give fufu to friends
          "Inah DID give fufu to his friends."

There is also a "focus particle" *nò* in Aghem that appears after a focused constituent. Sometimes the choice of whether to use word order or the particle *nò* to accomplish a particular focus task appears to be completely free (see section 10.1.1 for examples of word order as a focusing device in Aghem):

(33) a. fú kí mɔ̀ ñíŋ *nò* á kí-'bé
          rat SM AUX run FOC in compound
          "The rat RAN (i.e., did not walk) in the compound."

      b. fú kí mɔ̀ ñíŋ á kí-'bé   *nò*
          rat SM AUX run in compound FOC
          "The rat ran in the COMPOUND (not in the house)."

In Akan (Schachter 1985: 37) there is a "focus" particle *na* (ex. 34) and a "contrastive" particle *de* (ex. 35):

(34) Kwame *na* ɔbɛyɛ   adwuma no.
      Kwame FOC he:will:do work   the
      "It's Kwame who will do the work."

(35) Kwame *de*   ɔbɛkɔ,   na Kofi *de*   ɔbɛtena   ha.
      Kwame CONTR he:will:go and Kofi CONTR he:will:stay here
      "KWAME will go, but KOFI will stay here."

Overlay systems for marking pragmatic status of nominal elements are a combination of morphological case-marking systems and pragmatic status-marking systems. The essence of an overlay system is that one or more basic case markers are replaced ("overlaid") by the pragmatic status markers when a nominal element is singled out for special pragmatic treatment. Both Japanese and Korean have overlay systems for marking "topic" (defined in a language-specific sense). The topic marker in Japanese is *wa*. It can overlay either the subject marker *ga* (example 36b), the object marker *o* (36c), or other nominal case markers:

(36) a. *Unmarked*
          taroo ga hon o   katta
          Taro SUB book OBJ bought
          "Taro bought a book."

      b. taroo *wa* hon o katta
                TOP
          "As for Taro, he bought a book."

      c. hon *wa* taroo ga katta
             TOP
          "As for the book, Taro bought it."

In linguistic articles, English translations of Japanese clauses with *wa*-marked nominals typically employ the *"as for* X . . ."* left-dislocation construction. In fact Japanese *wa* has various functions, and is still a matter of some controversy (see, e.g., Hinds, Maynard, and Iwasaki 1987).

10.1.3   Cleft constructions

A **cleft construction** is a type of predicate nominal consisting of a noun phrase (NP_i) and a relative clause whose relativized NP is coreferential with NP_i (see section 11.5 on relative clauses). NP_i is commonly referred to as the "clefted constituent," and is normally found to the left of the rest of the clause, though it may appear in other positions. Cleft constructions can be formulated as follows:

(37) NP_i (COP) [. . . NP_i . . .]$_{S_{rel}}$

The form that S_{rel} (the relative clause) takes depends on what relativization strategies the language employs, i.e., it could be a nominalization, a participial clause, or a more prototypical relative clause (see section 11.5). Similarly, the presence or absence of a copula, COP, depends on the general structure of predicate nominal constructions in the language. As

stated above, the presence of COP is a clear indication that one is dealing
with a cleft construction. If COP is absent, the construction may still be a
cleft if the language allows predicate nominal constructions with no copular element (see section 6.1). In such a case, a cleft is distinguished from
plain dislocation in that the clause that follows the dislocated NP is a relative clause or other type of participant nominalization. In a very few languages, namely those that allow both predicate nominals with no copula
and relative clauses with no relativizer or other special morphology, some
structures may be indeterminate as to whether they are best thought of as
left-dislocation or clefting. Dera (Chadic) is apparently such a language:

(38)   wuni wun kapa kurei
        they ones plant corn
        "THOSE ONES plant corn" or "Those are the ones who plant corn."

Some examples of clefts in English include the following:

(39)   a. Home is [where the heart is 0   ]$_S$.
            NP$_i$ COP REL   NP$_i$
            (cf. "The heart is at home.")

        b. Lucretia is [whom I love 0   ]$_S$.
            NP$_i$ COP REL   NP$_i$
            (cf. "I love Lucretia.")

English has at least two types of cleft constructions. These have
traditionally been termed clefts and **pseudo-clefts**:

(40)   *Clefts* (it COP NP S$_{rel}$)
        a. It is Lucretia who grimaced.
        b. It's the duke whom Lucretia disdains.
        c. It's the duke who trod on poor Lucretia's watermelon.

(41)   *Pseudo-clefts* (NP COP S$_{rel}$)
        a. Lucretia is the one who grimaced.
        b. The duke is the one whom Lucretia disdains.
        c. The duke is the one who trod on poor Lucretia's watermelon.
        d. Home is where the heart is.

(42)   *Pseudo-clefts* (S$_{rel}$ COP NP)
        a. What happened was you blew a heater hose. (cf. "That you blew a heater
            hose happened")

b. What John ate was beans.
c. The one who grimaced was Yassar.
d. That which we have seen with our own eyes is what we are reporting to you. (both NPs contain relative clauses)

In fact, by our definition of cleft as a predicate nominal consisting of a noun phrase and a relative clause that relativizes that noun phrase, all of these construction types are clefts. "*It*-clefts" (ex. 40) and "*the one* clefts" (ex. 41a, b, and c) simply represent two different means that English employs to avoid having to use a headless relative clause (see section 11.5). The most "natural" (from the point of view of most of the world's languages) form of a cleft in English would involve a headless relative clause (41d, 42a, b, and the following):

(43)   ?Lucretia is who grimaced.
        ?The duke is whom Lucretia disdains.
        ?The duke is who trod on Lucretia's turnip.

Clefts in many languages exhibit the pattern NP COP headless-RC. However, headless relative clauses in English are generally avoided, at least in written and otherwise planned speech. For this reason a "dummy" element is employed, either as the subject (*it* in 40) or as the head (*the one* in 42c).

Prince (1978) provides an interesting and insightful analysis of the functions of various kinds of cleft constructions in English. This work could serve as a model for studies of the functions of pragmatically marked structures in other languages. However, one must always be aware that similar structures from one language to the next may or may not have similar functions. Therefore linguistic researchers should be careful not to project Prince's findings on data from another language without adequate empirical evidence from the language itself.

The following are examples of various types of clefts in other languages (data from Harries-Delisle 1978):

Headless relative clause
(44)   *Mandarin*
        Yohàn kàn-jiàn de shì ge nán rén
        John saw   REL be CL male person
        "Who John saw was a man (not a woman)."

(45)   *Indonesian*
bukan saya yang beladjar bahasa   indónésia
NEG   I   REL   study   language Indonesia
"I am not who is studying Indonesian."

(46)   *Participial phrase: German*
Der segelt   das ist mein Bruder.
the sail:PP that be my   brother
"The sailing (one), that is my brother."

(47)   *Nominalization: Amharic*
əssu naw yamattaw
3SG be   NOM:came
"He is who came." (lit.: "He is the 'comer'")

The following are examples from Malayalam (from Andrews 1985: 84–85). Example 48 is an uncleft clause. Examples 49a–d are clefts formed with various constituents. In Malayalam, the clefted constituent does not have to appear strictly to the left of the clause (though it may):

(48)   Kutti   innale   ammakkə aanaye   kotuttu
child:NOM yesterday mother:DAT elephant:DAT gave
"The child gave an elephant to the mother yesterday."

(49)   a. Kuttiy-aanə innale   ammakkə aanaye   kotutt-atə
child:NOM-is yesterday mother:DAT elephant:DAT gave-it
"The child is (he who) gave an elephant to the mother yesterday."

   b. Kutti   innale   ammakk-aanə aanaye   kotutt-atə
child:NOM yesterday mother:DAT-is elephant:DAT gave-it
"It is the mother that the child gave an elephant to yesterday."

   c. Kutti   innaley-aanə ammakkə aanaye   kotutt-atə
child:NOM yesterday-is mother:DAT elephant:DAT gave-it
"It is yesterday that the child gave an elephant to the mother."

   d. Kutti   innale   ammakkə aanayey-aan   kotutt-atə
child:NOM yesterday mother:DAT elephant:DAT-is gave-it
"The child gave an elephant to the mother yesterday."

?

Are there special devices for indicating pragmatic statuses in basic clauses, e.g., special constituent orders, left- and/or right-dislocation, affixes, or particles indicating referentiality, specificity, topic, focus, contrast, etc.?
Describe cleft constructions. If possible, give a characterization of their discourse functions.

What different types of pragmatic status is the grammar of this language
sensitive to?

....

10.2   Negation

A **negative** clause is one which asserts that some event, situation,
or state of affairs does *not* hold. Negative clauses usually occur in the context of some presupposition, functioning to negate or counter-assert that
presupposition. For example, if I say *Jorge didn't clean up the kitchen*, I
probably assume the addressee presupposes that Jorge did, or should have,
cleaned up the kitchen. In this respect, negative clauses are functionally
similar to contrastive focus clauses (see section 10.0.2), and consequently
negative and contrastive focus clauses are often formally similar. In this
section we will discuss and exemplify various ways in which languages are
known to express negative assertions. Except for Tagalog, Panare, and
Tennet, the examples in this section are cited in Horn (1978).

The most common negative strategies in any language are those
used to negate an entire proposition. These we will describe as **clausal
negation**, e.g., *I didn't do it*. Other types of negation are associated with
particular constituents of clauses, e.g., *I have no bananas*. This will be
referred to as **constituent negation**. Although the semantic effect of constituent negation can be very similar or identical to that of clausal negation,
constituent negation is always less common as a grammatical device than
clausal negation. In this section we will primarily discuss clausal negation.
Toward the end we will deal briefly with constituent negation.

One noteworthy feature of clausal negation is that most languages
possess more than one type. Sometimes the functional difference between
the various negative operations has to do with negation of existence vs.
negation of fact, negation of different aspects, different modes, or different
speech acts (e.g., refusal vs. simple negative assertion). In the following
paragraphs, we will describe lexical, morphological, and analytical expression of negation. After that we will describe a few of the functional and formal characteristics of clausal negation.

Lexical negation. As might be expected, lexical negation describes a situation in which the concept of negation is part and parcel of the lexical
semantics of a particular verb. For example, the verb *lack* in English can be

thought of as the lexical negative of *have*. However, it is sometimes difficult to isolate a particular verb as the lexical negative of some other verb. For example, is *stand* the lexical negative of *sit*, of *lie*, of *succumb*, or are these just all distinct verbs?

Morphological negation. Morphemes that express clausal negation are normally, if not always, associated with the verb. Many languages, e.g., Farsi as illustrated in 50a and b, employ a simple verbal prefix:

(50) a. *na*-xar-am
         NEG-buy-1SG
         "I didn't buy."

      b. *na*-mi-xar-am
         NEG-PRES-buy-1SG
         "I'm not buying."

As in the case of Farsi, it is very common for negative affixes to be reflexes of older negative particles (see below under analytic negation).

Negation is often tied up with other verbal inflections. For example, Nanai (Tungus) uses special tense markers in negative clauses (51c and d). Note also that the stem vowel is lengthened in the negative:

(51) a. xola-j-si
         read-PRES-2SG
         "You are reading."

      b. xola-xa-si
         read-PAST-2SG
         "You were reading."

      c. xola:-*si*-si
         read-NEG:PRES-2SG
         "You aren't reading."

      d. xola:-*ci*-si
         read-NEG:PAST-2SG
         "You weren't reading."

Analytic negation. There are two kinds of analytic negation: negative particles and finite negative verbs. Sometimes negative particles derive historically from negative verbs (see the Tennet examples below).

Negative particles are normally associated with the main verb of the clause. However, they may also be clause-level clitics. Negative particles can be invariant, such as the English *not* and its allomorph *-n't*, or Russian *ne*:

(52)   a. on *n^{j}e* igraet
            he NEG play
            "He doesn't play."

        b. *n^{j}e* igraj
            NEG play:IMP
            "Don't play!"

        c. on *n^{j}e* durak
            he NEG fool
            "He is not a fool."

Other negative particles may vary for kind of negation, clause type (imperative vs. declarative), tense, aspect, etc. See the Tennet, Tagalog, Mandarin, and Arabic examples below for illustrations of variant negative particles.

Multiple expression of negation. It is fairly common for negative constructions to involve multiple operators, either an affix and a particle, two particles, or a particle or affix plus a word order change. One might speculate that, since a negative assertion is communicatively so distinct from the corresponding affirmative, languages tend to develop very strong and easily perceived devices to express the difference. The problem with this speculation is that there also exist some languages in which the marker of a negative clause is perceptually quite weak. For example, in English the contracted form of the negative particle is often almost imperceptible, especially in certain environments, e.g., *I can talk* vs. *I can't talk*. In any case, it is true that languages often have multiple expressions of negation.

One example is French, in which two particles are used in negative clauses:

(53)   a. *Affirmative*
            Il   y-a   une   réduction pour les   étudiants.
            3SG EXIST INDEF discount   for   the:PL students
            "There is a discount for students."

b. *Negative*

Il   *n'*-y-a   *pas* de réduction pour les étudiants.
3SG NEG-EXIST NEG
"There is no discount for students."

In 53b both a negative particle *ne* (reduced to *n-* before the existential) and the particle *pas* are needed to make the clause negative.

Similarly, in Hausa, the negative particle *ba* occurs twice in a negative clause. Ungrammaticality or a different sense results if one of the instances of *ba* is omitted:

(54)   a. *Affirmative*
           yara   ne
           children 3PL
           "They are children."

        b. *Negative*
           ba yara   *ba* ne
           NEG children NEG 3PL
           "They are not children."

        c. *Affirmative*
           mace   zatahura wuta
           woman will:start fire
           "The woman will start the fire."

        d. *Negative*
           mace   *ba* zatahura wuta *ba*
           woman NEG will:start fire   NEG
           "The woman will not start the fire."

Different kinds of negation. In many languages the negative particle or affix varies depending on the tense, aspect, mode, or other factors. It is fairly common, for example, for negative imperatives to employ a different particle than negative assertions. This is true in Mandarin (see below), Hebrew (see section 10.3.2) and in Tennet (Nilo-Saharan, Surmic; examples courtesy of Scott Randall):

(55)   a. *ma* a-dúli   táttôk
           NEG IMPERF-break door
           "Don't break the door."

b. *ma* a-údâ   írá
NEG IMPERF-drink milk
"Don't drink the milk."

The negative particles for standard assertions in Tennet are *ɪrɔ́ŋ* and *ŋanní* (see examples 66 and 67 below).

Another typical distinction in negative particles is between plain negatives and negatives of existence. For example, in Tagalog, and most other Austronesian languages, there are two ways of saying "no." In Tagalog the particles are *wala* and *hindi*. *Wala* is the negative of existence. It is the appropriate negative response to a yes/no question relating to the existence or presence of some item:

(56)   a.   Mayroon ka bang pera?   "Do you have any money?"
        b.   Wala   "None."
              *Hindi

Hindi, on the other hand, is the standard means of responding negatively to non-existential propositions:

(57)   a.   Pupunta ka ba sa sayawan?   "Are you going to the dance?"
        b.   Hindi   "No."
              *Wala

In addition to being the negative responses to questions, *hindi* and *wala* are also the particles used to form negative clauses. Not surprisingly, the difference between the two particles is that *wala* negates existential propositions (ex. 58a, b) while *hindi* negates other sorts of propositions (ex. 59a, b):

(58)   a.   Wala akong pera   "I don't have any money."
        b.   Wala akong alam   "I don't know anything." (lit. "I lack knowledge.")

(59)   a.   Hindi ako papasok sa eskwela   "I'm not going to school."
        b.   Hindi ko alam   "I don't know."

Mandarin has at least three negative particles. The most common particle is *bu* (ex. 60a). The existential negative is *méi* (ex. 60b), and the negative particle used in imperatives is *bié* (ex. 60c):

(60)   a.   Tā *bu* hē   jiǔ
              3SG NEG drink wine
              "He doesn't/didn't drink wine."

b. Tā *méi* yǒu gēge
3SG NEG exist older:brother
"She doesn't have an older brother."

c. *Bié*   zǒu
NEG:IMP go
"Don't go!"

Many languages, among them Iraqi Arabic, employ one invariant negative particle in verbal predicates (predicates headed by a verb) as in 61a, and another in verbless predicates (e.g., predicate nominals, locationals, existentials, etc.) as in 61b, c, and d:

(61)   *Iraqi Arabic*

a. ʔəli *ma:* ra:h lidda:ʔire
Ali NEG went to:office
"Ali didn't go to the office."

b. ʔubu:jə *mu:* muha:mi
father:my NEG lawyer
"My father is not a lawyer."

c. haðə ššati *mu:* rəmli
this beach NEG sandy
"This beach is not sandy."

d. lwəktu:b *mu:* ʔili
the:letter NEG for:me
"The letter is not for me."

The second type of analytic negation involves a finite negative verb and a complement clause (see the introduction to chapter 11, and section 11.2). The test for whether a form that expresses negation is a verb or a particle is whether it has the morphosyntactic properties of finite verbs in general for the language. For example, a negative verb will take finite verbal inflectional morphology and will occur in the normal position of a verb. The affirmative verb, i.e., the verb that expresses the main semantic content of the clause, will be treated like a complement verb. That is, it may be introduced by a complementizer or take non-finite or irrealis verbal morphology. This negation strategy occurs primarily in verb-initial or verb-final languages. Following are some examples from various languages that employ a finite negative verb:

(62)   *Tongan* (Polynesian)
    a. Na'e-alu 'a   Siale
        COMPL-go ABS Charlie
        "Charlie went."

    b. Na'e-*'ikai* [ke 'alu 'a Siale]
        COMPL-NEG IRR go   ABS Charlie
        "Charlie didn't go."

The portion of clause 62b enclosed in brackets is a complement clause. It is marked as irrealis (a non-finite category in Tongan) and the negative stem *'ikai* takes inflectional morphology common to main verbs. It also occurs in the clause position characteristic of main verbs.

(63)   *Squamish* (Salish):
    Ha'u-č-0-ap   qaly-c'ic'a'p'
    NEG-AUX-PAST-2PL COMP-work
    "You (pl.) didn't work."

In this clause the stem that carries the negative sense, *ha'u*, takes all the verbal inflection, i.e., tense and person marking. It also occurs in the normal position for main verbs. The verb meaning "work," on the other hand, is clearly subordinated by the complementizer *qaly-*.

    Tongan and Squamish are both verb-initial languages. The following examples are from verb-final languages that employ a finite negative verb as a primary negation device:

(64)   *Diegeño* (Yuman)
    ʔnʸaː-č ʔ-aʔm-x   ʔ-*maːw*
    I-SUB   1SG-go-IRR 1SG-NEG
    "I didn't go."

In Diegeño both finite and complement verbs take person inflection. However, in this example it is clear that the verb meaning "go" is subordinate because it is marked with the irrealis suffix *-x*. Also the negative stem *maːw* occurs in clause-final position, as expected for main verbs.

    Although Evenki is a verb-final language, as illustrated in example 65a, the negative verb does not occur in final position, at least when the clause being negated has an overtly expressed direct object (65b):

(65)   *Evenki* (Tungus, Siberia)

   a. Bi dukuwu:n-ma duku-ca:-w   affirmative
       1SG letter-ACC   write-PAST-1SG
       "I wrote a letter."

   b. Bi dukuwu:n-ma ə-cə:-w   duku-ra   negative
       1SG letter-ACC   NEG-PAST-1SG write-PART
       "I didn't write a letter."

Nevertheless, since the stem that expresses the negative sense, ə, is inflected like a verb, and the other verb is inflected like a participle, it would still be appropriate to term this strategy a finite negative verb.

    Tennet employs two distinct negative particles depending on the aspect of the clause. One particle, *ɪrɔ́ŋ*, is used in imperfective aspect (ex. 66b) while the other, *ŋanní*, is used in perfective aspect (ex. 67b):

(66) a. k-á-čín-ι   anná Lokúli íyókó nɛ́kɔ   affirmative
      1-IMPERF-see-1 1SG (name) now DEM
      "I see Lokúli now."

    b. *ɪrɔ́ŋ* anná k-á-čín-ι   Lokúli íyókó nɛ́kɔ negative
      NEG 1SG 1-IMPERF-see-1 (name) now DEM
      "I don't see Lokúli now."

(67) a. k-í-čín-ι   anná Lokúli balwáz   affirmative
      1-PERF-see-1 1SG (name) yesterday
      "I saw Lokúli yesterday."

    b. *ŋanní* anná kι-čín   Lokúli balwáz   negative
      NEG 1SG 3:SUBJ-see (name) yesterday
      "I didn't see Lokúli yesterday."

There are two notable features of Tennet negatives. First, for both types of clausal negation the constituent order changes from VS to SV. Note that the first person singular pronoun follows the verb in 66a and 67a but precedes the verb in the negatives. This is a required grammatical feature of negative clauses in Tennet, and is not uncommon in other languages (see below). Second, in the perfective aspect (ex. 67) the verb goes into the subjunctive mode. This is the mode that occurs in certain complement clauses (see section 11.2). This fact is evidence that at least the particle *ŋanní* derives from a finite negative verb. However, it is clearly not a verb in the present-day language in that it takes none of the inflections common to verbs. It is an invariant particle.

Secondary modifications. So far we have discussed the primary devices that languages use to express a negative proposition. In addition to these primary devices, there are sometimes secondary devices that accompany them. To date, none of the following devices has been found to be the only indication of negation in a clause.

Alternative word order. Many VO languages employ a special word order in negative clauses. For example, Kru uses SVO order in affirmative clauses (68a) and SOV order in negative clauses (68b):

(68)   *Kru* (Niger-Congo, Ivory Coast)

    a. ɔ   tẽ kɔ́
        he:COMPL buy rice
        "He bought rice."

    b. ɔ   se kɔ̀ tẽ
        he:COMPL NEG rice buy
        "He didn't buy rice."

See also the Tennet examples above.

Change in tone. Many Niger-Congo languages employ a distinct tone on the verb or auxiliary for negative clauses. For example, the incompletive auxiliary in Igbo carries low tone in affirmative clauses (69a) but high tone in negative clauses (69b):

(69)   *Igbo* (Kwa, Niger-Congo)

    a. ò nà   àsá akwà
        she INCOMPL do wash
        "She is doing the wash."

    b. ò *ná-ghí*   àsá akwà
        she INCOMPL-NEG do wash
        "She has not done the wash."

Neutralization of tense–aspect distinctions. Sometimes there are fewer tense-aspect distinctions in the negative than in the affirmative. For example, Komi exhibits a present–future distinction in the affirmative (70a and b), but no such distinction in the negative (70c):

(70)   a. gižö   "He writes."
    b. gižas   "He will write."
    c. *oz* giž "He doesn't write" or "He won't write."

Similarly, Bembe allows two future tense markers, *ká* and *kà*, in affirmative clauses (71a and b), but only *kà* in negative clauses (71c):

(71)   *Bembe* (Bantu, Niger-Congo, Zambia)

    a. n-kà-boomba
       1SG-FUT:1-work
       "I'm about to work."

    b. n-ká-boomba
       1SG-FUT:2-work
       "I will work (later)."

    c. n-shi-kà-boomba
       1SG-NEG-FUT:1-work
       "I won't work."

    d. *n-shi-ká-boomba
       1SG-NEG-FUT:2-work

Special inflections. A few languages employ special person/number or tense/aspect/mode markers on verbs in negative clauses. These normally are reflexes of older structures in the language (see, e.g., the Tennet examples above). It is typically the case that negative clauses (along with other non-basic clause types) retain older morphosyntactic patterns. For example, in Kawaiisu, in past tense affirmative clauses the suffix is *-kɨdiine* (72a); in negative clauses, the suffix is *-keneeneene* (72b):

(72)   a. taʔnipuzi-a pɨkee-*kɨdiine* momoʔo-na
       man-SUB   see-PAST   woman-OBJ
       "Man saw woman."

    b. taʔnipuzi-a *yuweatɨ* pɨkee-*keneeneene* momoʔo-na
       man-SUB   NEG   see-PAST:3->3   woman-OBJ
       "Man didn't see woman."

Alternative case-marking patterns. In a few languages, special case-marking patterns occur in negative clauses. For example, in Russian, with certain transitive verbs the object occurs in the accusative case in affirmative clauses (73a) and in the genitive case in negative clauses (73b):

(73)   a. on zabudʲet tot   večer
       he forget:FUT that:ACC evening:ACC
       "He will forget that evening."

    b. on *n/e* zabud/et togo   vecera
       he NEG forget:FUT that:GEN evening:GEN
       "He will not forget that evening."

Non-clausal negation. So far we have discussed ways in which languages express negative assertions instantiated in propositions. In the following paragraphs we will discuss various ways in which specific clause *constituents* can be negated. We will begin with derivational negation, and will continue with negative quantifiers. Finally we will discuss briefly the notion of negative scope.

    Derivational negation. Occasionally languages will allow a stem to be transformed into its "opposite" by use of some derivational morphology. This can be termed **derivational negation**. English uses the prefixes *un-* and perhaps *non-* for this purpose:

(74)   *un*happy   *non*-smoker
       *un*selfish   *non*-past tense
       *un*reasonable *non*entity

In English *un-* is largely restricted to adjectival stems and *non-* to adjectival or nominal stems. Furthermore, neither of these is fully productive. In other languages, however, derivational negation can be more prevalent. For example, in Panare, many verb stems are built on a root plus a negative suffix *-(i)ka*. The resulting stem then embodies a concept which in some loose sense can be understood as the opposite of the concept embodied by the original root. For example:

(75) a. t-ama-yaj   chu
          1:3-throw:out-PAST 1SG
          "I threw it out."

      b. t-ama-*ika*-yaj   chu
          1:3-throw:out-NEG-PAST 1SG
          "I kept it/stored it/placed it."

(76) a. y-otawë-yaj
          3-get:dark-PAST
          "It got dark."

      b. y-otawë-*ika*-yaj   kën
          3-get:dark-NEG-PAST 3SG
          "He/she woke up."

This derivational operation is related to, but quite distinct from, standard inflectional negation. Standard negation in Panare is expressed via a postverbal particle *ka* (counter-expectation) or *pï* (consistent with expectations).

Negative quantifiers. Many languages employ quantifiers that are either inherently negative (e.g., English *none, nothing*) or are negated independently of clausal negation (e.g., *not many*). Most languages allow or require negative quantifiers to be accompanied by clausal negation. For example, in Russian the form *nikto* "nobody," when referring to the subject of a clause, must be accompanied by clausal negation:

(77)   a. *nikto*   nʲe   prišol
          nobody NEG came
          "Nobody came."

       b. **nikto* prišol

Standard English is exotic in disallowing this use of a "double negative:"

(78)   a. Nobody came.
       b. Nobody didn't come.   (means "everybody came," not "nobody came" as
                                 in Russian)

Negative scope. Sometimes constituent negation and clausal negation interact to cause variations in **negative scope**. Scope refers to the variable portions of a clause that can be negated. Clausal negation has scope over the entire clause. Constituent negation has scope over a particular constituent of the clause. Examples of variations in negative scope will be provided from English:

(79)   a. Not many people like Vonnegut.   *Scope*: subject quantifier only
       b. Many people do not like Vonnegut. *Scope*: entire clause

(80)   a. I deliberately didn't bump into her. *Scope*: entire clause
       b. I didn't deliberately bump into her. *Scope*: adverb only

(81)   a. I won't force you to marry Zelda.   *Scope*: entire clause
       b. I will force you not to marry Zelda. *Scope*: complement clause

---

?

What is the standard means of forming a negative clause in this language?
What secondary strategies are there? When are they used?
Is there constituent negation? Derivational negation?

How is morphology normally associated with negation employed in creative ways in discourse?

Additional reading: J. Payne (1985).

....

10.3   Non-declarative speech acts

Languages typically have different morphosyntactic devices that express what kind of speech act is being performed (Searle 1970). All languages have grammaticalized devices that show whether a clause is an assertion (declaratives), a request (interrogatives), or a command (imperatives). Such devices are often modal in character (see section 9.3.3 on the linguistic definition of mode). For example, questions and commands are irrealis in mode, therefore morphology associated with irrealis assertions often appears in questions and commands. However, declarative–interrogative–imperative does not describe a modal parameter *per se*. In this section we will look at various conventionalized means that languages employ to express these three speech act values.

The term "declarative" in traditional grammar refers to clauses that simply assert information. Often the term "declarative mode" will be found in the literature. In this book, and in linguistics in general, declarative is not a mode. In the tradition of speech act theory, the term **assertion** most closely approximates the traditional notion of declarative.

Declarative clauses are usually the normal, unmarked clause type. If there are special markings for speech act types, declarative is usually expressed via a zero marker. Tibetan is one exception to this generalization. In Tibetan, both declarative and interrogative clauses receive a special marker (examples courtesy of Scott DeLancey):

(82)   yoqöö mɔɔmɔɔ sɛɛ-pə-*ree*   declarative
       servant dumplings eat-PAST-DECL
       "The servant ate dumplings."

(83)   yoqöö mɔɔmɔɔ sɛɛ-qi-*ree*   declarative
       servant dumplings eat-FUT-DECL
       "The servant will eat dumplings."

(84)   yoqöö mɔɔmɔɔ sɛɛ-pə-*repɛɛ*   interrogative I
       servant dumplings eat-PAST-QP
       "Did the servant eat dumplings?"

(85)   yoqöö qhare sɛɛ-pə-rɛɛ?   interrogative II
        servant what eat-PAST-INTER
        "What did the servant eat?"

Since declarative clauses are usually the least-marked clause type, the remainder of this section will discuss various kinds of non-declarative speech acts as well as the ways that languages are known to express them.

10.3.1   Interrogatives

Languages always have some grammaticalized means of specifying that a particular utterance is to be understood as a request for information rather than an assertion. Such grammatical structures we will term **interrogative** clauses. In traditional English grammar the term interrogative is described as a "mode," along with declarative and imperative.

Within the class of interrogative clauses, languages typically distinguish two subtypes: those for which the information requested is a simple affirmation or disaffirmation (yes or no), and those for which the requested information is a more elaborate locution – a phrase, a proposition, or an entire discourse. In the following two subsections these two general types of interrogative clauses will be discussed.

10.3.1.1 Yes/no questions

We will use the term **yes/no questions** to refer to interrogative clauses for which the expected answer is either "yes" or "no." The following paragraphs discuss the various ways languages are known to form yes/no questions. Any given language may employ one or more of these strategies.

Intonation. Yes/no questions universally tend to involve distinctive intonation patterns. The intonation pattern employed in yes/no questions is usually rising, as in English, but is sometimes falling, as in Russian. Question intonation can either be the only indication that a clause is a question or it can accompany any of the other strategies listed below.

Word order. Many languages, especially languages that are of the VO constituent order type, employ distinctive constituent orders in yes/no questions. Usually this distinctive order involves an "inversion" (or reversal) of the order of subject and verb. This is very common in Austronesian and European languages. For example:

Malay

(86)   *Assertion*
        bapak datangkah nanti
        father come:FUT later
        "Father will come later."

(87)   *Question*
        datangkah bapak nanti
        come:FUT father later
        "Will father come later?"

English employs a somewhat exotic inversion system in yes/no questions. Instead of reversing the order of subject and main verb, English reverses the order of subject and auxiliary verb (88a and b). If the corresponding assertion contains no auxiliary, the "dummy" auxiliary *do* is inserted (88c):

(88)   a. Will he arrive on time?
        b. Can they bite corn nuts?
        c. Do you want to subsume these clause types?

In American English, simple subject–verb inversion occurs in predicate nominal, existential, and locational clauses (89a, b, and c); in British English this extends to possessive constructions (86d):

(89)   a. Is he a ringmaster?
        b. Are there cats under your flowerpots?
        c. Were you in the butterscotch pudding?
        d. Have you a match? (chiefly British)

Interrogative particle. Other than intonation, the most common means of forming a yes/no question universally is with an interrogative particle. This strategy is most common with OV languages, but does occur in VO languages as well. The question particle (QP) can be cliticized to the first constituent in the clause (either before or after), or at the end of the clause. Often the question particle can be omitted, leaving only intonation and the pragmatics of the situation to distinguish the clause as a question:

Tagalog

(90)   *Assertion*
        mabait si Pilar.
        "Pilar is kind."

(91)   *Question*
        mabait (*ba*) si Pilar?
        "Is Pilar kind?"

        Latin
(92)   erat-*ne*   te-cum
        he:was-QP you-with
        "Was he with you?"

        Zapotec
(93)   (*nee*) nuu bisoze-lu
        QP   is father-your
        "Is your father there?"

        Yagua
(94)   Jidyeetu-*víy*   júnaa-chara?
        your:daughter-QP cry-HABIT
        "Does your daughter cry?"

(95)   Sa-ya-*víy* Quityo-mú-jụ?
        3SG-go-QP Iquitos-LOC-DIR
        "Did he go to Iquitos?"

        Mandarin
(96)   tā   xihuan chī pǐngguǒ *ma*
        3SG like   eat apple   QP
        "Does she like to eat apples?"

        Wappo
(97)   eephi mansana paʔukh hak'she? *he*?
        3SG   apple   eat   like   QP
        "Does she like to eat apples?"

In Canadian and some other varieties of English a question particle is an alternative to subject–auxiliary inversion:

(98)   You want to feed my sled dogs, *eh*?

Tag questions. A **tag question** is a yes/no question consisting of a declarative clause plus a "tag" that requests confirmation or disconfirmation of the declarative clause. Usually tag questions are a secondary yes/no question device. That is to say, in languages that employ tag questions there is always some other, more fully grammaticalized means of forming yes/no questions. However, the tag is often the historical source for question

particles (see above). Spoken English uses tag questions in particular pragmatic environments. For example:

(99)   *English*
        She's leaving, *isn't she*?
        She's leaving, *right*?

These questions seem to imply that the speaker expects an affirmative
answer. The basic yes/no question strategy does not carry this pragmatic
expectation. The following are some additional examples of tag questions:

(100)   *Russian*
        tï   jevo slušil, *pravda*?
        you him heard true
        "You heard him, didn't you?"

(101)   *Lamani*
        u jan-wa cha, *koni ka*?
        he goes-he PRES NEG QP
        "He's going, isn't he?"

A tag question is sometimes a reduced form of a conjoined alternative clause:

(102)   *Mandarin* (Li and Thompson 1981: 546)
        a. nǐmen shi jiǔ diǎnzhōng kai mén de, *duì bu duì*?
            2PL   be nine o'clock   open door NOM right not right
            "You opened at nine o'clock, right?"

        b. wǒmen qu chī shuǐguǒ, *hǎo bu hǎo*?
            1PL   go eat fruit   good not good
            "Let's go eat some fruit OK?"

Functions. So far we have dealt with the various ways in which languages
form yes/no questions. In most languages, the morphosyntax of yes/no
questions is employed in several different ways in discourse. In the rest
of this section we will briefly survey some of the ways in which yes/no
questions are known to function. Since many of these are present at
least marginally in English, we will illustrate these functions primarily
from English. It should be kept in mind, however, that some of these
functions that are only marginal in English (e.g., intensification) are much
more well installed as discourse devices in other languages. Furthermore,

there may be other creative uses made of yes/no question structures that have yet to be attested.

    1 *To solicit information.* This is the basic use of yes/no questions:

(103)   "Is it time for class?"

    2 *To request action.* This is quite different from soliciting information:

(104)   "Could you close the window?"

        Spanish illustrates the difference between usages 1 and 2 in that there exist two distinct lexical verbs to describe the two senses of "asking:"

(105)   preguntar "to ask for information"
            pedir "to request a thing or some action"

(106)   Me preguntó qué hora fue. "He asked me what time it was."
            *Me pidió qué hora fue.

(107)   Me pidió un Bolívar. "He asked me for a Bolívar."
            *Me preguntó un Bolívar.

(108)   Me pidió escribir una carta. "He asked me to write a letter."
            *Me preguntó escribir una carta.

    3 *For rhetorical effect.* Rhetorical questions expect no answer:

(109)   "Are you always so messy?"

    4 *Confirmation* of information already possessed by the speaker:

(110)   "You're going, aren't you?"
            "Aren't you going?"

    5 *Intensification*:

(111)   "Did he ever yell!"

Although the clause type illustrated in 111 does not typically have question intonation, it does exhibit subject–auxiliary inversion common to yes/no questions.

10.3.1.2 *Question-word (information, content) questions*

    Questions that expect a more elaborate response than simply an affirmation or disaffirmation are called **question-word questions**, **content questions**, **information questions**, or **wh-questions**. The last term reflects the fact that in written English the question words nearly all contain a *w* and an *h*. Even though this mnemonic device may be helpful to speakers of English, we will not use this term in this book. Rather, we will employ the term "question-word questions."

Table 10.1   Question words of English

Question word	Relative pronoun	Meaning
who	who	human, subject
whom	whom	human, non-subject
what	–	non-human
where	where	location
why	why	reason
how	–	manner
when	when	time
which	which	generic

All languages have a set of special words that occur in question-word questions. These words are often similar or identical to a set of pronouns used elsewhere in the language, e.g., the relative pronouns or pronouns used to refer to non-specific, non-identified entities. For example, the set of question words in English is practically identical to the set of relative pronouns (see table 10.1).

In some dialects of English it is possible to use *what* and *how* as relative pronouns, e.g., *the house what I saw, the way how you did it*. In "standard" English, however, the generic complementizer *that* is more typical in these circumstances.

Often question words are similar to indefinite pronouns:

(112)   *Tamang*
khaima khaima klang-pa
when   when   play-INDEF
"Sometimes he plays"

Question words accomplish two tasks: (1) they mark the clause as a question; and (2) they indicate what information is being requested. For example, 113b–f are English questions formed from the declarative clause in 113a:

(113)   a. Zebedee threw stones at the herring.
   b. Who threw stones at the herring?
   c. What did Zeb throw 0 at the herring?
   d. What did Zeb throw stones at 0?

    e. What did Zeb do to the herring?

    f. Why did Zeb throw stones at the herring?

The presence of the special question word at the beginning of the clause marks the clause as a question. The actual question word chosen, plus a "gap" somewhere in the clause (indicated by a zero in examples 113c and d) or the pro-verb *do* (113e), specify what information the speaker is requesting the addressee to fill in.

    In VO languages, such as English, it is typical for the question word to appear at the beginning of the clause. This fact was observed by Greenberg (1966) in his universals 11 and 12. The following are some examples of clause-initial question words in a non-Indo-European language:

(114)   *Zapotec* (Zapotecan, Mexico)

    a. *tu*   biiya-lu?

       who saw-you

       "Whom did you see?"

    b. *zhi* bi'ni-lu?   "What did you do?"

    c. *tu* najii Betu?   "Who loves Betu?"

Sometimes the question word remains in the "normal" position (*in situ*), rather than "moving" to the front. This is especially common in OV languages like Japanese and Tibetan:

(115)   *Japanese* (Maynard 1987)

    Zentai   *doko* itteta   da?

    in:the:world where have:been COP

    "Where in the world have you been?"

(116)   *Tibetan*

    yoqöö *qhare* sɛɛ-pə-rɛɛ?

    servant what eat-PAST-INTER

    "What did the servant eat?"

However, in most OV languages the question word can either remain *in situ* or it can move to the front:

    Wappo

(117) a. *may* ce chici hak'she?

      who that bear like

      "Whom does that bear like?"

b. ce chici *may* hak'she?
   "Whom does that bear like?"

(118) a. *ita*   mi? yok'-okh hak'she?
          where you sit-INF   like
          "Where would you like to sit?"

       b. mi? yok'-okh hak'she *ita*?
          you sit-INF   like   where
          "Where would you like to sit?"

Some VO languages allow or require question words to remain *in situ*:

(119)   *Mandarin*
       a. *shei* kàn ni?
          who see you
          "Who saw you?"

       b. ni kàn *shei*?
          "Whom did you see?"

       c. ta   dao *nali*   qu?
          3SG to where go
          "Where did he go?"

The following are examples from Mangga Buang of Papua New Guinea (courtesy of Joan Healey):

(120) a. *Object*
          ataak vu   *vaati* vu hong?
          mother gave what to you
          "What did mother give you?"

       b. *Dative*
          ataak vu   vaahes   ti   vu *lati*?
          mother gave string:bag one to who
          "Who did mother give a string bag to?"

       c. *Location*
          ga-la   *tana* vasêên?
          you-went where yesterday
          "Where did you go yesterday?"

Many of the VO languages of eastern Africa require that question words remain *in situ*.

Question words can usually take case markers and/or adpositions. When a question word in an oblique role is fronted (sometimes **extracted**), the adposition may remain with the "gap" (121a) or it may go along with the question word (121b):

(121)   a.   *What* did you eat with 0?
        b.   *With what* did you eat 0?

Pied-piping is an informal term for the phenomenon illustrated in 121b.

10.3.2   Imperatives

Imperatives are verb forms or construction types that are used to directly command the addressee to perform some action, e.g., *Eat this!* Usually imperatives are understood to refer to second person subjects. Because it is so common and expected for the intended subject of an imperative clause to be the addressee, reference to the subject is not necessary and so the subject is often omitted. Imperatives typically allow fewer TAM contrasts than other construction types. This is because it is simply pragmatically impossible to command someone to perform acts with certain TAM operations, e.g., **Ate that!*, **Be having a baby!*, etc. In the following paragraphs we will discuss and exemplify certain formal properties of imperative constructions.

Imperatives sometimes take special verb forms. In Greenlandic Iñupiat, the distinction between declarative and imperative clauses is signaled by the morphological distinction between the verbal suffixes *-v* and *-gi*:

(122)   *Greenlandic*
        a.   iga-*v*-o-t
             cook-DECL-INTRNS-2
             "You are cooking (something)."

        b.   iga-*gi*-t
             cook-IMP-2
             "Cook (something)!"

Imperatives sometimes take special negation. In Greenlandic, the negative operator *-na* is used in imperatives (123a) and in dependent clauses (123b):

(123)   a. Attor-*na*-gu
            disturb-NEG-IMP:3SG
            "Do not disturb this."

    b. Attor-*na*-gu   iser-p-o-q
            disturb-NEG-INF:3SG enter-DECL-INTRNS-3SG
            "Without disturbing him, he came in."

This -*na* is distinct from the negative marker used in independent clauses. Note also that the third person singular non-finite verb suffix -*gu* is the same as the imperative marker. This is true only when the object is an identifiable third person argument.

    Imperatives are often associated with other irrealis modes (see section 9.3.3). For example, in modern Israeli Hebrew there is a specific verb form for imperatives (ex. 124a). However, the future can also be understood as an imperative (ex. 124b). The only way of forming a negative imperative is with the future form of the verb plus a special negative particle:

(124)   *Modern Israeli Hebrew*
    a. Shev
            sit(IMP)
            "Sit down!"

    b. Teshev
            sit(2SG.FUT.INDIC)
            "Sit down!" or "You will sit down."

    c. Hu lo' yoshev
            he NEG sit(MASC.SG.PRES.INDIC)
            "He is not sitting."

    d. *Lo' shev

    e. Lo' teshev
            NEG sit(2SG.FUT.INDIC)
            "You will not sit down."

    f. 'Al teshev
            NEG sit(2SG.FUT.INDIC)
            "Do not sit down!"

In Yagua the imperative and the future are exactly the same:

(125) a. Y-ą-maasa
       2SG-IRR-sit
       "Sit down" or "You will sit down."

   b. Vuryą-ą-murray
      1PL-IRR-sing
      "Let's sing" or "We will sing."

Sometimes imperatives affect case marking. For example, in Finnish P arguments normally occur in the morphological case traditionally termed "accusative" (126a). However, in imperatives the P argument occurs in the "nominative" case (126b):

(126) a. Maija   soi kala-*n*
       Maija:NOM ate fish-ACC
       "Maija ate fish."

   b Syö kala
      eat fish:NOM
      "Eat fish!"

Finally, in some languages different types of imperative exist. For example, in Panare, imperatives are distinguished by whether or not they involve motion. The suffix *-kë* indicates plain imperatives (127a), while the suffix *-ta'* expresses imperatives that involve motion (127b):

(127) a. akuíj*kë*
       a-kupi-*kë*
       NEU-bathe-IMPER
       "Bathe yourself!"

   b. y-o'kooma-*ta'*
      TRNS-lift-IMP:MVMT
      "Go lift it!"

?

How are yes/no questions formed?

How are information questions formed?

How are imperatives formed?

Are there "polite" imperatives that contrast with more direct imperatives?

Are there "first person" imperatives (e.g., *Let's eat*)? If so, how are they used?

---

11 Clause combinations

In previous chapters we have discussed several means of altering the form of verbs and nouns to shape the semantic force of the concepts they express. In every language there exist as well different ways of combining basic lexical items, such as verbs, to form more complex expressions. In this chapter we will discuss several construction types that involve combinations of verbs.

Most of the multi-verb constructions described in this chapter involve one **independent** clause and one or more **dependent** clauses. An independent clause is one that is fully inflected and capable of being integrated into discourse on its own (see section 2.2 on inflectional morphology). A dependent clause is one that depends on some other clause for at least part of its inflectional information. For example, in the following example, clause (b) is dependent on clause (a) because the subject and tense of clause (b) are only understood via the subject and tense of clause (a):

(1)   (a) He came in, (b) locking the door behind him.

Clause (b) by itself does not qualify as a fully inflected clause, able to be integrated into discourse on its own. Sometimes fully inflected verbs are called **finite** verbs, whereas dependent verbs are termed **non-finite**. However, this distinction must be understood as a continuum, as some verbs are dependent in one respect, but independent in another. Thus we may talk about one verb being *more* finite or *less* finite than another.

The present chapter will be organized according to six general types of multiple verb constructions: (1) serial verbs, (2) complement clauses, (3) adverbial clauses, (4) clause chains, (5) relative clauses, and

(6) coordination. These six construction types are arranged in such a way that the earlier ones represent the highest degree of grammatical integration between two verbs, whereas the later ones represent the lowest degree of grammatical integration. Another way of describing this arrangement is in terms of a continuum in which one end is a single clause, and the other end is two grammatically distinct clauses. A given language may possess any number of construction types that fall somewhere in between these extremes. In this chapter, we will discuss the six commonly occurring multiverb constructions:

One clause	Serial verbs	Complement clauses	Adverbial clauses	Clause chains	Relative clauses	Coordination	Two separate clauses

High degree of grammatical integration

No grammatical integration

11.1   Serial verbs

A serial-verb construction contains two or more verb roots that are neither compounded (see section 9.2) nor members of separate clauses. Serial verbs occur in all types of languages, but may be more common in languages that have little or no verbal morphology (isolating languages, see section 2.1). English marginally employs serial verbs in such constructions as the following:

(2)   *Run go get* me a newspaper.

In many other languages, serial verbs are a much more well installed characteristic of the grammar. Typically, verbs in a series will express various facets of one complex event. For example, the concept expressed by the English verb *bring* is divisible into at least two components, the picking up or taking of an object and the movement toward a deictic center. In many languages, this complex concept is embodied in a serial-verb construction (3a):

(3)   *Yoruba* (Bamgbose 1974)
     a. mo *mú* ìwé *wá* ilé
        I   take book come house
        "I brought a book home."

b. mo *mú* ìwé; mo sì *wá* ilé
I   take book I   and come house
"I took a book and came home."

Example 3b illustrates a pair of coordinate clauses that employ the same two verb roots as the serial construction in 3a. The formal factors that distinguish 3a as a serial construction are the following:

1 There is no independent marking of the subject of the second verb.
2 There is no independent tense/aspect marking of the second verb.
3 The intonation is characteristic of a single clause.

The following examples illustrate that in the Yoruba serial-verb construction, tense/aspect/mode information is carried by the first verb:

(4)   mò *n*   mú ìwé *bɔ*   (*wá)
I   PROG take book come:PROG come:PERF
"I am bringing a book."

In example 4 the auxiliary that signals progressive aspect occurs before the first verb. It is not repeated before the second verb. Nevertheless, the form of the verb meaning "come" must be consistent with progressive aspect, *bɔ*, rather than perfective aspect *wá*.

Example 5a illustrates that the negative particle is associated with the first verb. Nevertheless, negation has scope over the entire clause (see section 10.2 on negative scope). Example 5b illustrates that the negative cannot be associated with the second verb:

(5)   a. èmi *kò* mú ìwé wá
I.NEG not take book come
"I did not bring a book."

b. *èmi mú ìwé *kò* wá

In contrast to these serial constructions, in coordinate clauses each clause can have its own tense, aspect, and mode.

Another interesting formal characteristic of prototypical serial-verb constructions is that when a constituent of the second verb is clefted for pragmatic purposes, it moves to the front of the entire serial construction (see section 10.1.3 on clefts). Example 6a illustrates the same Yoruba clause with the constituent "to the house" clefted; 6b illustrates that such fronting cannot occur when the construction involves two separate clauses:

(6)   a. *ilé   ni* mo mú ìwé   wá
         house is I   take book come
         "It was to the house that I brought a book."

      b. **ilé ni* mo mú ìwé mo sì   wá
         I   and come

Some serial-verb constructions are less than prototypical in that some inflectional information may be carried by both verbs. For example, in Akan both verbs in a serial construction must have the same subject, but the subject is redundantly specified on both:

(7)   *Akan* (Schachter 1974)
         mede aburow migu   msum
         I:take corn   I:flow water:in
         "I pour corn into the water."

Sùpyìré and Minyanka are closely related Senufo languages of Mali, West Africa. In Sùpyìré both verbs in a serial construction may contain a reference to the subject (8), while in Minyanka, the subject reference in the second clause is omitted (9) (all the Sùpyìré examples in this section are courtesy of Bob Carlson. The Minyanka examples are courtesy of Dan Brubaker):

(8)   *Sùpyìré*
         pi-a   yì   yàha *pí-á*   kàrè fó Bàmàko e
         they-PERF them leave they:SUB-PERF go till Bamako to
         "They let them go to Bamako."

(9)   *Minyanka*
         pá   yì   yáhá kárì fó Bàmàkò nì
         they:ASP them leave go   till Bamako to
         "They sent them to Bamako." (lit.: "let them go")

One might say that the Minyanka serial-verb construction is "further along" in the diachronic path from fully independent clauses to compound verbs.

In Lahu, the difference between a serial construction and a clause chain (see section 11.4) is that in a clause chain non-final verbs may take a special particle, *-lɛ*. This particle may not appear on the final verb:

(10)   *Lahu* (Matisoff 1973)
         lâ   pɔʔ(*-lɛ*)   chèʔ(*-lɛ*) câ(*-*lɛ*) pə . . .
         tiger jump(-NF)   bite(-NF) eat(*-NF) finish
         "The tiger jumped (on them), bit into (them), and ate (them) up . . ."

In serial constructions, on the other hand, none of the verbs may take the non-final particle:

(11)   šúqhu nîqhu kə   lɔ?   chï ve
        pipes three put: into be: enough roll ?
        "He rolls enough to put into three pipes."

    The actual meaning of a serial-verb construction as a whole can often be ambiguous out of context. The following example from Thai is provided by Foley and Olson (1985):

(12)   John khàp rót chon   khwaay taay
        John drive car collide buffalo die
        a. John drove the car into a buffalo and it (*buffalo*) died.
        b. John drove the car into a buffalo and it (*car*) stalled.
        c. John drove the car into a buffalo and he (*John*) died.

Out of context this clause is ambiguous in the three ways illustrated above. In discourse, only the pragmatics of the situation can disambiguate.

    Semantically, serial-verb constructions often mean something slightly different than what the same series of verbs would mean if they were cast in separate clauses. However, if the semantics has changed very much, it is possible that one of the verbs in the series has been reanalyzed as an auxiliary. In fact, serial verbs are one major diachronic source for auxiliaries. In Lahu, some verb pairs are ambiguous, out of context, as to whether they are to be construed as a series of co-equal serial verbs, or as an auxiliary plus a main verb. Only the semantics reveal any difference whatsoever:

(13)   lɔ chê   a. beg to be there (verb series)
        beg be:there b. is begging (verb + auxiliary)

(14)   ga kì   a. is busy getting (verb series)
        get be:busy   b. must be busy (auxiliary + verb)

(15)   ta   ša   a. easy to begin (verb series)
        begin be:easy b. begin to be easy (auxiliary + verb)

    In many languages, serial verbs carry aspectual meaning. As such, they function as auxiliaries in languages that have a grammatically distinct class of auxiliaries. Grammatically, however, they are appropriately categorized as serial verbs, i.e., each verb has equal grammatical status, and neither one is clearly grammatically dependent on the other. Examples 16 and 17 are from Tok Pisin (Givón 1987):

(16)   *Finish φι completive*
        . . . em wokim paya pinis . . .
            she make fire finish
        "She got the fire started."

(17)   *Be φι continuative*
        . . . em brukim i-stap
            he break PRED-be
        "He keeps breaking (it)."

Examples 18 and 19 are from Sùpyìré:

(18)   *Come φι inchoative*
        . . . fó kà pi-í   m-*pá*   lyɛ
            till and they-SEQ CN-come be.old
        ". . . till they become old."

(19)   *Do φι distributive*
        u-a   cì   cyán-á *mà* hà
        she-PERF them drop-NF do DIST
        "She dropped them all over the place."

These Sùpyìré constructions are not prototypical serial verbs in that there is a grammatical marker of sequentiality or non-finiteness that is associated with one of the verbs in the series, i.e., there is some grammatical asymmetry between the two verbs. Nevertheless, such pairs do resemble serial verbs more closely than they resemble auxiliaries in that (a) auxiliaries constitute a small closed class of elements that distribute differently from the non-finite verbs in 18 and 19, and (b) the non-finite or sequential marking often occurs in constructions that are more clearly serial verbs, i.e., those in which the semantics has not changed (e.g., 8 above).

Verbs of motion are very useful in serial constructions. They are often exploited to express tense, aspect, or modal values. As such, they are well on their way to becoming auxiliaries. For example, it is very common for the verb meaning "go" to become a marker of future tense. This has happened in English (*He's going to get mad*), Spanish, and many other languages. In some languages, such as Sùpyìré, the construction type that gives rise to this use of the verb "go" is a serial construction:

(20)   Zànhe sí dùfugé   kɛ̀ɛ̀gɛ̀
        rain   go maize.DEF spoil
        "The rain will spoil the maize."

In Tibetan, motion verbs in a serial-like construction provide directional orientation for the action described by the other verb:

(21)   *Tibetan* (DeLancey 1990)
        qʰó   pʰoo   (cɛɛ) čĩ   pəréè
        he:ABS escape   NF   went PERF.DISJUNCT
        "He escaped away."

Serial verbs can also be a source for adpositions. For example, in Yoruba, the preposition that marks RECIPIENTS is transparently related to the verb meaning "give":

(22)   *Yoruba* (Stahlke 1970)
        mo sɔ   *fún*   ɔ . . .
        I   say give you
        "I said to you . . ."

In Efik, the verb meaning "give" has become a benefactive preposition:

(23)   *Efik* (Welmers 1973)
        nám útom ɛ̀mì *nə*   mì
        do   work this give me
        "Do this work for me!"

In Sùpyìré, and many other languages, the verb meaning "use" becomes a marker of the instrumental role. In Sùpyìré it has become a postposition:

(24)   U-a   lì *tàha-a* ɲùŋke   pwɔ̀
        she-PERF it use-NF head.DEF tie
        "She tied her hair with it."

?

Does the language have serial verbs (or "co-verbs" in the East Asian tradition)? Which verbs are most likely to occur in serial constructions?
Are there any that are losing their semantic content and becoming more like auxiliaries, adpositions, or TAM markers when they occur in serial constructions?

11.2   Complement clauses

A prototypical **complement clause** is a clause that functions as an argument (subject or object) of some other clause (Noonan 1985). A **main** (or **matrix**) clause is one that has another clause as one of its core arguments. However, a much wider range of clauses have been called "complements" in the literature. Sometimes a complement clause is said to be any clause that is **embedded** within another clause (Foley and Van Valin 1984).

The kinds of complement clause that we will discuss and illustrate in this section can be either subjects or objects of the matrix clause. For example:

(25)   **Subject complement**

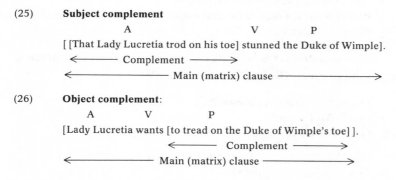

(26)   **Object complement**:

In English we usually place subject complements after the verb and replace the subject by the neuter pronoun *it*. This is called **postposing** of subject complements:

(27)   It stunned the Duke of Wimple that Lady Lucretia trod on his toe.

A clause can be both a complement *and* a matrix clause, i.e., it can be an argument of one clause and at the same time have a third clause as one of its own core arguments. For example:

(28)   [Lucretia wants [to believe [that that oaf is the Duke of Wimple]]].

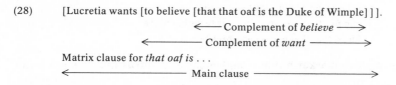

Complement clauses can be described as falling somewhere on a continuum defined in terms of its extremes, as follows:

"Non-finite complements"   "Finite complements"

⊢——⊣

We will refer to this continuum as the "complexity continuum."[1] It will guide our presentation of various kinds of complements in the following paragraphs. As we saw with causatives (section 8.1.1), the closer the structural integration between complement and main verb, the closer the conceptual integration is likely to be.

Prototypical **finite complements** are like independent clauses, as evidenced by the following characteristics:

1 They carry their own tense and aspect.
2 They express their subjects directly; subject reference is not restricted to that of the matrix clause.

Typical matrix verbs for finite complements are verbs of utterance and cognition (see, e.g., Givón 1980). For example:

(29)   *English finite object complements*
   a. I know *that it's raining.*
   b. I emphasized *that she knows Swahili.*

(30)   *English finite subject complements*
   a. *That it had rained* surprised me.
   b. It is well known *that she is terribly rude.*

Except for the complementizer *that*, each of the emphasized complement clauses in 29 and 30 could stand alone as a complete and understandable utterance in English. Each one is independently marked for tense and subject reference.

As might be expected, in VO languages object complements tend to follow the matrix verb:

(31)   *Mandarin*
   wǒ zhīdào *nèige rén   chī-le   sān   wǎn   fàn.*
   I   know   that person eat-PERF three bowl rice
   "I know that that person ate three bowls of rice."

The perfective marker in the complement verb shows that this is a finite complement.

In OV languages, object complements tend to precede the matrix verb:

(32)   *Wappo* (Charles Li and Sandra Thompson, p.c.)
?ah *ce   k'ew ew tum-tah* hatiskhi?
1sg that man fish buy-PAST know
"I know that man bought fish."

Again, the complement clause in 32 is a finite complement because it contains all of the inflectional information necessary to be an independent clause of the language.

Non-finite complements are more tightly knit, less independent, less like a separate clause from the matrix clause than are finite complements. Non-finite complements tend to have the following properties:

1   The identity of the subject is highly constrained. It often must be identical to the subject of the matrix verb.
2   Tense, aspect, and mode are highly constrained or not specified at all. The complement verb is usually non-finite.

Some examples of non-finite complements follow:

(33)   *English non-finite subject complements*
a. *To cook a meal like that* requires a lot of patience.
b. It isn't so easy *to do linguistics*.

(34)   *English non-finite object complements*
a. I enjoy *washing my car*.
b. She likes *to do linguistics*.

(35)   *Mandarin non-finite object complement*
wǒ yao *nian* (*-le) *shū*
1sg want read (-PERF) book
"I want to read a book."

In Mandarin it is ungrammatical to attach the perfective aspect marker to verbs that are complements of certain matrix verbs, such as *yao* "want."

(36)   *Wappo*
?ah *ce   k'ew ew tum-uhk* hak'se?
1sg that man fish buy-INF want
"I want that man to buy fish."

In this Wappo clause, the complement verb does not take an independent tense/aspect marker. Instead the infinitive suffix marks it as a non-finite verb.

Indirect questions are a subtype of complement clauses. English uses wh- type complementizers in indirect questions:

(37)   *English indirect questions – subject complements*
    a. *Whether they're here* is not known.
    b. It is a mystery to me *who saw you*.

Whether corresponds to yes/no type questions, while *what, when, where, who/whom, how, why*, and *which* correspond to question-word questions.

(38)   *English indirect questions – object complements*
    a. I wonder *whether they're here*.
    b. I wonder *who saw you*.

Indirect questions may share formal properties with interrogative clauses or relative clauses. For example, in Yoruba, *ti* is the complementizer used in relative clauses, and *woni* is a question word. In indirect questions, however, *ti* rather than *woni* is the complementizer:

(39)   Tale mo   okunrin *ti*   obinrin na lu
    Tale know man   that woman the hit
    "Tale knows which man the woman hit."

English can go either way:

(40)   a. I know *the year that Mary was born*.
    b. I know *which year Mary was born*.

In 40a the emphasized portion resembles a relative clause. It would express essentially the same thought as 40b, in which the complement resembles a question-word question.

?
    What kinds of complement clause does the language have?
    Are particular complement types common for particular classes of
    complement-taking verbs?
    Does the language allow subject and object complements, or just object
    complements?

11.3   Adverbial clauses

Adverbial clauses are those that serve an "adverbial" function (Longacre and Thompson 1985). They modify a verb phrase or a whole clause. They are not an argument of the clause. Sometimes adverbial clauses are termed "adjuncts" (as opposed to complements). This is a good term since the term "complement" implies completion, and a predicate does not express a complete proposition until all its argument positions are filled, i.e., completed. On other hand, adverbials attach to constructions that are already complete propositions. The adverbial simply adds some information to the proposition.

Sometimes adverbial clauses look like complements:

(41)   a. He ran *to get help*.   (purpose)
       b. We're sorry *that you feel that way*.   (reason)
       c. She went out, *locking the door behind her*. (sequence)

The adverbial clauses in these examples all have the same morphosyntax as certain complement types of English. Nevertheless, they are not complements because they do not constitute logical arguments of the main verb; rather, they simply add "adverbial" information, namely purpose, reason, and sequence respectively.

The kinds of information embodied in adverbial clauses are the same kinds of information expressed by adverbs, e.g., time, place, manner, purpose, reason, condition, etc. Examples of each of these will be provided in the following paragraphs. Most of these examples are from Longacre and Thompson (1985).

1 *Time*: We'll go *when Sandy gets here* (also *before, after*, etc.)

(42)   *Barai* (Papua New Guinea)
           Bae-*mo*-gana   e   ije   bu-ne   ke.
           ripe-PAST:SEQ-DS people these 3PL-FOC take
           "When it was ripe, these people took it." (takes one of several "sequence"
           markers)

2 *Location*: I'll meet you *where the statue used to be*.

(43)   *Turkish*
           Sen Erol-un   otur-dug-u   *yer*-e   otur.
           you Erol-GEN sit-OBJ-POSS place-DAT sit
           "You sit where Erol was sitting." (requires the word for "place")

3 *Manner*

    (a) She talks *like she has a cold*;
    (b) Carry this *as I told you*.

(44)   *Quechua*
        Alista-pan   kuura ni-*shan-naw*-qa.
        prepare-BEN3 priest say-REL-MAN
        "They prepared it for him like the priest said."

Manner clauses in Quechua take the marker for relative clauses in addition to the suffix that indicates manner. A literal translation of this clause might be ". . . the way that the priest said."

4 *Purpose*: He stood on his tiptoes *in order to see better*.

(45)   *Panare*
        T-yen-che'   e'ñapa tu'ñen   i'ya-ta-*tópe*
        IRR-take-GNO people medicine shaman-INCHO-PURP
        "People take medicine in order to become a shaman."

In Panare, the inflectional suffix *-tópe* marks a clause as being a purpose adverbial.

5 *Reason*: He got here early *because he wanted to get a good seat*.
      Most languages treat purpose and reason alike, e.g., Yoruba:

(46)   Vəru   *gàadà* dà shi səma
        go:out:PERF PURP IRR drink beer
        "He went out to drink beer." (purpose)

(47)   A-ta   abən *gàadà* aci ngaa
        eat-PERF food REASON he well
        "He ate because he was well." (reason)

The only formal difference between purpose and reason clauses in Yoruba is that the purpose clause contains the irrealis marker *dà*.

6 *Circumstantial*: He got into the army *by lying about his age*. (Typologically rare.)

7 Simultaneous

    (a) *While (we were) eating,* we heard a noise outside the window.
    (b) He woke up *crying.*

(48)   *Yavapai*
        Kwawa '-chkyat-a-k vak '-unuu-*t*-m   swach'skyap-ch vqaov-k
        hair   1-CUT-IRR-SS here 1-INCOMPL-SIM-DS scissors-SUB   break-SS
        yuny
        TNS
        "While I was cutting my hair the scissors broke."

8 Conditional

    Simple:
    (a) *If it's raining outside,* then my car is getting wet.
    (b) *If you step on the brake,* the car slows down.
    (c) *If you were at the party,* then you know about Sue and Fred.
        Hypothetical: *If I (were to see/saw) David,* I would speak Quechua with
        him.
        Counterfactual: *If you had been at the concert,* you would have seen Ravi
        Shankar.
        Concessive conditional: *Even if it rains,* we'll have our picnic.

Most languages use a subordinating morpheme like *if* in concessive conditionals, but some languages use a different morpheme than that which occurs in other types of conditionals:

(49)   *Mandarin*
        Jiùshi tā sòng gèi wǒ, wǒ dou bu yào.
        Even:if he give to 1SG 1SG still NEG want
        "Even if he gave it to me I wouldn't take it."

In spoken North American English, the form of a conditional clause is sometimes used to express non-conditional notions. These can be informally termed "speech act" conditionals in that they accomplish locutionary acts such as giving permission:

    "*Speech act*"
    If you're thirsty there's Coke in the refrigerator.

This is not a classic conditional clause in that even if the hearer is *not* thirsty, presumably the situation expressed in the main clause would still hold. Rather, this complex clause contains implicit propositions that can be phrased "It may be of interest to you to know that there's Coke in the refrigerator and I give you permission to have some."

9 *Negative conditional*: *Unless it rains*, we'll have our picnic (i.e., if and only if it does not rain, we will have our picnic).

10 *Concessive clause*
    (a) *Although she hates Bartok*, she agreed to go to the concert.
    (b) *Even though it's still early*, we'd better find our seats.

11 *Substitutive*: We barbecued chicken *instead of going out to eat*.

12 *Additive*: *In addition to having your hand stamped*, you also have to have your ticket stub.

13 *"Absolutive"*
    (a) *Having told a few bad jokes*, Harvey introduced the speaker.
    (b) *Seeing me*, Harvey hid behind his mother's skirt.

The distinguishing characteristic of "absolutive" adverbial clauses is that they simply present the general background for the situation expressed in the main clause. If the language seems to employ this sort of "absolutive" clause extensively, you should consider the possibility that they might more insightfully be analyzed as medial clauses (see section 11.4). In English these gerundive clauses really fall in between adverbial and medial clauses. However, because there are no canonical medial clauses in English, and because these gerundive clauses are not extremely common, it makes more sense for the purposes of this typology to think of them as a type of adverbial clause.

    How are adverbial clauses formed?
    What kinds of adverbial clauses are there, e.g., time, manner, purpose, reason, consequence, sequence, conditional?
    Can adverbial clauses occur in more than one place in a clause?
    If so, are there any differences in meaning associated with the various allowable positions for any given adverbial clause type?
    Among the conditionals, are there any subdivisions, e.g., contrafactual (*If I*

had done it differently, *that wouldn't have happened*), hypothetical (**If I were you**, *I'd
do it differently*)?
What restrictions are there on the TAM marking of conditional clauses?

....

11.4   Clause chaining, medial clauses, and switch reference

Since the mid-1960s there have been many studies dealing with
clause-chaining languages (McCarthy 1965, Healey 1966, Hetzron 1969,
1977, Longacre 1972, Olson 1973, Thurman 1975, Gerdel and Slocum 1976
inter alia). The paradigm examples of clause-chaining languages occur
in the highlands of New Guinea, both Irian Jaya and Papua New Guinea
(Elson 1964), though clause chaining is a well recognized phenomenon in
Australia (Austin 1980) and the Americas (Longacre 1985). In descriptions
of such languages there is normally a distinction drawn between "final"
and "non-final" clauses. These terms are based on the fact that in clause-
chaining languages, as identified in these previous studies, the sequentially
final clause in a clause chain is inflected for tense or aspect while the other
clauses are not. Longacre (1985: 264 and footnote 6) hypothesizes that,
though it is a logical possibility for languages to have clause chains in which
the more completely inflected clause occurs initially in the chain, no clear
examples of such languages had been documented. Since 1985, however,
some languages of this type have been documented (e.g., Panare), though it
remains the case that languages in which the more highly inflected clause
comes at the end of the chain seem to be in the majority and tend to employ
longer clause chains (T. Payne 1991).

More recently the term **medial** clause has begun to replace the
term non-final clause in descriptions of clause-chaining structures (Haiman
1987).[2] This term reflects the fact that this clause type occurs clause-
internally, i.e., in the "middle" of a clause chain. As defined by Longacre
(1985: 263), a medial clause is one which (a) has a reduced range of tense–
aspect possibilities in comparison to final clauses, (b) usually specifies
"subject" reference in terms of (i.e., as the same as or different from) the
subject of the final clause, and (c) usually directly expresses temporal relations such as "overlap" and "succession" with respect to other clauses in
the sequence. A clause-chaining language, then, is a language that employs
sequences of medial clauses completed by a final clause as a major discourse-
structuring device.

A prototypical **switch-reference** system is verbal inflection that indicates whether the subject of the verb is coreferential with (i.e., the same as) the subject of some other verb. For example in Yuman languages, such as Maricopa, the verbal suffix -*k* indicates that the subject of the verb is the same as the subject of the next verb in a sequence. The suffix -*m* indicates that the subject is different from the subject of the next verb (examples courtesy of Lynn Gordon):

(50)   *Maricopa* (Yuman, southwestern United States)
    a. Nyaa '-ashvar-*k* '-iima-k.
       I   1-sing-SS 1-dance-ASPECT
       "I sang and I danced."

    b. Bonnie-sh 0-ashvar-*m* '-iima-k.
       Bonnie-SUB 3-sing-DS 1-dance-ASPECT
       "Bonnie sang and I danced."

In Maricopa, switch-reference markers are distinct from verb agreement, i.e., they are a different inflectional category (note that both verbs "agree" with their subjects by way of prefixes). Hence there is a lot of redundancy. Sometimes, however, coreference markers are incorporated into the system of verb agreement. In this case the category of "third person" is subdivided into two, one for same reference and another for switch reference. Various terminology is used to refer to such systems, e.g., reflexive, fourth person, recurrent, etc. Yup'ik exhibits such a system:

(51) a. Dena-q quya-u-q   Toni-aq cinga-llra-0-ku.
       -ABS happy-INTRNS-3 -ABS   greet-because-3/3-DEP
      "Dena$_i$ is happy because she$_j$ greeted Tony."

    b. Dena-q quya-u-q Toni-aq cinga-llra-*mi*-ku.
                        -SS
      "Dena$_i$ is happy because she$_i$ greeted Tony."

The second clause in example 51a takes the standard verb agreement marking for third person acting on third person transitive verbs. The interpretation of 51a is that the actors mentioned in the two clauses are different. The second clause in 51b, on the other hand, takes a special suffix, -*mi*, which indicates that the actor of this clause is the same as the actor of the previous clause. Sometimes this suffix is called the "fourth person."

Table 11.1 Kâte switch-reference markers

	Overlap ("while")	Succession ("then")
SS	-huk	-ra
DS	-ha	-0

Table 11.2 Panare switch-reference markers

Operator	Temporal relation	Reference	Other relations conveyed
-séjpe	succession	actor = actor	purpose
-sé'ñape	succession	absolutive = patient	result
-ñépe	succession	actor ≠ actor	movement/purpose
-npan	overlap	actor = actor	none
-tááñe	overlap	actor = actor	none
-jpómën	anteriority	actor = actor	reason

More complex systems of switch reference occur in the languages of highland Papua New Guinea. For example, Kâte, illustrated in table 11.1, has a switch-reference system consisting of four markers (Longacre 1972).

(52) a. Fisi-*huk* na-wek
         arrive-SS ate-3SG
         "As he$_i$ arrived, he$_i$ was eating."

     b. Fisi-*ra*   na-wek
         arrive-SS ate-3SG
         "He$_i$ arrived, then he$_i$ ate."

     c. Mu-*ha*-pie   kio-wek
         speak-DS-3PL weep-3SG
         "As they spoke, he was weeping."

     d. Mu-*0*-pie   kio-wek
         speak-DS-3PL weep-3SG
         "After they spoke, he wept."

Some systems are even more complex than this. For example, in Panare, operators that indicate same- or switch-reference relations between clauses also indicate several temporal or logical relations. Table 11.2 illustrates these operators and the various relations they express (T. Payne 1991).

This table shows that interclausal coreference marking need not be based on the grammatical relation of subject only. Several languages, especially those that employ morphological ergativity as a basic case-marking strategy, have complex switch-reference systems in which some operators are anteceded by subjects while others are anteceded by objects or absolutives. This phenomenon has been documented in Australian languages (Austin 1980) and in Amerindian languages (Jones and Jones 1991 on Barasano).

The following is an extract from Kanite, a Papuan language. Not only does this language employ a special different subject morpheme, *ke*, but each medial clause is inflected for the subject of the *next* clause (Longacre 1972):

(53)   a.   his-u'a-*ke*-'ka,
            do-we-DS-you
            "If we do this,"

       b.   naki a'nemo-ka   hoya   ali-'ka,
            so   women-you garden work-you
            "you women work the garden,"

       c.   naki ali   ha'anoma hu-ne'atale-'ka,
            so   work finish   do-COMPL-you
            "when the work's finished"

       d.   popo hu-'ka, (e.) inuna kae-'ka,
            hoe do-you   weeds burn-you
            "hoe and burn the weeds"

       f.   naki ha'no hu-talete-*ke*-ta'a
            so   finish do-COMPL-DS-we
            "when that is finished,"

       g.   'naki viemoka-ta'a keki'yamo'ma ha'noma ne-his-i-*ana*
            so   men-we   fence   finish   FUT-do-it-1PL
            "we men will finish building the fence."

-ana in clause g marks the end of the chain.

Clause 53a is marked with *u'a*, indicating its own subject. Then *-ke* indicates that the next clause will have a different subject, and finally *-'ka* indicates that the next subject will be second person. Each of the following four clauses is marked with *-'ka* indicating that the following clause will have a second person subject. Same subject is indicated with zero. In clause f we have the *-ke* marker again, indicating that the final clause will have a different subject. After the *-ke* comes the form *-ta'a*, indicating that the final clause will have "we" as its subject. Clause g is the only final verb in this series. All others are medial, i.e., they cannot stand alone as full propositions. This is probably because of the *-'ka* markers. Notice that 53g has a tense marker, whereas none of the other verbs do.

?

> Does the language have any grammaticalized device that explicitly indicates whether a participant in one clause is the same as or different than some participant in another clause?
> If so, answer the following questions:
> (a) What direction does the dependency go? That is, does a marker signal coreferentiality with a yet to be mentioned participant, or an already mentioned participant? (Maybe both, depending on other factors.)
> (b) What can "antecede" one of these markers? That is, is coreferentiality always with respect to a "subject" participant, or can non-subject AGENT, or nominals of other grammatical relations also antecede a coreference form?
> (c) On what categories of elements can these markers go, e.g., verbs, nouns, conjunctions, etc.?
> Can one clause be inflected for the person/number of the subject of some other clause?
> Do the markers of interclausal coreference also carry other information, e.g., tense/aspect or semantic relations between clauses?
> How extensive is this phenomenon?

Additional reading: Haiman and Munro (1983).

11.5   Relative clauses

A **relative clause** is one that functions as a nominal modifier (Keenan 1985), for example:

(54)   The oaf *that [0 trod on Lady Lucretia's toe]*

The pertinent parts of a relative clause are the following:

1 The **head** is the noun phrase that is modified by the clause. In 54 the head is *the oaf*.
2 The **restricting clause** is the relative clause itself. In 54 the restricting clause is indicated in brackets.
3 The **relativized noun phrase** (NP_{rel}) is the element within the restricting

clause that is coreferential with the head noun. In 54 the NP_{rel} is represented as 0 (a gap).

4 The **relativizer** is the morpheme or particle that sets off the restricting clause as a relative clause. In 54 the relativizer is *that*. If the relativizer reflects some properties of the NP_{rel} within the restricting clause (e.g., humanness, grammatical relation in the restricting clause, etc.), then it can be termed a **relative pronoun** (see below).

There are several typological parameters by which relative clauses can be grouped. The parameters to be discussed and exemplified in this section are (1) the position of the clause with respect to the head noun, (2) the mode of expression of the relativized NP (sometimes called the "case recoverability strategy"), and (3) which grammatical relations can be relativized.

The first typological parameter by which relative clauses can vary is the position of the clause with respect to the head. Relative clauses can be **prenominal** (the clause occurs *before* the head), **postnominal** (the clause occurs *after* the head), **internally headed** (the head occurs within the relative clause), or they may be **headless**. Since relative clauses are noun modifiers, one might expect that they would occur in the same position as other noun modifiers, e.g., descriptive adjectives, numerals, etc. Though it is true that the position of the relative clause with respect to the head noun often is the same as the position of descriptive modifiers, there is a distinct tendency for relative clauses to be postnominal, even in languages for which descriptive modifiers are prenominal. This tendency is probably due to a universal pragmatic principle that shifts "heavy," i.e., long, phonologically complex, information to late in the clause. This is the same principle that motivates postposing of subject complements in English (see section 11.2). The following examples illustrate each of these types from several different languages.

Postnominal relative clauses are the most common type. Languages which are dominantly VO in main-clause constituent order always have postnominal relative clauses. English is such a language. The following examples are from Luganda, a Bantu language of Zaire:

(55) a. omukazi ya-kuba omusajja
          woman   she-hit   man
          "The woman hit the man."

      b. omusajja [omukazi gwe-ya-kuba]
          man   woman   REL-she-hit
          "the man that the woman hit"

Example 55a illustrates a plain transitive clause; 55b illustrates the same clause functioning as a relative clause to modify the noun *omusajja* "man." As is typical of VO languages, the relative clause follows the head noun.

Prenominal relative clauses occur in some OV languages.

(56)   *Japanese*
a. Yamada-san ga   sa'ru   o   ka't-te   i-ru
    Yamada-Mr. NOM monkey ACC keep-PART be-PRES
    "Mr. Yamada is keeping a monkey."

b. [*yamada-san ga ka'tte iru*] sa'ru
    "the monkey that Mr. Yamada is keeping"

c. [*sa'ru o ka'tte iru*] Yamada-san
    "the Mr. Yamada who is keeping a monkey"

Examples 56b and c illustrate two relative clauses based on the independent clause in 56a. In both of the relative clauses, the restricting clause comes before the head.

Example 57 illustrates an entire Turkish clause in which a relative clause modifies one of the nominals:

(57)   Eser [*uyuy-na*] kadïn-ï   tanyor
        Eser sleep-PART woman-ACC knows
        "Eser knows the woman who is sleeping."

Turkish is an OV language and, true to its type, it employs prenominal relative clauses. The head of the relative clause in 57 is *kadïn* "woman." This noun is preceded by the relative clause in brackets. Notice also that the verb within the relative clause is marked as a participle. This is a very common feature of relative clauses, especially in languages that have a lot of verbal morphology (polysynthetic languages). Even English has a marginal participial relative clause strategy:

(58)   a. Eser knows the [sleep-*ing*] woman.
        b. Eser sat on a [fall-*en*] log.
        c. Eser ripped up her [reject-*ed*] novel.

All of the italicized morphemes in these examples are markers of adjectives derived from verbs (participial verbs) of one type or another. Though traditional English grammar would not call such verb forms "clauses" at all, they fulfill our definition of relative clause. For many languages (e.g., Turkish) constructions analogous to these are the only means of modifying a noun phrase using anything like a clause, i.e., they function just like relative clauses even though they may not be very clause-like formally.

Internally headed relative clauses are those for which the head is within the relative clause. Many OV languages, including Bambara, a Niger-Congo language of West Africa, have internally headed relative clauses:

(59) a. ne ye so   ye
          1SG PAST horse see
          "I saw a horse."

      b. ce ye [ne ye so   *min* ye] san
          man PAST 1SG PAST horse REL see buy
          "The man bought the horse that I saw."

The relativizer *min* is the only thing that marks the clause in brackets as a relative clause in 59b. The head noun remains *in situ* within the relative clause and is not repeated external to the relative clause, as in the other examples above. Internally headed relative clauses can be thought of as another means of avoiding having a phonologically large and semantically complex modifier precede the head noun. It obviates the hearer having to "wait" until the relative clause has been uttered to learn what noun the clause modifies.

Headless relative clauses are those clauses which themselves refer to the noun that they modify. In general, languages in which nominal modifiers are themselves nouns are more likely to employ headless relative clauses as a major RC strategy than languages for which there is a distinct and large class of adjectives. English, and many other languages, can use headless relative clauses when the head noun is non-specific:

(60) a. [Whenever I'm afraid], I call her .
          (cf. "Any *time* that I am afraid . . .")

      b. [Whoever goes to the store] should get some water balloons.
          (cf. "Any *person* who goes to the store . . .")

Some languages use headless relative clauses whenever specific reference to the head is clear. Often the relative pronoun specifies as clearly as necessary, e.g., "who went to the store" = "the person who went to the store," "where I live" = "the place where I live," etc. Ndjuká (Surinam Creole) apparently employs headless relative clauses for both non-specific and specific referents (examples courtesy of George Huttar):

(61) a. [Di o   doo fosi] o wini.   Subject, non-specific
         REL FUT arrive first FUT win
         "Whoever arrives first will win."

      b. A mainsi ya a [di e   tan a ini se].   Subject, specific
         the eel   here COP REL CONT stay LOC inside sea
         "This eel is what (the one that) lives in the sea."

      c. A   daai go anga [di a   be puu].   Object, specific
         3SG turn go with REL 3SG ANT remove
         "He turned and returned with what (the ones) he had removed."

Sometimes headless relative clauses are hard to distinguish from complement clauses. They are, however, distinct at least at the semantic level. The following are examples of headless relative clauses (HRCs) and corresponding complement clauses (CCs) in English:

(62) a. HRC: *That which John said* annoyed her.
      b. CC: *That John said it/something/anything* annoyed her.

Notice that the semantic representation of 62a is ANNOY(x, y), i.e., the content of what John said annoyed her. The representation of 62b, on the other hand, is better represented as ANNOY(P, y). That is, it was not what he said that annoyed her, but the fact that he said anything at all. His *act* of saying is annoying rather than the specific *thing* he said. Here are some further examples:

(63) a. HRC: I hate *where I live*. (marginally acceptable to some?)
      b. CC: I know *where I live*.

The semantic representation of 63a would be HATE(x, y), where y is a *thing*, i.e., the particular place in the world where I live. The semantic representation of 63b, on the other hand, would be KNOW(x, P) where P is a *proposition*, i.e., "the place I live is located somewhere." It is not the same use of the verb *know* as in *I know your brother*.

(64) a. HRC: *Whoever goes to the store* has to buy me some rice.
      b. CC: I don't know *whether she'll go to the store*.

Example 64a is very similar in function to an adverbial (conditional) clause (see section 11.3): ***If someone goes to the store**, she has to buy me some rice*. In some languages this type of conditional clause is not distinct morphosyntactically from relative clauses. Example 64b is an embedded question.

It can be paraphrased as "I don't know the answer to the question 'Will she go to the store?'."

The second major parameter by which relative clauses can vary is how the NP$_{rel}$ is expressed. This parameter is sometimes stated as a "case recoverability" problem (e.g., Keenan 1985). That is, in any relative clause there must be some way of identifying the role of the referent of the head noun *within the relative clause*. The head noun itself functions in another clause (the "main") clause; however, it always has a coreferent within the relative clause (the NP$_{rel}$ in our terms). The role of that NP can be different from the role of the head noun within the main clause. For example, in 65a the head noun is the subject of the main clause verb *ate*. It is also the subject of the relative-clause verb *saw*. In 65b, however, the alligator is still the subject of *ate*, but it is now the object of the relative-clause verb:

(65) a. The alligator [that saw me] ate Alice.
      b. The alligator [that I saw] ate Alice.

These clauses can be considered to be reductions of the following two abstract structures:

(66) a. <u>The alligator</u> that [<u>the alligator</u> saw me] ate Alice.
          HEAD NOUN   NP$_{rel}$

      b. <u>The alligator</u> that [I saw <u>the alligator</u>] ate Alice.
          HEAD NOUN   NP$_{rel}$

Since the NP$_{rel}$ is left out in the surface structure of these clauses (65a, b), a problem arises as to how the hearer is to identify the grammatical relation of this invisible noun phrase within the bracketed clause. English solves this problem by simply leaving a conspicuous "gap" in the position where the NP$_{rel}$ would be if it were overtly expressed. This is called the **gap strategy**. This strategy works for languages that have a fairly fixed constituent order, i.e., those for which grammatical relations are expressed via the position of the core nominals in a clause. In such languages a missing argument is very obvious. However, if the language allows many constituent orders, and/or if grammatical relations are specified via some device other than constituent order, the gap strategy may leave the relative clause ambiguous.

Furthermore, the gap strategy is only effective in recovering the grammatical relation of the NP$_{rel}$ in verb-medial languages. For example, Isthmus Zapotec is a VAP language that allows an NP$_{rel}$ to be coded with a gap, but for which the gap is useless as a case recovery strategy:

(67)   a. najii Juan junaa
         loves John woman
         "John loves a woman."

       b. najii junaa Juan
         "A woman loves John."

       c. junaa ni   najii Juan 0
         woman REL loves John
         "A woman that John loves."

       d. junaa ni najii 0 Juan
         "A woman that loves John."

Examples 67a and b show that constituent order is in fact one way of determining the grammatical relations of A and P arguments in transitive clauses. Example 67c shows that when the NP_{rel} is the object of the relative clause, the gap appears in the object position, i.e., after the subject. Example 67d illustrates that when the NP_{rel} is the subject of the relative clause, the gap appears in the subject position. Notice, however, that 67c and d are identical. The gap is an abstract symbol that does not actually have any phonetic realization (though sometimes there may be intonational cues as to where such gaps appear). In fact the grammatical relation of the NP_{rel} is simply unrecoverable in these clauses out of context. In context, of course, the pragmatics of the situation would normally disambiguate. These examples show that though case recoverability is an important property of relative clauses, at times a certain amount of ambiguity is tolerated. However, the fact that the gap strategy is potentially ambiguous in VAP languages that do not have overt marking of grammatical relations, such as Zapotec, explains why this strategy is uncommon in such languages. The same holds true for APV languages.

     If the gap strategy is insufficient, the language is likely to use a more explicit device to express the grammatical relation of the NP_{rel}. The next device we will discuss is termed **pronoun retention**. In this strategy a pronoun that explicitly references the grammatical relation of the NP_{rel}, by its position, its form, or both, is retained within the relative clause. Pronoun retention is used in many types of relative clauses in spoken English:

(68)   That's the guy who [I can never remember *his* name].

In this clause the NP_{rel} is coded by the pronoun *his*.

(69)   We've got sixteen drums here that we don't even know what's in *them*.
         (heard on a television news interview)

Here is an example of the pronoun retention strategy in modern
Israeli Hebrew (Keenan 1985: 146):

(70)   ha-sarim   she [ha-nasi   shalax *otam* la-mitsraim]
         DEF-ministers REL DEF-president sent   them to-Egypt
         "the ministers that the president sent to Egypt"

In this relative clause, the pronoun *otam* "them," referring to the ministers,
is retained within the relative clause in the position and form required of
direct objects.

Samoan uses the pronoun retention strategy when the NP$_{rel}$ has
any role other than AGENT or PATIENT:

(71)   'o   le mea sa nofo **ai** le fafine
         PRES ART place PAST stay PRN ART woman
         "the place where the woman stayed." (lit.: the place the woman stayed
         there")

In this example the pronoun *ai* refers to the NP$_{rel}$ in the position and form
a location is normally expressed with respect to the verb *nofo*, which could
perhaps be glossed "to stay at."

It is rare for pronoun retention to be used to relativize the subject
of the relative clause in any language. For example, the following RC is
ungrammatical in Hebrew:

(72)   *ha-ish   she [*hu* makir oti]
         DEF-man REL he knows me
         "*The man who he knows me."

Keenan (1985) claims that Urhobo (Kwa, Niger-Kordofanian, Nigeria) and
Yiddish are the only languages which clearly employ the pronoun retention
strategy to relativize the subject position.

Many languages employ a special form called a **relativizer** to identify a clause as a relative clause. Often the relativizer is the same form as a
complementizer (see section 11.2). For example, English can employ the
relativizer *that* (normally unstressed):

(73)   The man *that* I saw.
         The man *that* saw me.

The bed *that* I slept in.
?The house *that* I went to.

A prototypical relativizer does not constitute a reference to the NP_{rel} and thus cannot itself help recover the role of the NP_{rel} in the relative clause. This is evidenced by the fact that the complementizer cannot be preceded by prepositions specifying the role of the NP_{rel}:

(74)   *The bed *in that* I slept.
        *The house *to that* I went.

Instead, in such circumstances a different kind of form must be used to introduce the relative clause. This is called a **relative pronoun**:

(75)   The bed *in which* I slept.
        The house *where* I went.

Relative pronouns are typically similar to other pronouns in the language, either the question words or the pronouns used to refer to non-specific, indefinite items (see section 10.3.1.2 on the parallel between relative pronouns and question words in English). Relative pronouns can be thought of as combining the functions of a plain relativizer and a clause-internal pronoun that refers to the relativized NP. English allows the relative pronoun strategy (Rel Pro), a relativizer plus gap strategy (Rel + gap), and an unmarked "no relativizer" plus gap strategy (No Rel). Sometimes all three are allowed in the same environment, and it is difficult to determine what semantic nuances are conveyed, if any, by the various allowable structures. The following illustrate some English possibilities and impossibilities:

(76)   a. Rel Pro   the man who saw me
        b. Rel + gap   the man that saw me
        c. No Rel   *the man [0 saw me]

(77)   a. Rel Pro   the man whom [I saw]
        b. Rel + gap   the man that [I saw 0]
        c. No Rel   the man [I saw 0]

(78)   a. Rel Pro   the place where I live
        b. Rel + gap   *the place that I live
        c. No Rel   the place I live

(79) a. Rel Pro   the reason why I came
      b. Rel + gap   the reason that I came
      c. No Rel   the reason I came

(80) a. Rel Pro   ?the way how he did it (acceptable to some speakers)
      b. Rel + gap   the way that he did it
      c. No Rel   the way he did it

(81) a. Rel Pro   the table which he put it on
      b. Rel + gap   the table that he put it on
      c. No Rel   the table he put it on

Lango, a Nilotic (Nilo-Saharan) language of Uganda, employs a relativizer *àmê* that is invariant, no matter what the inherent properties or grammatical relation of the NP$_{rel}$ are (Noonan 1992). The following are examples of RCs in which various classes of NP$_{rels}$ are subject (82a), object (82b), and oblique (82c):

(82) a. lócə *àmê* márô   gwôk
          man REL 3SG:like dog
          "the man that likes the dog"

      b. lyècc   *àmê* rwòt àmìttò   wìllò
          elephant REL king 3SG:want buy:INF
          "the elephant that the king wants to buy"

      c. dákô   *àmê* rwòt òlègò   òbáŋá pìrè
          woman REL king 3SG:pray:PERF God   because:of
          "the woman that the king prayed to God because of"

In contrast to the English relativizer *that* and the Lango relativizer *àmê*, the element that introduces a relative clause in Chickasaw can be inflected for the role of the NP$_{rel}$ in the relative clause. The following examples show that the form *yamma* "that" takes subject marking, *-at*, when the NP$_{rel}$ is the subject of the RC (*the woman saw the dog*, 83a), and takes object marking when the NP$_{rel}$ is the object of the RC (83b):

(83)   *Chickasaw* (Munro 1983: 230)
      a. ihoo   *yamm-at* ofi' pìs-tokat   illi-tok
          woman that-SUB dog see-PAST:DEP:SS die-PAST
          "The woman that saw the dog died."

      b. ihoo-at   ofi' *yamma* pìs-tokã   illi-tok
          woman-SUB dog that   see-PAST:DEP:DS die-PAST
          "The woman that the dog saw died."

This is evidence that in Chickasaw *yamma* constitutes a reference to the NP_{rel} and thus can be termed a relative pronoun, rather than simply a relativizer.

Finally, in outlining the typology of relative clauses in a language, it is important to specify for each type of relative clause encountered *which* elements can be relativized. Keenan and Comrie (1977) observe that any given relative-clause strategy will allow relativization on a continuous segment of the following hierarchy:

subject > direct object > indirect object > oblique > possessor

For example, according to Keenan and Comrie, no language allows relativization on subjects and indirect objects but not on direct objects using a single strategy. Also, Keenan and Comrie assert that in any given language, if one position on this hierarchy is relativizable, all positions to the *left* will also be relativizable, though not necessarily with the same strategy. For example, some languages allow relativization of subjects, but no other clausal arguments; no language, however, allows relativization of direct objects but not subjects. Different case recoverability strategies (e.g., gap, pronoun retention, etc.) may be employed for different positions, but there will never be a language which allows relativization on one position while not allowing it on a position to the left. For example, standard written English allows relativization on all positions on this hierarchy, except possessor:

(84) a. I hate the alligator that 0 ate Mildred.   subject
      b. I hate the alligator that Mildred saw 0.   direct object
      c. I hate the alligator that Mildred threw the ball to 0. indirect object
      d. I hate the alligator that Mildred rode on 0.   oblique
      e. I hate the alligator that Mildred is bigger than 0.   oblique
      f. *I hate the alligator that 0 teeth are huge.   possessor

For every relative clause strategy noted in the grammar sketch, be sure to clarify which "positions" (i.e., grammatical relations) can be relativized with that strategy. Chances are the more explicit strategies (relative pronoun, pronoun retention, internal head) will be used to relativize arguments farther down (to the right) the hierarchy than the less explicit strategies. For example, possessors can be relativized in English using the more explicit relative pronoun strategy (ex. 85a) even though they cannot, usually, be relativized using the gap (85b) or relativizer (85c) strategies:

(85)   a. I hate the alligator whose teeth are huge.
        b. *I hate the alligator 0 teeth are huge.
        c. *I hate the alligator that('s) teeth are huge.

Of course, this characterization of the relativizability hierarchy depends on the questionable assumption that every language has identifiable grammatical relations such as subject, object, and indirect object. In languages for which grammatical relations are either organized according to some other system (e.g., ergative/absolutive) or for which grammatical relations are not clearly identifiable at all, the concept of a relativizability hierarchy may not be very useful. Nevertheless, for a good number of languages it can be possible and insightful to determine how and whether Keenan and Comrie's predictions apply.

?

What kind or kinds of relative clauses does the language have?

(a) Prenominal?
(b) Postnominal?
(c) Internally headed?
(d) Headless?
(e) Correlative?

What positions on the following relativizability hierarchy can be relativized?

subject > direct object > indirect object > oblique > possessor

What RC type or "case recoverability strategy" is used for each position?

11.6   Coordination

Languages often have morphosyntactic means of linking two clauses of equal grammatical status. Such linkage is termed **coordination**. It is distinct from **subordination** in that in subordination, one clause is grammatically dependent on the other. All of the dependent clause types discussed in the previous sections (i.e., complement clauses, adverbial clauses, and relative clauses) may be considered to be examples of subordinate clauses. However, there is really not much commonality to this broad group of clause types other than grammatical dependency. Therefore, the notion of "subordinate clause" is not very useful as a universal linguistic category (see Haiman and Thompson 1984).

Coordination is sometimes difficult to distinguish from mere juxtaposition of clauses in discourse. In fact, in spoken discourse some kind of morphosyntactic clause linkage, either coordination or subordination, may be evident at nearly all clause junctures. Many readers will be familiar with the English colloquial narrative style that inserts *and . . .* or *and then . . .* after each clause. In general, the fact that two clauses are grammatically coordinated simply asserts that (1) the two clauses have more or less the same function in terms of the event structure of the text (e.g., they both code events, they both code non-events, they both code foregrounded information, or they both code background information, etc.), and (2) they are presented as being conceptually linked in some way.

Interpropositional (logical) relations that often obtain between coordinate clauses include conjunction, disjunction, and exclusion. Coordinating devices used to distinguish these relations will be discussed in this section. It should be kept in mind, however, that just about any semantic relation between clauses in discourse can obtain in a coordinate structure. Section 12.1.2 describes one framework for analyzing the interpropositional relations in a text.

Often some strategies for conjoining clauses are identical to strategies for conjoining noun phrases. For example, English uses the conjunction *and* for both phrasal and clausal conjunction:

(86)   John *and* Mary   NP + NP
        John cried *and* Mary laughed.   clause + clause

However, it is also common for there to be special strategies for conjoining clauses that are not used for conjoining phrases. For example, the English *but* does not easily function as a noun phrase conjunction:

(87)   *John *but* Mary   NP + NP
        John cried *but* Mary laughed.   clause + clause

The simplest means of conjoining two clauses is what J. Payne (1985) describes as the **zero strategy**. This is where two phrases or clauses are simply juxtaposed. According to J. Payne, most languages probably allow the zero strategy at least as a stylistic variation. Some languages, however, use it more extensively than do others. Vietnamese is a language that uses the zero strategy extensively in both phrasal and clausal coordination (examples from Watson 1966: 170, as quoted in J. Payne 1985: 26):

(88) a. Nháng tiráp   [tilêt,   callóh, acôq]
          we   prepare basket spear   knife
          "We prepare baskets, spears, and knives."   NP coordination

      b. Do chô   [tôq cayâq,   tôq apây]
          she return to   husband to   grandmother
          "She returns to (her) husband and
          to (her) grandmother."   PP coordination

      c. Do [chô   tôq cayâq,   chô   tôq apây]
          she return to   husband return to   grandmother
          "She returns to (her) husband and
          returns to (her) grandmother."   VP coordination

The most common means of indicating conjunction is by the use
of a **coordinating conjunction** such as *and* in English. For VO languages
this conjunction normally occurs in between the two conjoined clauses:

(89)   Robespierre fell out of favor *and* the revolutionaries killed him.

However, sometimes in VO languages the coordinating conjunction follows the first element of the second clause:

(90)   *Yoruba*
          mo mú ìwé; mo **sì**   wá   ilé
          I   take book I   and come house
          "I took a book and I came home."

For OV languages, the coordinating conjunction comes either between the two conjoined elements, as in Farsi (91a, b, c), or after the last
element, as in Walapai (93):

(91)   *Farsi (from J. Payne 1985: 28)*
      a. Jân [xandid *va*   dast   tekân dâd]$_{VP}$
          John smiled and hand sign   gave
          "John smiled and waved."   VP coordination

      b. Jân [puldar *va*   mašhur]$_{AP}$ bud
          John rich   and famous   was
          "John was rich and famous."   adj. coordination

      c. [Jân   raft *va*   Meri dast   tekân dâd]$_{CL}$
          John left and Mary hand sign   gave
          "John left and Mary waved."   clausal coordination

The form that conjoins two elements is often the same as the operator that encodes the comitative sense of *with*. In Walapai (Yuman), both instrumental and comitative elements are signaled with the enclitic *-m*. Example 92 illustrates this *-m* in its common role as an instrumental case marker (Redden 1966: 160–61, as cited in J. Payne 1985: 30):

(92)   ɲa-č   ɲikwáì-č-a   avon-a-*m*   taθ-k-wíl
        1SG-NOM clothes-PL-DEF soap-DEF-with wash-1SG-CONT
        "I washed the clothes with soap."

This *-m* operator also functions as a phrasal and clausal coordinator:

(93)   Wàlpáìkwáùk háìkùkwáùk-m   íče
        Walapai:speech white:man:speech-with we:speak
        "We speak Walapai and English."

Such isomorphism among the instrumental, comitative, and coordinating operators is extremely common in the world's languages.

Latin possesses a "negative conjunctive" particle *nec*, in addition to the affirmative conjunction *et*. The meaning of the negative conjunctive particle can be characterized as "and not" in English (Kühner and Stegmann 1955: 48, as cited in J. Payne 1985: 37):

(94)   eques Romanus [*nec*   infacetus *et*   satis   litteratus]$_{AP}$
        knight Roman   and:not dull   and moderately literate
        "a not dull and moderately literate Roman knight"

Unlike the English translation "not . . . and," the negative conjunctive particle in Latin does not have scope over the entire conjoined phrase. In other words, only dullness is negated in the Latin example, whereas the English translation could be taken as ambiguous as to whether "moderately literate" should be taken as being negated as well.

In the following paragraphs we will briefly discuss the logical relations of conjunction and disjunction.

Conjunction is primarily a logical relationship between propositions. If the conjunction of two propositions is true then each of the component propositions is true. By this definition, nearly any two propositions in discourse could be considered conjoined.

Disjunction, like conjunction, is a logical relationship between propositions. If the logical disjunction of two propositions is true, then one or both of the component propositions can be true. There is no particular reason why a language would grammaticalize exactly this notion of disjunction, and it is quite rare for languages to employ a device specifically for this purpose. English *or* tends to express a more exclusive notion of disjunction if both component clauses are affirmative:

(95)   He came in through the window or he broke down the door.

That is, 95 would normally assert that one of the conjoined propositions holds true but the other one does not. The word *either* reinforces this interpretation. In fact, in discourse this use of *or* without *either* is quite rare. Instead *or* without *either* is used almost exclusively when one or both of the component propositions is negated. In this case *or* ceases to convey logical disjunction:

(96)   I didn't break the window or the door.

Under any natural circumstances this clause expresses the *conjunction* of *I didn't break the window* and *I didn't break the door*. Therefore it is simply inaccurate to characterize *or* as a disjunctive particle in English. Logical disjunction is but one, relatively rare, function of this particle.

In other languages it is similarly rare for logical disjunction to have its own unique morphosyntax. If disjunction is expressed at all it will usually be via some periphrastic device such as "I might have broken the window and I might have broken the door." In Yagua one interesting case of disjunction is expressed via the use of contrastive pronouns:

(97)   a. Ra-dyéétya-ręę-kyey,
            1SG-know-POT-EVID
            "I want to know"

        b. níí-numáá-tiy   vátan-tán-dyé-ryéy,   munuñú-niy,
            3SG:PRN-now-COND curse-cause-DAY-1SG savage-NIY
            "if HE cursed me, the savage,"

        c. ráñiy   vátan-tán-dye-ryéy.
            1SG:PRN curse-cause-DAY-1SG
            "or I cursed myself."

In this case the speaker is not claiming that either the savage or the speaker himself did the cursing, but only that one did and the other did not. The use of contrastive pronouns alone codes the disjunctive relation between 97b and 97c.

?

How are the following kinds of logical relations between clauses typically expressed?

(a) Conjunction (a and b)/(neither a nor b)?

(b) Disjunction (a or b)?

(c) Exclusion (a and not b)?

---

12   Conclusions: the language in use

12.0   Discourse analysis and linguistic analysis

Discourse is intentional communication among people. Much of human communication involves language, therefore the study of discourse typically involves the study of language. However, discourse and language are two potentially independent fields of investigation. Because they are independent, each can provide evidence for claims made in the other – if they were identical, or notational variants of the same phenomenon, then generalizations made in one domain based on evidence from the other would be meaningless.

For example, AGENT is a concept that is useful in human communication (discourse). AGENTS exist quite apart from language (see section 3.2.0). Subject (as defined in this book), on the other hand, is a linguistic concept. It does not exist apart from its role as a category in linguistic structures. If AGENT and subject were simply two names for the same concept, generalizations such as "in this sentence the AGENT is the subject," or "AGENT is the primary candidate for subjecthood" would be tautologous. One could not meaningfully explain anything about AGENT in terms of subject or vice versa.

The term **discourse analysis** is used in different ways by linguists, anthropologists, sociologists, and philosophers (see Schiffrin 1994 for a survey of approaches to discourse analysis). In this section, I will make an important distinction between *linguistic analysis* of discourse and discourse *interpretation*. Much of what has been called discourse analysis in the previous literature would fall under the heading of discourse interpretation in this characterization. For example, if I examine a text and divide it up into "paragraphs" based on my understanding of the propositional

342

information in the text, e.g., when the speaker finishes talking about one thing and begins talking about another, then I am *interpreting* the text. However, if I look at the same text and divide it up according to the use of certain particles, referential devices, pauses, and intonational patterns, I am engaged in *linguistic analysis* of the text.

Interpretation certainly has a role in linguistic analysis, but interpretation and analysis are not the same thing. For example, I may interpret the paragraphing in a text based on the propositional content alone. Then, I may analyze the text according to the morphosyntactic cues sprinkled within it. If I am able to successfully keep my interpretation independent of my analysis, then some meaningful, *scientifically valid*, generalizations may result, e.g., "particle X marks paragraph boundaries." However, if I let interpretation into my analysis, e.g., by *defining* particle X as a marker of paragraph boundaries, or deciding ahead of time where paragraph boundaries are by looking for particle X, then no meaningful generalization is possible.

The point at which a sociologist who studies discourse becomes a sociolinguist who studies language is when he/she makes scientifically valid generalizations (predictions, explanations) using empirical linguistic data as evidence. Much understanding of the functions of morphosyntactic devices is based on interpretation, and hypotheses are generated through interpretive judgments. Nevertheless, linguistics as a discipline derives its independence from its distinctively empirical methodologies and perspectives. Sociologists and literary scholars do not need linguists if interpretation is their only concern.

In this chapter, we will first describe some general properties of discourse that tend to be reflected in language. In section 12.2 a survey of various discourse genres will be presented. Finally, in section 12.3 several topics that may be treated in a concluding section of a grammatical description are suggested.

12.1   Continuity (cohesion) and discontinuity

Discourse is human communication. A **text** is a linguistic artifact – a record of language used during a portion of discourse. Text, then, normally consists of strings of clauses, i.e., linguistic instantiations of propositions. However, not every string of clauses is a text. In order to be a text, a series of clauses must *hang together* in certain definable ways. This is because discourse hangs together. If a text does not reflect the cohesive character of discourse, then it is dysfunctional, just as if it did not reflect the referential or temporal character of discourse. Thus text exhibits **cohesion** or **continuity**.

There are three kinds of continuity that will concern us here: **topic continuity**, **action continuity** and **thematic continuity** (Givón 1983a). This division is somewhat arbitrary since the categories clearly overlap and interact with each other to a high degree. Also, there are probably kinds of continuity that are not captured under these headings. Nevertheless, this tripartite division is reasonably well defined, and will serve as a convenient framework within which a field linguist might organize observations regarding the discourse-structuring devices of a language.

Topic continuity refers to the fact that discourse tends to evoke the same referents over and over again. Pronouns and other referential devices are morphosyntactic means of expressing this kind of continuity, as well as its converse, topic *discontinuity*, i.e., the introduction of new, unexpected referents.

Action (or event, or situation) *continuity* refers to the fact that discourse tends to develop along certain parameters, e.g., location (X happened here, Y happened there), time (first X happened then Y happened, then Z happened), or logic/causation (X happened because of Y, Y happened so that Z). Different kinds of discourse, or **genres** (see section 12.2), rely on different organizational parameters to a greater or lesser degree. Foregrounding and backgrounding are defined in relation to the particular parameter employed, e.g., foregrounded clauses denote progress along the major organizational parameter, whereas backgrounded clauses provide ancillary, supportive information (Longacre 1976, Hopper and Thompson 1980). Tense/aspect marking and clause connectors are morphosyntactic devices that aid speakers and hearers in expressing and recovering this kind of continuity.

Thematic continuity refers to the fact that discourse tends to revolve around recurring "themes," e.g., "how to make a blowgun," or "latest styles." Inference is probably the major process whereby thematic continuity is recovered. However, devices that normally express other kinds of continuity also may be used, by extension, to express or reinforce thematic continuity. Thematic continuity is probably the most difficult kind of discourse continuity for linguists to deal with precisely because there is so little in the way of empirical evidence that identifies it. The most promising results so far are drawn from experimental studies (e.g., Tomlin 1995). Unfortunately, the methodologies developed in such studies are not particularly amenable to implementation in a field situation. Nevertheless, some important general principles may be forthcoming from this research.

It should be noted that the term "theme," and related expressions, such as "thematic" or "thematicity," has been used in a variety of senses by linguists. We will use this term in the sense of Jones (1977) to mean the "main idea" of a text or portion of text. Themes in this sense are expressed via propositions akin to titles, rather than via referring expressions. This use departs rather significantly from the way the term is used by Mathesius, Halliday, Grimes, and others. For these linguists, theme is identified as the "point of departure" for a proposition. It is a piece of information functioning on the clause level rather than a "main idea" that has relevance over an entire text or portion of text. Some linguists, following in the tradition of Mathesius *et al.*, go so far as to define theme completely formally as the "left-most constituent of a sentence" (Brown and Yule 1983: 126). For descriptive linguists, it is extremely important to keep definitions of formal and functional categories independent of one another. Otherwise, statements regarding the functions of formal structures are tautologous (see above).

12.1.1   Topic (referential) continuity

The kinds of structure that are likely to function in the domain of topic continuity are:

1   anaphoric zeros;
2   verb coding (or anaphoric/grammatical agreement);
3   unstressed (clitic) pronouns;
4   stressed (independent) pronouns;
5   demonstrative pronouns;
6   full noun phrases;
7   specified noun phrases;
8   modified noun phrases;
9   special constituent orders, e.g., fronting;
10   "voice" alternations, e.g., active, passive, antipassive, and inverse;
11   "switch-reference" systems.

Of course, these structures also are sensitive to functional influences other than topic continuity and discontinuity. Nevertheless, a full topic continuity study of a language would need to take into account any and all of these options that exist in the language.

At the highest level, referential devices have one of two functions in the domain of topic continuity: either they code initial appearances of a referent on the discourse stage or they code appearances of a referent that is already on the discourse stage. In other words, whenever a referent is mentioned in a text it is either already "on stage" or it is being brought "onto stage." It is safe to say that languages *always* possess distinct structures that characteristically code these two functions. Any grammar sketch should describe at least this aspect of the referential system. Some of the terminology that has been used for this distinction is:

Initial appearance	*Subsequent appearance*
coming onto stage	already on stage
new	given (Halliday 1967)
switch	continuing
previously inactivated	activated (Chafe 1987)
discontinuous	continuous (Givón 1983a)

This distinction may be relevant within a clause or within a higher-level unit. For example, switch-reference systems (see section 11.4) typically indicate whether a referent is the same as or different from a referent in a neighboring clause even though all referents are "on stage" in terms of the discourse as a whole. Very different structures are used to indicate that an important referent is being mentioned for the very first time in the discourse ("brand new" in terms of Prince 1981).

It should be noted that the crucial criterion is whether the referent is "on stage," not whether it has already been mentioned in the text. There are various ways in which a referent can be brought onto the discourse stage without necessarily being overtly mentioned. Thus the first actual textual mention of a referent need not be an introduction of that referent. Referents are often treated as "given" when they are first mentioned. Some ways in which referents can be brought "onto stage" without explicit mention are:

Presence in the discourse context:
I hope he's not vicious. (one pedestrian to another as a large dog approaches)

Perpetually present:
The sun was out. (no need to say "There is a sun that sometimes comes out")
I love you. (speech act participants are always "on stage")

Part of a discourse "frame":
We had dinner at Fat City last night. The waitress spilled coffee on me. (the restaurant frame includes waiters/waitresses)

Rhetorical suspense:
The executioner smiled. (first line of a short story)

In spite of the many extragrammatical ways in which referents get onto the discourse stage, all languages also provide morphosyntactic devices to explicitly accomplish this function. Also, a referent that has appeared earlier in the text may subsequently have been removed from the discourse stage. In this case it may have to be "re-introduced."

In addition to the brute binary distinction between initial mention and subsequent mention, there are many more functional principles that are known to impinge on referential systems. Prince (1981) provides a good framework within which a more detailed description of the topic-continuity-related devices of a language might be couched.

One function not developed by Prince is the notion of "deployability" or "importance." This notion reflects the fact that not all initial mentions are created equal. Some referents are "destined" to figure prominently in the subsequent discourse whereas others are just passing through. Languages typically possess alternative coding devices to reflect this distinction. For an obvious example, Wright and Givón (1987) demonstrate that in spoken North American English a noun phrase preceded by the demonstrative *this* serves to introduce referents that are destined to figure prominently in the subsequent discourse. For example, example 1 below sounds odd because the use of *this guy* sets the reader up to expect the subsequent discourse to involve the indicated referent:

(1) I was sitting there reading a newspaper when *this guy* walks up to me. It was the *New York Times*, and I was fascinated by a front-page story about linguistics. After I finished reading it I went home. < end >

Example 2 is a more natural use of this expression:

(2) I was sitting there reading a newspaper when *this guy* walks up to me and says, "Hey lady, you got a quarter for a cuppa coffee?" He looked familiar somehow, so I asked him . . .

On the other hand, the standard expression using the article *a* tends to refer to new referents that are not going to be particularly important in the subsequent text (cf. *a newspaper*, *a quarter*, and *a cuppa coffee* in 2).

All of the above observations serve to illustrate that there is more to referential coding choices than simply the given vs. new distinction.

Givón (1983a, b, c) proposes a **scalar** notion of topic continuity. That is, any referent ("topic" in Givón's terminology) is mentioned more or less often than the others. The more often it is mentioned, the more it contributes to the sense that the text "hangs together." Referents that are mentioned often are sometimes said to be more **continuous** or more **topical** than others. There are several factors that enter into the degree of topicality evidenced by a referent. These factors can be divided into **inherent** characteristics of the referents themselves and **context-imparted** factors. These are briefly outlined below:

1 *Inherent topicality (topic-worthiness)*. Humans are inherently more likely to be mentioned in human discourse than are non-humans, entities that control events than entities that are passively affected by events, etc.
2 *Context-imparted topicality*. Speech act participants (first and second persons) are highly likely to be mentioned in any discourse. Entities that are visible to speaker and hearer at the moment of speaking are more likely to be mentioned than random objects in the world. Referents that have already been mentioned are more likely to be mentioned again than are random referents in the world.

The quantitative methodology developed by Givón and colleagues is a way of determining how topical any referent is at any given point in a text according to the last mentioned kind of context-imparted topicality. Although the methodology only measures one kind of topicality, it has the advantage of being rigorous and non-circular. Once topicality is measured, referential devices can be ranked in terms of the average topicality values of the referents they code.

Additional reading: Chafe (1980 and the articles therein), Hopper and Thompson (1984).

12.1.2   Thematic continuity

Speech is necessarily linear, since sounds are uttered one at a time in a continuous stream. Ideas, on the other hand, are hierarchically structured. They are grouped topically, and some thoughts can be broken down into lots of subthoughts or concepts. Not all thoughts are related to one another "head-to-tail," conceptually speaking, the way linguistic units are in the speech stream. One problem that the grammar of any language must deal with is how to represent such hierarchically structured ideas by means of a linear speech stream. Often morphosyntactic devices sprinkled in the speech stream help speakers express and hearers recover the hierarchical nature of discourse. For example, indentation is a way of indicating certain "high-level" boundaries in written text, as are chapter headings, section headings, etc. These are formal devices (as formal as any morphological device in spoken language) present in the morphology of the text that delimit the hierarchical structure of the text. Natural spoken texts also exhibit morphological signals of hierarchical structure usually in the form of particles and special intonational patterns.

In spite of the fact that every language employs some morphosyntactic devices to express hierarchical thematic structure, the most common "device" is inference. In a certain sense, *all* of the information gleaned from a text is inferred. People speak in order to communicate, and so they use every resource at their disposal to make their own message obvious, and to reconstruct in their own minds a coherent version of what the other participants are trying to say. The morphosyntactic structures of a shared language constitute one set of tools for accomplishing these tasks. However, assumptions regarding context, attitudes, perceptions, and knowledge of the interlocutors also help the process along. Inference is the process of reconstructing the meaning intended by another discourse participant using all tools available, including but not limited to linguistic structure. The message is not the words; the words (and other linguistic units) are merely tools that aid in constructing and reconstructing meaning.

When we say that thematic structure is normally inferred, however, we are not using "infer" in this general sense that *all* meaning in discourse is inferred; rather, we mean that thematic structure is often not expressed by overt morphosyntactic cues. Hearers use their knowledge of the propositional content of the text alone to infer the thematic structure. For example, in the following brief text, there are no overt markers of the semantic relation that holds between the two parts:

(3)   I'm hungry. Let's go to the Fuji gardens.

However, most English speakers readily identify the first part as representing a "problem" for which the second part is a "solution" (Mann and Thompson 1987). How do we know this? We infer it from our understanding of the informational content of each part. This inference is similar to the inferential process that takes place in languages (such as Sierra Popoluca, see section 7.3.2) that rely heavily on pragmatics to distinguish grammatical relations (see chapter 7). Longer texts can be assigned hierarchical structures based on just this kind of inference. For example, Mann and Thompson (1987) assign the structure in figure 12.1 to a brief newspaper article.

This kind of display can be useful for investigating the functions of various grammatical structures, including clause types, particles, and constituent orders. For example, in Yagua it was found that certain presentative constructions commonly occur at major hierarchical boundaries (T. Payne 1992). There are several frameworks within which the thematic structure of the message content of a text can be diagrammed, including: **rhetorical structure theory** (Mann and Thompson 1985, 1987), and **Story Grammar** (Rumelhart 1975). Individual languages, genres, or particular texts may be more or less amenable to one or another of these frameworks.

Of course, this work would be considered discourse *interpretation* rather than *linguistic analysis* given the characterization provided in section 12.1. The interpretive nature of applying hierarchical thematic structures to texts is confirmed by the fact that different observers will apply different hierarchical structures to the same text. However, as also mentioned in section 12.1, there is definitely a place for interpretation in discourse analysis. For instance, after having diagrammed a text, you might look at the distribution of some particle or other morphosyntactic device whose meaning has not been adequately identified. In many cases, one's understanding of the functions of that device will be greatly enhanced by the exercise of interpretation.

In a descriptive grammar, a linguistic researcher might describe some semantic principles on which texts are hierarchically structured, and any morphosyntactic devices that contribute to the interpretation of that hierarchical structure. Finally, one may want to diagram the thematic structure of a few short texts of various genres, and give clear, non-circular answers to the following question: How is the thematic structure of this

1 Farmington police had to help control traffic recently,

2 when hundreds of people lined up to be among the first applying for jobs at the yet-to-open Marriot Hotel.

3 The hotel's help-wanted announcement – for 300 openings – was a rare opportunity for many unemployed.

4 The people waiting in line carried a message, a refutation of claims that the jobless could be employed if only they showed enough moxie.

5 Every rule has exceptions,

6 but the tragic and too-common tableaux of hundreds or even thousands of people snake-lining up for any task with a paycheck illustrates a lack of jobs,

7 not laziness.

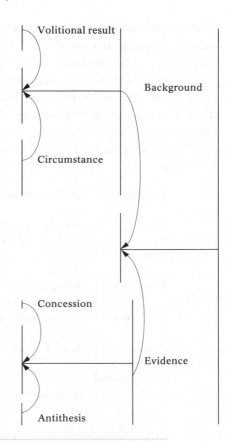

Volitional result

Background

Circumstance

Concession

Evidence

Antithesis

Figure 12.1 Rhetorical structure analysis of a newspaper article (Mann and Thompson 1987)

text encoded in the morphosyntax, if at all? It is important to be careful in this section to support all assertions with concrete examples.

12.1.3   Action continuity

Different kinds of discourse are organized according to different principles. For example, narrative discourse (see section 12.2.2) is normally organized according to time: first X happened, then Y happened, etc. The **events** in a narrative are those propositions that are related to one another sequentially, i.e., those that clearly end before the next one begins

(Labov and Waletzky 1967). Sometimes the series of propositions that express the events of a narrative is referred to as the "time line," the "main event line," or the "backbone" of the text. In a good narrative, however, there is always a great deal of very important information that is not on the main event line. For example, the following narrative excerpt has been divided into events and non-events. Non-events have been tagged as to whether they express descriptive, evaluative, or non-sequential information (based on Grimes' 1975 analysis of p. 1 of *Out of the Silent Planet* by C. S. Lewis):

Descriptive	The last drops of the thundershower had hardly ceased falling
EVENT	when the Pedestrian stuffed his map into his pocket,
EVENT	settled his pack more comfortably on his tired shoulders
EVENT	and stepped out from the shelter of a large chestnut tree into the middle of the road.
Descriptive	A violent yellow sunset was pouring through a rift in the clouds to the westward,
Descriptive	but straight ahead over the hills the sky was the colour of dark slate.
Descriptive	Every tree and blade of grass was dripping,
Descriptive	and the road shone like a river.
Non-sequential	The Pedestrian wasted no time on the landscape
EVENT	but set out at once with the determined stride of a good walker
Descriptive	who has lately realized that he will have to walk further than he intended.
Descriptive	That indeed was his situation.
Non-sequential	If he had chosen to look back,
Non-sequential	which he did not,
Evaluative	he could have seen the spire of Much Nadderby,

If one were to ask for a synopsis of "what happened?" in this excerpt, the simple response would be: "Some Pedestrian stuffed a map into his pocket, settled his pack on his shoulders, stepped out of the shelter of a chestnut tree and started walking." These are the EVENTS described by the clauses in the excerpt. This sequence of events can be considered the **foreground information**. All the other information sets the scene, or describes other, sometimes hypothetical, related situations. This supportive material is often called the **background information**.

In a procedural text (see section 12.2.4), the foregrounded information would consist of those clauses that express the steps in the procedure. Backgrounded clauses would be comments on why one does this, descriptions of the materials, tools, etc. In a hortatory discourse, the foregrounded information would be those clauses that express the behaviors the speaker is trying to elicit from the hearer (see below for descriptions of various discourse genres).

"Foreground" information is not the same as the "most important" information in a text. It may be more accurate to say that the foregrounded material is the framework on which the important information is hung. For example, Linde and Labov (1975) make the distinction between a "chronicle" and a narrative. A chronicle is essentially a narrative without background material. It is the kind of text often elicited by the parental question "What did you do today?:"

> I got up. I got dressed. I ate breakfast. I washed up. I walked to school. I played . . .

Without evaluative, supportive material, the text has no "point," other than to appease the nosy parent. The real significance of a narrative, as well as any other kind of text, often is carried in the "backgrounded" clauses. For example, many fables would hardly be worth quoting without the "moral of the story."

12.1.4   Episodic prominence

In addition to continuity and discontinuity, discourse also exhibits various kinds of prominence. Some morphosyntactic devices used to highlight or ascribe prominence to clause elements are described in chapter 10 on pragmatically marked structures. In a section on episodic prominence in a grammar sketch, you may want to describe recognizable, preferably grammaticalized, ways in which speakers of the language draw special attention to certain longer spans of discourse.

12.1.4.1 *Climax/peak*

Climax in narrative describes the point at which rhetorical tension is released. A climax must be preceded by a build-up of tension, and followed by some sort of resolution. "Climax" does *not* necessarily refer to the end of a discourse. Climactic points are often characterized by unusual morphosyntactic structures. For example, in the story of "Little Red Riding Hood" tension builds as Little Red senses something strange about her "grandmother," who is really Big Bad Wolf in disguise:

(4)   a. LR: My what big eyes you have Grandma!
        b. BBW: The better to see you with my dear.
        c. LR: My what big ears you have Grandma!
        d. BBW: The better to hear you with my dear.
        e. LR: My what big teeth you have Grandma!
        f. BBW: The better to EAT you with my dear!

Clause f in this sequence can be characterized as a climax. Tension mounts in clauses a–e as the audience, aware that "Grandma" is in fact the wolf in disguise, anticipates this revelation to Little Red. In this example, the only special morphosyntactic device that signals the climax is special intonation. In many languages, other "emphatic" or stylistically marked devices may occur. For example, in Yagua, special inflection of intransitive verbs of motion is used at points of episodic climax (T. Payne 1990a). Other languages may use cleft constructions, special constituent orders, or particles at such points.

Peak refers to a point in a narrative discourse where events are presented in rapid succession, with little backgrounded material interspersed. It is in some sense "the important part" of the story. Climax and peak are certainly related phenomena, but they are logically distinct. The same sort of phenomena associated with climax are also commonly associated with peaks. Additional morphosyntactic correlates of narrative peaks include unusually short sentences, longer paragraphs, neutralization of tense/aspect marking, and increased frequency of "emphatic" particles.

12.1.4.2 Intensification

Rhetorical questions are clauses that have the morphosyntactic form of questions, but which do not expect a literal answer. Rather, they function to "highlight" or intensify an assertion. Rhetorical questions are particularly common in persuasive and expressive discourse, and are typically characterized by unusual intonation patterns. For example, a politician attempting to generate support for a war might culminate his speech by saying something like:

(5)   Who will save our great nation from this dire threat?

Of course, the politician is not naïvely questioning his audience concerning some information they have and he does not; rather, he is trying to elicit a response such as "*We* will!" If the build-up portion of his discourse has been successful, this response will be obvious to all concerned. Rhetorical questions that seem to require "yes" or "no" responses (see section 10.3.1.1) are sometimes used to assert that certain propositions ought to be obvious. For example:

(6)   Shall we continue to be humiliated by this foreign despot?

The obvious answer to this "question," assuming that the discourse has been effective to this point, is "No!"

In other situations a rhetorical question might be used to convey the speaker's emotional commitment to a proposition. For example, in an argument, if I take offense at something my interlocutor says, I might respond:

(7)   How can you say that?!?!

The combination of question marks and exclamation points is one graphic means sometimes used in English writing to represent the intonation of "incredulity" associated with such rhetorical questions. Of course the function of this clause in the context of an argument is not at all to request information; rather, it is an intensive way of saying "I am offended by what you just said."

Occasionally even in narrative discourse, rhetorical questions will be used to express intensive assertions. For example:

(8)   Did he ever yell!

This clause is in the grammatical form of a question, but with the right intonation is really an intensive assertion meaning "He really yelled."

Negation is also sometimes used in this way:

(9)   a. Did that bother you?
       b. Oh no, nothing like that.

When uttered with appropriate "sarcastic" intonation, 9b can express an intensive assertion: "Of course that really bothered me." For some languages this is much more integral a part of normal discourse than it is in English.

Finally, rhetorical questions are often, as in English, posed in the negative:

(10)   Didn't I tell you to take out the trash?

Again, with the appropriate intonation and in the right context, this clause would be likely to express an intensive assertion "I told you to take out the trash!" or imperative "Take out the trash!"

?

What are the discourse functions of the various referential devices? That is, which code highly continuous referents, and which code highly discontinuous referents?

Related questions: how are referents introduced into narrative and/or conversational discourse?

Are referents introduced differently depending on whether or not they are "destined" to figure prominently in the following text? (That is, does the language clearly distinguish introductions of "discourse manipulable" referents?)

Are there different coding devices used to introduce referents that have some honorific status?

How is tense/aspect marking deployed in discourse? (Answer will probably vary according to genre.)

What morphosyntactic devices are used to signal the "events" in a narrative discourse? What about the "non-events," i.e., collateral descriptive material?

What devices are used to ascribe special prominence to portions of text?

Can you isolate the *kinds* of prominence that the language is sensitive to?

Are there special morphosyntactic devices characteristically used at the climax or peak of a narrative?

Is there a recognizable peak in other genres?

Are rhetorical questions and/or negation used as "highlighting" devices in discourse? Give examples.

12.2   Genres

The following sections constitute a possible list of genres, with well-known examples from the English tradition, and/or questions you might ask to elicit texts of various genres. Beware, however, of texts elicited in this manner. It is always better to record a text in its natural setting, e.g., when a father actually *is* exhorting his son prior to marriage, rather than in a hypothetical context. However, such opportunities are frustratingly rare.

12.2.1   Conversation

Conversation is probably the universal default discourse type. However, conversation does not easily qualify as a "genre" in that there is no consistent and obvious "organizational parameter" that provides its structure. Rather, any and all of the organizational parameters that define the other genres are used cooperatively or competitively by the various interactants in a conversation as each sees fit. In fact, most discourse employs a combination of organizational principles. Conversation, however, takes this truism to an extreme.

The most obvious structural feature of conversation is the **turn** (see Sacks, Schegloff and Jefferson 1974). A turn is a contiguous portion of a conversation in which one participant speaks. A coherent conversation consists of a series of turns taken by the various conversational participants. Communities (if not languages) typically employ various morphosyntactic and gestural devices to initiate, nurture, yield, and hold a turn.

Turn-initiating devices are signals used to indicate that a participant has a contribution to make. Another way of stating this is that the participant "wants the floor" (Sacks, Schegloff and Jefferson 1974). In English such signals include inhaling audibly, raising the eyebrows, and using interjections such as *but . . . , well . . .* , etc.

Turn-nurturing devices are used by conversational participants who do not have the floor to encourage those who do have the floor to continue. In English such devices include the ubiquitous *Uh huh . . .* as well as less stylized expressions such as *Really?, Cool*, or just an interested look. In many speech communities, nurturing devices appear to be more central to all kinds of discourse than they are in European communities. For example, in many languages, it is common for an interlocutor to repeat the entire expression or portion of the contribution of another to encourage the other to continue. This phenomenon is so common in languages we have worked with in both Americas and in Africa that we are tempted to call it a universal of storytelling style. For example, the following was recorded in Panare. A and B represent the two participants in the exchange:

(11)   A: He was picking fruit.
         B: Ummmmmm
         A: Big fruit.
         B: Big fruit.

A: Bigger than around here.
B: Ummmmmmm
A: Like this big.
B: Big.

Panare consultants often had difficulty recounting stories unless there was another Panare speaker who could provide encouragement and ask appropriate questions to keep the turn-taking rhythm of the narrative alive.

Turn-yielding devices include special intonation patterns and even grammatical particles. These are used to signal that a participant is finished with a particular contribution, and that the floor is open for others. Question intonation is often used to elicit a response from an interlocutor, even if the clause is not an actual question.

Finally, floor-holding devices indicate that a speaker is not finished with his/her contribution. Often speakers need a chance to formulate their thoughts, but do not want to "give up the floor" while they are thinking, so they use "fillers" or "hesitation particles" to occupy their turn while they are pondering the rest of their contribution. In English such particles include: *er, um, well uh, so,* etc.

12.2.2   Narrative

Narratives are stories. That is, they are portions of discourse in which a speaker describes a set of events in the real world or some imagined world. The events of a narrative are usually (but not necessarily) related to one another according to time, i.e., chronologically prior events are described before other events. The following sections describe some common subtypes of narrative. There may be additional types that have not been listed.

12.2.2.1 *Personal experience*

Some examples of personal experience narratives are:

(a) How I spent my summer vacation.
(b) What happened on my hunting trip.

Ways to elicit personal experience narratives:

(a) "Did you ever have an experience where you almost died?"
(b) "Tell me about your trip to . . ."
(c) Take advantage of significant events in the community, e.g., "Tell me about

the fire at Vicente's house," or "Where were you when the lights went out/earthquake struck/hurricane hit?," "What did you do for Carnaval?," etc. Try to be as specific as possible, and to focus on activities that are especially important to the consultant. For example, "You killed eleven monkeys? That's amazing. How did it happen?" is better than "Tell me about what you did yesterday."

12.2.2.2 *Historical*

Some examples of **historical narratives** are:

(a) War stories. Most areas of the world have experienced significant violent conflicts within the lifetime of living individuals. These are especially rich sources of personal experience and historical narratives. Stories that "go the rounds" may have become polished and stylized. Such stories may provide valuable insights into the characteristics of planned speech – the precursor to a written tradition. However, these stories are not likely to reflect everyday narrative style.

(b) "What was life like under the colonial government?" This is especially relevant for Africa and insular Asia. However, the results may be politically sensitive, especially if the person says that life was better under the colonial system.

(c) "How was this community founded?"

12.2.2.3 *Folk stories*

Technically, folklore consists of stories about real or imagined ancestors. Folk stories may contain supernatural elements, but are not primarily concerned with explaining natural phenomena. They are the stories that define a community. Counterparts in the English-language tradition would be King Arthur, Robin Hood, Daniel Boone, and Davy Crockett.

Questions to ask:

(a) "Do you know any stories about the ancestors?"

(b) "Was there ever a time when animals could talk?"

12.2.2.4 *Mythology*

This genre may merge with folklore. In some communities there is a recognizable distinction. In such systems mythology would consist of stories that rely heavily on the supernatural and which typically deal with explanations for the current state of the world. Folklore, on the other hand, consists of tales that rely less on the supernatural, and do not necessarily purport to explain anything about the world. Some examples of mythological narratives are the Greek myths, Paul Bunyan, and the first eight chapters of Genesis.

Questions to ask:

(a) "Was there ever a time when animals could talk?"
(b) "What is the origin of X?" (where X is a culturally significant plant, animal, body part, geographic landmark or group of people)
(c) "How did the world begin?"
(d) "Was the world ever covered with water?"

12.2.3   Hortatory

Hortatory discourses are attempts on the part of the speaker to get the hearer to do something, or to act in a certain way. Languages differ as to how hortatory discourse is handled. Some (especially in West Africa) have specific "hortatory" constructions; others use commands; still others use first person plural forms. For example a North American parent is likely to be heard saying something like the following to a child: "We don't throw food at mommy." Some examples of hortatory discourses are didactic sermons, and scoldings or parental lectures.

Questions to ask:

(a) "What would you tell your daughter/son just before marriage?"
(b) "My kid is doing terribly in school. What should I tell him?"

12.2.4   Procedural

Procedural discourses are instructions on how to do something. This is seldom a natural genre. Beware of elicited procedural discourses. Attempts to elicit procedural discourses are likely to result in hortatory speech. Procedural discourse, like narrative, is usually organized according to time. The foregrounded portions of a procedural text are the clauses that refer to the "steps" in the procedure.

Examples of procedural discourse include recipes and instructions on how to assemble a swing set.

Questions to ask:

(a) "How do you make a blowgun?"
(b) "Great meal! How did you cook it?"

12.2.5   Expository

Expository discourse is an attempt to explain something. This is another uncommon genre. Attempts to elicit expository texts, especially around topics related to cosmology, are likely to result in folklore or mythology. Expository discourse may be organized according to location if the subject matter is concrete, or logic if the subject matter is an abstract or technical concept. Examples of expository discourse include expository sermons and technical articles/textbooks.

Questions to ask:

(a)   "Why do you hunt when the moon is full?"
(b)   "Which animals do you hunt at night? Why?"
(c)   "Where are your gardens located? Why?"
(d)   "What is this thing? What is it for?" (demonstrating some complex object, idea, or organism)

12.2.6   Descriptive

People occasionally want to describe the characteristics of something, someone or some abstract concept. This is another uncommon genre, and you may have difficulty eliciting clear examples. Some examples of descriptive discourse are a classified advertisement for a house and the scene-setting section of a novel or short story.

Questions to ask:

(a)   "What is the place you grew up in like?" (or "What is community X like?").
(b)   "What is your house like?"
(c)   "What is your father/brother like?" (Be careful here: male researchers especially should be careful not to appear nosy with respect to females.)

12.2.7   Ritual speech

Ritual speech consists of prescribed discourse types used in religious or other ceremonial contexts. This is a very common genre, but can be difficult to elicit. Some examples of ritual speech are prayers, religious liturgy such as might be heard at weddings, funerals, coming-of-age celebrations, healing rituals, and rituals employed in conflict resolution. In the Philippines and Indonesia, as well as other areas of the world, poetry and song are commonly employed as means of resolving local conflicts.

? ....

> What discourse genres are demonstrably distinct in this language? Exemplify
> and discuss the significant characteristics of each.

....

12.3   Miscellaneous and conclusions

What else is particularly interesting about this language? The following sections provide some suggested headings. However, any particular
grammar sketch should not be limited to these headings.

12.3.1   Idiomatic expressions / proverbs

Idiomatic expressions are turns of phrase that mean more than
what the actual words contained in the expression would lead one to
expect. There may be a fine line between idiomatic expressions and proverbs. Some languages (especially in Africa) place great importance on
proverbs. For this reason they may function almost as idiomatic expressions. Some common English idiomatic expressions are: *to get dolled up, to
fathom* (*I can't fathom that*), etc.

Proverbs: *Look before you leap, A stitch in time saves nine, the
calm before the storm, The grass is always greener, birds of a feather, Haste
makes waste*, etc.

The following are a few of the thousands of proverbs that exist in
Sùpyìré, a Senoufo language of Mali, West Africa (from Carlson 1994).
Carlson provides literal translations of these proverbs, but few interpretations. This is because the functions of most proverbs are highly context-
dependent, i.e., there is seldom one objective "meaning" of a proverb apart
from a specific conversational context. For some of the following proverbs,
however, readers will be able to infer possible contexts:

(12)   Sùpyà lù-wùlì-gé   puní ɲyɛ na   u   tà-à   mɛ́.
        person water-bathe-DEF:CLS all NEG PROG CLS get-IMPERF NEG
        "All of a person's bath water doesn't get on him/her."

(13)   Nɔɔ-gɔ   jyí-fóó   u   kú bérè.
        wound-CLS wash-AGENT CLS CLS cause:pain:in:wound
        "The one who washes a wound causes pain."

(14)   Ntasènmii naha-fóó   ɲyɛ na   fyàà mɛ́.
        toad:CLS herd-AGENT NEG PROG hurry NEG
        "A toad herd doesn't hurry."

(15)   Mu ahá   kàkɔɔ ɲyɛ ú   u   kùlùshî-bire   jóólì, u   ɲyi-i
        you COND lizard see CLS:COMP PROG trousers-short:CLS sew   CLS eye-CLS
        màha mpyi `nɛŋ-ké   tà-fworoŋ-ké   na.
        HAB be   tail-DEF:CLS LOC-go:out-DEF:CLS on
        "If you see a lizard sewing trousers, his eye is on the hole for his tail."

12.3.2   Sound symbolism

All languages have some words that are supposed to sound like
the concept they express. Some such words in English include *splash*, *thud*,
and *flutter*. Sometimes words expressing sound symbolism are described as
onomatopoeic expressions, or as **ideophones**. In many languages, such
expressions are more common in discourse, especially narrative discourse
of various types, than they are in the European languages. Often such
expressions are characterized by unusual phonological properties, and
may even exhibit reduced inflectional possibilities. For example, Yagua
contains a number of sound-symbolic expressions. Many of these expressions have highly specific functions in discourse. The following are a few of
many possible examples:

(16)   pu̧u̧   "thump" (an animal or person falling down)
        pǫǫ   (sound of a spear or arrow)
        tyę́ę́   (sound of someone hitting something with a club)
        juus   (sound of someone blowing)
        rǫ́ǫ́   "scrape"
        siyǫ́ǫ́   "slice" (through flesh)
        kanekïï   (sound of someone tumbling into something)
        típye   "crash" (something hard, with many parts falling, e.g., a tree or a
                  house)

The following words are obviously sound-symbolic in origin, but
no longer have a meaning that can be directly associated with a particular
sound. Comparable expressions in English might be *phew!* to express the
idea of a narrow escape or *tsk, tsk* (a tongue tip click) to express disgust:

(17)   jiiiin   "yikes!"
        jayo   "ouch!"
        vañu   "let's go/hurry."
        kíí   "huh?"
        tiiy   "no soap" (expression of unfulfilled expectation)

While most of these are transparently sound-symbolic because their phonology is so distinct from that of normal words in Yagua (e.g., the vowel in *jiiiin*) is much longer than any vowel in a normal word would be), some can be classified as sound words only on the basis of their morphosyntactic behavior. For example, it is clear that *vañu* "let's go" is not a normal verb in Yagua because it takes none of the verbal inflections or derivations. Furthermore, this expression, and many of the others, is often used repetitively:

(18)   Vañu, vañu!   "C'mon, let's go!"

?
>   Does the language make extensive and productive use of sound symbolism?
>   What are some common ideophones?
>   How is the phonological system of ideophones and sound symbolism different than that of the rest of the language?
>   How is the morphology different? How is the syntax different?

12.3.3   Typological findings

While the bulk of this guide has been dedicated to delineating known ranges of typological diversity, field linguists should not lose sight of the fact that any given language may transcend the known range of diversity. As stated in the Introduction, a great deal is now known about the universal properties and range of variation among languages. However, this impressive body of knowledge should not be seen as a straitjacket that determines what one expects to find in any given language. After all, this body of knowledge was only acquired as grammatical descriptions of previously unknown languages progressively added to linguists' conceptualizations of what is possible in a human language. There is no particular reason to expect that this process has miraculously ended. Future descriptions will certainly expand and refute much of what is currently "known" about language. Every language exhibits unique typological characteristics. A superior grammatical description will highlight the unique features and overall "character" of the language being described, using the known typologies as reference points.

"Character" is a concept that cannot be defined objectively. It has to do with a combination of dominant features and the subjective "feel" one has while listening to and speaking the language. For example, Yagua is a verb-initial language that employs a large number of verbal derivational suffixes. Constructing and comprehending sentences in Yagua is largely a matter of accurately conceptualizing verbal derivations and morphophonemics. The syntax of sentence constituency requires much less processing effort. In other words, syntactic rules are few and simple, while derivational morphology bears most of the functional complexity. A skilled orator in Yagua is one who can construct intricate derivational patterns. Other languages may require a great deal of effort to acquire and use the inflectional paradigms, while derivation remains minimal. A successful reference grammar will contain insightful qualitative observations (not value judgments) at various points in the description. These observations will impart a sense of dignity and respect for the language and for its speakers.

?

What are the features of this language that are particularly interesting? What typological surprises does it present?

How does this work contribute to our understanding of the notion "possible human language?" What directions for further research do you recommend and/or plan to undertake yourself?

Can you qualitatively describe the "character" of this language? What are its dominant features?

What are the characteristics of a skilled orator in this language?

Can you provide some explicit examples that will contribute to the reader's sense of how this language is used? Some possibilities might be jokes, prayers, metaphorical expressions, or other culturally relevant discourse samples.

Appendix 1 Elicited and text data

Both text and elicited data are essential to good descriptive linguistics. They each have advantages and disadvantages. The linguistic researcher needs to be aware of these in order to make the best use of all the data available. Even as chopsticks are no good for eating soup and a spoon is awkward for eating spaghetti, so elicited and text data each have their own areas of usefulness. The linguistic researcher will be handicapped in conceptualizing a linguistic system if he/she attempts to use one type of data to accomplish a task best performed by the other type.

In the following paragraphs, I will first define and present some characteristics of text and elicited data. Then I will list the areas of linguistic analysis that each type of data is best suited to. Finally, I will suggest some ways in which text and elicited data might be managed in the course of a linguistic field program. This discussion is mostly directed to fieldworkers who are not working in their native language. However, many of the principles mentioned should also be helpful to mother-tongue linguistic researchers.

A1.1 Definitions

Here I will use the word "text" to mean any sample of language that accomplishes a non-hypothetical communicative task. By contrast, "elicitation" (or "elicited data") refers to samples of language that accomplish hypothetical communicative tasks.

The social task of elicited language samples is to fulfill a metalinguistic request on the part of a linguist, e.g., "How do you say 'dog'?" The response would not actually refer to any concept, either referential or non-referential. No particular dog or characteristic of dogs in general would be communicated. The task of the response would be to accommodate the inquirer by providing a reasonable analog to some hypothetical utterance in another language. So elicited utterances, like all intentional human behavior, do fulfill tasks. It is just that the communicative tasks they fulfill are "hypothetical," in the sense just described.

"Text" may include very short utterances, for example greetings. Similarly, "elicitation" could include multi-sentence language samples. Length of utterance is simply not a defining characteristic of either elicitation or text. Longer utterances are more likely to qualify as text, but there is no necessary connection. My experience is that longer utterances, even when in response to metalinguistic queries, tend to evolve into real text, as it is difficult for most speakers to maintain a hypothetical perspective on their speech for an extended period of time. Most people need to be taught to speak in terms of hypothetical knowledge. Metalinguistic queries tend to be interpreted as non-hypothetical, especially when a language consultant is new on the job. For example, I once asked a consultant "How do you say 'Yero kissed Dena'?" She responded with "He would never do that!" Scribner (1979) provides a fascinating empirical study of the relation between speech based on general knowledge and speech based on hypothetical knowledge.

A1.2   Properties of text and elicited data

Good text data are uncontrolled, open-ended, and dynamic. A text will contain forms that never appear in elicitation. It will also contain forms that appear in elicitation, but in sometimes obviously and sometimes subtly different usages. There is much idiosyncrasy in text. That is, forms are used in novel ways in order to accomplish very specific communicative tasks. Sometimes these are referred to as "nonce" usages. For example, a sentence like *He psycho-babbled away our two-hour appointment* might arise in a particular communication situation, even though the verb *to psycho-babble* is probably not a part of the lexicalized vocabulary of most English speakers. One wonders how such a sentence could possibly be elicited! Such idiosyncrasy in text is more common than one might expect and often provides great insights into speakers' ways of thinking and conceptualizing their experience.

In addition to learning the uncontrolled, flexible, and idiosyncratic aspects of a language, the fieldworker also needs to be aware of its regular, systematic, and predictable aspects. Elicited data are controlled, limited, and static. Phonology is probably the most rule-governed and systematic area of language, though even in phonology there is communicationally based and idiosyncratic variation.

The controlled, systematic, and rule-dominated parts of language are best approached with an emphasis on elicited data. These would include:

1 phonology (excluding intonation);
2 morphophonemics;
3 inventory of derivational morphology (which derivational operations apply to which roots, etc.);
4 inflectional inventory (determining the range of inflectional possibilities for person and number "agreement" and case marking);
5 pronoun inventory (isolating the entire set of free pronouns);
6 lexical inventory (acquiring the words for a large number of culturally significant things and activities).

Notice that in elicitation there is an emphasis on obtaining "inventories" of various coding possibilities. This is because languages typically employ a small number of forms in text, though many more forms are possible. For example, a declarative sentence with a second person subject is very rare in texts. This is because people do not often inform other people concerning activities of the person spoken to, e.g., *You are baking bread.* Questions are much more natural in such a context. Nevertheless, a description of the language would be incomplete if the second person declarative forms were missing. Elicitation is essential to the completion of paradigm charts. Often the meaning of a particular operator is not clear until the entire set of operators that could replace it is identified. Entire paradigms are rarely obtained by inspection of texts. The same observation can be applied to syntactic constructions. For example, whether a particular transitive construction is a passive or an ergative depends at least partially on whether there exists a corresponding "active" construction. Similarly, the precise function of AVP word order may not be apparent until minimal pairs with VAP order are obtained. Text data may exhibit AVP and VAP orders, but in text examples there are usually so many other formal differences that the precise contribution of word order to the observed semantic differences is obscured. True minimal pairs are usually obtainable only through elicitation.

The more pragmatic, semantic, and subtle parts of language are best analyzed via a large body of text data, supplemented by elicitation where necessary. This would include:

1 intonation;

2 constituent order;

3 inflectional morphology (determining the precise functions, including tense/aspect/mode);

4 voice (alignment of grammatical relations and semantic roles of verbal arguments);

5 sentence-level particles (evidentials, validationals, and pragmatic highlighting particles);

6 clause combining (including relativization, complementation, adverbial clauses, and clause chaining);

7 lexical semantics (determining the nuances associated with various lexical choices, including derivational morphology and pronouns).

A1.3   Suggestions for managing text and elicited data

In all of these areas there should properly be an "interchange" between elicitation and text. One excellent method of conducting field interviews is to start with a well-transcribed text (sometimes this is not obtainable until the phonological system has been learned, i.e., several months into the field program). The text, then, provides the context for elicited language samples. For example, in a text about spearing monkeys, verbs in the hunting domain will arise in their appropriate case frames. These verbs and case frames can then be used by the linguist to structure elicited examples. This practice reduces the danger of attempting to elicit culturally nonsensical sentences (like "Yero kissed Dena" in a culture where kissing is considered abhorrent and Yero and Dena are well known to the consultant). The linguist and the consultant go over the text sentence by sentence, with the consultant commenting on the meanings of each sentence (this scenario assumes a bilingual but not necessarily literate consultant). The linguist takes notes on these comments in the margins of the printed text and elicits utterances around the sentences that appear in the text. For example, if the meaning of a particular morpheme is not clear, the linguist may ask if the sentence is possible without that morpheme. What, according to the consultant's interpretation, semantic nuances change when the morpheme is removed? Can different word orders be employed? What would the speaker have meant if he/she had said ACB instead of ABC?

All utterances elicited in this way should be clearly marked as elicited in whatever filing system is employed. Proposed semantic or pragmatic nuances should also be checked carefully with other consultants. The first inclination for many consultants regarding grammatically acceptable variants of a sentence is to say "They mean the same thing." Needless to say, the linguist should not take a consultant's first attempt at contrastive semantic shadings as definitive. Some consultants are better than others at introspecting about their language and operating in hypothetical communicative situations. Also, some linguistic alternations have no consistent semantic effects. They either really do "mean the same thing" or their semantic differences vary from context to context, speaker to speaker, or even day to day for the same speaker.

I sometimes suggest beginning fieldwork in a language with a heavy emphasis on elicitation (derived from text as much as possible, as outlined above), moving toward a greater reliance on text material as the fieldworker begins to internalize the systematic properties of the language. Perhaps a rule of thumb would be to begin with 90 percent elicited data, and 10 percent text data, then move gradually to 90 percent text data and 10 percent elicited data some time in the second year. Consistent with this progression, the fieldworker should begin by studying the systematic aspects of language and gradually move toward the less systematic, more idiosyncratic aspects (see above).

Text data should be distinguished from elicited data in whatever cataloging system is employed. The functions of these two types of data are so different that they should be kept formally distinct as much as possible. In an automated filing system, one can either mark each record as elicited or text, or one can keep elicited data in a completely different database from text data. I have done it both ways. In my text database I have "comment" records interspersed with the records that constitute the body of the text. Each comment has the same record number as the record it is a comment about, with the addition of the characters "cm N" where N is a number. The characters "cm" simply identify the record as an elicited sentence – not part of the text – while the number allows multiple comments on any given text record. For example, the reference field containing "FAO16.1 cm 1" indicates that this record is the first comment record attached to the record FAO16.1. If I want to just look at or print the text, I can filter out all records that contain "cm" in the reference field. I also have another entire database set up for elicited data. These files are distinguished by their filenames from the files containing text data. Wimbish (1993) provides excellent suggestions on how to organize a linguistically oriented database.

Text and elicited data are both essential to a well-rounded field program. Each is useful for particular purposes. This functional difference makes a formal distinction between the two types of data essential.

Appendix 2 Sample reference grammars

The following is a list of reference grammars that may serve as examples of how a grammatical description may be organized. These grammars have been judged as "successful" by an informal panel of professional and student linguists who have actually used reference grammars in their research. They provide alternative organizational schemes to the one offered in the body of the present work. In general, the criterion for whether a grammar is "successful" or not is whether reliable information can be gleaned from it fairly quickly by readers who may not be at all familiar with the language being described. Other helpful characteristics include an insightful description of the sociological and cultural context in which the language is used, well-glossed examples, transparent terminology, and an inclusive index.

In formulating an outline for a grammar sketch or reference grammar, it is very important to keep in mind that the inclusiveness of the work will be in direct proportion to the author's familiarity with the language, and resources available for fieldwork. While a complete reference grammar for every language on Earth is ideal, exigencies of fieldwork and limitations on funding and time make it necessary at times to limit the scope of a description. For a language that is completely undocumented, a concise ten-page sketch may be extremely useful, while for a language that has been well studied, and may be spoken by a large number of speakers, a more detailed reference grammar would probably be necessary. It is important for a fieldworker to accurately estimate the level of detail of a proposed reference grammar in proportion to available resources.

Africa

Carlson, Robert J. 1994. *A Grammar of Supyire: Kampwo Dialect*. Berlin: Mouton de Gruyter.

Dimmendaal, Gerrit Jan. 1983. *The Turkana Language*. Dordrecht, Holland, and Cinnaminson, NJ: Foris.

Kimenyi, Alexandre. 1980. *A Relational Grammar of Kinyarwanda*. Berkeley: University of California Press.
Noonan, Michael. 1992. *A Grammar of Lango*. Berlin and New York: Mouton de Gruyter.

Asia
Driem, George van. 1987. *A Grammar of Dumi*. Berlin and New York: Mouton de Gruyter.
   1993. *A Grammar of Limbu*. Berlin and New York: Mouton de Gruyter.
Haspelmath, Martin. 1993. *A Grammar of Lezgian*. Berlin and New York: Mouton de Gruyter.
Hewitt, B. G. 1979. *Abkhaz*. London: Croom Helm.
Kuno, Susumu. 1973. *The Structure of the Japanese Language*. Cambridge, MA: MIT Press.
Lehmann, Thomas. 1989. *A Grammar of Modern Tamil*. Pondicherry, India: Pondicherry Institute of Linguistics and Culture.
Li, Charles N. and Sandra A. Thompson. 1981. *Mandarin Chinese: a Functional Reference Grammar*. Berkeley and Los Angeles: University of California Press.

Amerindian
Cole, Peter. 1982. *Imbabura Quechua*. London and Dover, NH: Croom Helm.
Craig, Colette Grinevald. 1977. *The Structure of Jacaltec*. Austin: University of Texas Press.
Derbyshire, Desmond C. 1979. *Hixkaryana*. London: Croom Helm.
Gamble, Geoffrey. 1978. *Wikchamni Grammar*. Berkeley: University of California Press.
Gordon, Lynn. 1986. *Maricopa Morphology and Syntax*. Berkeley: University of California Press.
Kimball, Geoffrey D. 1991. *Koasati Grammar*. Lincoln: University of Nebraska Press.
Munro, Pamela. 1976. *Mojave Syntax*. New York: Garland Press.
Payne, Doris L. and Thomas E. Payne. 1990. Yagua. In *Handbook of Amazonian Languages*, vol. II, ed. by Desmond C. Derbyshire and Geoffrey Pullum, 249–474. Berlin: Mouton.
Pitkin, Harvey. 1984. *Wintu Grammar*. Berkeley: University of California Press.
Press, Margaret L. 1978. *Chemehuevi: a Grammar and Lexicon*. Berkeley: University of California Press.
Rice, Keren. 1989. *A Grammar of Slave*. Berlin and New York: Mouton de Gruyter.
Rood, David. 1976. *Wichita Grammar*. New York: Garland Press.
Watkins, Laurel. 1984. *A Grammar of Kiowa*. Lincoln: University of Nebraska Press.
Weber, David J. 1989. *A Grammar of Huallaga (Huanuco) Quechua*. Berkeley: University of California Press.
Williams, Marianne (Mithun). 1976. *A Grammar of Tuscarora*. New York: Garland Press.
Zepeda, Ofelia. 1983. *A Papago Grammar*. Tucson: University of Arizona Press.

Australia
Austin, Peter. 1981. *A Grammar of Diyari, South Australia*. Cambridge Studies in Linguistics 32. Cambridge University Press.

Dixon, R. M. W. 1972. *The Dyirbal Language of North Queensland.* Cambridge University Press.

Evans, Nicholas. 1995. *A Grammar of Kayardild: with Historical–Comparative Notes on Tangkic.* Berlin and New York: Mouton de Gruyter.

Heath, Jeffrey. 1978. *Ngandi Grammar, Texts and Dictionary.* Canberra: Australian Institute of Aboriginal Studies.

Merlan, Francesca. 1982. *Mangarayi.* London: Croom Helm.

    1994. *A Grammar of Wardaman: a Language of the Northern Territory of Australia.* Berlin and New York: Mouton de Gruyter.

Austronesia

Antworth, Evan L. 1979. *Grammatical Sketch of Botolan Sambal.* Manila: Linguistic Society of the Philippines.

Dixon, R. M. W. 1988. *A Grammar of Boumaa Fijian.* University of Chicago Press.

Dougherty, Janet. 1983. *West Futuna-Aniwa: an Introduction to a Polynesian Outlier Language.* Berkeley: University of California Press.

Durie, Mark. 1985. *A Grammar of Acehnese on the Basis of a Dialect of North Aceh.* Dordrecht, Holland, and Cinnaminson, NJ: Foris.

Harrison, Sheldon P. 1976. *Mokilese Reference Grammar.* Honolulu: University Press of Hawaii.

Jensen, John Thayer. 1977. *Yapese Reference Grammar.* Honolulu: University Press of Hawaii.

Lee, Kee-dong. 1975. *Kusaiean Reference Grammar.* Honolulu: University Press of Hawaii.

Lichtenberk, Frantisek. 1983. *A Grammar of Manam. Oceanic Linguistics Special Publication 18.* Honolulu: University of Hawaii Press.

Schachter, Paul and Fe T. Otanes. 1972. *Tagalog Reference Grammar.* Berkeley: University of California Press.

Sohn, Ho-min. 1975. *Woleaian Reference Grammar.* Honolulu: University Press of Hawaii.

Topping, Donald and Bernadita Dugca. 1973. *Chamorro Reference Grammar.* Honolulu: University Press of Hawaii.

Miscellaneous

Berman, Ruth Aronson. 1978. *Modern Hebrew Structure.* Tel-Aviv: University Publication Projects.

Lewis, Geoffrey L. 1991. *Turkish Grammar.* Oxford and New York: Oxford University Press.

Press, Ian. 1986. *A Grammar of Modern Breton.* Berlin and New York: Mouton de Gruyter.

Saltarelli, Mario. 1988. *Basque.* London and New York: Routledge.

Underhill, Robert. 1993. *Turkish Grammar:* Cambridge, MA: MIT Press.

Papuan languages

Davies, John. 1981. *Kobon.* Amsterdam: North-Holland.

Foley, William. 1991. *The Yimas Language of New Guinea.* Stanford University Press.

Franklin, K. J. 1971. *A Grammar of Kewa.* New Guinea and Canberra: Linguistic Circle of Canberra.

Haiman, John. 1980. *Hua, a Papuan Language of the Eastern Highlands of New Guinea*. Amsterdam: John Benjamins.

Reesink, Ger. 1987. *Structures and their Functions in Usan: a Papuan Language of Papua New Guinea*. Amsterdam and Philadelphia: John Benjamins.

Notes

Introduction

[1] This book focuses exclusively on morphosyntactic description. Most grammars or grammar sketches of under-documented languages would also include a chapter, or at least a major section, on the phonology, or sound system, of the language. The reader is referred to the extensive literature on phonological description for help in writing the phonology section. A good place to start would be Spencer (1996) and the references cited therein.

[2] Here I wish to interpret the term "other things" in the broadest sense possible, i.e., I make no claims as to whether the *signifié* (the item signaled, or coded, by language form) is a real-world item, a "message world" item, a "mental concept," a connotation, a denotation, etc. The characteristic of language that is of interest to this discussion is that it is **representational**, i.e., it represents something else (even if the something else happens to be language itself). The precise nature of what it is that language represents is not at issue here. My personal view is that the notion of **cognitive model** proposed by Lakoff (1987) will prove to be an extremely fruitful source of insight into the nature and structure of the concepts expressed by linguistic expressions, and the ways in which form is shaped by that content. However, it is not necessary to share this view in order to agree that linguistic units are used by speakers to represent *something*.

[3] This concept and terminology is reminiscent of Hockett's (1954) "item-and-process" model of grammatical description. Along with most current approaches to grammatical description, we consciously adopt the item-and-process model, and accept the implications of teleology that go along with it. I have tried to be consistent with terminology used by most linguists in adopting the term "operation" for particular morphosyntactic devices with conceptual effect in specific languages, and reserving the term "process" for broad strategies for encoding those operations, e.g., plural formation in English is a morphological *operation*, whereas suffixation is a kind of morphological *process*. Though terminology varies widely in this area, I believe this distinction, though perhaps confusing to some, will be generally understandable to linguists of various theoretical persuasions.

The distinction between an operation and a process becomes more difficult to maintain as one transcends morphology and begins to examine analytic (syntactic) structures. This is due to the fact that syntax is more determined by universal functional principles (such as iconicity) than is morphology. For example, left-dislocation is an appropriate syntactic analogy to prefixation in morphology. It is defined entirely in terms of the structural change involved, and thus is not inherently tied to any particular conceptual content in any given language. Nevertheless, there is a distinct universal tendency for left-dislocation to code a particular function, namely contrastive focus (see chapter 10). This tendency is so strong that linguists may actually think of left-dislocation as synonymous with the functional term "contrastive focus." Many formal devices, such as "passive," have been given functional-sounding labels precisely because they have such strong associations with particular functions. For these reasons, we will in practice dispense with the operation/process distinction in syntax.

2 Morphological typology

[1] Following standard notation in descriptive linguistics, we will use square brackets, [ ], to indicate phonetic representation and slashes, / /, to indicate phonemic representation. Any good introduction to phonetics or phonology will define these terms and other notation that appears in this section. For example, see Burquest and Payne (1994).

3 Grammatical categories

[1] The term "fourth person" has been used in a variety of ways in the literature. None of the previous uses of this term describes a function that is not covered by some other term employed in this book. Therefore we will not attempt to survey the various uses of this term.

[2] See section 8.1 for a discussion of the difference between semantic and syntactic argument structure.

[3] An additional complication, which will be dealt with more fully in chapters 7 and 8, is that many verbs have more than one argument structure. This is another way of saying that verbs have different "senses." For example, the verb *grow* has at least two senses (meanings): to increase in size, and to foster an increase in size on the part of some other object. In the first sense, the argument structure contains only a PATIENT:

"My ivy plant keeps growing," while in the second sense there is an AGENT and a PATIENT: "He grows marijuana for a living."

[4] See DeLancey (1990) for an alternative definition of AGENT. I believe DeLancey's definition of AGENT as "the first CAUSE in the clause" is essentially compatible with Fillmore's definition plus the notion of "message world." That is, the clause is the linguistic unit within which message world scenes are perspectivized. Insofar as the "instigator of the action" is equivalent to the "first CAUSE," and the message world "scene" is equivalent to the "clause," the two definitions become near restatements of one another.

Foley and Van Valin (1984) describe a functional continuum between two "macroroles," ACTOR and UNDERGOER. The prototypical ACTOR is an AGENT and the prototypical UNDERGOER a PATIENT in the classic Case Grammar sense. This is their method of preserving an objectivist definition of AGENT and PATIENT while still accounting for the variability in grammatical coding of these roles.

[5] The terms "ergative," "absolutive," "topic," and others used to refer to morphological cases will be defined in chapter 7. For now it is important simply to note that the ergative is a distinct case form.

[6] Factive verbs are not to be confused with verbs that take factive complements. These are discussed in section 11.2.

[7] Literally: "They two went all over the place thinking in their heart." Women who have had children are always referred to as dual in Yagua.

4 Constituent order typology

[1] Of course the grammatical clause consisting of a "subject" and "predicate" is not the only possible linguistic instantiation of a proposition. In conversation, in

particular, propositions are often expressed in shorter linguistic forms, such as phrases, interjections, incomplete structures, etc. Furthermore, propositions can be instantiated in non-linguistic media as well, or not instantiated at all, i.e., they may be inferred (see Sperber and Wilson 1986). For the purposes of a reference grammar, however, the field linguist will want to limit the domain of discussion to conventionalized linguistic instantiations of propositions.

2 See chapter 7 for a more detailed history and critique of the notions of grammatical relations, including subject and object.

3 Even though *do* is sometimes thought of as "semantically empty," it certainly can express important pragmatic information, such as contrastive focus (see section 10.0.2).

5 Noun and noun-phrase operations

1 These examples are in the standard Tagalog orthography. The form spelled "mga" is pronounced [máŋa].

2 These are perfectly acceptable sentences in Yagua; however, neither one represents the normal way of expressing these thoughts. The verb *dííy*, meaning "kill," in particular is normally used with more complex morphology to express the idea of "mortal," e.g., *vųųvyų dííyasara*, "our mortal bodies," literally "our destined to be killed things." The idea of "killing" in Yagua is usually expressed with a more specific verb indicating the manner of killing. The verb *dííy* is also not the normal way of expressing the idea of "to see." Clauses like 19b do occur commonly in folktales, but they are given a gloss corresponding to "An alligator came into his sight" or "His vision rested on an alligator." There is another verb *junúúy* that glosses the English verb *see* more exactly.

6 Predicate nominals and related constructions

1 Locomotion clauses are those in which someone or something changes place, such as *She fell into a vat of sausage dye*. These are distinct from clauses that do not express an explicit change of place, such as *She fell*.

2 Clark follows traditional English grammar by using the term "definiteness" for the pragmatic status described in this book as "identifiability."

7 Grammatical relations

1 See the Introduction, section 0.2.1, on the form–meaning relationship in language, and section 3.2 on the definition of the term "argument" for descriptive linguists.

2 Similarly, fast-food restaurants in the United States have a highly automated way of making cheeseburgers-with-everything. This is a *useful* category because many North Americans want cheeseburgers with everything. However, once this is made into an automated category, it drives even more people to choose cheeseburgers-with-everything because to ask for something slightly different is more complicated and therefore takes longer. So the category, once grammaticalized, becomes a kind of self-fulfilling prophecy where people choose it *just because it is a category*, and not necessarily because it is the best solution to the problem they are facing. The very establishment of a category creates or accentuates a need for that category.

3 **Oblique** is sometimes also considered to be a grammatical relation but not a core grammatical relation. I prefer to consider obliques to be those nominal clause elements that do not bear a grammatical relation to the verb. Oblique arguments can be thought of as those that are objects of prepositions in English. They are optional sentence adjuncts, akin to adverbials (see

sections 3.4 and 11.3). The status of indirect object is dubious in many languages. Usually clause elements that are called indirect objects have the same formal properties as either direct objects or obliques.

4 By AGENT-like here, we mean the argument which most closely approximates the ideal of the initiating, controlling participant in the scene described by the proposition. We do not refer to *inherent* properties of the verbal arguments, as described in the "topic-worthiness hierarchy" in section 7.3.2. That is, in a sentence like:

(i) The change in schedule made me late.

the phrase *the change in schedule* is the A because it is presented as being the entity that controls the specific event of being late, even though a first person, *me*, is much higher on the hierarchy of inherent agentivity. The notion of inherent agentivity refers to the fact that certain kinds of entities are inherently quite likely to be coded as AGENTS, but does not by any means preclude the fact that such entities are often found in other roles as well.

5 The terms nominative and accusative are from the grammars of classical languages. To a large extent their use in those grammars corresponds to the definitions given here. However, the terms in the classical languages refer strictly to morphological cases. The markers that signal those cases are often used in many other ways in addition to marking A, S, and P arguments. For example, the "accusative" case in Latin occurs on objects of certain prepositions. Here we are using the terms nominative and accusative to describe groupings of semantico-syntactic roles, no matter how those roles are instantiated in the morphosyntax. So we may, for example, refer to a particular noun phrase as a "nominative" noun phrase if it is an S or an

A argument, whether or not it is marked by a distinct nominative case marker. More commonly, certain syntactic rules may refer to the nominative category, whether or not the case-marking system of the language is organized on a nominative/accusative basis (Anderson 1976). This same sort of practice was observed in the section on noun phrases where it was noted that possessors are often referred to as "genitives" even in languages that have no morphologically distinct genitive case. Any morphosyntactic units that are glossed with terms from familiar languages should not necessarily be expected always to correspond exactly to the operators that bear those glosses in the familiar languages.

6 Dixon (1994: 203) describes a marginal example of a type IV system in the Iranian language Rushan. However, he describes this system as "unstable," and it appears from the discussion that it may be an unusual arrangement even in that language.

7 The following discussion, indeed this entire chapter, owes much to the work of R. M. W. Dixon (1972, 1979, 1994) and Bernard Comrie (1978a).

8 There is some additional complexity to this hierarchy, especially in the areas of agreement and pronouns. This complexity derives partially from the complexity and frequent idiosyncrasy of agreement and pronominal systems in general, and partially from the fact that some languages do not distinguish first and second persons on this hierarchy. That is, first and second persons (agreement or pronouns), are considered equally likely to be agentive, but both outrank third persons. Such systems do not counterexemplify the generalization that items to the left outrank items to the right in systems that rely on pragmatics to distinguish A from P. They simply do not rely on pragmatics to distinguish A from P

when one argument is first and the other second person. A true counterexample would be a language in which an item to the right was treated pragmatically as more likely to be an AGENT than some item to the left.

9 R. M. W. Dixon (p.c.) suggests that noun incorporation (ex. 45) is universally sensitive to the ergative/absolutive distinction. I agree 90 percent with this suggestion. However, with noun incorporation, there often are enough complications in the system that I would hesitate to say unequivocally that ergative/absolutive is always the relevant syntactic alignment. For example, the expression *This medicine is doctor-recommended* (incorporation of A argument) is possible in English. In fact, I find that in most languages noun–verb incorporation is not necessarily sensitive to grammatical relations at all. Often any noun that is in some way associated with the verb can be incorporated. Such nouns *often* are S or O, but there does not seem to be a direct correlation. A few examples from English in which incorporated nouns are not S or O would be *You will be pay-deducted, I will spoon-feed him, We baby-sat for four hours.*

8 Voice and valence adjusting operations

1 Technically, applicatives of transitive verbs do not increase valence numerically. However, because they do bring a peripheral participant onto "center stage," they are treated with other valence increasing devices. See section 8.1.2 for fuller discussion.

2 Technically, inverse constructions do not decrease valence numerically. However, because they do downplay the centrality of a controlling argument, they are treated with other valence decreasing devices. See section 8.2.3 for fuller discussion.

3 The decision whether to use direct or inverse in Cree is not the *same* as the decision to use passive or active; it is just the same *kind* of decision, i.e., it is a speaker option with pragmatic effects. Cree also has a grammatically distinct passive construction, so the direct vs. inverse alternation is quite independent of the active vs. passive alternation.

9 Other verb and verb-phrase operations

1 The signs of grammaticalization include: (1) formal simplification and (2) semantic bleaching. The "markers" of English inceptive and completive aspects are the complement-taking verbs *begin* and *finish*. They neither take on special form, nor convey any idiosyncratic semantic overtones when occurring in inceptive or completive clauses. This is in contrast to the verb *have*, for example, which does have special semantics and special formal properties when occurring as a marker of perfect aspect or deontic mode:

(i) *Perfect aspect*
     They'*ve* fallen.
(ii) *Deontic mode*
     They *hæftə* go now.

In the lexical use of the verb *have*, the contractions illustrated in these clauses are much more unusual:

(iii) *Lexical use*
      They have two dollars.
      ??They've two dollars.
      ??They hæftə dollars./??They hæf two dollars.

Phonological contraction is a formal indication of grammaticalization. The semantic indication that grammaticalization has taken place with the aspectual and modal use of *have* is that the meanings of (i) and (ii) are quite different from the standard lexical use of *have* to mean something like "possess."

Finish and *begin* as complement-taking verbs, on the other hand, convey pretty much the same concepts as they do when the complement is not a clause:

(iv) *Lexical use*
  He finished the bookcase.
  He began Mozart's sonata in G.

Of course, grammaticalization is a process rather than an event. Therefore, any given operator may be more or less grammaticalized. Verbs that have been grammaticalized as aspectual auxiliaries in English include *have* and *go*. *Will* is an archaic lexical verb (meaning "want") that is now used almost exclusively as a future tense auxiliary. *Ought* is related to the lexical verb *owe*, and *can* is related to the lexical verb *know*. But these modal auxiliaries have diverged so significantly from their lexical sources that it is difficult for native speakers to discern any formal or functional connection. Interestingly, in all of these cases the auxiliary reflects the more conservative, older, form.

10 Pragmatically marked structures
[1] Foley and Van Valin (1984) use the term topicalization for 26b and left-dislocation for 26c. Here we do not adopt this terminology for two reasons. (1) In the interests of maintaining a truly universal perspective, we avoid using functional terms, such as topicalization, to describe morphosyntactic devices. This is because structures that are analogous from one language to the next may not have analogous functions. (2) To consider 26c to be left-dislocation entails that the leftward NP is external to the clause. From the field linguist's point of view there is no independent evidence for this entailment. In fact, it would seem to imply that there are four levels of grammatical integration, one of which is unattested in English:

Fronted but clause-internal (unattested in English)
Left-dislocation   Beans I like.
Topicalization   (As for) beans, I like them.
Apposition   Beans. What a great lunch.

A survey of the literature reveals no other sources that use Foley and Van Valin's terminology.

11 Clause combinations
[1] The terminology and the concept of a "complexity continuum" stems from class lectures presented by Sandra Thompson in 1979. The notion of a typology of complement types is represented in many works, including notably Givón (1984).
[2] Haiman (1987) uses the term "medial verb" to describe the morphologically distinct verb type that heads non-final clauses. Longacre (1985), however, seems to use the terms medial clause and non-final clause interchangeably.

References

Adams, Karen L. and Nancy Faires Conklin. 1973. Toward a theory of natural
classification. *Chicago Linguistic Studies* 9.1–10.

Allen, Keith. 1977. Classifiers. *Language* 53.285–311.

Anderson, John. 1971. *The Grammar of Case: towards a Localist Theory*. Cambridge
University Press.

1977. *On Case Grammar*. Cambridge University Press.

Anderson, Stephen R. 1976. On the notion of subject in ergative languages. In *Subject and
Topic*, ed. by Charles N. Li, 1–24. New York: Academic Press.

1977. On mechanisms by which languages become ergative. In *Mechanisms for
Syntactic Change*, ed. by Charles N. Li, 317–32. Austin: University of Texas
Press.

1982. Where's morphology? *Linguistic Inquiry* 13.4.571–612.

1985a. Typological distinctions in word formation. In *Language Typology and
Syntactic Description*, vol. III: *Grammatical Categories and the Lexicon*, ed. by
Timothy Shopen, 3–56. Cambridge University Press.

1985b. Inflectional morphology. In *Language Typology and Syntactic Description*,
vol. III: *Grammatical Categories and the Lexicon*, ed. by Timothy Shopen,
150–201. Cambridge University Press.

Anderson, T. 1988. Ergativity in Päri, a Nilotic OVS language. *Lingua* 75.289–324.

Andrews, Avery. 1985. The major functions of the noun phrase. In *Language Typology and
Syntactic Description*, vol. III: *Grammatical Categories and the Lexicon*, ed. by
Timothy Shopen, 62–154. Cambridge University Press.

Austin, Peter. 1980. Switch reference in Australian languages. In *Studies of Switch
Reference*, ed. by Pamela Munro. UCLA Papers in Syntax 8.1–54. Los Angeles:
University of Southern California.

1981. *A Grammar of Diyari, South Australia*. Cambridge Studies in Linguistics 32.
Cambridge University Press.

Bamgbose, A. 1974. On serial verbs and verbal status. *Journal of West African Linguistics*
9.17–48.

Barnes, Janet. 1990. Classifiers in Tuyuca. In *Amazonian Linguistics: Studies in Lowland
South American Languages*, ed. by Doris L. Payne, 273–92. Austin: University
of Texas Press.

Barshi, Immanuel and Doris L. Payne. 1996. The interpretation of "possessor raising" in a
Maasai dialect. In *Proceedings of the Sixth International Nilo-Saharan
Linguistics Conference*, ed. by M. Lionel Bender and Thomas J. Hinnebusch.
Afrikanistische Arbeitspapiere 45. Cologne: Institut für Afrikanistik,
Universität zu Köln.

Baugh, John and Joel Sherzer. 1984. *Language in Use: Readings in Sociolinguistics.* Englewood Cliffs: Prentice-Hall.

Bauman, Richard. 1977. *Verbal Art as Performance.* Prospect Heights: Waveland Press.

Bauman, Richard and Joel Sherzer (eds.). 1974. *Explorations in the Ethnography of Speaking.* Cambridge University Press.

Besnier, Niko. 1986. Register as a sociolinguistic unit: defining formality. In *Social and Cognitive Perspectives on Language*, ed. by Christopher J. Hall and Mary McGinnis, 25–63. Southern California Occasional Papers in Linguistics, 11. Los Angeles: University of Southern California Press.

Bloomfield, Leonard. 1956. *Eastern Ojibwa: Grammatical Sketch, Texts and Word List.* Ann Arbor: University of Michigan Press.

Boas, Franz. 1911. *Handbook of American Indian Languages.* Smithsonian Institution; Bureau of American Ethnology; Bulletin 40.

Borgman, D. M. 1990. Sanuma. In *Handbook of Amazonian Languages*, vol. II, ed. by Desmond C. Derbyshire and Geoffrey Pullum, 15–248. Berlin: Mouton.

Brown, Gillian and George Yule. 1983. *Discourse Analysis.* Cambridge University Press.

Burling, Robbins. 1970. *Man's Many Voices.* New York: Holt, Rinehart, and Winston.

Burquest, Donald and David Payne. 1994. *Phonological Analysis: a Functional Approach.* Dallas: Summer Institute of Linguistics.

Bybee, Joan. 1985. *Morphology: Typological Studies in Language*, vol. IX. Amsterdam: John Benjamins.

Carlson, Robert. 1994. *A Grammar of Supyire, Kampwo Dialect.* Berlin: Mouton de Gruyter.

Carlson, Robert and Doris L. Payne. 1989. Genitive classifiers. In *Proceedings of the Fourth Pacific Linguistics Conference*, 87–119.

Casad, Eugene H. 1982. Cora locationals and structured imagery. Unpublished doctoral dissertation, University of California, San Diego.

Chafe, Wallace L. 1970. *Meaning and the Structure of Language.* University of Chicago Press.

   1976. Givenness, contrastiveness, definiteness, subjects, topics and point of view. In *Subject and Topic*, ed. by Charles N. Li, 25–55. New York: Academic Press.

   (ed.) 1980. *The Pear Stories: Cognitive, Cultural and Linguistic Aspects of Narrative Production.* Norwood, NJ: Ablex.

   1987. Cognitive constraints on information flow. In *Coherence and Grounding in Discourse*, ed. by Russell C. Tomlin, 21–51. Amsterdam and Philadelphia: John Benjamins.

Chafe, Wallace L. and Johanna Nichols (eds.). 1986. *Evidentiality: the Linguistic Coding of Epistemology.* Norwood, NJ: Ablex.

Chambers, J. K. and Peter Trudgill. 1980. *Dialectology.* Cambridge University Press.

Chapman, S. and Desmond C. Derbyshire. 1991. Paumarí. In *Handbook of Amazonian Languages*, vol. III, ed. by Desmond C. Derbyshire and Geoffrey Pullum, 161–352. Berlin: Mouton.

Chomsky, Noam. 1982. *Some Concepts and Consequences of the Theory of Government and Binding.* Linguistic Inquiry Monograph 6. Cambridge, MA: MIT Press.

Clark, Eve V. 1978. Locationals: existential, locative and possessive constructions. In *Universals of Human Language*: vol. IV: *Syntax*, ed. by Joseph H. Greenberg, 85–126. Stanford University Press.

Clark, Eve V. and H. Clark. 1979. When nouns surface as verbs. *Language* 55.767–811.

Comrie, Bernard. 1974. Causatives and universal grammar. *Transactions of the Philological Society* 1–32.

    1978a. Ergativity. In *Syntactic Typology: Studies in the Phenomenology of Language*, ed. by Winfred P. Lehmann, 329–94. Austin: University of Texas Press.

    1978b. *Aspect* (2nd printing). Cambridge University Press.

    1989. *Language Universals and Linguistic Typology* (2nd edition). University of Chicago Press.

Comrie, Bernard and Sandra A. Thompson. 1985. Lexical nominalization. In *Language Typology and Syntactic Description*, vol. III: *Grammatical Categories and the Lexicon*, ed. by Timothy Shopen, 349–98. Cambridge University Press.

Corbett, Greville G. 1991. *Gender*. Cambridge University Press.

Craig, Colette Grinevald. 1977. *The Structure of Jacaltec*. Austin: University of Texas Press.

    1986. *Noun Classes and Categorization*. Typological Studies in Language, 7. Amsterdam and Philadelphia: John Benjamins.

Croft, William. 1990. *Typology and Universals*. Cambridge University Press.

Dahlstrom, Amy. 1991. *Plains Cree Morphosyntax*. New York and London: Garland.

De Guzman, Vida. 1978. *Syntactic Derivation of Tagalog Verbs*. Oceanic Linguistics Special Publications 16. Honolulu: University Press of Hawaii.

DeLancey, Scott. 1982. Aspect, Transitivity and Viewpoint. In *Tense–aspect: between Semantics and Pragmatics*, ed. by Paul J. Hopper, 167–84. Amsterdam and Philadelphia: John Benjamins.

    1990. Ergativity and the cognitive model of event structure in Lhasa Tibetan. *Cognitive Linguistics* 1.289–321.

    1991. The origins of verb serialization in modern Tibetan. *Studies in Language* 15.1.1–23.

Dik, Simon. 1981. On the typology of focus phenomena. In *Perspectives on Functional Grammar*, ed. by Teun Hoekstra, Harry Van der Hulst, and Michael Moortgat. Dordrecht: Foris.

Dixon, R. M. W. 1968. Noun classes. *Lingua* 21.104–25.

    1972. *The Dyirbal Language of North Queensland*. Cambridge University Press.

    1977. Where have all the adjectives gone? *Studies in Language* 1.19–80.

    1979. Ergativity. *Language* 55.59–138.

    1994. *Ergativity*. Cambridge Studies in Linguistics 69. Cambridge University Press.

Dorian, Nancy C. 1981. *Language Death: the Life Cycle of a Scottish Gaelic Dialect*. Philadelphia: University of Pennsylvania Press.

Dowty, David. 1987. Thematic proto-roles, subject selection and lexical semantic defaults. Paper presented at the 1987 LSA annual meeting.

Dryer, Matthew. 1988. Object–verb order and adjective–noun order: dispelling a myth. *Lingua* 74.185–217.

    1991. SVO languages and the OV:VO typology. *Journal of Linguistics* 27.2.443–82.

1994. The discourse function of the Kutenai inverse. In *Voice and Inversion*, ed. by T. Givón. Typological Studies in Language 28.65–99. Amsterdam and Philadelphia: John Benjamins.

Du Bois, John W. 1980. Beyond definiteness: the trace of identity in discourse. In *The Pear Stories: Cognitive, Cultural and Linguistic Aspects of Narrative Production*, ed. by Wallace L. Chafe, 203–74. Norwood, NJ: Ablex.

1985. Competing motivations. In *Iconicity in Syntax*, ed. by John Haiman. Typological Studies in Language 6.343–66. Amsterdam and Philadelphia: John Benjamins.

1987. The discourse basis of ergativity. *Language* 63.4.805–55.

Edmondson, B. 1988. A descriptive grammar of Huastec (Potosino dialect). Unpublished doctoral dissertation, Tulane University.

Elson, Benjamin F. (ed.). 1964. *Verb Studies in Five New Guinea Languages*. Norman: University of Oklahoma, Summer Institute of Linguistics.

England, Nora. 1988. *Introducción a la lingüística: idiomas mayas*. Antigua, Guatemala: Proyecto lingüístico Francisco Marroquín.

Fasold, Ralph W. 1992a. *The Sociolinguistics of Society: Introduction to Sociolinguistics*, vol. I (5th edition). Oxford, UK and Cambridge, MA: Blackwell.

1992b. *The Sociolinguistics of Language: Introduction to Sociolinguistics*, vol. II (5th edition). Oxford, UK and Cambridge, MA: Blackwell.

Fillmore, Charles J. 1968. The case for case. In *Universals in Linguistic Theory*, ed. by Emond Bach and Robert T. Harms, 1–88. New York: Holt, Rinehart, and Winston.

1976. Topics in lexical semantics. In *Current Issues in Linguistic Theory*, ed. by Peter Cole, 76–138. Bloomington: Indiana University Press.

1977. The case for case reopened. In *Syntax and Semantics*, vol. VIII: *Grammatical Relations*, ed by P. Cole and J. M. Sadock, 59–81. New York: Academic Press.

Foley, William A. and Mike Olson. 1985. Clausehood and verb serialization. In *Grammar Inside and Outside the Clause: Some Approaches to Theory from the Field*, ed. by Johanna Nichols and Anthony C. Woodbury, 17–60. Cambridge University Press.

Foley, William and Robert Van Valin. 1984. *Functional Syntax and Universal Grammar*. Cambridge University Press.

1985. The packaging of information in the clause. In *Language Typology and Syntactic Description*, vol. I: *Clause Structure*, ed. by Timothy Shopen, 282–364. Cambridge University Press.

Frachtenberg, Leo J. 1913. *Coos Texts*. Columbia University Contributions to Anthropology 1. New York: Columbia University Press.

Franchetto, Bruna. 1990. Ergativity and nominativity in Kuikuro and other Cariban languages. In *Amazonian Linguistics: Studies in Lowland South American Languages*, ed. by Doris L. Payne, 407–27. Austin: University of Texas Press.

Gerdel, F. and M. Slocum. 1976. Paez discourse, paragraph and sentence structure. In *Discourse Grammar: Studies in Languages of Colombia*, vol. I ed. by Robert E. Longacre and F. Woods, 259–443. Dallas: Summer Institute of Linguistics.

Gildea, Spike. 1992. Comparative Cariban morphosyntax: on the genesis of main clause morphosyntax. Doctoral dissertation, University of Oregon.

1994. Semantic and pragmatic inverse: "inverse alignment" and "inverse voice" in Carib of Surinam. In *Voice and Inversion*, ed. by T. Givón. Typological Studies in Language 28.65–99. Amsterdam and Philadelphia: John Benjamins.

Givón, T. 1979. *On Understanding Grammar*. New York: Academic Press.

1980. The binding hierarchy and the typology of complements. *Studies in Language*, 4.3.333–77.

1982a. Logic vs. pragmatics, with human language as the referee. *Journal of Pragmatics* 6.81–133.

1982b. Transitivity, topicality, and the Ute impersonal passive. In *Syntax and Semantics*, vol. XV: *Studies in Transitivity*, ed. by Paul Hopper and Sandra Thompson, 143–60. New York: Academic Press.

1983a. Topic continuity in discourse: an introduction. In *Topic Continuity in Discourse: a Quantitative Cross-language Study*, ed. by T. Givón. Typological Studies in Language 3.1–41. Amsterdam and Philadelphia: John Benjamins.

1983b. Topic continuity and word-order pragmatics in Ute. In *Topic Continuity in Discourse: a Quantitative Cross-language Study*, ed. by T. Givón. Typological Studies in Language 3.141–214. Amsterdam and Philadelphia: John Benjamins.

1983c. Topic continuity in discourse: the functional domain of switch reference. In *Switch Reference and Universal Grammar*, ed. by John Haiman and Pamela Munro. Typological Studies in Language 2.51–82. Amsterdam and Philadelphia: John Benjamins.

1984. *Syntax: a Typological Functional Introduction*, vol. I. Amsterdam and Philadelphia: John Benjamins.

1987. Serial verbs and the mental reality of "event." Final NEH progress report, University of Oregon department of linguistics (ms.).

1990. *Syntax: a Functional–Typological Introduction*, vol. II. Amsterdam and Philadelphia: John Benjamins.

(ed.). 1994. *Voice and Inversion*. Typological Studies in Language 28. Amsterdam and Philadelphia: John Benjamins.

Green, Georgia. 1981. Some wherefores of English inversions. *Language* 56.582–601.

Greenberg, Joseph H. 1954. A quantitative approach to the morphological typology of language. *Interactional Journal of American Linguistics* 26.178–94.

1963. Some universals of grammar with particular reference to the order of meaningful elements. In *Universals of Language*, ed. by Joseph H. Greenberg. Cambridge, MA: MIT Press.

1966. *Language Universals, with Special Reference to Feature Hierarchies*. Janua Linguarum. Series minor, 59. The Hague: Mouton.

Greenberg, Joseph H., Charles A. Ferguson, and Edith A. Moravcsik (eds.) 1978. *Universals of Human Language*, 4 vols. Stanford University Press.

Grice, H. Paul. 1975. Logic and conversation. In *Syntax and Semantics*, vol. III: *Speech Acts*, ed. by Peter Cole and J. Morgan, 41–58. New York: Academic Press.

Grimes, Barbara (ed.). 1992. *Ethnologue* (12th edition). Consulting editors: Richard S. Pittman and Joseph E. Grimes. Dallas: Summer Institute of Linguistics.

Grimes, Joseph. 1975. *The Thread of Discourse*. The Hague: Mouton.

Haiman, John. 1980. The iconicity of grammar. *Language* 56.515–40.

1983a. Iconic and economic motivations. *Language* 59.781–819.

1983b. On some origins of switch-reference marking. In *Switch Reference and Universal Grammar*, ed. by John Haiman and Pamela Munro. Typological Studies in Language 2.105–28. Amsterdam and Philadelphia: John Benjamins.

1987. On some origins of medial-verb morphology in Papuan languages. University of Manitoba, Winnipeg (ms.).

Haiman, John, and Pamela Munro (eds.). 1983. *Switch Reference and Universal Grammar*. Typological Studies in Language 2. Amsterdam and Philadelphia: John Benjamins.

Haiman, John and Sandra A. Thompson. 1984. "Subordination" in universal grammar. *Proceedings of the Berkeley Linguistics Society* 10.510–23.

Hale, Kenneth. 1983. Warlpiri and the grammar of non-configurational languages. *Natural Language and Linguistic Theory* 1.1–43.

1992. Language endangerment and the human value of linguistic diversity. *Language* 68.1.35–42.

Halliday, M. A. K. 1967. Notes on transitivity and theme in English. *Journal of Linguistics* 3. Part I: 37–81. Part II: 199–244.

Harries-Delisle, Helga. 1978. Coordination reduction. In *Universals of Human Language*, vol. IV: *Syntax*, ed. by Joseph H. Greenberg, Charles A. Ferguson, and Edith A. Moravcsik, 515–84. Stanford University Press.

Harris, Alice C. 1990. Alignment typology and diachronic change. In *Language Typology 1987: Systematic Balance in Language*, ed. by Winfred P. Lehman, 67–90. Amsterdam and Philadelphia: John Benjamins.

Haspelmath, Martin. To appear. Les constructions à possesseurs externes dans les langues de l'Europe. In *Actance et valence dans les langues d'Europe*, ed. by Jack Feuillet. Berlin: Mouton de Gruyter.

Hawkins, John A. 1983. *Word Order Universals*. New York: Academic Press.

1994. *A Performance Theory of Order and Constituency*. Cambridge University Press.

Healey, Phyllis M. 1966. *Levels and Chaining in Telefol Sentences*. Pacific Linguistics Series B.5. Canberra: Australian National University.

Heath, Jeffrey. 1976. Antipassivization: a functional typology. *Proceedings of the Second Annual Meeting of the Berkeley Linguistics Society*.

1978. *Ngandi Grammar, Texts and Dictionary*. Canberra: Australian Institute of Aboriginal Studies.

Heine, Bernd and Mechthild Reh. 1984. *Grammaticalization and Reanalysis in African Languages*. Hamburg: Helmut Buske.

Heitzman, Allene, 1982. Some cohesive elements in Pajonal Campa narratives. Ms., Summer Institute of Linguistics, Peru.

Hetzron, R. 1969. *The Verbal System of Southern Agaw*. Berkeley: University of California Press.

1977. *The Gunnan-Gurage Languages*. Naples: Istituto Orientale di Napoli.

Hewitt, B. G. 1979. Aspects of verbal affixation in Abkhaz (Abzui dialect). *Transactions of the Philological Society* 211–38.

Hill, Jane and Kenneth Hill. 1980. Metaphorical switching in modern Nahuatl: change and contradiction. In *Papers from the Sixteenth Regional Meeting of the Chicago Linguistics Society*, 121–33. Chicago Linguistics Society.

Hinds, John, Senko K. Maynard, and Shoichi Iwasaki. 1987. *Perspectives on Topicalization: the Case of Japanese "wa."* Amsterdam and Philadelphia: John Benjamins.

Hockett, Charles F. 1954. Two models of grammatical description. *Word* 10.210–31.

Hopper, Paul J. 1979. Aspect and foregrounding in discourse. *Syntax and Semantics*, vol. XII: *Discourse and Syntax*, ed. by T. Givón, 213–41. New York: Academic Press.

(ed.) 1982. *Tense-aspect: between Semantics and Pragmatics*. Amsterdam and Philadelphia: John Benjamins.

1991. On some principles of grammaticization. In *Approaches to Grammaticalization*, vol. I, ed. by Elizabeth Closs Traugott and Berndt Heine, 17–35. Amsterdam and Philadelphia: John Benjamins.

Hopper, Paul J. and S. A. Thompson. 1980. Transitivity in grammar and discourse. *Language* 56.251–99.

1984. The discourse basis for lexical categories in universal grammar. *Language* 60.4.703–52.

Horn, Laurence R. 1978. Some aspects of negation. In *Universals of Human Language*, vol. IV: *Syntax*, ed. by Joseph H. Greenberg, Charles A. Ferguson, and Edith Moravcsik. 127–210. Stanford University Press.

Howse, James. 1844. *A Grammar of the Cree Language, with which is Combined an Analysis of the Chippeway Dialect*. London: J. G. F. and J. Rivington.

Hyman, Lawrence. 1971. Consecutivization in Fe? Fe?. *Journal of African Languages* 10.29–43.

Jaggar, Phillip. 1984. Referential choice in Hausa narrative. Doctoral dissertation, University of California, Los Angeles.

Jelinek, Eloise. 1984. Empty categories, case and configurationality. *Natural Language and Linguistic Theory* 2.39–76.

1988. The case split and pronominal arguments in Choctaw. In *Configurationality: the Typology of Asymmetries*, ed. by László Marácz and Pieter Muysken, 117–41. Dordrecht: Foris.

Johnson-Laird, P. N. 1981. Comprehension as the construction of mental models. *Philosophical Transactions of the Royal Society of London* B295.353–74.

1983. The coherence of discourse. In *Mental Models*, ed. by P. Johnson Laird. 356–95. Cambridge University Press.

Jones, Linda Kay. 1977. *Theme in English Expository Discourse*. Edward Sapir Monograph Series in Language, Culture and Cognition 2. Lake Bluff, IL: Jupiter Press.

Jones, Wendell and Paula Jones. 1991. *Barasano Syntax*. Studies in the Languages of Colombia 2. Dallas: Summer Institute of Linguistics and University of Texas at Arlington.

Keenan, Edward L. 1985. Relative clauses. In *Language Typology and Syntactic Description*, vol. II: *Complex Constructions*, ed. by Timothy Shopen, 141–70. Cambridge University Press.

Keenan, Edward L. and Bernard Comrie. 1977. NP accessibility and universal grammar. *Linguistic Inquiry* 8.63–100.

Keenan, Edward L. and Elinor Ochs. 1979. Becoming a competent speaker of Malagasy. In *Languages and their Speakers*, ed. by Timothy Shopen, 113–60. Cambridge, MA: Winthrop.

Kemmer, Suzanne. 1993. *The Middle Voice*. Amsterdam and Philadelphia: John Benjamins.

Kimenyi, Alexander. 1980. *A Relational Grammar of Kinyarwanda*. Berkeley: University of California Press.

Klavans, Judith. 1985. The independence of syntax and phonology in cliticization. *Language* 61.95–120.

Krauss, Michael. 1992. The world's languages in crisis. *Language* 68.1.4–10.

Kühner, R. and C. Stegmann. 1955. *Ausfürliche Grammatik der lateinischen Sprache: Satzlehre*, vol. II. Leverkusen: Gottschalk.

Kuno, Susumo. 1976. Subject, theme and the speaker's empathy – a reexamination of relativization phenomena. In *Subject and Topic*, ed. by Charles N. Li, 137–53. New York: Academic Press.

Labov, William and Joshua Waletzky. 1967. Narrative analysis: oral versions of personal experience. In *Essays on the Verbal and Visual Arts, Proceedings of the 1966 Annual Spring Meeting of the American Ethnological Society*, ed. by June Helm, 12–44. Seattle: University of Washington Press.

Lakoff, George. 1987. *Women, Fire and Dangerous Things: What Categories Reveal about the Mind*. University of Chicago Press.

Langacker, Ronald W. 1987. *Foundations of Cognitive Grammar*, vol. I. Stanford University Press.

Lehman, Christian. 1991. Grammaticalization and related changes in contemporary German. In *Approaches to Grammaticalization*, vol. I, ed. by Elizabeth Closs Traugott and Berndt Heine, 493–535. Amsterdam and Philadelphia: John Benjamins.

Lehmann, Winfred P. 1973. A structural principle of language and its implications. *Language* 49.47–66.

Levinson, Stephen C. 1983. *Pragmatics*. Cambridge University Press.

Li, Charles N. (ed.). 1976. *Subject and Topic*. New York: Academic Press.

Li, Charles N. and Sandra A. Thompson. 1976. Subject and topic: a new typology of language. In *Subject and Topic*, ed. by Charles N. Li, 457–90. New York: Academic Press.

    1981. *Mandarin Chinese: a Functional Reference Grammar*. Berkeley and Los Angeles: University of California Press.

Linde, Charlotte and William Labov. 1975. Spatial networks as a site for the study of language and thought. *Language* 50.924–39.

Longacre, Robert. 1972. *Hierarchy and Universality of Discourse Constituents in New Guinea Languages: Discussion*. Washington DC: Georgetown University Press.

    1976. *An Anatomy of Speech Notions*. Lisse: Peter de Ridder Press.

    1985. Sentences as combinations of clauses. In *Language Typology and Syntactic Description*, vol. II: *Complex Constructions*, ed. by Timothy Shopen, 235–86. Cambridge University Press.

Longacre, Robert and Sandra A. Thompson. 1985. Adverbial clauses. In *Language Typology and Syntactic Description*, vol. II: *Complex Constructions*, ed. by Timothy Shopen, 171–234. Cambridge University Press.

Lord, Carol. 1973. Serial verbs in transition. *Studies in African Linguistics* 4.269–96.

1976. Evidence for syntactic reanalysis: from verb to complementizer in Kwa. In *Papers from the Parasession on Diachronic Syntax*, ed. by Sanford B. Seever, Carol A. Walker, Salikoko S. Mufwere, and Robert Peter Ebert, 179–91. Chicago Linguistics Society.

Mann, William C. and Sandra A. Thompson. 1985. *Rhetorical Structure Theory: Description and Construction of Text Structures*. Information Sciences Institute Reprint Series 86–174. Los Angeles: University of Southern California.

1987. *Rhetorical Structure Theory: a Framework for the Analysis of Texts*. Information Sciences Institute Reprint Series, 87–185. Los Angeles: University of Southern California.

Mathesius, V. 1939 [1947] O tak zvaném aktuálním len ení v etném [On the so-called Functional Sentence Perspective]. Reprinted in *Čestina a obecny jazykozpyt* [The Czech Language and General Linguistics], 234–42. Prague.

Matisoff, J. A. 1973. *The Grammar of Lahu*. Berkeley and Los Angeles: University of California Press.

Matthews, P. H. 1991. *Morphology* (2nd edition). Cambridge University Press.

Maynard, Senko K. 1987. Thematization as a staging device in the Japanese narrative. In *Perspectives on Topicalization: the Case of Japanese "wa"*, ed. by John Hinds, Senko K. Maynard, and Shoichi Iwasaki, 57–82. Amsterdam and Philadelphia: John Benjamins.

McCarthy, J. 1965. Clause chaining in Kanite. *Anthropological Linguistics* 7.59–70.

Merlan, Francesca. 1985. Split intransitivity: functional oppositions in intransitive inflection. In *Grammar Inside and Outside the Clause: Some Approaches to Theory from the Field*, ed. by Johanna Nichols and Anthony C. Woodbury, 324–62. Cambridge University Press.

Mervis, Carolyn and Eleanor Rosch. 1981. Categorization of natural objects. *Annual Review of Psychology* 32.89–115.

Minsky, Marvin. 1975. A framework for representing knowledge. In *Theoretical Issues in Natural Language Processing*, ed. by Bonnie Nash-Webber and Roger Schank, 118–30. Cambridge, MA: Yale University Press.

Mithun, Marianne. 1984. The evolution of noun incorporation. *Language* 60.847–93.

1986. Evidential diachrony in Northern Iroquois. In *Evidentiality: the Linguistic Coding of Epistemology*, ed. by Wallace Chafe and Johanna Nichols, 89–112. Norwood, NJ: Ablex.

1987. Is basic word order universal? In *Coherence and Grounding in Discourse*, ed. by Russell Tomlin. Typological Studies in Language 11.281–328. Amsterdam and Philadelphia: John Benjamins.

1991. Active/agent case marking and its motivations. *Language* 67.3.510–46.

Mosel, Ulrike and Even Hovdhaugen. 1992. *Samoan Reference Grammar*. Oslo: Scandinavian University Press.

Mühlhäusler, Peter and Rom Harré. 1990. *Pronouns and People: the Linguistic Construction of Social and Personal Identity*. Oxford, UK, and Cambridge, MA: Basil Blackwell.

Munro, Pamela. 1983. When "same" is not "not different." In *Switch Reference and Universal Grammar*, ed. by John Haiman and Pamela Munro, 223–43. Amsterdam and Philadelphia: John Benjamins.

1984. The syntactic status of object possessor raising in Western Muskogean. *Proceedings of the Tenth Annual Meeting of the Berkeley Linguistics Society*, 634–49.

Nelson, Francis W. 1983. *Dialectology: an Introduction*. New York: Longman.

Nichols, Johanna. 1986. Head-marking and dependent-marking grammar. *Language* 62.1.56–119.

Noonan, Michael. 1985. Complementation. In *Language Typology and Syntactic Description*, vol. II: *Complex Constructions*, ed. by Timothy Shopen, 42–140. Cambridge University Press.

1992. *A Grammar of Lango*. Berlin and New York: Mouton de Gruyter.

Ochs, Elinor. 1988. *Culture and Language Development: Language Acquisition and Language Socialization in a Samoan Village*. Cambridge University Press.

Olson, M. L. 1973. *Barai Sentence Structure and Embedding*. Santa Ana, CA: Summer Institute of Linguistics.

Payne, Doris L. 1985a. Review of *Word Order Universals*, by John Hawkins. *Language* 61.462–66.

1985b. Inflection and derivation: is there a difference? In *Proceedings of the First Annual Pacific Linguistics Conference*, ed. by Scott DeLancey and Russel Tomlin, 247–78. Eugene: University of Oregon.

1986. Basic word order in Yagua clauses: implications for word order universals. In *Handbook of Amazonian Languages*, vol. I, ed. by Desmond C. Derbyshire and Geoffrey Pullum, 440–65. Berlin: Mouton.

1990. *The Pragmatics of Word Order: Typological Dimensions of Verb-initial Languages*. Berlin and New York: Mouton.

1992a. Nonidentifiable information and pragmatic order rules in 'O'odham. In *Pragmatics of Word Order Flexibility*, ed. by Doris L. Payne. Amsterdam and Philadelphia: John Benjamins.

1992b. Towards a more adequate approach to "focus" phenomena. *Journal of African Languages and Linguistics* 13.2.205–17.

Payne, Doris L. and Thomas E. Payne. 1990. Yagua. In *Handbook of Amazonian Languages*, vol. II, ed. by Desmond C. Derbyshire and Geoffrey Pullum. Berlin: Mouton.

Payne, John R. 1985. Complex phrases and complex sentences. In *Language Typology and Syntactic Description*, vol. II: *Complex Constructions*, ed. by Timothy Shopen, 3–41. Cambridge University Press.

Payne, Judith and David Payne. 1991. The pragmatics of split intransitivity in Asheninca. Paper read at the Symposium on Arawakan Linguistics, 47th International Congress of Americanists, New Orleans.

Payne, Thomas E. 1982. Role and reference related subject properties and ergativity in Yup'ik Eskimo and Tagalog. *Studies in Language* 6.1.75–106.

    1984. Locational relations in Yagua narrative. *Work Papers of the Summer Institute of Linguistics*, University of North Dakota, 28.157–92.

    1987. Pronouns in Yagua discourse. *International Journal of American Linguistics* 53.1.1–21.

    1990a. Estatividad y movimiento. *Montalban: Revista de la Universidad Católica "Andrés Bello,"* Caracas, Venezuela. 99–136.

    1990b. Transitivity and ergativity in Panare. In *Amazonian Linguistics: Studies in Lowland South American Languages*, ed. by Doris L. Payne, 429–53. Austin: University of Texas Press.

    1991. Medial clauses and interpropositional relations in Panare. *Cognitive Linguistics* 2–3.247–81.

    1992. *The Twins Stories: Participant Coding in Yagua Narrative*. Berkeley: University of California Press.

    1994. The pragmatics of voice in a Philippine language: actor-focus and goal-focus in Cebuano narrative. In *Voice and Inversion*, ed. by T. Givón. Typological Studies in Language 28.317–64. Amsterdam and Philadelphia: John Benjamins.

Perlmutter, David M. 1980. Relational grammar. In *Syntax and Semantics*, vol. XIII: *Current Approaches to Syntax*, ed. by Edith A. Moravcsik and Jessica R. Wirth, 195–229. New York: Academic Press.

Pike, Kenneth Lee. 1947. *Phonemics: a Technique for Reducing Languages to Writing*. Ann Arbor: University of Michigan Press.

Plank, Frans (ed.). 1979. *Ergativity: Towards a Theory of Grammatical Relations*. London and New York: Academic Press.

    (ed.). 1984. *Objects: Towards a Theory of Grammatical Relations*. London and Orlando, FL: Academic Press.

Powlison, Paul. 1987. *Yagua Mythology: Epic Tendencies in a New World Mythology*. Dallas: Summer Institute of Linguistics.

Prince, Ellen F. 1978. A comparison of WH-clefts and it-clefts in discourse. *Language* 54.883–907.

    1981. Toward a taxonomy of given–new information. In *Radical Pragmatics*, ed. by Peter Cole. New York: Academic Press.

Redden, J. A. 1966. Walapai II: morphology. *International Journal of American Linguistics* 32.141–63.

Reed, Irene, Osahito Miyaoka, Steven Jacobson, Paschal Afcan, and Michael Krauss. 1977. *Yup'ik Eskimo Grammar*. Fairbanks: Alaska Native Language Center and Yup'ik Language Workshop, University of Alaska.

Reinhart, Tanya. 1982. *Pragmatics and Linguistics: an Analysis of Sentence Topics*. Bloomington: Indiana University Linguistics Club.

Rosch, Eleanor. 1977. Classification of real-world objects: origins and representations in cognition. In *Thinking: Readings in Cognitive Science*, ed. by Philip Johnson-Laird and P. C. Wason. Cambridge University Press.

Rosch, Eleanor and B. Lloyd (eds.). 1978. *Cognition and Categorization*. Hillsdale, NJ: Erlbaum Associates.

Rosen, Carol. 1983. The interface between semantic roles and initial grammatical relations. In *Studies in Relational Grammar*, vol. II, ed. by David Perlmutter and Carol Rosen, 71–113. University of Chicago Press.

Rumelhart, D. 1975. Notes on a schema for stories. In *Representation and Understanding: Studies in Cognitive Science*, ed. by D. Bobrow and A. Collins, 211–36. New York: Academic Press.

Sacks, H., Emanuel Schegloff, and G. Jefferson. 1974. A simplest systematics for the organization of turn-taking for conversation. *Language* 50.696–735.

Sadock, Jerrold M. 1986. Some notes on noun incorporation. *Language* 62.19–31.

Sankoff, Gillian. 1980. *The Social Life of Language*. Philadelphia: University of Pennsylvania Press.

Sapir, Edward. 1911. The problem of noun incorporation in American languages. *American Anthropologist* 13.250–82.

Saussure, Ferdinand de. 1915. *A Course in General Linguistics*, trans. by C. Bally and A. Ferdlinger. New York: Philosophical Library.

Schachter, Paul. 1974. A non-transformational account of serial verbs. *Studies in African Linguistics*, supplement 5.253–70.

———. 1977. Reference-related and role-related properties of subjects. In *Syntax and Semantics*, vol. VIII: *Grammatical Relations*, ed. by Peter Cole and Jerrold M. Sadock, 279–306. New York: Academic Press.

———. 1985. Parts-of-speech systems. In *Language Typology and Syntactic Description*, vol. III: *Grammatical Categories and the Lexicon*, ed. by Timothy Shopen. 3–61. Cambridge University Press.

Schank, Roger. 1972. Conceptual dependency: a theory of natural language understanding. *Cognitive Psychology* 3.552–631.

Schank, Roger, and R. Abelson. 1977. *Scripts, Plans, Goals, and Understanding*. Hillsdale, NJ: Lawrence Erlbaum.

Schiffrin, Deborah. 1994. *Approaches to Discourse*. Cambridge, MA, and Oxford, UK: Blackwell.

Scribner, Sylvia. 1979. Modes of thinking and ways of speaking: culture and logic reconsidered. In *New Directions in Discourse Processing*, ed. by Roy O. Freedle, 223–43. Norwood, NJ: Ablex.

Searle, John R. 1970. *Speech Acts: an Essay in the Philosophy of Language*. Cambridge University Press.

Seki, Luci. 1990. Kamaiurá (Tupí-Guaraní) as an active–stative language. In *Amazonian Linguistics: Studies in Lowland South American Languages*, ed. by Doris L. Payne, 367–92. Austin: University of Texas Press.

Sherzer, Joel. 1977. The ethnography of speaking: a critical appraisal. In *Georgetown University Round Table on Languages and Linguistics*, ed. by Muriel Saville-Troike, 43–58. Washington, DC: Georgetown University Press.

Shibatani, Masayoshi. 1985. Passives and related constructions: a prototype analysis. *Language* 61.4.821–48.

———. 1991. Grammaticization of topic into subject. In *Approaches to grammaticalization*, vol. II, ed. by Elizabeth Closs Traugott and Bernd Heine, 93–134. Amsterdam and Philadelphia: John Benjamins.

Shopen, Timothy. 1985. *Language Typology and Syntactic Description*, 3 vols. Cambridge University Press.

Silverstein, Michael. 1976. Hierarchy of features and ergativity. In *Grammatical Categories in Australian Languages*, ed. by R. M. W. Dixon. Linguistic Series 22.112–71. Canberra: Australian Institute of Aboriginal Studies.

Simons, Gary F. 1983. *Language Variation and Limits to Communication*. Dallas: Summer Institute of Linguistics.

Spencer, Andrew. 1996. *Phonology: Theory and Description*. Oxford, UK, and Cambridge, MA: Blackwell.

Sperber, Dan and Deirdre Wilson. 1986. *Relevance: Communication and Cognition*. Oxford: Blackwell.

Stahlke, H. 1970. Serial verbs. *Studies in African Linguistics* 1.60–99.

Steele, Susan. 1981. *An Encyclopedia of AUX: a Study in Cross-linguistic Equivalence*. Linguistic Inquiry Monographs, 5. Cambridge, MA: MIT Press.

Thompson, Chad. 1989. Voice and obviation in Athabaskan and other languages. Doctoral dissertation, University of Oregon.

Thompson, Sandra A. 1988. A discourse approach to the cross-linguistic category "adjective." In *Explaining Language Universals*, ed. by John A. Hawkins, 167–85. Oxford and New York: Blackwell.

To appear. Discourse motivations for the core–oblique distinction as a language universal. In *Functionalism in Linguistics*, ed. by Akio Kamio. Berlin: Mouton de Gruyter.

Thurman, Robin. 1975. Chuave medial verbs. *Anthropological Linguistics*. 17.342–52.

1986. *Basic Constituent Orders: Functional Principles*. London: Croom Helm.

1995. Focal attention, voice, and word order: an experimental, cross-linguistic study. In *Word Order in Discourse*, ed. by P. Downing and M. Noonan, 517–54. Amsterdam and Philadelphia: John Benjamins.

Traugott, Elizabeth Closs and Bernd Heine (eds.). 1991. *Approaches to Grammaticalization*, vol. II. Amsterdam and Philadelphia: John Benjamins.

Trudgill, Peter. 1986. *Dialects in Contact*. New York: Blackwell.

Tucker, Archibald N. and John T. Ole Mpaayei. 1955. *A Maasai Grammar, with Vocabulary*. Publications of the African Institute, Leyden, 2. London and New York: Longmans and Green.

Ultan, Russell. 1978. Some general characteristics of interrogative systems. In *Universals of Human Language*, vol. IV: *Syntax*, ed. by Joseph H. Greenberg, 211–48. Stanford University Press.

Vendler, Zeno. 1967. *Linguistics in Philosophy*. Ithaca, New York: Cornell University Press.

Vennemann, Theo. 1974. Topics, subjects and word order: from SXV to SVX via TVX. In *Historical Linguistics*, ed. by John M. Anderson and Charles Jones. North-Holland Linguistics Series 12.339–76. Amsterdam: North-Holland.

Voegelin, C. F. and F. M. Voegelin. 1977. *Classification and Index of the World's Languages*. New York: North-Holland.

Wallace, Stephen. 1982. Figure and ground: the interrelationships of linguistic categories. In *Tense and Aspect*, ed. by Paul J. Hopper, 201–23. Amsterdam and Philadelphia: John Benjamins.

Watson, R. 1966. Clause to sentence gradations in Pacoh. *Lingua* 16:166–88.

Watters, John. 1979. Focus in Aghem. In *Aghem Grammatical Structure*, ed. by Lawrence Hyman. University of Southern California Occasional Papers in Linguistics 7. Los Angeles: University of Southern California.

Weber, David J. 1986. Information perspective, profile and patterns in Quechua. In *Evidentiality: the Linguistic Encoding of Epistemology*, ed. by Wallace Chafe and Joanna Nichols, 137–55. New York: Ablex.

1989. *A Grammar of Huallaga (Huanuco) Quechua*. Berkeley: University of California Press.

Weisemann, Ursula (ed.). 1986. *Pronominal Systems*. Tübingen: Gunter Narr.

Welmers, William E. 1973. *African Language Structures*. Berkeley: University of California Press.

Wimbish, John. 1993. *The Linguist's Shoebox*. Waxhaw, NC: Summer Institute of Linguistics.

Wise, Mary Ruth. 1971. *Identification of Participants in Discourse: a Study of Aspects of Form and Meaning in Nomatsiguenga*. Summer Institute of Linguistics Publications in Linguistics and Related Fields 28. Dallas: Summer Institute of Linguistics.

Wright, Suzanne and T. Givón. 1987. The pragmatics of indefinite reference: quantified text-based studies. *Studies in Language* 11.1–33.

Zipf, Paul. 1949. *Human Behavior and the Principle of Least Effort: an Introduction to Human Ecology*. New York: Hafner.

Zwicky, Arnold. 1973. Linguistics as chemistry: the substance theory of semantic primes. In *A Festschrift for Morris Halle*, ed. by S. Anderson and P. Kiparsky. New York: Holt, Rinehart, and Winston.

Index of languages, language families, and language areas

Subject index

absolutive
  case, 135
  diagram, 166
  grammatical relation, 129–33
  pivot for relativization in Dyirbal, 164
  union of S and P, 75
absolutive clauses, 320
accusative, 134, 166
action continuity, 344, 351–53
action nominalizations, 224–25
action verbs, 58–59
action-processes, 59
active systems, 144
additive clauses, 320
addressee, 263
adjectives, 63–65
  in English, 65
  as predicates, 111–12
  order in noun phrases, 86
adjuncts, 317
adpositional phrases, 86–88
adpositions, 86–88
  complex, 87
  distinguished from case marking,
    100–102
  distinguished from nouns, 87
  distinguished from verbs, 87
  grammatical category, 32
  head of phrase, 31
advanced tongue root, 29
adverbial clauses, 306, 316–20
adverbial modifiers, 35
adverbs, 49, 69–70
adversative passive, 208
affected, 172
affix, 21
afterthought topicalization, 273

agent, 49–50
  of cause, 176
  conceptual notion, 47
  contrasted with "subject," 342
  in defining grammatical relations,
    129–30, 132
  independent of topicality, 141
  often chosen as topic, 262
agent nominalization, 226–27
agent-worthiness, 150
agentivity hierarchy, 150
agglutinating, 27, 28–29, 30
agreement, 42–44, 84
  grammatical, 275
alienable possession, 40–41, 104–107
allomorph, 23
analytic causatives, 181
analytic expression, 9–11
analytic nominalizations, 225
analytic passives, 206
analytic reflexives, 200–201
anaphoric agreement, 345
anaphoric clitics, 42–44, 46
anaphoric zeros, 345
anaphoricity, 42–44, 102, 250
animacy, 128, 150
anticausatives, 198, 218
antipassives, 219–20
  in relative clauses, 164–65
  valence decreasing devices, 196
  voice, 345
aorist, 217
applicatives, 186–91
  in Athabaskan, 259
  and semantic roles, 62
  in Tagalog, 54
applied object, 186